Teacher Edition

STRATEGIES for Writers

Level E – Recommended for Grade 5 and Above

Authors

Leslie W. Crawford, Ed.D.
Georgia College & State University

Rebecca Bowers Sipe, Ed.D.
Eastern Michigan University

Consulting Author

Ken Stewart
Master Teacher
Bexley Middle School
Bexley, Ohio

Zaner-Bloser

Zaner-Bloser proudly presents a strategic and innovative approach to writing instruction that makes it easier to improve students' writing. **Strategies for Writers, A Complete Writing Program** is...

THE NEXT Step in Writing Instruction for Students

- **Rubric**-based instruction is logical and effective, so students always know what's expected and what to do.

- The writing process is taught with special emphasis on prewriting and revising, so students are guided smoothly through these challenging areas.

- Specific types of writing are modeled in an upbeat, conversational way throughout, so students are engaged and eager to write.

- Grammar is taught in conjunction with writing, so students learn how grammar is best applied to writing.

STRATEGIES
for Writers

The NeXT Step in Teaching Writing

- Instruction is **Rubric**-based, so teaching is focused and learning becomes more independent.

- Complete writing instruction is provided in one program, so it's easy for teachers to teach the writing process, different types of writing, and grammar.

- Units are self-contained, so they can be taught in any order.

- A School-Home Connection Blackline Master is provided in every unit, so teachers can easily communicate with families.

The NeXT Step in Writing Assessment

- Assessment is **Rubric**-based, so students know exactly what they need to do to succeed.

- Instruction supports major national, state, and NCTE standards, so students learn the skills necessary to succeed in writing assessment.

- Global rubrics that can be used as pretest and posttest rubrics are available in the Teacher Edition Appendix.

Wherever your students' writing skills are, Strategies for Writers will take them to the next step!

The Authors Tell Us
How They Take Students' Writing to THE NEXT Step

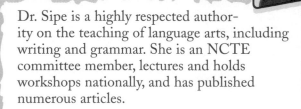

Leslie W. Crawford, Ed.D.

Co-author of *Strategies for Writers*

" *Strategies for Writers* goes beyond modeling and analyzing writing. The rubric is central to the learning process. Students analyze a model, using a rubric, then use it to guide and evaluate their writing. *"*

Dr. Crawford is an honored language arts educator and Fulbright Scholar who has contributed to many educational publications. In addition to co-authoring *Strategies for Writers,* Dr. Crawford is also co-author of Zaner-Bloser's *9 Good Habits for All Readers*.

Dr. Crawford received his Doctorate in Education from the University of California, Berkeley. He was Dean of the John H. Lounsbury School of Education at the Georgia College & State University from 1996 to 2001 and is currently a professor of Early Childhood and Middle Grades Education at the same university.

Rebecca B. Sipe, Ed.D.

Co-author of *Strategies for Writers*

" Through the use of rubrics, *Strategies for Writers* gives students the tools they need to think about their writing in a critical and reflective way. We help students understand the many requirements of writing, then support their efforts to build original compositions. *"*

Dr. Sipe is a highly respected authority on the teaching of language arts, including writing and grammar. She is an NCTE committee member, lectures and holds workshops nationally, and has published numerous articles.

Dr. Sipe began her career in education as a classroom teacher and received her Doctorate in Education from Boston University. She is currently Assistant Professor of English Education at Eastern Michigan University.

Kenneth Stewart, *Master Teacher*

Mr. Stewart has been teaching for over 30 years and is currently an eighth grade language arts teacher at Bexley Middle School in Ohio. He received his Master of Arts degree from the University of Dayton. Mr. Stewart is known for his development of a cooperative learning teaching philosophy. He has received many commendations and honors, including Outstanding Educator in his district in 2001.

Lee Bromberger, *Assessment Specialist*

Mr. Bromberger received his Master of Arts, English, from Marquette University and is currently the K–12 Language Arts Curriculum Co-Chair at Mukwonago High School in Wisconsin. He is known for his research on the correlation of writing standards to assessment, which he presented at the NCTE national convention in 2001. Mr. Bromberger has also authored various publications on writing and grammar.

The Program Components

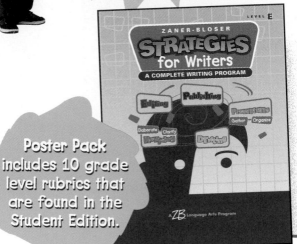

Units can
be taught
in any order!

Teacher Edition gives complete guidelines that make writing instruction easy for teachers.

Practice the Strategy Notebook provides guided practice for the strategies being taught in the unit.

Pages may be reproduced.

Poster Pack includes 10 grade level rubrics that are found in the Student Edition.

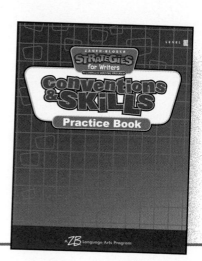

Student Edition contains the step-by-step writing instruction students need, modeled in an upbeat, conversational way throughout the program.

Conventions & Skills Practice Book Student Edition provides students with complete conventions and skills instruction for their level.

Conventions & Skills Practice Book Teacher Edition is fully annotated and easily makes conventions and skills instruction an important part of the program.

Level E book covers shown.

in Writing Instruction for Students

Rubric-Based Instruction Helps Students Succeed

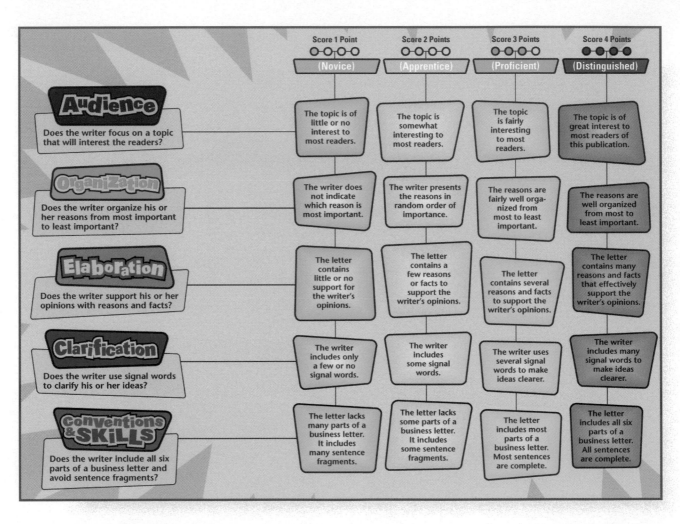

	Score 1 Point (Novice)	Score 2 Points (Apprentice)	Score 3 Points (Proficient)	Score 4 Points (Distinguished)
Audience Does the writer focus on a topic that will interest the readers?	The topic is of little or no interest to most readers.	The topic is somewhat interesting to most readers.	The topic is fairly interesting to most readers.	The topic is of great interest to most readers of this publication.
Organization Does the writer organize his or her reasons from most important to least important?	The writer does not indicate which reason is most important.	The writer presents the reasons in random order of importance.	The reasons are fairly well organized from most to least important.	The reasons are well organized from most to least important.
Elaboration Does the writer support his or her opinions with reasons and facts?	The letter contains little or no support for the writer's opinions.	The letter contains a few reasons or facts to support the writer's opinions.	The letter contains several reasons and facts to support the writer's opinions.	The letter contains many reasons and facts that effectively support the writer's opinions.
Clarification Does the writer use signal words to clarify his or her ideas?	The writer includes only a few or no signal words.	The writer includes some signal words.	The writer uses several signal words to make ideas clearer.	The writer includes many signal words to make ideas clearer.
Conventions & Skills Does the writer include all six parts of a business letter and avoid sentence fragments?	The letter lacks many parts of a business letter. It includes many sentence fragments.	The letter lacks some parts of a business letter. It includes some sentence fragments.	The letter includes most parts of a business letter. Most sentences are complete.	The letter includes all six parts of a business letter. All sentences are complete.

Level E rubric shown.

Students succeed when they have clear guidelines and expectations for their writing. **Strategies for Writers** provides clear guidelines because the rubric is central to its instructional plan.

- The **Rubric** in each chapter is specific to the type of writing and strategies being taught.

- In the beginning of each chapter, the **Rubric** is introduced and the students are taught how to use it by applying it to a model.

- Throughout the chapter, the strategies being taught support the points of the **Rubric**.

- In the **Practice the Strategy Notebook**, the same **Rubric** appears again for students to evaluate their own writing.

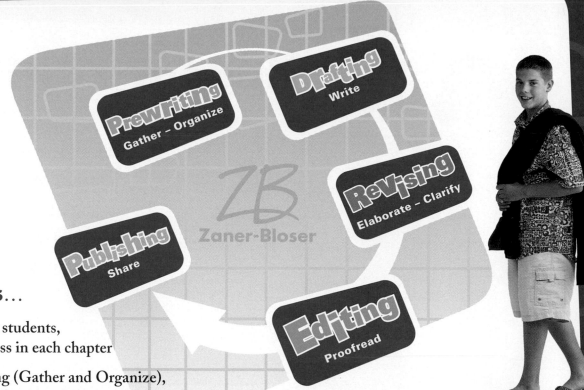

The Writing Process in **Strategies for Writers**...

- Uses writing partners that walk students, step-by-step, through the process in each chapter

- Has two strategies for prewriting (Gather and Organize), so students are well prepared before they begin writing

- Has two strategies for revising (Elaborate and Clarify) that give students clear guidelines for improvement

- Is successful in teaching students that writing is a recursive process, so they are continually encouraged to improve

Conventions & Skills in **Strategies for Writers**...

are taught on three different levels:

 A short lesson on the Editing page of each chapter focuses on one skill.

 For students who need further instruction, a complete lesson is provided in the back of the Student Edition for the same skill introduced on the Editing page.

 50 grade-level appropriate lessons (a full year's worth of instruction) are available in the **Conventions & Skills Practice Book.**

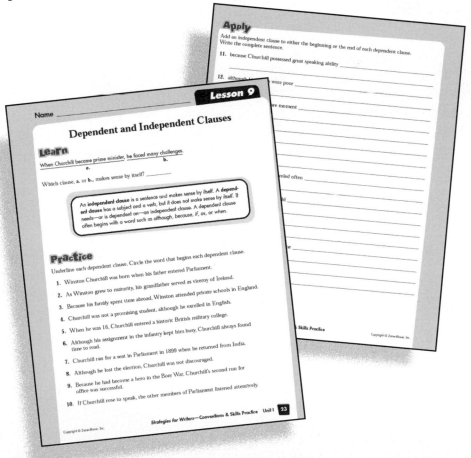

Level E **Conventions & Skills Practice Book** pages shown.

The Student Edition

An engaging, step-by-step instructional plan empowers students to take their writing to the next step.

THE NEXT Step

Model

Student writing partners in each chapter walk students, step-by-step, through an entire writing process to create a specific type of writing.

Halle
Writer of a
Letter to the Editor

Name: Halle
Home: Florida
Favorite Clothes: old jeans my big sister used to wear
Hobby: taking care of my dog, two cats, gerbil, and parrot
Favorite Book: *The Incredible Journey* by Sheila Burnford
Assignment: letter to the editor

213

Conversational text throughout the Student Edition engages students and makes learning fun.

Prewriting

Gather
Use what I read and learn from others to form an opinion about a topic.

"I love pets! That's why I got so upset when I learned that our local animal shelter is in big trouble. The people who work and volunteer there have way too much to do. The staff really cares about animals—like I do—but they don't get enough money or help. I decided something had to be done!

"First, I wanted to learn as much as I could about animal shelters. I found some good newspaper and magazine articles at the library. The librarian helped me find some information on the Internet, and I talked to people at the local shelter. Here are some of the notes I took on what I learned."

Opinion

An **opinion** is a belief, often strong, that cannot be proven to be true.

My Notes About the Local Animal Shelter
- The shelter finds homes for animals, provides shelter for strays, helps people find lost pets, educates people about owning pets, helps control rabies and other diseases, and investigates pet abuse and neglect.
- The shelter is understaffed. Cages get cleaned only once a week. Animals get little time outside their cages.
- The shelter needs volunteers to care for and play with the animals, help get animals ready for adoption, clean cages and play areas, raise money, talk to school classes about the shelter, answer telephones, and do many other tasks.

Go to page 104 in the **Practice Notebook!**

214 **Persuasive Writing** • Letter to the Editor

Level E Student Edition pages shown.

During Prewriting, writing partners model the prewriting strategies of gathering and organizing information.

Prewriting

Organize
Make an outline to focus and support my opinion.

"After reading over my notes on the animal shelter, I decided to write a letter to the editor of our local newspaper. I will encourage the people in our town, especially the kids, to volunteer at the shelter and help make it a great place for animals and people.

"The **Rubric** reminds me to organize my reasons from most important to least important. I decided to use an outline to do that. I've got three main points. They'll be the Roman numerals I., II., and III. I'll make I. my most important reason."

I. The shelter provides important services.
  A. It finds homes for animals.
  B. It helps people find lost pets.
  C. It helps control rabies and other diseases.
  D. The staff investigates pet abuse and neglect.
II. Staff is working hard, but there aren't enough people.
  A. There is only one staff person for every 40 animals.
  B. Cages get cleaned only once a week.
  C. Animals do not get much play time.
III. Community is not helping enough with money.
  A. Shelter needs more equipment and supplies.
  B. Our town spends more on holiday decorations than on the animal shelter.

Outline

An **outline** shows the main points or reasons and supporting details or facts in a piece of writing. Each main point or reason should have a Roman numeral. Each supporting detail should have a capital letter. An outline can be written in sentences or phrases—but not a combination of both.

the Strategy
Practice Notebook!

Persuasive Writing • Lett

A variety of graphic organizers helps students organize their information.

Prewriting

Organize Make an outline to focus and support my opinion.

Below is part of a topic outline that a writer made using the notes on page 104. Read his notes.

I. Problems with the school grounds
   A. Litter and trash
   B. Bike racks tipped over
   C. Bushes overgrown and unhealthy
   D. New plantings needed
   E. Sports fields need cleaning
   F. New paint needed in many places

II. Benefits of making school grounds more attractive
   A. More pleasant to come to school
   B. Increased pride among students
   C. Increased respect from parents, other adults, and community members
   D. Increased school spirit from working together on a project

Now it's time for you to practice this strategy. You will help this writer organize each section of his letter. Decide which of the problems listed in the first section (I.) of his outline is most important. Write the letter of that problem (A.–F.) below and explain why you think it is the most important. Then decide which of the benefits (II.) is most important. Write its letter (A.–D.) and explain your choice.

Most Important Problem: _____

Most Important Benefit: _____

106   **Persuasive Writing** · Letter to the Editor

Guided Practice

After each step is modeled, students are directed to their **Practice the Strategy Notebook** to practice.

Drafting

Write Draft my letter to the editor. State my opinion, support it, and sum up my argument.

your own writing

Now it's time for you to practice this strategy. On these two pages, draft your own letter to the editor, using your outline on page 107. Start with your opinion, support it, and sum up your argument at the end of your letter. You do not need to include all the parts of a business letter, such as the heading and salutation, in this draft.

108   **Persuasive Writing** · Letter to the Editor

Level E **Practice the Strategy Notebook** pages shown.

Prewriting

Organize Make an outline to focus and support my opinion.

your own writing

Now it's time for you to practice this strategy. Make an outline below for your own letter to the editor. You can use a sentence outline or a topic outline. Use your notes on page 105. Outline only the reasons you will use to support your opinion. Put them in order from most important to least important. Use another sheet of paper if you need more room.

I. _____
   A. _____
   B. _____
   C. _____

II. _____
   A. _____
   B. _____
   C. _____

III. _____
   A. _____
   B. _____
   C. _____

Now go back to Halle's work on page 216 in the Student Edition.

Persuasive Writing · Letter to the Editor   107

Level E **Practice the Strategy Notebook** page shown.

Apply to

After students practice the strategy, they can immediately apply the strategy to their own work. Then, they are directed back to their Student Edition to go on to the next step.

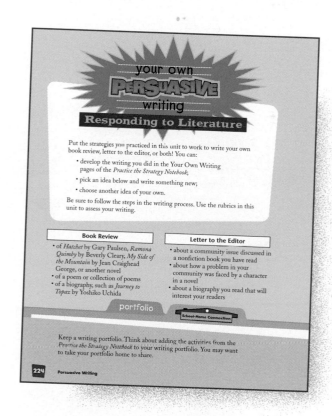

your own **PERSUASIVE** *writing*

Responding to Literature

Put the strategies you practiced in this unit to work to write your own book review, letter to the editor, or both! You can:

- develop the writing you did in the Your Own Writing pages of the *Practice the Strategy Notebook*;
- pick an idea below and write something new;
- choose another idea of your own.

Be sure to follow the steps in the writing process. Use the rubrics in this unit to assess your writing.

Book Review	**Letter to the Editor**
• of *Hatchet* by Gary Paulsen, *Ramona Quimby* by Beverly Cleary, *My Side of the Mountain* by Jean Craighead George, or another novel • of a poem or collection of poems • of a biography, such as *Journey to Topaz* by Yoshiko Uchida	• about a community issue discussed in a nonfiction book you have read • about how a problem in your community was faced by a character in a novel • about a biography you read that will interest your readers

portfolio   School-Home Connection

Keep a writing portfolio. Think about adding the activities from the *Practice the Strategy Notebook* to your writing portfolio. You may want to take your portfolio home to share.

224   Persuasive Writing

Level E Student Edition page shown.

At the end of each unit, writing prompts help students apply the writing strategies to other content areas.

in Teaching Writing

The Teacher Edition

A complete, step-by-step guide makes it easy for teachers to improve students' writing.

Tips from a master classroom teacher are provided for classroom activities designed to improve students' writing and communication skills.

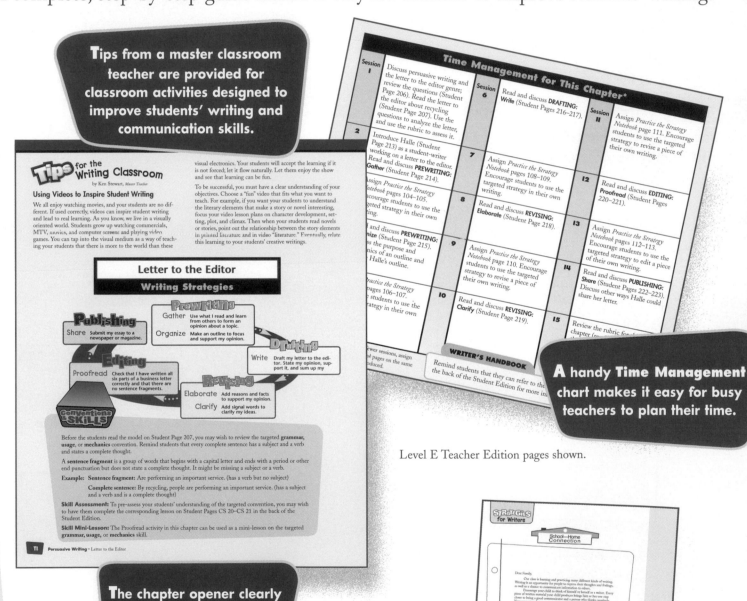

A handy **Time Management** chart makes it easy for busy teachers to plan their time.

Level E Teacher Edition pages shown.

The chapter opener clearly displays the writing process with the strategies being taught.

Blackline masters keep families informed and involved.

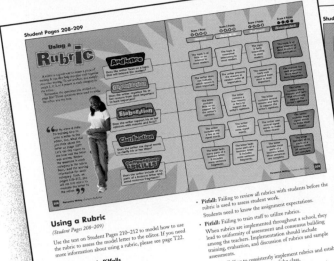

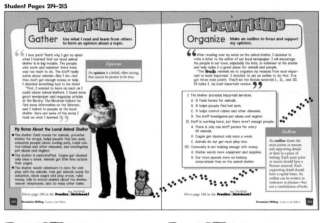

The rubric is introduced early in each chapter, so teaching is focused and students know from the start what is expected of them.

Teaching suggestions are provided to help meet the needs of every student.

The Teacher Edition is fully annotated and student pages are clearly displayed, so it's easy for teachers to stay organized.

Clear instructions are provided for teachers to guide their students, step-by-step, through the writing process.

Practice the Strategy Notebook assignments are highlighted and clearly described.

Level E Teacher Edition pages shown.

in Writing Assessment

The **Rubric** provides clear guidelines for students to assess other students' writing, for students to assess their own writing, and for teachers to assess students' writing.

Level E Student Edition pages shown.

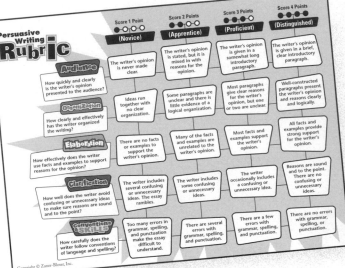

Level E rubric shown.

Global rubrics that can be used as pretest and posttest rubrics are available in the Teacher Edition Appendix.

During the publishing step of the writing process, students use the **Rubric** to assess both the writing partner's writing and any of their own writing that was developed within the chapter.

THE NEXT Step

Standardized Test-Taking

Strategies for Writers supports students' success on the **Terra Nova Basic Battery** by developing students' abilities in these key areas:

- Demonstrate an understanding of topic sentences.
- Demonstrate an understanding of concluding sentences.
- Demonstrate an understanding of connective and transitional words and phrases.
- Demonstrate an understanding of supportive statements.
- Demonstrate an understanding of sequence of ideas.
- Demonstrate an understanding of relevance of information.
- Focus on a topic and develop an organized response.

Strategies for Writers supports students' success on the **Stanford 9 Achievement Test** by developing students' abilities in these key areas:

- Demonstrate an understanding of the descriptive writing mode.
- Demonstrate an understanding of the narrative writing mode.
- Demonstrate an understanding of the expository writing mode.
- Demonstrate an understanding of the persuasive writing mode.
- Produce writing that has clear and coherent paragraphs that develop a central idea.
- Produce writing that shows evidence of considering audience and purpose.
- Produce writing that is developed by progressing through the writing process (i.e., prewriting, drafting, revising, and editing successive versions).
- Produce writing that demonstrates grade-level appropriate knowledge of grammar, usage, and mechanics.

Strategies for Writers supports students' success on the **ITBS (Iowa Tests of Basic Skills)** by developing students' abilities in these key areas:

- Produce writing that demonstrates an understanding of capitalization.
- Produce writing that demonstrates an understanding of punctuation.
- Produce writing that demonstrates an understanding of usage and expression.

NCTE/IRA Standards

Strategies for Writers aligns with these **NCTE/IRA** Standards:

Students adjust their use of spoken, written, and visual language (e.g., conventions, style, vocabulary) to communicate effectively with a variety of audiences and for different purposes.

Students employ a wide range of strategies as they write and use different writing process elements appropriately to communicate with different audiences for a variety of purposes.

Students apply knowledge of language structure, language conventions (e.g., spelling and punctuation), media techniques, figurative language, and genre to create, critique, and discuss print and non-print texts.

Students conduct research on issues and interests by generating ideas and questions and by posing problems. They gather, evaluate, and synthesize data from a variety of sources (e.g., print and non-print texts, artifacts, people) to communicate their discoveries in ways that suit their purpose and audience.

Students use a variety of technological and information resources (e.g., libraries, databases, computer networks, video) to gather and synthesize information and to create and communicate knowledge.

Students use spoken, written, and visual language to accomplish their own purposes (e.g., for learning, enjoyment, persuasion, and the exchange of information).

Table of Contents

Table of Contents

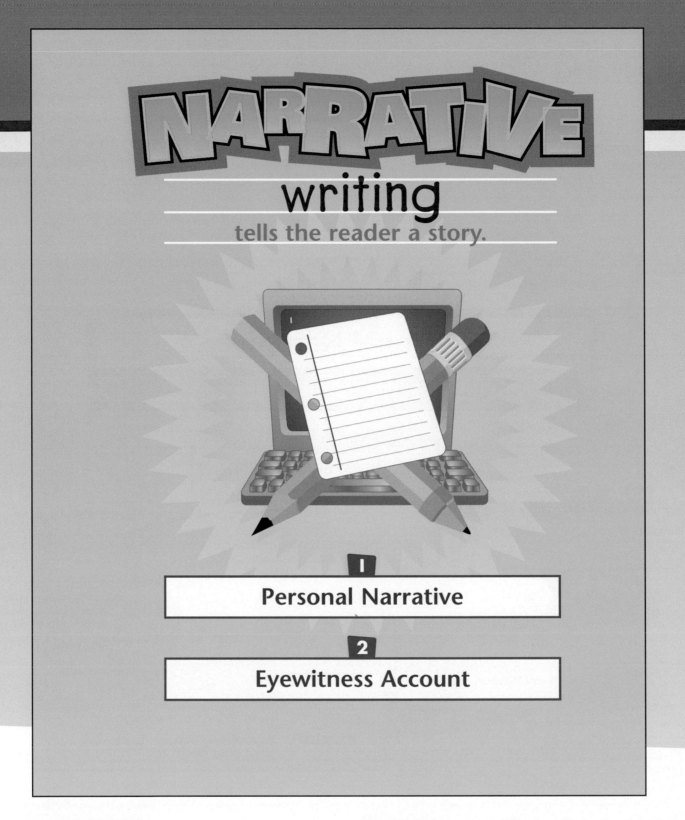

NARRATIVE writing

tells the reader a story.

1 Personal Narrative

2 Eyewitness Account

Defining Narrative Writing

Begin this unit by sharing one or two personal stories with students. These stories might recall the best day of your summer vacation, a funny/exciting/scary thing that happened to you, or your first/best day of teaching. Be sure to tell each story in chronological order. If you prefer, read two short nonfiction stories of your choice.

Read the unit opener (Student Page 9) with your students. Emphasize that the primary purpose of narrative writing is to tell a story. Guide the class in a discussion of the kinds of narrative writing. Discuss

- the reasons why personal narratives, eyewitness accounts, and letters CAN be examples of narrative writing and

- the reasons why some other types of writing, such as persuasive essays, editorials, and research reports, CAN'T be examples of narrative writing.

 **for the Writing Classroom**

by Ken Stewart, *Master Teacher*

Committing to a Philosophy of Student Cooperation, Ownership, and Personalization Education (SCOPE)

Too often teachers spend too much of their time disciplining students rather than teaching. It is not uncommon to hear an educator complaining about wasting as much as fifty percent or more of his/her time on discipline. Many of these problems may be the result of how a classroom is structured.

In a language arts setting teachers should always encourage oral (includes listening) and written communication. To do this, you are encouraged to structure a classroom that allows students to cooperate, to have ownership in how they learn, and to personalize the learning so it becomes meaningful.

By using **cooperative** learning, students are guided to cooperate in order to solve problems to achieve a common goal. You, as the teacher, take on the role of facilitator. This requires the teacher to accept that there are different roads to get to a destination. At times these roads may be longer or shorter, but the key is that we all get there.

Giving students **ownership** in how they learn seems to frighten many educators. Give your students "teacher-guided, decision-

Personal Narrative

Writing Strategies

Prewriting

Gather — Look at photographs to get ideas. Pick a photo that reminds me of a personal experience.

Organize — Organize my thoughts in a storyboard.

Drafting

Write — Draft the body of my personal narrative by writing one or more sentences about each picture on my storyboard.

Revising

Elaborate — Write an introduction and a conclusion that will interest my reader.

Clarify — Replace overused words and clichés with more exact words and fresh language.

Editing

Proofread — Make sure I have avoided run-on sentences by joining compound sentences correctly.

Conventions & Skills

Publishing

Share — Submit my personal narrative to a magazine.

Before the students read the model on Student Pages 11–13, you may wish to review the targeted **grammar, usage,** or **mechanics** convention. Remind students that when two sentences are joined, they become a compound sentence. Explain that compound sentences can be joined by placing a comma and a coordinating conjunction (*and, but,* or *or*) or a semicolon between the sentences.

Examples: I had fun at camp, **and** I can't wait to go back.

I had fun at camp; I can't wait to go back.

Skill Assessment: To pre-assess your students' understanding of the targeted convention, you may wish to have them complete the corresponding lesson on Student Pages CS 2–CS 3 in the back of the Student Edition.

Skill Mini-Lesson: The Proofread activity in this chapter can be used as a mini-lesson on the targeted **grammar, usage,** or **mechanics** skill.

making empowerment." Establish well-defined criteria (specific to the writing genre being taught) and give your students options as to how to reach those criteria. Within the parameters of your lesson, give your students freedom to design how they will accomplish their tasks. Try it; you may be surprised.

Personalization is the ability to make school and the "real" world one and the same. You need to set aside time for the students to share their writings, to discuss their thoughts, and to understand how their ideas are part of a larger picture. Help them understand that they are not just writing for a grade, but that they are writing to communicate valuable ideas worthy of thought, discussion, and action (whenever possible).

For one to move from a dictator/lecturer style of teaching to a facilitator/coach style, you need to make a commitment to all three areas: cooperation, ownership, and personalization. By doing so, you will be meeting the needs of most of your students most of the time. You may also find that competition is reduced and an attitude of working with others will replace it. As often as possible, everyone's needs will be met and incidents of conflict will be greatly reduced.

(See "More Tips for the Writing Classroom: SCOPE Philosophy" on page T31 for four easy steps to set up this progressive type of classroom.)

Time Management for This Chapter*

Session 1	Discuss the personal narrative genre; review the questions (Student Page 10). Read "Don't Call Me Goldilocks" (Student Pages 11–13). Use the questions to analyze the article. Use the rubric to assess it.	Session 6	Read and discuss **DRAFTING: Write** (Student Pages 22–23).	Session 11	Assign *Practice the Strategy Notebook* page 12. Encourage students to use the targeted strategy to revise a piece of their own writing.
2	Introduce Janell (Student Page 19) as a student-writer working on a personal narrative. Read and discuss **PREWRITING: Gather** (Student Page 20).	7	Assign *Practice the Strategy Notebook* page 9. Encourage students to use the targeted strategy in their own writing.	12	Read and discuss **EDITING: Proofread** (Student Pages 28–29).
3	Assign *Practice the Strategy Notebook* pages 6–7. Encourage students to use the targeted strategy in their own writing.	8	Read and discuss **REVISING: Elaborate** (Student Pages 24–25).	13	Assign *Practice the Strategy Notebook* page 13. Encourage students to use the targeted strategy to edit a piece of their own writing.
4	Read and discuss **PREWRITING: Organize** (Student Page 21). Discuss the purpose and mechanics of a storyboard and analyze Janell's storyboard.	9	Assign *Practice the Strategy Notebook* pages 10–11. Encourage students to use the targeted strategy to revise a piece of their own writing.	14	Read and discuss **PUBLISHING: Share** (Student Pages 30–33). Discuss other ways Janell could share what she has written.
5	Assign *Practice the Strategy Notebook* page 8. Encourage students to use the targeted strategy in their own writing.	10	Read and discuss **REVISING: Clarify** (Student Pages 26–27).	15	Review the rubric for this chapter (reprinted on *Practice the Strategy Notebook* pages 14–15). Ask pairs of students to use the rubric to discuss and evaluate Janell's essay.

WRITER'S HANDBOOK

* To complete the chapter in fewer sessions, assign the *Practice the Strategy Notebook* pages on the same day the targeted strategy is introduced.

Remind students that they can refer to the Writer's Handbook in the back of the Student Edition for more information.

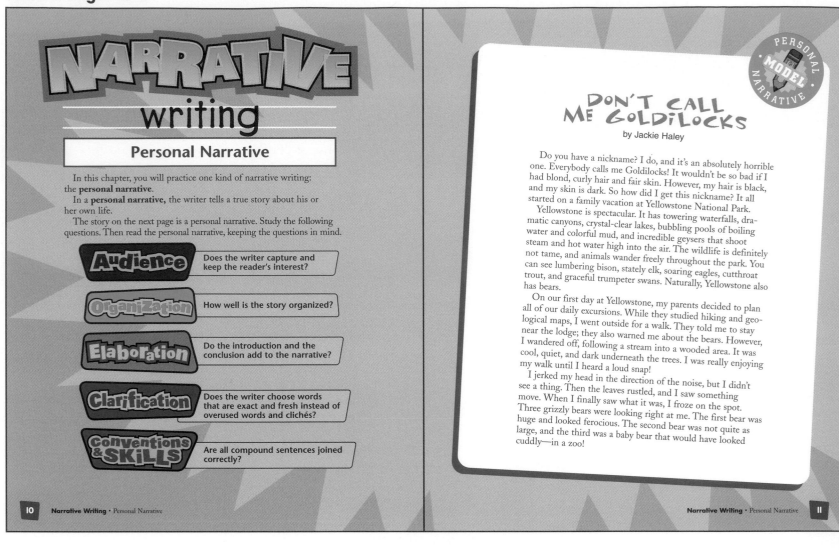

Introduce the Genre:
Personal Narrative

Ask student volunteers to tell stories about any of the following:

- their best birthday
- the best day of their summer vacation
- the day they learned an important lesson
- their very first day of school

Explain that students are telling narratives. One type of narrative writing is the *personal narrative*. In this type of writing, the author writes a story about an event in his/her life. Emphasize that personal narratives are written in first person.

Conclude by telling students that they are going to study and practice strategies for writing a personal narrative.

Discuss the Questions

(Student Page 10)

Read the questions on Student Page 10 aloud. Point out the five categories and be sure students are clear on their meaning in the context of writing. Possible points to discuss:

Audience: The writer must keep the audience in mind. It is important to capture the reader's attention right away and keep it throughout the piece of writing.

Organization: Different types of writing lend themselves to different organizational strategies. A personal narrative usually describes an event in the order it occurred.

Elaboration: A good writer fully explains a topic by elaborating. Writing an introduction and a conclusion that interest the reader is an effective way to elaborate.

Clarification: A good writer replaces overused words and clichés with more exact words and fresh language.

Conventions & Skills: Writers who join compound sentences correctly make their writing easier for the audience to read and understand.

Read the Model:
Personal Narrative

(Student Pages 11–13)

Read "Don't Call Me Goldilocks" aloud.

I couldn't move a muscle, but my mind was racing. What did my parents say about bears? How was I supposed to get away from them? I tried to calm down. The bears didn't look too unhappy; that was good. I remembered that Mom said bears have a good sense of smell and bad eyesight. I hoped I didn't smell too good, and I really hoped they couldn't see me very well. She had also said that bears could run over 30 miles per hour. I took a deep breath and decided that I was in serious trouble.

I don't know how long I stood there, but it seemed like forever. I was starting to panic when I heard a low voice say, "Stay calm. I'm right behind you." I cannot tell you how happy I was to hear Dad's voice! He said not to look at the bears; he told me to back away quietly and carefully. As I moved backward very slowly, I knew the three bears were watching me closely.

After several long minutes, Dad said, "I think we're okay now, so turn around and follow me. Don't say a word until I do." When we reached the clearing, he grabbed me and hugged me. "What were you thinking?" he asked in a voice that shook a little. "You could have been killed!"

What could I say? I glanced back and breathed a long sigh of relief. The bears weren't anywhere in sight.

As we hurried toward the lodge, Dad turned to me and said, "Guess we'll have to call you Goldilocks from now on. You could have gotten into a lot of trouble with those three bears today." I sighed; I knew what was coming. Dad went in and announced to everyone that he had saved me. He described the three bears and my predicament in great detail and with elaborate gestures. I got lots of hugs and lectures that afternoon, and, unfortunately, I also got a nickname.

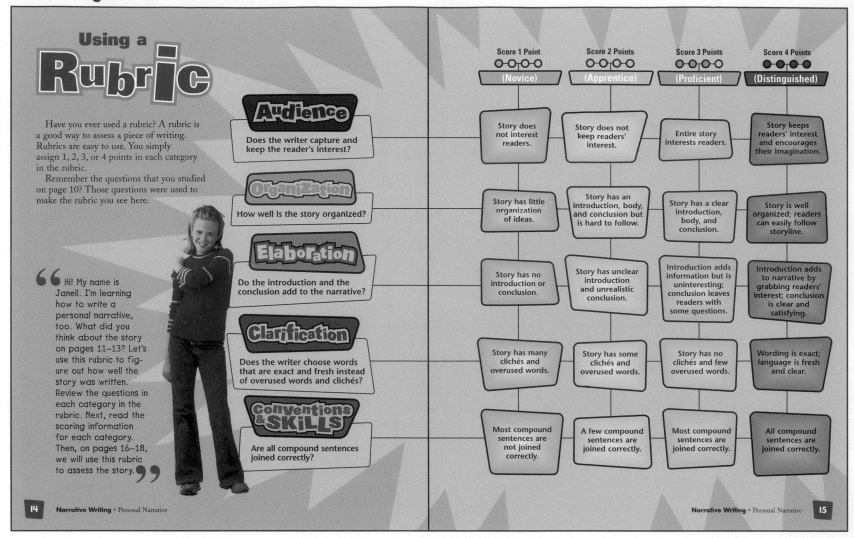

Using a Rubric

(Student Pages 14–15)

Explain that a rubric is a tool for assessing a piece of writing. The rubric on these pages will be used to evaluate a personal narrative. Tell students that a rubric helps a reader focus on key elements in writing (audience, organization, elaboration, clarification, and conventions and skills).

Read the questions aloud and point out that they are the same questions that were listed before the model personal narrative.

Guide students in a discussion of the rubric. Read the four descriptors that go with each question, and take a moment to explain the relationship between a point score and the terms *novice, apprentice, proficient,* and *distinguished*. (A novice or beginner's performance, for example, will not be as skilled as someone who has more experience.)

Remind students that this is a model personal narrative, so it should do well in all areas of the rubric.

Use Student Pages 16–18 to model the use of the rubric in evaluating a piece of writing.

A Few Words About Rubrics

by Rebecca Sipe, *Program Author*

What are rubrics and why are they important to teachers? Rubrics are a way to help define clearly the qualities in student writing. Though teachers may choose to emphasize different traits, rubrics frequently address areas such as **audience, organization, elaboration** (i.e., adding information), **clarification** (including areas such as **voice**), and **conventions** (grammar and spelling). Each trait will be broken down into levels (e.g., novice, apprentice, proficient, distinguished), and each level will describe the writer's demonstration of proficiency with that trait.

When teachers and students work with a rubric, we can use it to talk with students about the strengths and weaknesses of their papers and to show them how to improve their work.

We've all heard that teachers can't agree on how to evaluate or assess writing. That just isn't true. When we take time to consciously identify the traits and levels of quality reflected in student writing, it is easy for teachers—and even parents and students—to reach agreement on assessment.

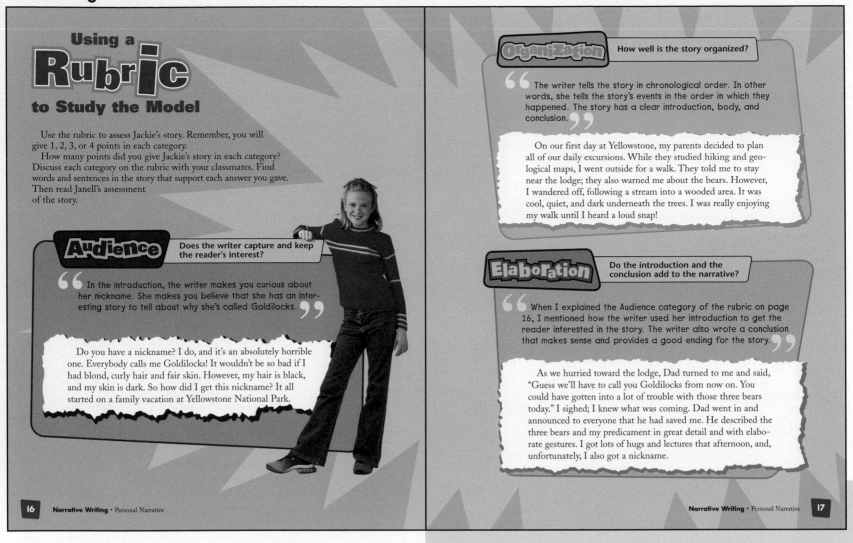

Using a Rubric to Study the Personal Narrative

(Student Pages 16–18)

Read the questions and answers on Student Pages 16–18. Discuss whether students agree or disagree with each point in Janell's assessment of the story. For example, do students agree that the writer captures and keeps the reader's interest? Can they think of a better way to capture or keep the reader's interest?

Note on Conventions & Skills: Remind students that this rubric focuses attention on an important skill: joining compound sentences correctly. However, students should always check their writing for correct spelling, punctuation, and capitalization.

Meeting Students' Needs:
Second Language Learners

The compound sentence is sometimes difficult to grasp. Write related simple sentences on strips of cardboard. Then make additional cardboard strips with *and, but,* and *or* printed on them. Also make strips with a comma (,) and a semicolon (;) on them. Guide students as they create and punctuate compound sentences with the cardboard strips.

Students Who Need Extra Help

Some students will need guidance in understanding the importance of chronological order in personal narratives. To stress this point, ask students to reread the model narrative and list the main events as they occur. Emphasize the importance of order by encouraging the students to use words such as *first, next, then, finally,* and *in the end.*

Gifted Students

Challenge students to retell/rewrite the model story, or another short nonfictional story, from the perspective of another character in the story. For example, students could retell/rewrite the model story from the father's perspective. Remind them that the narrator should speak/write in first person.

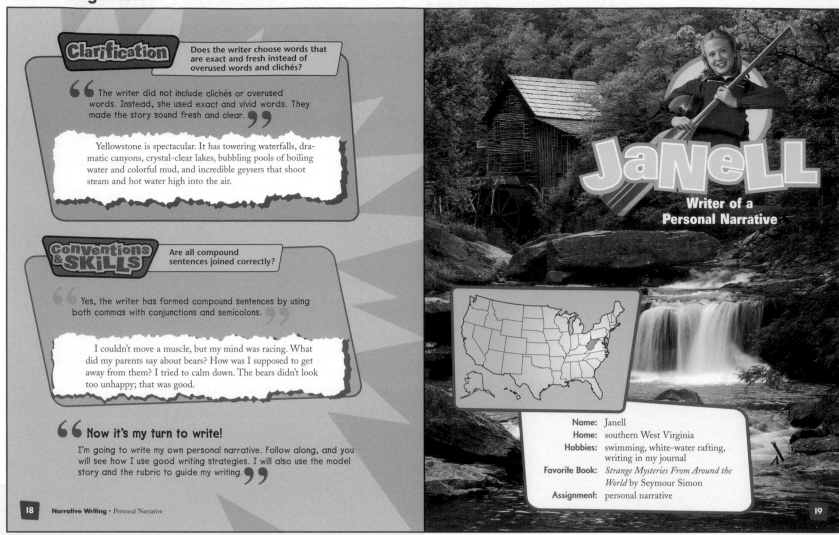

Clarification — Does the writer choose words that are exact and fresh instead of overused words and clichés?

"The writer did not include clichés or overused words. Instead, she used exact and vivid words. They made the story sound fresh and clear."

Yellowstone is spectacular. It has towering waterfalls, dramatic canyons, crystal-clear lakes, bubbling pools of boiling water and colorful mud, and incredible geysers that shoot steam and hot water high into the air.

Conventions & Skills — Are all compound sentences joined correctly?

"Yes, the writer has formed compound sentences by using both commas with conjunctions and semicolons."

I couldn't move a muscle, but my mind was racing. What did my parents say about bears? How was I supposed to get away from them? I tried to calm down. The bears didn't look too unhappy; that was good.

"**Now it's my turn to write!**

I'm going to write my own personal narrative. Follow along, and you will see how I use good writing strategies. I will also use the model story and the rubric to guide my writing."

18 Narrative Writing • Personal Narrative

JaNeLL
Writer of a Personal Narrative

Name: Janell
Home: southern West Virginia
Hobbies: swimming, white-water rafting, writing in my journal
Favorite Book: *Strange Mysteries From Around the World* by Seymour Simon
Assignment: personal narrative

19

Unlocking Text Structure:
Personal Narrative

The structure of any writing depends upon how information is organized. To help your students unlock the structure of the personal narrative, you may wish to use the graphic organizer in this unit. The storyboard lends itself to understanding the process of writing a personal narrative.

Help your students define the terms *chronological* and *sequential*. Then review some of the stories you and your students have told one another using the storyboard graphic as a guide. Explain that chronological or sequential order is essential in writing a personal narrative.

Janell:
Writer of a Personal Narrative

(Student Page 19)

Read the information about Janell to learn more about her.

Make sure students understand that Janell will write her own personal narrative in this chapter. Discuss what she might choose to write about. Check to see if students' suggestions reflect a clear understanding of the narrative mode of writing.

Point out that Janell will go through all the steps in the writing process: Prewriting, Drafting, Revising, Editing, and Publishing. At each stage she will demonstrate a good writing strategy and explain how she used it. Students should watch for key words, such as **Gather, Organize, Write, Elaborate, Clarify, Proofread,** and **Share**.

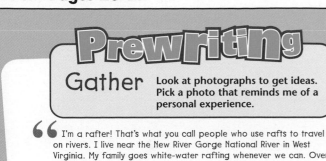
Prewriting
Gather
Look at photographs to get ideas. Pick a photo that reminds me of a personal experience.

" I'm a rafter! That's what you call people who use rafts to travel on rivers. I live near the New River Gorge National River in West Virginia. My family goes white-water rafting whenever we can. Over the years, my parents have taught me all about staying safe on rivers. Rafting can be dangerous, so I need to know what I'm doing.

"When my teacher asked us to write personal narratives, I decided to look at pictures of rafting in our family album. I knew that those pictures would help me remember some of my experiences. I discovered that I had many good stories locked up in my memory! "

Go to page 6 in the **Practice the Strategy Notebook!**

20   Narrative Writing • Personal Narrative

Prewriting
Organize
Organize my thoughts in a storyboard.

" I know from the **Rubric** that organization is important. When I looked at the pictures, I remembered so many stories. There was so much to tell! I decided to make a storyboard. A storyboard could help me organize my thoughts. Then I could write a great story about rafting! "

> **Storyboard**
>
> A **storyboard** is a series of pictures. The pictures show the main events of a story in the order they happen.

Go to page 8 in the **Practice the Strategy Notebook!**

Narrative Writing • Personal Narrative   21

Prewriting Gather

Strategy: Look at photographs to get ideas. Pick a photo that reminds me of a personal experience.

(Student Page 20)

Read the text with students. Then study and discuss the picture. Ask students to suggest a possible storyline, based on the picture. [**Possible responses: The boat overturned, and they fell into the water; the life jackets saved their lives.**]

Practice the Strategy Notebook!

Assign pages 6–7 in the *Practice the Strategy Notebook*. (Your Own Writing sections should be used as time and students' abilities permit.) Explain that the students will practice this Gather strategy with a different topic. Suggested responses for the *Practice the Strategy Notebook* appear in the Appendix at the back of this Teacher Edition.

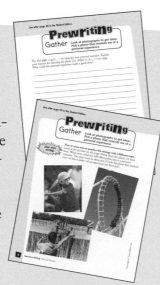

Prewriting Organize

Strategy: Organize my thoughts in a storyboard.

(Student Page 21)

Explain that writing can be organized in many different ways. A graphic organizer is one way to organize information in preparation for writing.

Ask which strategy Janell is using to organize her information. Review the definition of *storyboard* on the page. Then direct attention to Janell's storyboard.

Practice the Strategy Notebook!

Assign page 8 in the *Practice the Strategy Notebook*. Allow students plenty of time to complete this activity. If necessary, they can go back to the Gather step to get more ideas for their own storyboards.

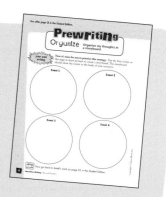

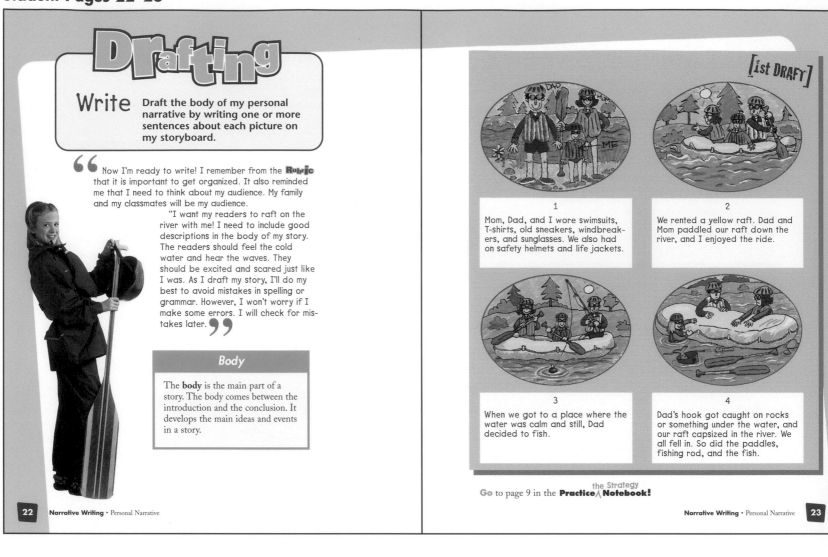

Drafting Write

Strategy: Draft the body of my personal narrative by writing one or more sentences about each picture on my storyboard.

(Student Pages 22–23)

Begin by asking students what it means to write a rough draft. Be sure they understand that a draft is a temporary or "rough" form of writing. A draft will be changed and corrected several times before it is ready for readers. Then have a student read Janell's sentences for the class, or read them yourself.

Ask students why Janell is not worried about making mistakes in spelling and grammar as she writes her draft. **[Possible response: She is eager to get her ideas down on paper during the drafting stage. She will do her best with spelling and grammar and correct her errors during the revising and editing stages.]**

Refer to the Rubric: The student spokesperson will refer to the rubric throughout the chapter. Remind students to get into the habit of referring back to the rubric so they fully understand its use as a tool for shaping their writing.

the Strategy Practice ∧ Notebook!

Assign page 9 in the *Practice the Strategy Notebook*. Be sure students can explain why they wrote certain sentences. Have volunteers read their sentences. Then ask the class if they are written in the first person. Also ask students to determine whether the sentences are written in chronological, or sequential, order.

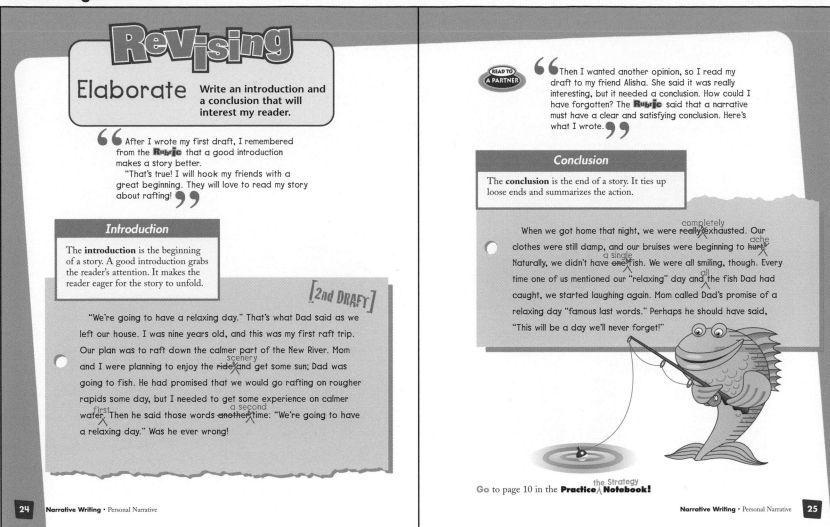

Revising Elaborate

Strategy: Write an introduction and a conclusion that will interest my reader.

(Student Pages 24–25)

Ask a student to take the part of Janell and read her words to the class.

Ask a different student to identify the strategy Janell will use. **[Response: Write an introduction and a conclusion that will interest my reader.]** Read the information about the purposes of an introduction and conclusion in the boxes. Guide students as they study Janell's introduction and conclusion. Invite them to add words and details that make the introduction and conclusion more interesting. For example, students might include a description of how Janell felt as she left the house to go on the raft trip or what the family looked like when they returned home that night.

Practice the Strategy Notebook!

Assign *Practice the Strategy Notebook* pages 10–11. Ask volunteers to share their revised introductions and conclusions with the class.

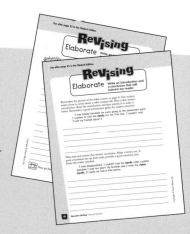

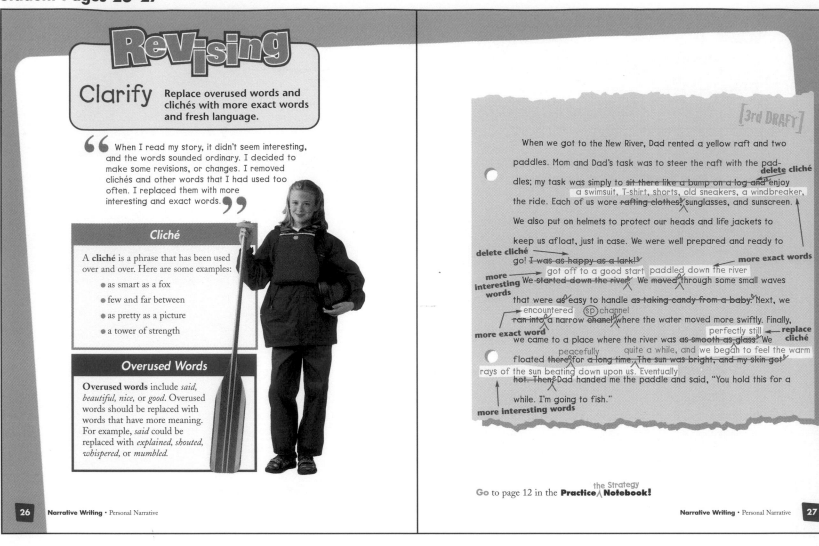

Revising Clarify

Strategy: Replace overused words and clichés with more exact words and fresh language.

(Student Pages 26–27)

Ask a student to take the part of Janell and read her words to the class. Have other students explain why Janell's revisions make the wording more exact and the language fresher.

Invite students to suggest other overused words and clichés that they have heard or read too many times. Ask them to think of fresher, more exact ways to express the same ideas.

Practice the Strategy Notebook!

Assign *Practice the Strategy Notebook* page 12. Ask volunteers to share their revised sentences with the class.

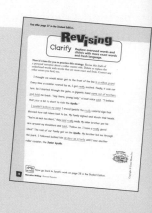

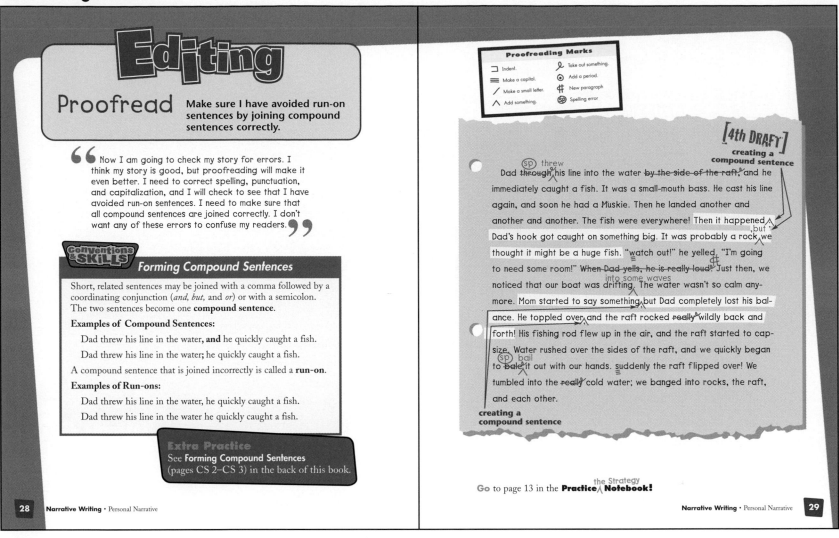

Editing   Proofread

Strategy: Make sure I have avoided run-on sentences by joining compound sentences correctly.

(Student Pages 28–29)

Discuss the difference between revising and editing. Be sure that students understand that in the revising step they look for ways to make their personal narratives clearer, more interesting, and more complete. In the editing step, they look for errors in spelling, punctuation, and grammar.

Ask a volunteer to read Janell's words to the class. Remind the students that good writers search for spelling, punctuation, and grammar errors when they proofread. Explain that it is also helpful to focus on specific errors, especially the kinds of skills that students may have had problems with in the past.

Practice the Strategy Notebook!

Assign *Practice the Strategy Notebook* page 13. If necessary, review the proofreading marks and demonstrate their use on the chalkboard.

Extra Practice: Conventions & Skills Student Edition

If you did not use Student Pages CS 2–CS 3 as a pre-assessment tool and your students need more practice in writing complete sentences, you may wish to assign these pages now.

Conventions & Skills Practice

For more targeted practice related to this skill, see these lessons in the optional *Conventions & Skills Practice Book*:

Lesson   1: Complete Subjects and Complete Predicates
Lesson   2: Simple Subjects and Simple Predicates
Lesson   3: Compound Subjects and Compound Predicates
Lesson 10: Avoiding Fragments, Run-ons, Comma Splices
Lesson 20: Coordinating and Subordinating Conjunctions
Lesson 41: Writing Sentences Correctly
Lesson 47: Commas
Lesson 48: Using Semicolons

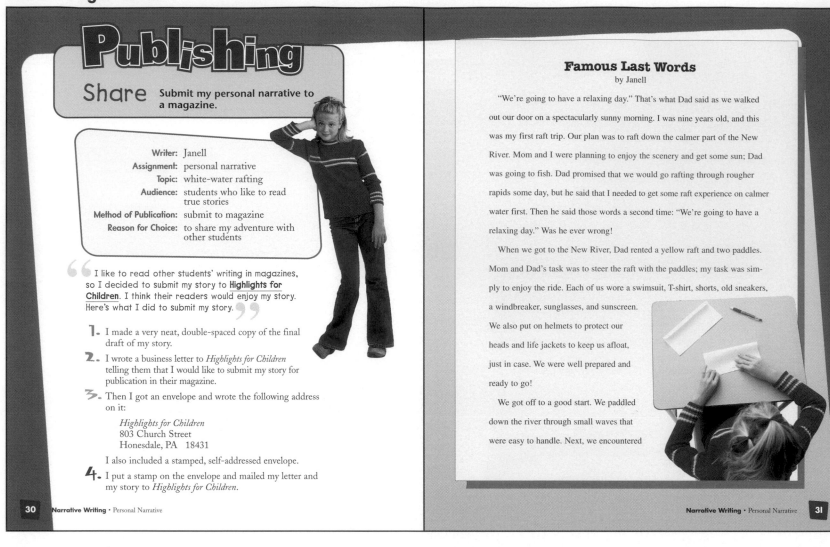

Publishing

Share Submit my personal narrative to a magazine.

Writer: Janell
Assignment: personal narrative
Topic: white-water rafting
Audience: students who like to read true stories
Method of Publication: submit to magazine
Reason for Choice: to share my adventure with other students

"I like to read other students' writing in magazines, so I decided to submit my story to **Highlights for Children**. I think their readers would enjoy my story. Here's what I did to submit my story."

1. I made a very neat, double-spaced copy of the final draft of my story.

2. I wrote a business letter to *Highlights for Children* telling them that I would like to submit my story for publication in their magazine.

3. Then I got an envelope and wrote the following address on it:

   Highlights for Children
   803 Church Street
   Honesdale, PA 18431

   I also included a stamped, self-addressed envelope.

4. I put a stamp on the envelope and mailed my letter and my story to *Highlights for Children*.

30 **Narrative Writing** • Personal Narrative

Famous Last Words
by Janell

"We're going to have a relaxing day." That's what Dad said as we walked out our door on a spectacularly sunny morning. I was nine years old, and this was my first raft trip. Our plan was to raft down the calmer part of the New River. Mom and I were planning to enjoy the scenery and get some sun; Dad was going to fish. Dad promised that we would go rafting through rougher rapids some day, but he said that I needed to get some raft experience on calmer water first. Then he said those words a second time: "We're going to have a relaxing day." Was he ever wrong!

When we got to the New River, Dad rented a yellow raft and two paddles. Mom and Dad's task was to steer the raft with the paddles; my task was simply to enjoy the ride. Each of us wore a swimsuit, T-shirt, shorts, old sneakers, a windbreaker, sunglasses, and sunscreen. We also put on helmets to protect our heads and life jackets to keep us afloat, just in case. We were well prepared and ready to go!

We got off to a good start. We paddled down the river through small waves that were easy to handle. Next, we encountered

Narrative Writing • Personal Narrative 31

Publishing Share

Strategy: Submit my personal narrative to a magazine.

(Student Pages 30–33)

Challenge students to think of other ways Janell could share what she has written. Ask if they think the strategy she chose was appropriate.

Using the Rubric

Ask students to work in pairs to use the rubric (reprinted on pages 14–15 of the *Practice the Strategy Notebook*) to evaluate Janell's paper. After each pair has made its decision, ask students to compare and discuss their evaluations.

a narrow channel where the water moved more swiftly. Finally, we came to a place where the river was perfectly still. We floated peacefully for quite a while, and we felt the warm rays of the sun beating down upon us. Eventually, Dad handed me the paddle and said, "You hold this while I fish."

Dad threw his line into the water, and he immediately caught a fish, a small-mouth bass. He cast his line again, and soon he had a muskie. Then he landed another and another and another. The fish were everywhere! Then it happened; Dad's hook got caught on something big. It was probably a rock, but we thought it might be a huge fish. "Watch out!" he yelled. "I'm going to need some room to get my line loose!"

Just then, we noticed that our boat was drifting into some waves that weren't so calm. Mom started to say something, but Dad completely lost his balance. He toppled over, and the raft rocked wildly back and forth! His fishing rod flew up in the air, and the raft started to capsize. Water rushed over the sides of the raft, and we quickly began to bail it out with our hands. Suddenly the raft flipped over! We tumbled into the cold water, banging into rocks, the raft, and each other. Then we noticed that everything was floating away. We managed to snag the paddles and the fishing rod, but the lucky fish were long gone. We struggled to turn the raft right side up and finally crawled in. We were soaking wet and more than a little cranky!

By the time we got home that night, we were completely exhausted. Our clothes were still damp, our bruises were beginning to ache, and we didn't have a single fish. We were all smiling, though. Every time one of us mentioned our "relaxing" day and all the fish Dad caught, we started laughing again. Mom called Dad's promise of a relaxing day his "famous last words." Perhaps he should have said, "This will be a day we'll never forget!"

Janell Smith
123 Main St.
Pleasantview, WV 12345

Highlights for Children
803 Church Street
Honesdale, PA 18431

USING the Rubic for Assessment

Go to pages 14–15 in the **Practice Notebook!** Use that rubric to assess Janell's paper. Try using the rubric to assess your own writing.

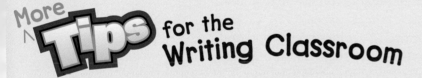

More Tips for the Writing Classroom

SCOPE Philosophy

Four easy steps to establish a SCOPE classroom:

1. Be prepared for your lesson. Always increase your knowledge of your subject matter by researching the most current advances in whatever you are teaching. Make sure all materials necessary to complete the task at a high level are readily available. Emphasize the importance of working together, stressing cooperation and collaboration over competition.

2. Have open discussions about the expectations of achieving criteria (specific to writing genre) and the time frame in which this work is to be completed. After having established this, you should make an effort to fit your lessons to the skill levels of the students.

3. Model what you consider to be outstanding work for a particular lesson. While modeling, continually get student input and be willing to make adjustments (if the student suggestions improve the lesson) whenever possible.

4. Evaluate student work and then allow the students to evaluate their own work. Then engage the students in a discussion to understand why their work was superior, average, or poor. Finally, have the students express, verbally or in writing, how they may improve their work, and if possible, allow them to do so.

You are now on your way to establishing a classroom that will meet the needs of each individual student as well as your own. In the following chapters there will be specific "Teacher Tips" that will help you continue your journey.

School–Home Connection

Dear Family,

In *Strategies for Writers,* your child is learning and practicing the writing process. This process is very important in helping people establish good writing skills and will help your child to develop communication skills that he or she will use throughout life.

The writing process is made up of five basic steps, which build on each other to help the writer produce a finished product—a piece of written work. The five steps are Prewriting, Drafting, Revising, Editing, and Publishing.

The first step is Prewriting. This is where the writer does two very important things—Gather and Organize information. When writers Gather, they may do formal research, such as looking up information in books and encyclopedias. They may also do informal research, such as talking to people or recalling their own experiences. They write lists, jot down notes, and do interviews. When writers Organize, they put information they have gathered into a form that will help them make sense of all they have learned, such as a web, a chart, or an outline.

The second step in the writing process is Drafting. Once a writer has gotten all the information necessary and organized that information, he or she writes the first version of a document—a first draft. It will be messy, and it may be full of mistakes, but that's the way it should be. The first draft will go through many changes before it becomes the final draft. The important thing is for the writer to get his or her ideas down on paper.

The next step is Revising. This is where the first draft becomes the second and then the third draft. The Revising step is made up of two smaller steps—Elaborating and Clarifying. When writers elaborate, they add missing facts, interesting details, descriptions, and other necessary information. When writers clarify, they make sure their writing says what they want it to say. They rearrange sentences and paragraphs, cut out unnecessary information, and make sure their writing is clear and concise.

The fourth step in the writing process is Editing. Now all those mistakes in grammar, punctuation, and spelling get ironed out. When they edit, writers proofread their work, find mistakes, and correct them.

The final step is Publishing. A final draft can be published in many ways. A writer may choose to type a neat copy and put it in a presentation folder to be turned in. A writer may submit the final draft to a newspaper or magazine. Many writers choose to publish their work on-line. The method of publication depends on the kind of writing.

As you can see, writing is a process. Very few, if any, writers can sit down once and write a perfect final draft. The steps in the writing process are the keys to good writing. *Strategies for Writers* is designed to help your child understand these steps and become comfortable using them.

You may wish to copy the letter above and send it home with your students.

Books on Teaching Writing

Jorgensen, Karen L. *The Whole Story: Crafting Fiction in the Upper Elementary Grades.* Portsmouth, NH: Heinemann, 2001.

The author takes students through the crafts of building characterization, discovering setting, clarifying plot, finding themes, and refining their stories. An appendix of blackline masters includes strategies to help students in grades 4–6 through the process of crafting fiction.

Anderson, Carl. *How's It Going?: A Practical Guide to Conferring with Student Writers.* Portsmouth, NH: Heinemann, 2001.

This source offers samples of the structured conferences that the author advocates. He demonstrates various techniques and strategies to help both the teacher and the student refine their participation.

Murray, Donald M. *Shoptalk: Learning to Write with Writers.* Portsmouth, NH: Boynton/Cook, 1990.

This collection of quotations is taken from a wide variety of writers on all aspects of the writing process. It includes comments from writers both famous and obscure. One example is from James Thurber: "Don't get it right, get it written."

Johnson, Paul. *Making Books: Over 30 Practical Book-Making Projects for Children.* Markham, Ont.: Pembroke, 2000.

Almost half of these projects, arranged from easy to complex, are designed for children in grades 3–6. The author explains the genres and the skills related to them. He deals with the informational, persuasive, and narrative writing modes.

 **for the Writing Classroom**

by Ken Stewart, *Master Teacher*

Establishing a Cooperative Atmosphere

If you establish a cooperative atmosphere from the first day of school, students will be encouraged to communicate openly in their writing and class discussions. An important component of the cooperative classroom is cooperative learning groups. However, placing students in groups without established guidelines or without practicing "how to work with group members" may be a prescription for failure. Follow these simple steps to give students experiences in becoming cooperative learners.

1. Post five easy-to-follow classroom rules:

   Rule 1: Always do your best work.

   Rule 2: When you think you have done your best, challenge yourself to make it better.

   Rule 3: Stay on task and be responsible for your own actions.

   Rule 4: When working in a group, use a 12-inch voice. (Speak softly.)

   Rule 5: Share all information and respect others' ideas. If one member of your group understands the lesson, all the members should understand.

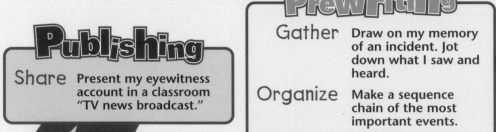

Before the students read the model on Student Pages 35–37, you may wish to review the targeted **grammar, usage, or mechanics** convention. Explain to students that they will be learning about subject pronouns, object pronouns, and pronouns that show ownership.

Examples: **He** told a story. (subject pronoun)

The teacher encouraged **him**. (object pronoun)

The student shared **his** eyewitness account. (pronoun that shows ownership)

Skill Assessment: To pre-assess your students' understanding of the targeted convention, you may wish to have them complete the corresponding lesson on Student Pages CS 4–CS 5 in the back of the Student Edition.

Skill Mini-Lesson: The Proofread activity in this chapter can be used as a mini-lesson on the targeted **grammar, usage,** or **mechanics** skill.

2. Create mini-lessons that give your students lots of opportunities to use cooperative learning in a variety of ways.

3. When introducing a cooperative learning style, allow at least five minutes for the whole class to process the positives and negatives of the experience. Offer encouragement for positive behaviors; allow students to suggest improvements.

4. Create a fun activity to allow students to process why working on a team is often better than working individually.

(See "More Tips for the Writing Classroom: Cooperative Classroom Decoding Activity," page T46.)

Time Management for This Chapter*

Session		Session		Session	
1	Discuss the eyewitness account genre; review the questions (Student Page 34). Read "The New Madrid Earthquake" (Student Pages 35–37). Use the questions to analyze the article. Use the rubric to assess it.	6	Read and discuss **DRAFTING: Write** (Student Pages 46–47).	11	Assign *Practice the Strategy Notebook* page 23. Encourage students to use the targeted strategy to revise a piece of their own writing.
2	Introduce William (Student Page 43) as a student-writer working on an eyewitness account. Read and discuss **PREWRITING: Gather** (Student Page 44).	7	Assign *Practice the Strategy Notebook* pages 20–21. Encourage students to use the targeted strategy in their own writing.	12	Read and discuss **EDITING: Proofread** (Student Pages 50–51).
3	Assign *Practice the Strategy Notebook* pages 16–17. Encourage students to use the targeted strategy in their own writing.	8	Read and discuss **REVISING: Elaborate** (Student Page 48).	13	Assign *Practice the Strategy Notebook* pages 24–25. Encourage students to use the targeted strategy in their own writing.
4	Read and discuss **PREWRITING: Organize** (Student Page 45). Discuss the purpose and mechanics of a sequence chain and analyze William's sequence chain.	9	Assign *Practice the Strategy Notebook* page 22. Encourage students to use the targeted strategy to revise a piece of their own writing.	14	Read and discuss **PUBLISHING: Share** (Student Pages 52–55). Discuss other ways William could share what he has written.
5	Assign *Practice the Strategy Notebook* pages 18–19. Encourage students to use the targeted strategy in their own writing.	10	Read and discuss **REVISING: Clarify** (Student Page 49).	15	Review the rubric for this chapter (reprinted on *Practice the Strategy Notebook* pages 26–27). Ask pairs of students to use the rubric to discuss and evaluate William's eyewitness account.

WRITER'S HANDBOOK

*To complete the chapter in fewer sessions, assign the *Practice the Strategy Notebook* pages on the same day the targeted strategy is introduced.

Remind students that they can refer to the Writer's Handbook in the back of the Student Edition for more information.

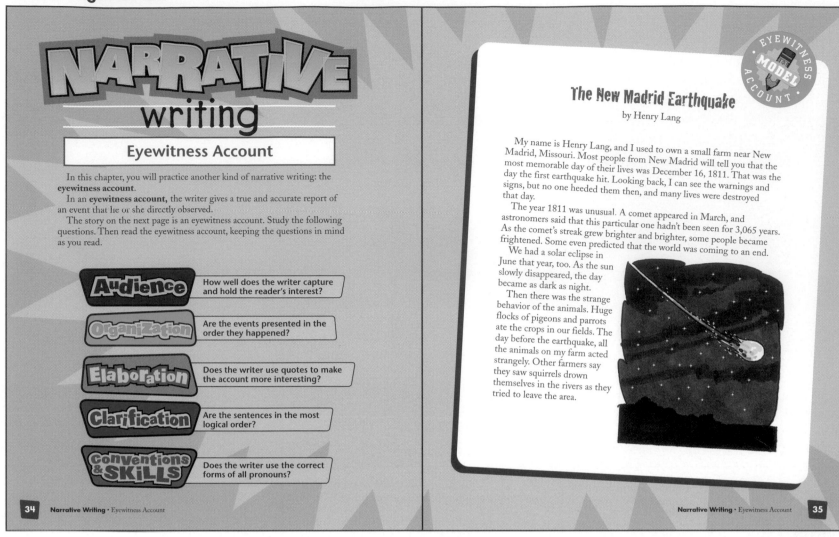

NARRATIVE writing

Eyewitness Account

In this chapter, you will practice another kind of narrative writing: the **eyewitness account.**

In an **eyewitness account,** the writer gives a true and accurate report of an event that he or she directly observed.

The story on the next page is an eyewitness account. Study the following questions. Then read the eyewitness account, keeping the questions in mind as you read.

Audience How well does the writer capture and hold the reader's interest?

Organization Are the events presented in the order they happened?

Elaboration Does the writer use quotes to make the account more interesting?

Clarification Are the sentences in the most logical order?

Conventions & Skills Does the writer use the correct forms of all pronouns?

34   **Narrative Writing** • Eyewitness Account

The New Madrid Earthquake
by Henry Lang

My name is Henry Lang, and I used to own a small farm near New Madrid, Missouri. Most people from New Madrid will tell you that the most memorable day of their lives was December 16, 1811. That was the day the first earthquake hit. Looking back, I can see the warnings and signs, but no one heeded them then, and many lives were destroyed that day.

The year 1811 was unusual. A comet appeared in March, and astronomers said that this particular one hadn't been seen for 3,065 years. As the comet's streak grew brighter and brighter, some people became frightened. Some even predicted that the world was coming to an end.

We had a solar eclipse in June that year, too. As the sun slowly disappeared, the day became as dark as night.

Then there was the strange behavior of the animals. Huge flocks of pigeons and parrots ate the crops in our fields. The day before the earthquake, all the animals on my farm acted strangely. Other farmers say they saw squirrels drown themselves in the rivers as they tried to leave the area.

Narrative Writing • Eyewitness Account   35

Introduce the Genre:
Eyewitness Account

Ask student volunteers to name the most interesting and/or important events they have seen. Invite two or three students to tell the stories of the events that they witnessed.

Tell students that the stories they have told are a kind of narrative. They are called eyewitness accounts. In this type of narrative writing, the writer gives a true and accurate report of an event that he or she has directly observed. Emphasize that eyewitness accounts are written in first person and that they include precise facts and details.

Conclude by telling students that they are going to study and practice strategies for writing an eyewitness account.

Discuss the Questions

(Student Page 34)

Read the questions on page 34 aloud. Point out the five categories and be sure students are clear on their meaning in the context of writing. Possible points to discuss:

Audience: The writer must keep his/her audience in mind. It is important to capture the reader's attention right away and keep it.

Organization: Different types of writing lend themselves to different organizational strategies. An eyewitness account should describe events in the order in which they occurred.

Elaboration: A good writer fully explains a topic by elaborating. The use of quotes is a good way to elaborate.

Clarification: A good writer makes sure that sentences are in a logical order.

Conventions & Skills: Writers who observe conventions, including using the correct form of pronouns, make their writing easier for their audience to read and understand.

Read the Model:
Eyewitness Account

(Student Pages 35–37)

Read "The New Madrid Earthquake" aloud. Point out that the information about the earthquake is true, but Henry Lang is a fictitious person. He represents the experiences of the many people who lived through the earthquake.

"Something's wrong here," I said. "What on earth is happening?" Well, something was wrong, but it wasn't on the earth. It was deep within the earth.

I was sleeping soundly on the night of December 15 when the house began to shake, moving my bed violently back and forth. I was tossed on the floor, with my leg bent under me. I heard my leg break, and a sharp pain hit me. All this time, the ceiling was collapsing, and the walls were cracking and falling. A sound like thunder welled up from beneath the house, deep within the earth. Then I heard my neighbors shrieking and calling, "Help us! Save us!" I wanted to get up and help them, but the pain in my leg was too fierce.

I don't know exactly how long the earth quaked that night. It seemed like hours to me. The air was moist and smelly, and even my candle couldn't shine through the thick darkness. I lay on the floor alone, waiting and wondering.

Smaller tremors hit throughout the night, but by morning the air had cleared. When I managed to crawl outside, I couldn't believe my eyes. Trees were split, homes were destroyed, fires burned, and injured people wandered around in disbelief. The ground had opened up near my house, and the gaping crack was filled with a thick, brown bubbling substance. My neighbors and I agreed on one thing that day. Never before had we seen a sight so fearsome or so grim.

That night was the beginning of many tremors along the Mississippi River valley. A large earthquake struck again in January. In February, we had the worst one. It caused the strangest things to happen. It temporarily turned a part of the Mississippi River into a waterfall, and another section of the river ran backwards for a while. That's when I decided to leave New Madrid for good.

Today I live in Ohio. Putting my life back together hasn't been easy, but eventually I saved enough money to buy more farmland. The day I paid for it, I looked at my new fields and said, "No one ever owns the land. It has a life and mind of its own. We only get to use it for a while."

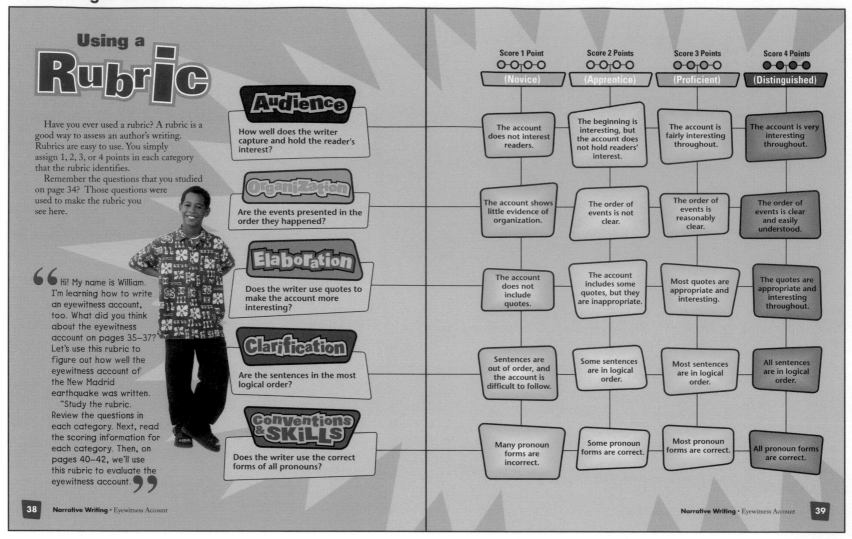

Using a Rubric

(Student Pages 38–39)

Use the text on Student Pages 40–42 to model the use of the rubric in evaluating a piece of writing. For more information on using a rubric, please see page T22.

When and How to Share Rubric Information With Parents

by Lee Bromberger, *Assessment Specialist*

While classroom teachers who utilize rubrics will have many opportunities throughout the school year to introduce, explain, illustrate, and apply rubrics with their students, opportunities to share rubrics with parents will not be as plentiful. Therefore, the classroom teacher must be sure to seize those moments with direct parent contact and also creatively develop other forms by which to communicate the role that rubrics play in developing and evaluating student writing.

Direct parent contact opportunities include the following:

- Open House
- Beginning of the Year/Introductory Class Materials
- Parent-Teacher Conferences

Providing copies of class rubrics at either the Open House or through class materials sent home allows parents to review rubric standards at their leisure. While most rubrics are self-explanatory, teachers may wish to attach a commentary of the rubric, which could include a brief summary of the document's usefulness, as well as a description as to how the rubric will be implemented in class. An invitation to call should parents have questions would be an effective way in which to conclude this introductory information.

The Open House forum allows teachers the opportunity to highlight various rubrics used. One practical method to direct attention to a rubric would be to display an enlarged rubric on a classroom wall. A creative method might involve elementary students making a "rubric placemat" for their desks, which parents could then take home. By showcasing their rubric, teachers can indicate the importance of the rubric within the course curriculum.

The rubric can function as an effective tool during the parent-teacher conference when teachers review a writing sample with the parent(s), explaining how the rubric provides an accurate picture of the assignment's strengths and/or weaknesses. Students could choose the writing sample to be reviewed from within a class writing folder or writing portfolio. Illustrating the implementation of the rubric as an assessment tool with an actual piece of student writing would help to prepare the parent for future assignments employing rubric assessment.

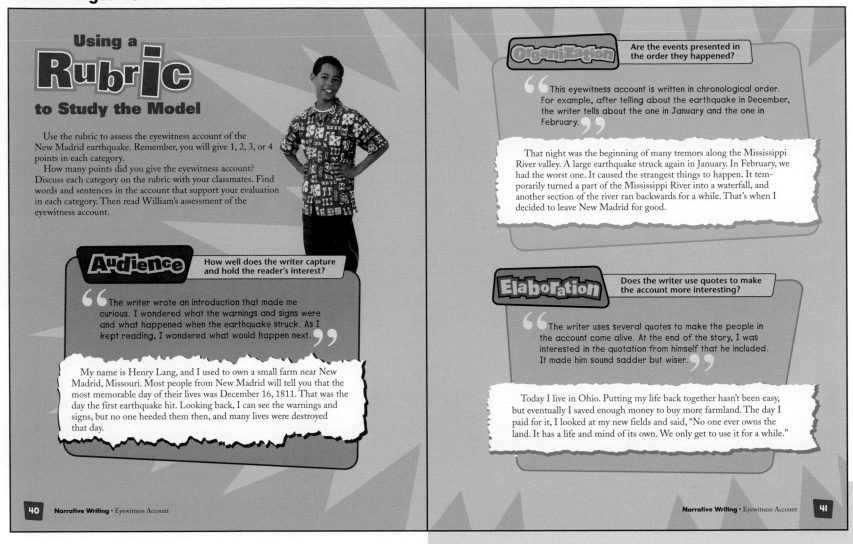

Using a Rubric to Study the Eyewitness Account

(Student Pages 40–42)

Read the questions and answers on Student Pages 40–42. Discuss whether students agree or disagree with each point in William's assessment of the account. For example, do students agree that the writer captures and holds the reader's interest? Can they think of a better way to capture the reader's interest?

Note on Conventions & Skills: Remind students that this rubric focuses attention on an important skill: using the correct forms of pronouns. However, students should always check their writing for spelling, punctuation, and capitalization.

Be sure students have a good grasp of the features of an eyewitness account, as well as key aspects of the rubric.

Meeting Students' Needs:
Second Language Learners

The second language learner may encounter difficulty with objective-case pronouns. To aid these students, write phrases such as *to him, for her,* and *beside them* on the board and ask students to read them aloud. Have them draw an arrow from the preposition to the pronoun, or object of the preposition. This will reinforce the correct use of pronouns used as objects.

Students Who Need Extra Help

Guide students to identify people whose quotes would be relevant to eyewitness accounts. Also ask for examples of quotes that would not be relevant. Then guide students as they write and punctuate some of their quotes on the chalkboard.

Gifted Students

Challenge students to locate eyewitness accounts of events that interest them, including scientific discoveries such as Alexander Graham Bell's first words over the telephone or historical events such as the first walk on the moon. Invite students to share their findings with the class.

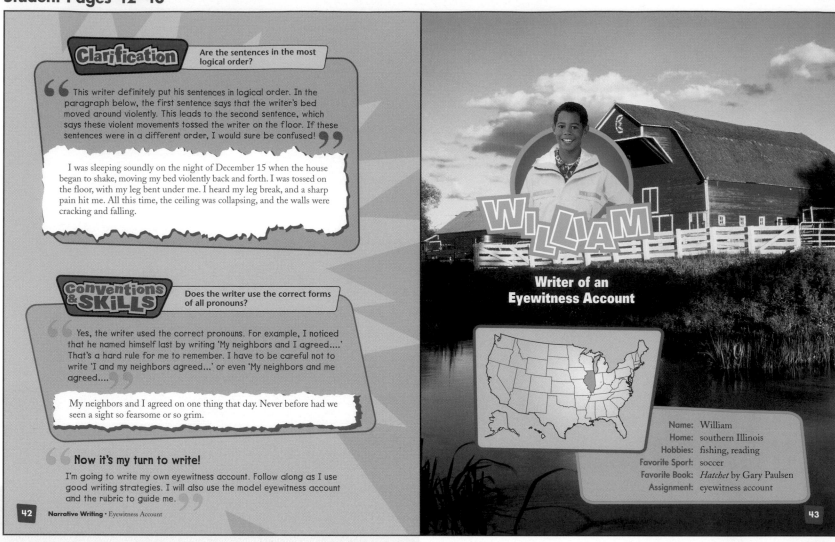

Clarification Are the sentences in the most logical order?

❝ This writer definitely put his sentences in logical order. In the paragraph below, the first sentence says that the writer's bed moved around violently. This leads to the second sentence, which says these violent movements tossed the writer on the floor. If these sentences were in a different order, I would sure be confused! ❞

I was sleeping soundly on the night of December 15 when the house began to shake, moving my bed violently back and forth. I was tossed on the floor, with my leg bent under me. I heard my leg break, and a sharp pain hit me. All this time, the ceiling was collapsing, and the walls were cracking and falling.

Conventions & SKILLS Does the writer use the correct forms of all pronouns?

❝ Yes, the writer used the correct pronouns. For example, I noticed that he named himself last by writing 'My neighbors and I agreed....' That's a hard rule for me to remember. I have to be careful not to write 'I and my neighbors agreed...' or even 'My neighbors and me agreed....

My neighbors and I agreed on one thing that day. Never before had we seen a sight so fearsome or so grim.

❝ **Now it's my turn to write!**

I'm going to write my own eyewitness account. Follow along as I use good writing strategies. I will also use the model eyewitness account and the rubric to guide me. ❞

42   **Narrative Writing** • Eyewitness Account

WILLIAM!

Writer of an Eyewitness Account

Name:	William
Home:	southern Illinois
Hobbies:	fishing, reading
Favorite Sport:	soccer
Favorite Book:	*Hatchet* by Gary Paulsen
Assignment:	eyewitness account

43

Unlocking Text Structure:
Eyewitness Account

The structure of any writing depends upon how information is organized. To help your students unlock the structure of the eyewitness account, you may wish to use the graphic organizer in this unit. The sequence chain lends itself to understanding the process of writing an eyewitness account. Review the definitions of *chronological* and *sequential*. Emphasize that chronological or sequential order, which your students studied in relation to personal narratives in Chapter 1, is equally essential in an eyewitness account.

William:
Writer of an Eyewitness Account

(Student Page 43)

Read the information about William. Make sure students understand that he will write his own eyewitness account in this chapter. Discuss what he might choose to write about in his account. Check to see if students' suggestions reflect an understanding of the narrative mode of writing.

Point out that William will complete the steps in the writing process: Prewriting, Drafting, Revising, Editing, and Publishing. At each stage William will demonstrate a good writing strategy and explain how he used it. Students should watch for key words, including **Gather, Organize, Write, Elaborate, Clarify, Proofread,** and **Share**.

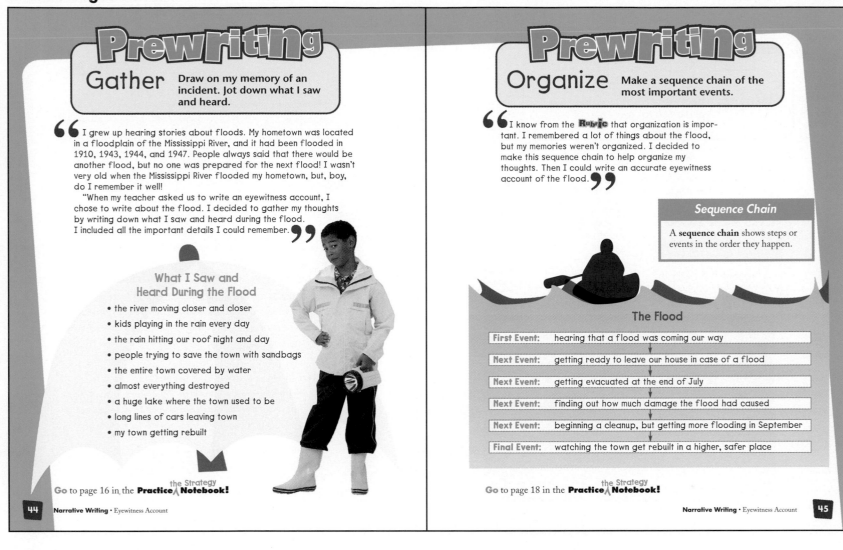

Prewriting

Gather
Draw on my memory of an incident. Jot down what I saw and heard.

> I grew up hearing stories about floods. My hometown was located in a floodplain of the Mississippi River, and it had been flooded in 1910, 1943, 1944, and 1947. People always said that there would be another flood, but no one was prepared for the next flood! I wasn't very old when the Mississippi River flooded my hometown, but, boy, do I remember it well!
>
> "When my teacher asked us to write an eyewitness account, I chose to write about the flood. I decided to gather my thoughts by writing down what I saw and heard during the flood. I included all the important details I could remember."

What I Saw and Heard During the Flood
- the river moving closer and closer
- kids playing in the rain every day
- the rain hitting our roof night and day
- people trying to save the town with sandbags
- the entire town covered by water
- almost everything destroyed
- a huge lake where the town used to be
- long lines of cars leaving town
- my town getting rebuilt

Go to page 16 in the **Practice the Strategy Notebook!**

44 Narrative Writing • Eyewitness Account

Prewriting

Organize
Make a sequence chain of the most important events.

> I know from the **Rubric** that organization is important. I remembered a lot of things about the flood, but my memories weren't organized. I decided to make this sequence chain to help organize my thoughts. Then I could write an accurate eyewitness account of the flood.

Sequence Chain

A **sequence chain** shows steps or events in the order they happen.

The Flood

First Event:	hearing that a flood was coming our way
Next Event:	getting ready to leave our house in case of a flood
Next Event:	getting evacuated at the end of July
Next Event:	finding out how much damage the flood had caused
Next Event:	beginning a cleanup, but getting more flooding in September
Final Event:	watching the town get rebuilt in a higher, safer place

Go to page 18 in the **Practice the Strategy Notebook!**

Narrative Writing • Eyewitness Account 45

Prewriting Gather

Strategy: Draw on my memory of an incident. Jot down what I saw and heard.

(Student Page 44)

Read the text with students. Then study and discuss the phrases that William recorded. Ask students to speculate upon the possible eyewitness accounts that William might be able to write. **[Possible responses: what happened the day the town flooded; how William and his family were evacuated; how the town was rebuilt]**

Practice the Strategy Notebook!

Assign pages 16–17 in the *Practice the Strategy Notebook.* (Your Own Writing sections should be used as time and students' abilities permit.) Explain that the students will practice this Gather strategy with a different topic. Suggested responses for the *Practice the Strategy Notebook* appear in the Appendix at the back of this Teacher Edition.

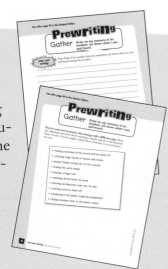

Prewriting Organize

Strategy: Make a sequence chain of the most important events.

(Student Page 45)

Explain that a graphic organizer can help organize information in preparation for writing. Ask which graphic organizer William is using to organize his information. Review the definition of a sequence chain on the page. Then direct attention to William's sequence chain.

Practice the Strategy Notebook!

Assign pages 18–19 in the *Practice the Strategy Notebook.* Allow students plenty of time to complete this activity. If necessary, they can go back to the Gather step to find or create more phrases for their eyewitness accounts.

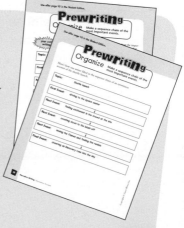

Drafting

Write
Draft my account by writing one paragraph for every part of my sequence chain.

"Now I'm ready to write! I want my readers to see and hear and feel what the flood was like. I will write a paragraph for every event in my sequence chain so my readers can easily follow what happened. You can read the first part of my draft on the next page. As I draft my account, I won't worry about making mistakes in spelling or grammar. I'll write now and check for mistakes later."

Paragraph

A **paragraph** is a group of sentences that focus on one main idea or thought.

[1st DRAFT]

The Flood

First Event: hearing that a flood was coming our way

   That summer, I heard stories on the news about broken levees and floods upstream. I knew that the Mississippi had flooded many times in the past. I heard that Valmeyer had been flooded in 1910, 1943, 1944, and 1947. I wondered if this was the year that it would happen again.

Next Event: getting ready to leave our house in case of a flood

   The rain fell steadily that year. During June and July, my friends and I played in the rain almost every day. My mother worried as the water rose. I got boxes from the grocery store. I walked around those boxes for weeks. She would look around our house and frown. Then she began to make lists. She said that we had to decide what we'd take if we had to leave. She said that we needed to decide now. She and I filled the boxes with important papers, photographs, and other favorite things.

Next Event: getting evacuated at the end of July

   At the end of July, we were evacuated. The flood was on its way. My father and me loaded the boxes into the car. Then we packed some clothes and left. As we drove away, we stared sadly at our house.

Go to page 20 in the **Practice** the Strategy **Notebook!**

Drafting Write

Strategy: Draft my account by writing one paragraph for every part of my sequence chain.

(Student Pages 46–47)

Begin by asking students what it means to write a rough draft. Be sure they understand that a draft is a temporary or "rough" form of a narrative. A draft should be changed and corrected, possibly several times, before it is finished. Then ask a student to read William's words aloud, or read the words yourself.

Ask why William is not too concerned about making mistakes in spelling and grammar as he writes his draft. [**Possible response: While he will do his best with spelling and grammar, he is eager to get the events of his story down on paper at the drafting stage.**]

Refer to the Rubric : The student spokesperson will refer to the rubric throughout the chapter. Remind students to get into the habit of referring back to the rubric so they fully understand its use as a tool for shaping their writing.

Practice the Strategy Notebook!

Assign pages 20–21 in the *Practice the Strategy Notebook*. Review the basics of good paragraph structure with your students, including topic sentence, supporting sentences, and indentation. When they have completed their rough drafts, invite volunteers to share some of their paragraphs. Ask the class to assess paragraph structure and determine whether each paragraph has been written in the first person.

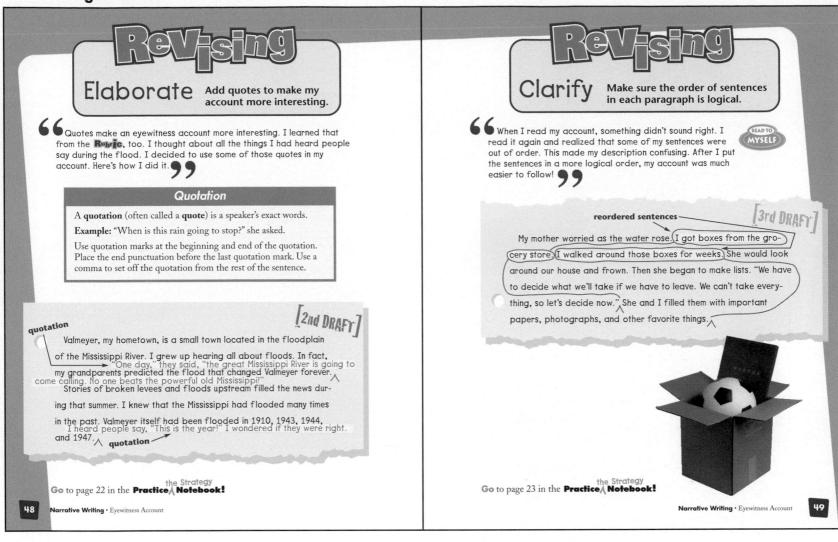

ReVising Elaborate

Strategy: Add quotes to make my account more interesting.

(Student Page 48)

Ask a student to take the part of William and read his words to the class.

Ask a different student to identify the strategy William will use. **[Response: Add quotes to make my account more interesting.]** Guide students as they study the quotes used in the text. Invite them to suggest other quotes that might be included. For example, students might like to know what people had said about the earlier floods of the Mississippi River.

ReVising Clarify

Strategy: Make sure the order of sentences in each paragraph is logical.

(Student Page 49)

Ask a student to read William's words to the class. Discuss why William's revisions make the order of the sentences more logical.

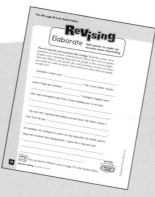

the Strategy
Practice ∧ Notebook!

Assign *Practice the Strategy Notebook* page 22. Ask volunteers to share the quotes they have written with the class.

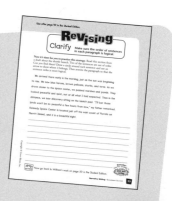

the Strategy
Practice ∧ Notebook!

Assign *Practice the Strategy Notebook* page 23. Ask volunteers to share their revised sentences with the class.

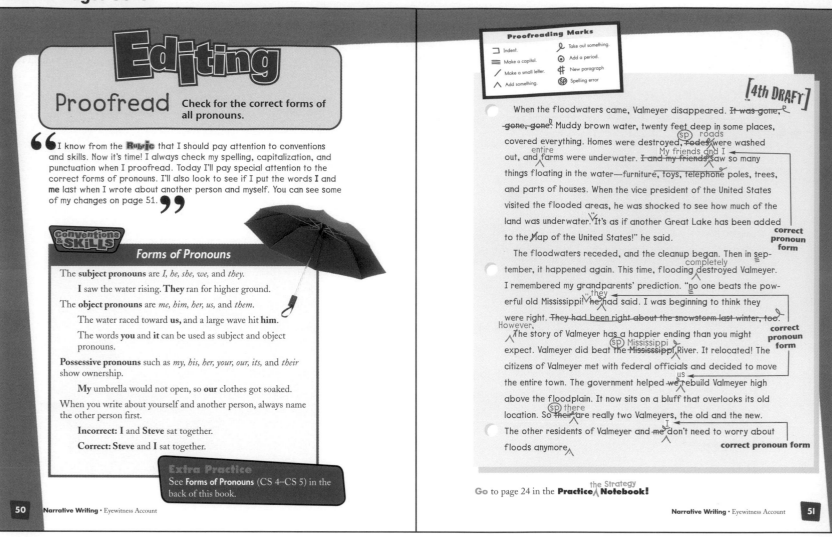

Editing Proofread

Strategy: Check for the correct forms of all pronouns.

(Student Pages 50-51)

Discuss the difference between revising and editing. Make sure students understand that in the revising step they reread their draft to look for ways to make it more complete, more interesting, and easier to understand. In the editing step, they look for spelling and grammar errors.

Ask a volunteer to read William's words to the class. Remind students that good writers search for spelling, punctuation, and grammar errors when they proofread. Explain that students should also focus on specific areas that have given them problems in the past.

Extra Practice: Conventions & Skills Student Edition

If you did not use Student Pages CS 4–CS 5 as a pre-assessment tool, and your students need more practice in using the correct form of pronouns, you may wish to assign these pages now.

Conventions & Skills Practice

For more targeted practice related to this skill, see these lessons in the optional *Conventions & Skills Practice Book*:

Lesson 13: Personal and Possessive Pronouns
Lesson 31: Subject and Object Pronouns
Lesson 32: Pronouns in Pairs
Lesson 33: Using *I* or *Me*

Practice the Strategy Notebook!

Assign *Practice the Strategy Notebook* pages 24–25. If necessary, review the proofreading marks and demonstrate their use on the chalkboard.

Share

Present my eyewitness account in a classroom "TV news broadcast."

Writer: William
Assignment: eyewitness account
Topic: the flooding of Valmeyer, Illinois
Audience: classmates
Method of Publication: oral presentation
Reason for Choice: to share my eyewitness account as if I were on a television news program

❝ I like to watch the news on television. I especially like it when a reporter gives an eyewitness account. Here's what I did to turn my eyewitness account into a TV news broadcast. ❞

1. I used my computer to make a neat copy of my account. I made it easy to read by putting extra space between lines.

2. I wrote this introduction to my news story: "Hello! My name is William, and I am here with an update on the flooding in Valmeyer, Illinois."

3. I practiced reading the introduction and the account aloud. I even recorded myself on a tape recorder. I made sure to speak clearly and not rush.

4. I put a table and chair at the front of the classroom.

5. I made a cardboard sign with the name of a TV station. Then I put the sign on the table facing the audience.

6. I presented the eyewitness account as if I were really on television.

Higher and Drier
by William

I'm standing on a bluff overlooking the Mississippi River. I am in the town of Valmeyer, Illinois. I am also looking down upon the town of Valmeyer, Illinois. How is that possible? Let me tell you about the flood that hit when I was little.

Before the flood, Valmeyer, my hometown, was located in the floodplain of the Mississippi River. I grew up hearing all about floods. In fact, my grandparents predicted the flood that changed Valmeyer forever. "One day," they said, "the great Mississippi River is going to come calling. No one beats the powerful old Mississippi!"

Stories of broken levees and floods upstream filled the news during that summer. I knew that the Mississippi had flooded many times in the past. Valmeyer itself had been flooded in 1910, 1943, 1944, and 1947. I heard people say, "This is the year!" I wondered if they were right.

Publishing   Share

Strategy: **Present my eyewitness account in a classroom "TV news broadcast."**

(Student Pages 52–55)

Challenge students to think of other ways William could share what he has written. Discuss whether they agree that this strategy was appropriate.

Using the Rubric

Ask students to work in pairs to use the rubric (reprinted on pages 26–27 of the *Practice the Strategy Notebook*) to evaluate William's paper. After each pair has reached its decision, ask pairs to compare their results and discuss the reasons for their decisions.

The rain fell steadily on the Mississippi Valley that year. It rained for 49 days straight. I wasn't very old, but I remember those rains. During June and July, my friends and I played in the rain almost every day. Sometimes we'd help the people fill sandbags to protect our town in case it flooded. The river was usually four miles from town. However, it was creeping closer every day.

My mother worried as the water rose. She would look around our house and frown. Then she began to make lists. "We have to decide what we'll take if we have to leave. We can't take everything, so let's decide now." I got boxes from the grocery store. She and I filled them with important papers, photographs, and other favorite things. I walked around those boxes for weeks.

At the end of July, we had to leave. The flood was on its way. My father and I loaded the boxes and some clothes into the car. As we drove away, we stared back at our house. "We'll be safer on higher ground," my father said sadly.

When the floodwaters came, Valmeyer disappeared. Muddy brown water, twenty feet deep in some places, covered everything. Homes were destroyed, roads were washed out, and entire farms were underwater. My friends and I saw so many things floating in the water—furniture, toys, telephone poles, trees, and parts of houses. When the vice president of the United States visited the

54 **Narrative Writing** • Eyewitness Account

flooded areas, he was shocked to see how much of the land was underwater. "It's as if another Great Lake has been added to the map of the United States!" he said.

The floodwaters receded, and the cleanup began. Then in September, it happened again. This time, flooding completely destroyed Valmeyer. I remembered my grandparents' prediction. "No one beats the powerful old Mississippi!" they had said. I was beginning to think they were right.

However, the story of Valmeyer has a happier ending than you might expect. Valmeyer did beat the Mississippi River. It relocated! The citizens of Valmeyer met with federal officials and decided to move the entire town. The government helped us rebuild Valmeyer high above the floodplain. It now sits on a bluff that overlooks its old location. So there are really two Valmeyers, the old and the new. The other residents of Valmeyer and I don't need to worry about floods anymore.

USING the Rubric for Assessment

Go to page 26 in the **Practice Notebook!** Use that rubric to assess William's paper. Try using the rubric to assess your own writing.
the Strategy

55 **Narrative Writing** • Eyewitness Account

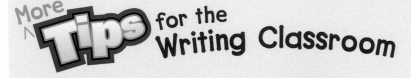

More Tips for the Writing Classroom

Cooperative Classroom Decoding Activity

Create a puzzle sheet. (The Food Puzzle on page T48 is a good example. You may duplicate that puzzle or create a similar one related to your curriculum.)

At first, have your class work on the puzzle individually for two minutes. Interrupt and invite the students to work with a partner. Next, ask them to work in small groups. Finally, ask them to work as a whole class. Before each transition, ask students how much of the puzzle has been completed.

Answers to the Food Puzzle: 1. lettuce 2. Turkey 3. lima beans 4. bread 5. apple 6. prune 7. grease 8. beet 9. turnip 10. thyme

Debrief:

The debriefing process is very important because it gives your students the opportunity to evaluate the lesson. Use the following procedure to debrief:

1. Ask the class whether working individually or with group members was more effective. Have them verbalize why.

2. Review the class rules and discuss the successes and the areas that need improvement.

your own NARRATIVE writing

Science

Put the strategies you practiced in this unit to work to write your own personal narrative, eyewitness account, or both! You can:

- develop the writing you did in the Your Own Writing pages of the *Practice the Strategy Notebook*;

- pick an idea below and write something new;

- choose another idea of your own.

Be sure to follow the steps in the writing process. Use the rubrics in this unit to assess your writing.

Personal Narrative	**Eyewitness Account**
• my most interesting science experiment or project • a scientific or nature discovery of my own • how I started my rock, insect, or other kind of collection	• a fireworks display • a hot-air balloon or air show • a tornado or hurricane • an eclipse

portfolio

School-Home Connection

Keep a writing portfolio. Think about adding the activities from the *Practice the Strategy Notebook* to your writing portfolio. You may want to take your portfolio home to share.

Your Own Writing
Narrative Writing for Science

Assign either one or both genres to the students. Before they begin writing, review key information about each genre. Decide whether you wish students to:

- Choose one of the topics on this page in the Student Edition.

- Complete one of the pieces they partially drafted in the Your Own Writing pages in the *Practice the Strategy Notebook*.

- Generate a completely new idea.

Portfolio/School-Home Connection

Encourage the students to keep portfolios of their writing. You may also wish to duplicate and distribute the School-Home Letter included in this unit.

Work-in-Progress Portfolio

Remind students to review this portfolio often to revise existing pieces that have not been published. Encourage students to share pieces of their Work-in-Progress Portfolios with family members who can help in editing.

Published Portfolio

Encourage students to choose pieces from their Published Portfolios to share with family members.

Food Puzzle

Directions: Fill in the blanks using the names of foods or food products.

1. The impatient wife said to her husband, "Hurry, dear. _____ be going."

2. The city of Istanbul is in the country of _____.

3. People who have been in the capital of Peru could be called _____

    _____.

4. One young person asking another for money: "Man, can you give me some

    _____?"

5. One of the major geographical features of the Eastern Seaboard is the

    _____achian Mountains.

6. If you trim a tree, you _____ it.

7. Athens is the capital of _____.

8. The tired, overworked father came in the door and said, "Boy, I'm

    _____ tonight."

9. When you smell something you don't like, you might _____ your nose at it.

10. The night watchman left his watch at home so he called his wife for the

    _____.

Purpose: To help students gain understanding of working in a group. See page T46 for more information and answers. This page may be duplicated for classroom use.

T48

DESCRIPTIVE

writing

describes something to the reader.

1
Descriptive Essay

2
Observation Report

Defining Descriptive Writing

Begin this unit by asking your students to write a description of a specific object, person, place, or event that they all saw on the previous day. For example, you might ask students to describe an assembly, a plant or animal that was in your room, or a person who visited your classroom. Invite volunteers to share their descriptions with the class. Discuss the details they did and did not include.

Read the unit opener (Student Page 57) with your students. Discuss why descriptive essays, observation reports, and responses to literature are examples of descriptive writing. **[They all describe something in detail.]** Then discuss other

types of writing that would not be examples of descriptive writing (e.g., adventure stories or how-to essays). Discuss why these examples are not descriptive writing. **[They tell a story or explain how to do something, but they do not describe an object, person, place or event.]**

Emphasize the importance of using sensory details (what the writer hears, sees, smells, touches, and tastes) in all descriptive writing.

Tips for the Writing Classroom

by Ken Stewart, *Master Teacher*

Using Student/Teacher Writing Models

If your students are having a problem understanding the criteria you are looking for in a piece of writing, use a "not-so-perfect" student or teacher sample to model the revision process with their input. By doing so, you allow your class to be actively engaged in the revision process. Their critical thinking skills of analysis, synthesis, and evaluation will be challenged as they discuss and dissect the writing sentence by sentence, phrase by phrase, or word by word. As you work through the writing,

encourage your students (as a class) to voice their changes so that they have the opportunity to compare their suggestions. Finally, encourage them to choose the best suggestions and support their choices.

Follow these simple steps:

1. Choose a student's piece of writing to personalize the lesson. (It is helpful to save students' work for future use. Ask the students for permission before sharing with the class.)
2. Make copies for each student to correct.
3. Display an overhead transparency of the writing.
4. Read the writing aloud, and then go back and read it sentence by sentence, and ask for specific changes (nouns,

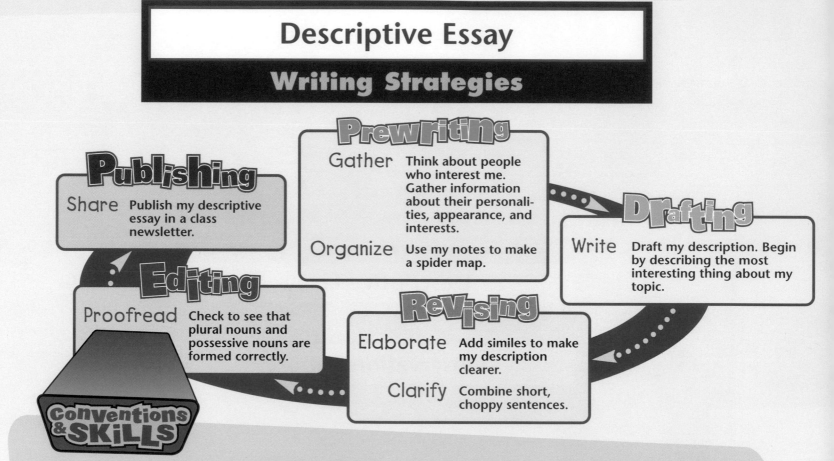

Before students read the model on Student Pages 59–61, you may wish to review the targeted **grammar, usage,** or **mechanics** convention. Remind students that most plural nouns are formed by adding *-s* or *-es* to the singular form. Some nouns change their spelling or remain unchanged in their plural form. Also remind students that the possessive form of singular and plural nouns that do not end in *s* is formed by adding an apostrophe and *-s*. Only an apostrophe is needed to form the possessive of plural nouns that already end in *s*.

Examples: The **students** received new books. (singular noun made plural by adding *-s*)

The **men** carried the boxes. (plural form that does not require *-s*)

The **student's** books are on the desk. (possessive form of a singular noun)

The **students'** books are in their lockers. (possessive form of a plural noun)

Skill Assessment: To pre-assess your students' understanding of the targeted convention, you may wish to have them complete the corresponding lesson on Student Pages CS 6–CS 7 in the back of the Student Edition.

Skill Mini-Lesson: The Proofread activity in this chapter can be used as a mini-lesson on the targeted **grammar, usage,** or **mechanics** skill.

verbs, adjectives, adverbs, punctuation, clarity, etc). Use the proofreading marks in the Student Edition.

5. After you and the class have made your changes, reread the piece and analyze why the revised version is better.

Your modeling will literally show the students how this process works and exactly what they need to do to improve their own writing. Have your students start revising their own writing (with or without partners).

When modeling a writing lesson, focus on these guidelines:

1. Make sure the purpose for writing is clear and the content is well developed and presented in a unique way.

2. Make sure the writing follows a logical order, flows naturally, and transitions well.

3. Make sure the writer keeps the audience engaged.

4. Make sure word choices are specific and interesting.

5. Make sure sentence structure is varied (length, clauses, phrases) and paragraphs are well structured.

6. Make sure grammar, mechanics, and spelling are correct.

Have students store the revised writing in their notebooks.

(See "More Tips for the Writing Classroom: Writing Model Sample," page T61.)

Time Management for This Chapter*

Session		Session		Session	
1	Discuss the descriptive essay genre; review the questions (Student Page 58). Read "Sarah the Sound Engineer" (Student Pages 59–61). Use the questions to analyze the article. Use the rubric to assess it.	**6**	Read and discuss **DRAFTING: Write** (Student Pages 70–71).	**11**	Assign *Practice the Strategy Notebook* page 35. Encourage students to use the targeted strategy to revise a piece of their own writing.
2	Introduce Joseph (Student Page 67) as a student-writer working on a descriptive essay. Read and discuss **PREWRITING: Gather** (Student Page 68).	**7**	Assign *Practice the Strategy Notebook* pages 32–33. Encourage students to use the targeted strategy in their own writing.	**12**	Read and discuss **EDITING: Proofread** (Student Pages 74–75).
3	Assign *Practice the Strategy Notebook* pages 28–29. Encourage students to use the targeted strategy in their own writing.	**8**	Read and discuss **REVISING: Elaborate** (Student Page 72).	**13**	Assign *Practice the Strategy Notebook* pages 36–37. Encourage students to use the targeted strategy to edit a piece of their own writing.
4	Read and discuss **PREWRITING: Organize** (Student Page 69). Discuss the purpose and mechanics of a spider map and analyze Joseph's spider map.	**9**	Assign *Practice the Strategy Notebook* page 34. Encourage students to use the targeted strategy to revise a piece of their own writing.	**14**	Read and discuss **PUBLISHING: Share** (Student Pages 76–77). Discuss other ways Joseph could share what he has written.
5	Assign *Practice the Strategy Notebook* pages 30–31. Encourage students to use the targeted strategy in their own writing.	**10**	Read and discuss **REVISING: Clarify** (Student Page 73).	**15**	Review the rubric for this chapter (reprinted on *Practice the Strategy Notebook* pages 38–39). Ask pairs of students to use the rubric to discuss and evaluate Joseph's essay.

WRITER'S HANDBOOK

* To complete the chapter in fewer sessions, assign the *Practice the Strategy Notebook* pages on the same day the targeted strategy is introduced.

Remind students that they can refer to the Writer's Handbook in the back of the Student Edition for more information.

Introduce the Genre:
Descriptive Essay

Explain to students that they are going to play a game called "Who Am I?" Ask them each to think of someone that everyone in the class knows and write a description of that person. You may wish to limit their choices, such as people in the news or people from history. When students have completed their writing, ask volunteers to read their descriptions aloud. Then encourage other students to guess the identity of the person who has been described.

Explain that the writing they have just completed is called descriptive writing. One type of descriptive writing is the *descriptive essay*. In this type of descriptive writing, the author gives a clear and detailed picture of a person, place, thing, or event.

Tell students that in this chapter, they are going to study and practice strategies for writing a descriptive essay.

Discuss the Questions
(Student Page 58)

Read the questions on Student Page 58 aloud. Point out the five categories and be sure students are clear on their meaning in the context of writing. Possible points to discuss:

Audience: The writer must keep his/her audience in mind and include details that will interest them.

Organization: Different types of writing lend themselves to different organizational strategies. A descriptive essay should begin with the most interesting information about the topic and stay focused on that topic.

Elaboration: A good writer fully explains a topic by elaborating. One way to elaborate is to include similes that make a description clearer.

Clarification: A good writer combines short, choppy sentences to make the description easier to read.

Conventions & Skills: Writers who observe conventions, such as forming plural nouns and possessive nouns correctly, make their writing easier to understand.

Read the Model:
Descriptive Essay
(Student Pages 59–61)

Read "Sarah the Sound Engineer" aloud.

Sarah likes her job because she spends the day listening to interesting information and music. Tex likes Sarah's job because the floor underneath her desk is as cool as a cave.

When Sarah gets home from work each day, she takes off her sunglasses and lets her long auburn hair out of its barrette. It flows like a waterfall over her shoulders. Then she puts on her favorite outfit: jeans and a T-shirt. She has trouble finding jeans that are short enough. She is only 5 feet, 1 inch tall, as short as a minute, her father says.

After changing clothes, Sarah turns on classical music, waters her plants, listens to phone messages, returns calls, and cooks dinner. In the evening, she often visits with friends or her sister Meg, who lives in the same town. Sarah and Meg go out to eat at least once a week, usually at their favorite Mexican restaurant.

Sometimes Sarah just stays home and reads. She uses a computer and a scanner. The scanner transmits words from printed pages to the computer, and then the computer reads the words aloud, just like a person. Sarah also has a small computer called Braille'n Speak. It has buttons for the braille alphabet, the raised dots that blind people touch to read. Sarah uses this machine to type in braille or to turn braille dots into printed words. It can read for her, too. Like Tex, both of these machines help Sarah "see."

While Sarah reads, Tex usually sleeps. A large black Labrador retriever, he has been trained to help her. Tex seems as smart as most people. Absolutely nothing escapes his attention. When he is working, he always wears a harness that Sarah holds in her left hand. He watches traffic, pauses at steps, and understands Sarah's commands.

You can see Sarah and Tex all around town. They get on buses, cross busy streets, ride elevators, and sometimes buy lunch at a vendor's stand. They go to restaurants, ice cream shops, concerts, and friends' homes. It's hard to talk about Sarah without talking about Tex. They are a team.

Sarah's life is a lot like most people's lives, but she is different in one way. She never travels alone. She always has the help of a friend named Tex.

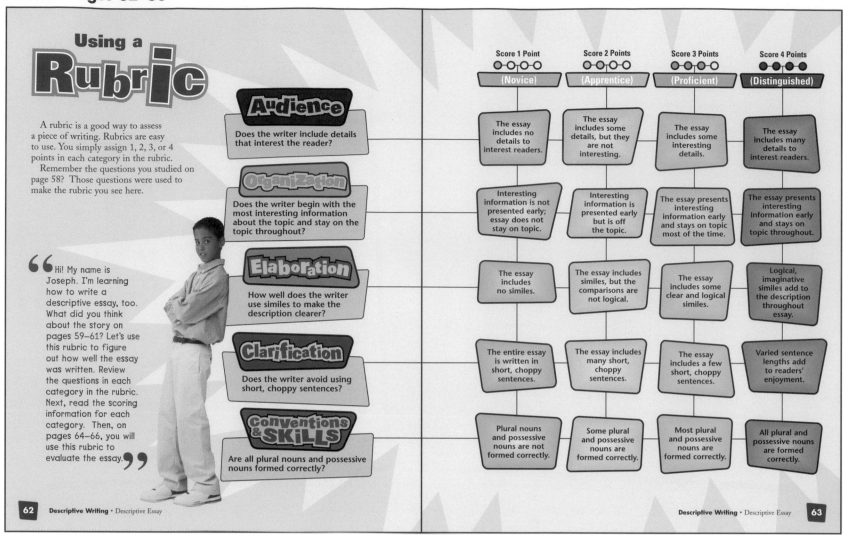

Using a Rubric

(Student Pages 62–63)

Use Student Pages 64–66 to model the use of the rubric in evaluating a piece of writing. For more information on using a rubric, see "Using a Rubric" on page T22.

Differentiating Rubrics for Assignments

by Lee Bromberger, *Assessment Specialist*

The ease with which rubrics can be designed and varied for many classroom assignments at all grade levels accounts for their growing popularity, especially with writing assignments. Listed below are some fundamental guidelines for developing and/or adapting rubrics.

- **Determine the objective(s) of the writing assignment.** A class that has recently practiced writing effective introductions should expect the teacher to pay close attention to those introductions when evaluating their writing. "Introductions" could then become a focus of the assignment rubric.

- **Tailor the rubric to the specific writing students shall complete.** If students are writing a narrative, design rubrics that incorporate narrative elements throughout the rubric

hierarchy. Depending on the grade level, narrative rubrics might evaluate plot, character development, inclusion of setting, dialogue, etc. Similarly, a rubric tailored to descriptive writing might focus on the writer's use of descriptive words, sensory details, spatial organization, etc.

- **Borrow successful rubrics from colleagues, applying changes that meet your assignment's objective(s).** Why reinvent the wheel? Sometimes a well-prepared existing rubric, tried and true, can be the appropriate assessment tool with one or two changes.

- **Comb your textbook's teacher resource materials.** Many teacher editions include rubrics that correlate with textbook writing assignments. Like rubrics you borrow from your colleagues, these rubrics may be directly applicable as they exist or easily modified to meet your assignment objective(s).

Differentiating rubrics offers classroom teachers at all grade levels an opportunity to be creative while also reviewing the learning objectives of specific writing assignments. Sharing these rubrics with students, highlighting the components of the rubric itself, allows for clear communication of expectations and a productive assignment for students and teachers.

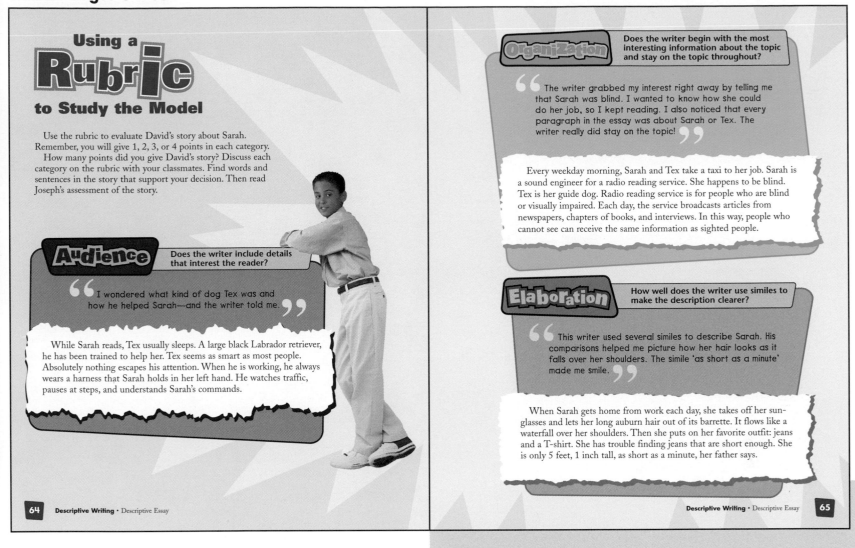

Using a Rubric to Study the Model

Use the rubric to evaluate David's story about Sarah. Remember, you will give 1, 2, 3, or 4 points in each category.

How many points did you give David's story? Discuss each category on the rubric with your classmates. Find words and sentences in the story that support your decision. Then read Joseph's assessment of the story.

Audience
Does the writer include details that interest the reader?

" I wondered what kind of dog Tex was and how he helped Sarah—and the writer told me. "

While Sarah reads, Tex usually sleeps. A large black Labrador retriever, he has been trained to help her. Tex seems as smart as most people. Absolutely nothing escapes his attention. When he is working, he always wears a harness that Sarah holds in her left hand. He watches traffic, pauses at steps, and understands Sarah's commands.

Organization
Does the writer begin with the most interesting information about the topic and stay on the topic throughout?

" The writer grabbed my interest right away by telling me that Sarah was blind. I wanted to know how she could do her job, so I kept reading. I also noticed that every paragraph in the essay was about Sarah or Tex. The writer really did stay on the topic! "

Every weekday morning, Sarah and Tex take a taxi to her job. Sarah is a sound engineer for a radio reading service. She happens to be blind. Tex is her guide dog. Radio reading service is for people who are blind or visually impaired. Each day, the service broadcasts articles from newspapers, chapters of books, and interviews. In this way, people who cannot see can receive the same information as sighted people.

Elaboration
How well does the writer use similes to make the description clearer?

" This writer used several similes to describe Sarah. His comparisons helped me picture how her hair looks as it falls over her shoulders. The simile 'as short as a minute' made me smile. "

When Sarah gets home from work each day, she takes off her sunglasses and lets her long auburn hair out of its barrette. It flows like a waterfall over her shoulders. Then she puts on her favorite outfit: jeans and a T-shirt. She has trouble finding jeans that are short enough. She is only 5 feet, 1 inch tall, as short as a minute, her father says.

64 Descriptive Writing • Descriptive Essay

Descriptive Writing • Descriptive Essay 65

Using a Rubric to Study the Descriptive Essay

(Student Pages 64–66)

Read the questions and answers on Student Pages 64–66. Discuss whether students agree or disagree with each point in Joseph's assessment of the essay. For example, do students think that the use of similes adds to the descriptive essay? Can they think of other similes that could make the essay even better?

Note on Conventions & Skills: Remind students that this rubric focuses on an important skill: forming plural and possessive nouns. However, students should always check their writing for correct spelling, punctuation, and capitalization.

Be sure students have a good grasp of the features of a descriptive essay, as well as key aspects of the rubric.

Meeting Students' Needs:
Second Language Learners

Second language learners may need help in understanding the concept of a simile. List familiar adjectives, such as *smart, soft, quick,* and *slow.* Then ask students to match the adjectives to pictures of animals. Guide them in forming similes such as "slow as a turtle" or "smart as a fox." Also encourage them to form other similes, such as "cold as ice" and "sharp as a knife."

Students Who Need Extra Help

To help students with plural nouns, prepare flashcards. Write a regularly or irregularly formed plural noun or a singular noun on the front of each card. On the back, identify it as singular, plural, or singular and plural. Have students practice identifying whether each noun is singular or plural. Include *mice, geese, children, men, women, oxen,* and *sheep.*

Gifted Students

Challenge students to find and share examples of similes from books and songs. Be sure they can identify the two things that are being compared.

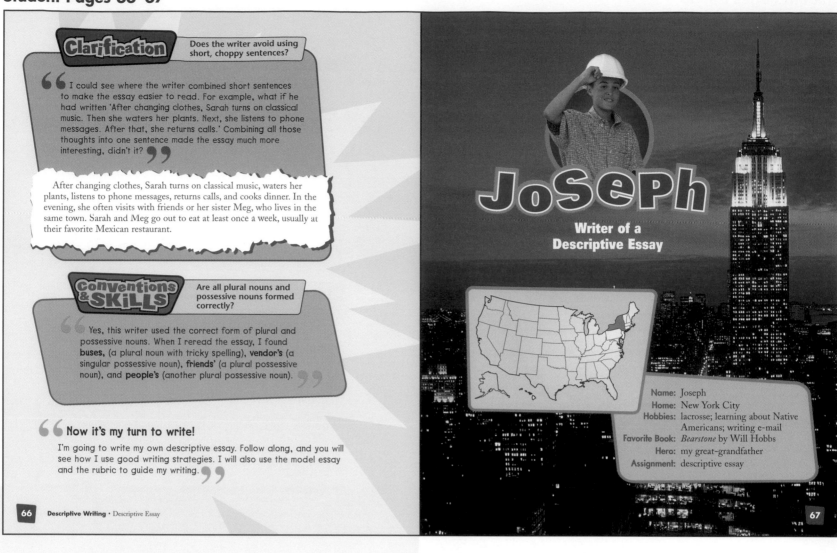

Clarification — Does the writer avoid using short, choppy sentences?

" I could see where the writer combined short sentences to make the essay easier to read. For example, what if he had written 'After changing clothes, Sarah turns on classical music. Then she waters her plants. Next, she listens to phone messages. After that, she returns calls.' Combining all those thoughts into one sentence made the essay much more interesting, didn't it? "

After changing clothes, Sarah turns on classical music, waters her plants, listens to phone messages, returns calls, and cooks dinner. In the evening, she often visits with friends or her sister Meg, who lives in the same town. Sarah and Meg go out to eat at least once a week, usually at their favorite Mexican restaurant.

Conventions & Skills — Are all plural nouns and possessive nouns formed correctly?

" Yes, this writer used the correct form of plural and possessive nouns. When I reread the essay, I found **buses,** (a plural noun with tricky spelling), **vendor's** (a singular possessive noun), **friends'** (a plural possessive noun), and **people's** (another plural possessive noun). "

" **Now it's my turn to write!**
I'm going to write my own descriptive essay. Follow along, and you will see how I use good writing strategies. I will also use the model essay and the rubric to guide my writing. "

66   **Descriptive Writing** · Descriptive Essay

JoSeph
Writer of a Descriptive Essay

Name: Joseph
Home: New York City
Hobbies: lacrosse; learning about Native Americans; writing e-mail
Favorite Book: *Bearstone* by Will Hobbs
Hero: my great-grandfather
Assignment: descriptive essay

67

Unlocking Text Structure:
Descriptive Essay

The structure of any writing depends upon how information is organized. To help your students unlock the structure of the descriptive essay, you may wish to use the graphic organizer in this unit, the spider map.

The purpose of a spider map is to organize details about a single topic. The details are written on the spider's "legs." Explain that all of these details are equally important and help present a clear picture, or description, of the topic.

Joseph:
Writer of a Descriptive Essay

(Student Page 67)

Read the information about Joseph.

Be sure students understand that Joseph will write his own descriptive essay in this chapter. Discuss what he might choose to write about. Check to see that student suggestions reflect an understanding of the descriptive mode of writing.

Point out that Joseph will complete all the steps in the writing process: Prewriting, Drafting, Revising, Editing, and Publishing. At each stage he will demonstrate a good writing strategy and explain how he used it. Students should watch for key words, including **Gather, Organize, Write, Elaborate, Clarify, Proofread,** and **Share**.

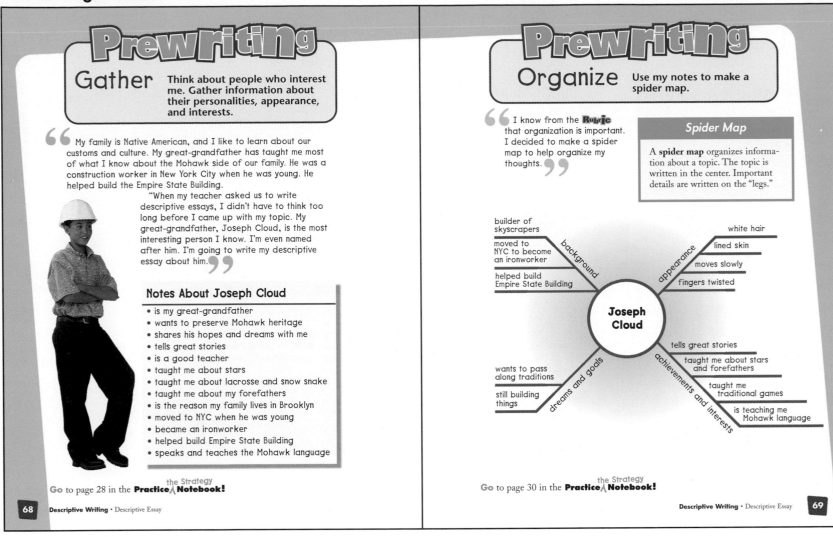

Prewriting

Gather
Think about people who interest me. Gather information about their personalities, appearance, and interests.

" My family is Native American, and I like to learn about our customs and culture. My great-grandfather has taught me most of what I know about the Mohawk side of our family. He was a construction worker in New York City when he was young. He helped build the Empire State Building.

"When my teacher asked us to write descriptive essays, I didn't have to think too long before I came up with my topic. My great-grandfather, Joseph Cloud, is the most interesting person I know. I'm even named after him. I'm going to write my descriptive essay about him. "

Notes About Joseph Cloud
- is my great-grandfather
- wants to preserve Mohawk heritage
- shares his hopes and dreams with me
- tells great stories
- is a good teacher
- taught me about stars
- taught me about lacrosse and snow snake
- taught me about my forefathers
- is the reason my family lives in Brooklyn
- moved to NYC when he was young
- became an ironworker
- helped build Empire State Building
- speaks and teaches the Mohawk language

Go to page 28 in the **Practice the Strategy Notebook!**

68 — Descriptive Writing · Descriptive Essay

Prewriting

Organize
Use my notes to make a spider map.

" I know from the **Rubric** that organization is important. I decided to make a spider map to help organize my thoughts. "

Spider Map
A **spider map** organizes information about a topic. The topic is written in the center. Important details are written on the "legs."

Spider map:
- **background**
  - builder of skyscrapers
  - moved to NYC to become an ironworker
  - helped build Empire State Building
- **appearance**
  - white hair
  - lined skin
  - moves slowly
  - fingers twisted
- **achievements and interests**
  - tells great stories
  - taught me about stars and forefathers
  - taught me traditional games
  - is teaching me Mohawk language
- **dreams and goals**
  - wants to pass along traditions
  - still building things

Center: **Joseph Cloud**

Go to page 30 in the **Practice the Strategy Notebook!**

69 — Descriptive Writing · Descriptive Essay

Prewriting Gather

Strategy: Think about people who interest me. Gather information about their personalities, appearance, and interests.

(Student Page 68)

Read the text with students. Study and discuss the notes that Joseph recorded. Ask students to explain whether they think that Joseph Cloud will be an interesting topic for a descriptive essay.

Practice the Strategy Notebook!

Assign pages 28–29 in the *Practice the Strategy Notebook*. (Your Own Writing sections should be used as time and students' abilities permit.) Explain that the students will practice this Gather strategy with a different topic. Suggested responses for the *Practice the Strategy Notebook* appear in the Appendix in the back of this Teacher Edition.

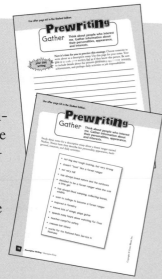

Prewriting Organize

Strategy: Use my notes to make a spider map.

(Student Page 69)

Explain that writing can be organized in many different ways. A graphic organizer is one way to organize details in preparation for writing.

Ask which strategy Joseph is using to organize his information. Review the definition of a spider map. Then direct attention to Joseph's spider map.

Practice the Strategy Notebook!

Assign pages 30–31 in the *Practice the Strategy Notebook*. Allow students plenty of time to complete this activity. If necessary, students can go back to the Gather step to get more ideas from their notes.

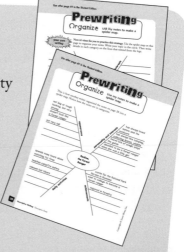

D**r**afting

Write
Draft my description. Begin by describing the most interesting thing about my topic.

66 Now I'm ready to write! First, I need to choose the most interesting thing about my great-grandfather. Lots of things about him interest me, but I have to think about my audience. It will be my classmates. I think they will be interested in the fact that my great-grandfather helped build the Empire State Building. I'll start with that! You can read my first paragraph on the next page. 99

[**1st DRAFT**]

○ Joseph Clouds journey began in 1928. He was nineteen years old and living in upstate New York. Like many Mohawk mens, he knew that he could earn better wages working in construction. By the Fall of 1930, he was working on one of New York Cities' grandist projects. It was the construction of the Empire State Building. Like other Mohawk ironworkers, Joseph Cloud was not afraid of heights. He was sure-footed on the steel girders. He and other Mohawks helped build many of the skyscraper's along the east coast. Many of them settled in New York City. They lived in brooklyn. Joseph Cloud did.

most interesting thing
dangerous

66 As I write the rest of my essay, I want my class-mates to be able to picture my great-grandfather, as if he is standing right in front of them. I will write detailed descriptions about what he looks like, what kind of person he is, and what his life has been like. I won't worry about making mistakes in spelling or grammar right now. I will just do my best and check for mistakes later. 99

Go to page 32 in the **Practice the Strategy Notebook!**

D**r**afting   Write

Strategy: Draft my description. Begin by describing the most interesting thing about my topic.

(Student Pages 70–71)

Begin by asking students what it means to write a rough draft. Be sure they understand that a draft is a temporary or "rough" form of a descriptive essay. A draft should be changed and corrected, possibly several times, before it is finished. Then have a student read Joseph's words for the class, or read the words yourself.

Ask students why Joseph is not overly concerned about making mistakes in spelling and grammar as he writes his draft. **[Possible response: He is eager to get the description of his great-grandfather down on paper at the drafting stage. He will do his best with spelling, punctuation, and grammar and check for mistakes during the revising stage.]**

Refer to the Rubric: The student spokesperson will refer to the rubric throughout the chapter. Remind students to get into the habit of referring back to the rubric so they fully understand its use as a tool for shaping their writing.

Practice the Strategy Notebook!

Assign pages 32–33 in the *Practice the Strategy Notebook*. Be sure students can explain why they chose a certain aspect of their topic as the most interesting point. Ask volunteers to read what they have written. Invite classmates to ask questions about this part of the description. Remind students that they should include as many sensory details as possible as they write descriptions.

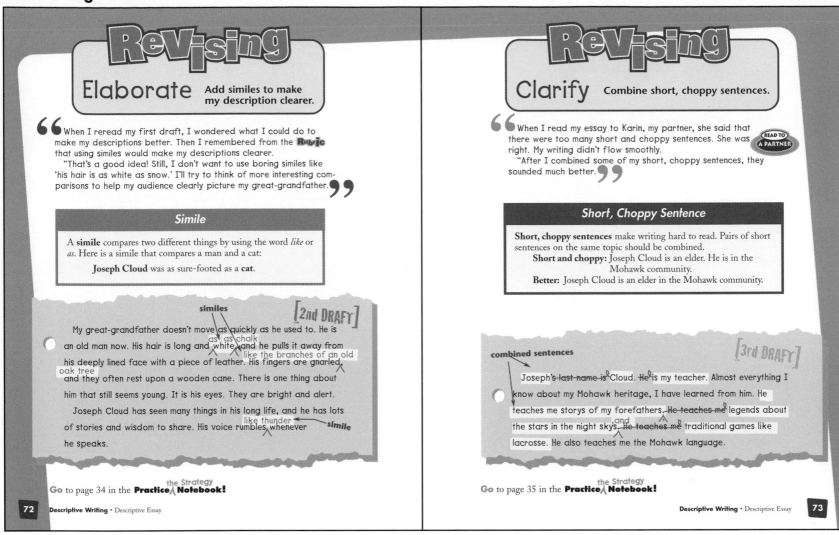

ReVising Elaborate

Strategy: Add similes to make my description clearer.

(Student Page 72)

Ask a student to take the part of Joseph and read his words to the class.

Explain that one good way to create a picture in a reader's mind is to include similes, comparisons that use the words *like* or *as*. As students study the similes, have them identify the two things that are being compared.

the Strategy
Practice ∧ Notebook!

Assign *Practice the Strategy Notebook* page 34. Ask volunteers to explain the similes they found. Stress that some comparisons using the words *like* or *as* are not similes because they do not compare two different things. For example the sentence, "That coat looks like mine," does not contain a simile, even though it uses the word *like*. This sentence compares two similar things: two coats.

ReVising Clarify

Strategy: Combine short, choppy sentences.

(Student Page 73)

Ask a volunteer to read Joseph's words to the class.

Ask students to explain how and why Joseph's revisions turned the short, choppy sentences into more readable descriptive sentences.

the Strategy
Practice ∧ Notebook!

Assign *Practice the Strategy Notebook* page 35. Ask volunteers to share their revised sentences with the class.

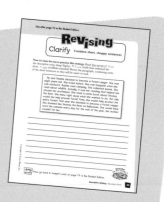

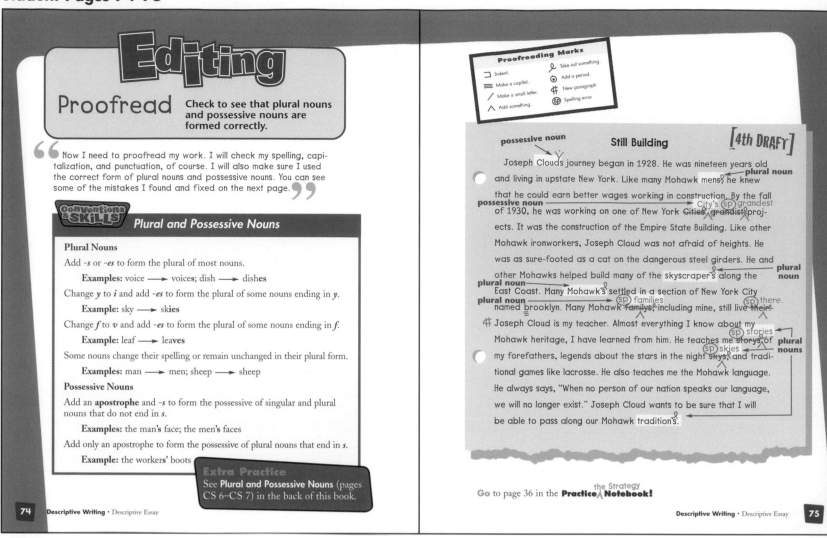

Editing

Proofread

Check to see that plural nouns and possessive nouns are formed correctly.

"Now I need to proofread my work. I will check my spelling, capitalization, and punctuation, of course. I will also make sure I used the correct form of plural nouns and possessive nouns. You can see some of the mistakes I found and fixed on the next page."

Conventions & SKILLS

Plural and Possessive Nouns

Plural Nouns

Add *-s* or *-es* to form the plural of most nouns.

    Examples: voice ⟶ voice**s**; dish ⟶ dish**es**

Change *y* to *i* and add *-es* to form the plural of some nouns ending in *y*.

    Example: sky ⟶ sk**ies**

Change *f* to *v* and add *-es* to form the plural of some nouns ending in *f*.

    Example: leaf ⟶ lea**ves**

Some nouns change their spelling or remain unchanged in their plural form.

    Examples: man ⟶ men; sheep ⟶ sheep

Possessive Nouns

Add an **apostrophe** and *-s* to form the possessive of singular and plural nouns that do not end in *s*.

    Examples: the man**'s** face; the men**'s** faces

Add only an apostrophe to form the possessive of plural nouns that end in *s*.

    Example: the workers**'** boots

Extra Practice
See **Plural and Possessive Nouns** (pages CS 6–CS 7) in the back of this book.

Proofreading Marks

⊐ Indent.   ⌐ Take out something.
⟌ Make a capital.   ⊙ Add a period.
/ Make a small letter.   ⌗ New paragraph
∧ Add something.   (sp) Spelling error

Still Building   [4th DRAFT]

possessive noun

Joseph Clouds journey began in 1928. He was nineteen years old and living in upstate New York. Like many Mohawk mens, he knew that he could earn better wages working in construction. By the fall of 1930, he was working on one of New York Cities grandist projects. It was the construction of the Empire State Building. Like other Mohawk ironworkers, Joseph Cloud was not afraid of heights. He was as sure-footed as a cat on the dangerous steel girders. He and other Mohawks helped build many of the skyscrapers along the East Coast. Many Mohawk's settled in a section of New York City named brooklyn. Many Mohawk familys, including mine, still live their.

Joseph Cloud is my teacher. Almost everything I know about my Mohawk heritage, I have learned from him. He teaches me storys of my forefathers, legends about the stars in the night skys, and traditional games like lacrosse. He also teaches me the Mohawk language. He always says, "When no person of our nation speaks our language, we will no longer exist." Joseph Cloud wants to be sure that I will be able to pass along our Mohawk tradition's.

Go to page 36 in the **Practice the Strategy Notebook!**

Editing   Proofread

Strategy: Check to see that plural nouns and possessive nouns are formed correctly.

(Student Pages 74–75)

Discuss the difference between revising and editing. Be sure that students understand that in the revising step they reread their draft to look for ways to improve the completeness, accuracy, and interest level of their descriptive essay. In the editing step, they look for errors in spelling, grammar, and punctuation.

Ask a volunteer to read Joseph's words to the class. Remind students that good writers search for all kinds of spelling, punctuation, and grammar errors when they proofread. They also focus on the kinds of skills they have had problems with in the past.

Extra Practice: Conventions & Skills Student Edition

If you did not use Student Pages CS 6–CS 7 as a pre-assessment tool, and your students need more practice in forming plural and possessive nouns, you may wish to assign these pages now.

Conventions & Skills Practice

For more targeted practice related to this skill, see these lessons in the optional *Conventions & Skills Practice Book*:

    Lesson 12: Plural and Possessive Nouns
    Lesson 14: The Present Tense
    Lesson 45: Apostrophes

Practice the Strategy Notebook!

Assign *Practice the Strategy Notebook* pages 36–37. If necessary, review the proofreading marks and demonstrate their use on the chalkboard.

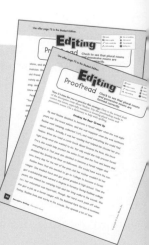

Publishing   Share

Strategy: Publish my descriptive essay in a class newsletter.

(Student Pages 76–77)

Challenge students to think of other ways Joseph could share what he has written. Discuss whether they agree that this strategy was appropriate.

Using the Rubric

Ask students to work in pairs to use the rubric (reprinted on pages 38–39 of the *Practice the Strategy Notebook*) to evaluate Joseph's paper. After each pair has reached its decision, ask students to compare and discuss their results.

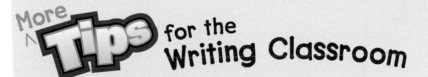

More Tips for the Writing Classroom

Writing Model Sample

You may use this writing sample, focusing on setting, to demonstrate revisions. Make copies for students and create an overhead transparency. Leave space to write revisions.

Setting (original)

Wethertin Elementary had been there for years. It was made of wood and a layer of old paint. There were four windows on each side of the building. An old door marked the entry way. The roof was rusted tin.

Setting (revised)

Wethertin Elementary had been there for years. It was made of *rotting* wood and a *chipping* layer of *blue* paint. There were four windows on each side of the building. *Each pane of glass had a "t" across it.* An old *wooden* door *that had been painted dark blue* marked the entry way. The roof, rusted tin, *had leaked for years.*

School–Home Connection

Dear Family,

In this program, your child will be learning and practicing five types of writing—Expository, Narrative, Descriptive, Persuasive, and Writing for a Test.

Expository writing is writing that explains or informs. It can be a report, a set of directions, or an essay. It can't be a fictional story or a persuasive letter. Your child will be learning and practicing two examples of expository writing— the research report and the compare-and-contrast essay.

Narrative writing is writing that tells a story. It can be an adventure story, a mystery, or a personal story. It can't be a set of instructions or a research report. Your child will be learning and practicing four examples of narrative writing—the personal narrative, the eyewitness account, the fable, and the mystery.

Descriptive writing paints pictures with words. It is meant to help the reader "see" what the writer is writing about. Descriptive writing can describe a person, place, event, or thing. Your child will be learning and practicing two examples of descriptive writing—the descriptive essay and the observation report.

Persuasive writing is meant to convince the reader to agree with a writer's opinion. Sometimes, persuasive writing calls for action on the reader's part. Persuasive writing includes advertising, letters to the editor, and some speeches. Persuasive writing is not meant to tell a story or entertain. Your child will be learning and practicing two examples of persuasive writing—the persuasive essay and the letter to the editor.

Writing to take a test is different from any other kind of writing. To write for a test, a writer needs a specific set of skills. Your child will work with these skills in the last unit in the Student Edition.

You may wish to copy the letter above and send it home with your students.

Books on Teaching Writing

Graves, Donald. *Writing: Teachers and Children at Work.* Portsmouth, NH: Heinemann, 1983.

An indispensable text on teaching writing to children, this introductory book offers helpful advice on where to begin, how to respond to children's work, how to confer with young writers, and how to publish students' writing. Written for teachers of grades 1–6, the "Actions" in each chapter serve as strategies both for your teaching and for students' writing.

Wilde, Jack. *A Door Opens: Writing in Fifth Grade.* Portsmouth, NH: Heinemann, 1993.

This author gives serious attention to genre and strategies. Much is presented anecdotally, but many lists are included. Wilde uses a single broad topic to demonstrate the steps and strategies of persuasion and report writing. However, he also covers choosing a genre, topic selection, and note taking, along with the genres of fiction, poetry, informational writing, personal narrative, and writing across the curriculum.

Clark, Roy Peter. *Free to Write: A Journalist Teaches Young Writers.* Portsmouth, NH: Heinemann, 1995.

The author is a professional writer who follows the model of journalism and uses the real world as the source of all writing. He has students write every day, gathering and sifting information, seeking a focus, building momentum, rethinking and correcting their work, and working to reach their audience. Strategies are designed mainly for fifth graders but are applicable at other grade levels. The presentation is primarily anecdotal but loaded with tips and strategies. Genres include news stories, letters to the editor, and narrative.

Portalupi, JoAnn, and Ralph Fletcher. *Nonfiction Craft Lessons: Teaching Information Writing K-8.* Portland, ME: Stenhouse, 2001.

Divided into chapters for K–2, 3–4, and 5–8, this book includes more than 25 one-page descriptions of strategies for aspects of all steps of the writing process. The book focuses on informative writing, with lessons specific to persuasion, comparison, how-to writing, and biography.

Tips for the Writing Classroom

by Ken Stewart, *Master Teacher*

Creating Tutorial Groups

Tutorial groups allow students, under the watchful eye of the teacher, to take on the role of tutor with their peers. Tutorial groups provide peer editing but place more ownership and responsibility on the student group to understand what constitutes good writing. Students who participate in tutorial groups not only write their own pieces, but they are able to read and analyze other student works. This, in turn, helps everyone improve his/her own writing. Use of the more

formal tutorial group should be limited to three to four times throughout the year. The more informal "partner peer editing" should take place on a more regular basis.

Ideally, tutorial groups should consist of four team members (no fewer than three). Each member must have a copy of the paper being discussed.

The following are six steps to establish successful tutorial groups:

Step 1. (5 minutes) Review the expectations and specific criteria established for a particular type of paper. Distribute a copy of the Tutorial Groups blackline master (page T77) to each tutorial group. Discuss the sheet's contents and explain as needed.

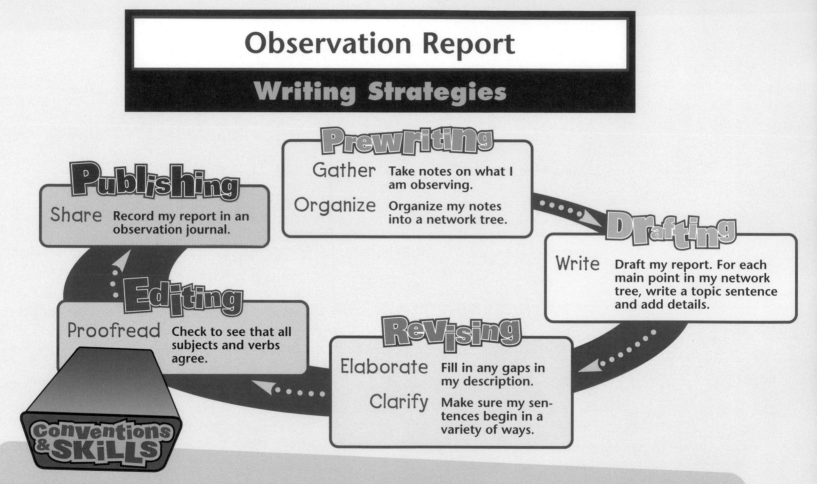

Observation Report

Writing Strategies

Prewriting
Gather — Take notes on what I am observing.
Organize — Organize my notes into a network tree.

Drafting
Write — Draft my report. For each main point in my network tree, write a topic sentence and add details.

Revising
Elaborate — Fill in any gaps in my description.
Clarify — Make sure my sentences begin in a variety of ways.

Editing
Proofread — Check to see that all subjects and verbs agree.

Publishing
Share — Record my report in an observation journal.

Conventions & Skills

Before students read the model on Student Page 79, you may wish to review the targeted **grammar, usage,** or **mechanics** convention, subject-verb agreement. Remind students of the basic rules: singular subjects require singular verbs. Plural subjects require plural verbs. Add *-s* or *-es* to the verb when the subject is singular. Do not add *-s* or *-es* when the subject is plural.

Examples: The **report includes** interesting details. (singular subject and singular verb)

The **reports cover** many different topics. (plural subject and plural verb)

Skill Assessment: To pre-assess your students' understanding of the targeted convention, you may wish to have them complete the corresponding lesson on Student Pages CS 8–CS 9 in the back of the Student Edition.

Skill Mini-Lesson: The Proofread activity in this chapter can be used as a mini-lesson on the targeted **grammar, usage,** or **mechanics** skill.

Step 2. (10–15 minutes) Have each student read the paper completely without making any marks. Then, without conferring with any other team member, each person should write specific comments on his/her copy of the paper. Students should work silently.

Step 3. (10-15 minutes) The person whose paper is being discussed must read his/her paper orally (softly) in the "voice" in which it was written. The reader should stop and ask for comments along the way. This allows students to clarify comments they wrote earlier.

Step 4. (2–3 minutes) Each person should make at least one positive comment about the paper. Model this for students.

Step 5. Have each tutorial group member sign the paper. This means they have done their best work and followed the tutorial steps.

Step 6. Have the writer keep the papers and notes for reference when rewriting the paper. Remind students that the comments are only suggestions to think about ways to improve a paper.

Note: You may want to model the tutorial process for the class before beginning.

(See "More Tips for the Writing Classroom: Establishing Criteria for Use During Tutorials," page T75.)

Time Management for This Chapter*

Session		Session		Session	
1	Discuss the observation report genre; review the questions (Student Page 78). Read "New Mexico Piñon Pines" (Student Page 79). Use the questions to analyze the report. Use the rubric to assess it.	**6**	Read and discuss **DRAFTING: Write** (Student Pages 88–89).	**11**	Assign *Practice the Strategy Notebook* page 47. Encourage students to use the targeted strategy to revise a piece of their own writing.
2	Introduce Rebecca (Student Page 85) as a student-writer working on an observation report. Read and discuss **PREWRITING: Gather** (Student Page 86).	**7**	Assign *Practice the Strategy Notebook* pages 44–45. Encourage students to use the targeted strategy in their own writing.	**12**	Read and discuss **EDITING: Proofread** (Student Pages 92–93).
3	Assign *Practice the Strategy Notebook* pages 40–41. Encourage students to use the targeted strategy in their own writing.	**8**	Read and discuss **REVISING: Elaborate** (Student Page 90).	**13**	Assign *Practice the Strategy Notebook* pages 48–49. Encourage students to use the targeted strategy to edit their own writing.
4	Read and discuss **PREWRITING: Organize** (Student Page 87). Discuss the purpose and mechanics of a network tree and analyze Rebecca's tree.	**9**	Assign *Practice the Strategy Notebook* page 46. Encourage students to use the targeted strategy to revise a piece of their own writing.	**14**	Read and discuss **PUBLISHING: Share** (Student Pages 94–97). Discuss other ways Rebecca could share what she has written.
5	Assign *Practice the Strategy Notebook* pages 42–43. Encourage students to use the targeted strategy in their own writing.	**10**	Read and discuss **REVISING: Clarify** (Student Page 91).	**15**	Review the rubric for this chapter (reprinted on *Practice the Strategy Notebook* pages 50–51). Ask pairs of students to use the rubric to discuss and evaluate Rebecca's report.

WRITER'S HANDBOOK

* To complete the chapter in fewer sessions, assign the *Practice the Strategy Notebook* pages on the same day the targeted strategy is introduced.

Remind students that they can refer to the Writer's Handbook in the back of the Student Edition for more information.

Introduce the Genre:
Observation Report

Begin your introduction by sharing a detailed description of a place, thing, or event that you have observed in nature. Then ask two or three volunteers to share descriptions of places, things, or events that they have seen in nature.

Explain that the descriptions you have shared are called *observation reports*. Emphasize that observation reports are written in first person and include vivid details that appeal to all the senses.

Tell students they are going to study and practice strategies for writing an observation report.

Discuss the Questions

(Student Page 78)

Read the questions on Student Page 78 aloud. Point out the five categories and be sure students are clear on their meaning in the context of writing. Possible points to discuss:

Audience: Writers must keep their audience in mind and choose details that will interest this audience.

Organization: Good writers use well-organized paragraphs in all their work, including observation reports.

Elaboration: Good writers fully explain a topic by elaborating. Filling in gaps in a description is a good way to elaborate.

Clarification: Good writers make descriptions lively by beginning sentences in different ways.

Conventions & Skills: Writers who check to see that their subjects and verbs agree make their writing easier for their audience to read and understand.

Read the Model:
Observation Report

(Student Page 79)

Read "New Mexico Piñon Pines" aloud.

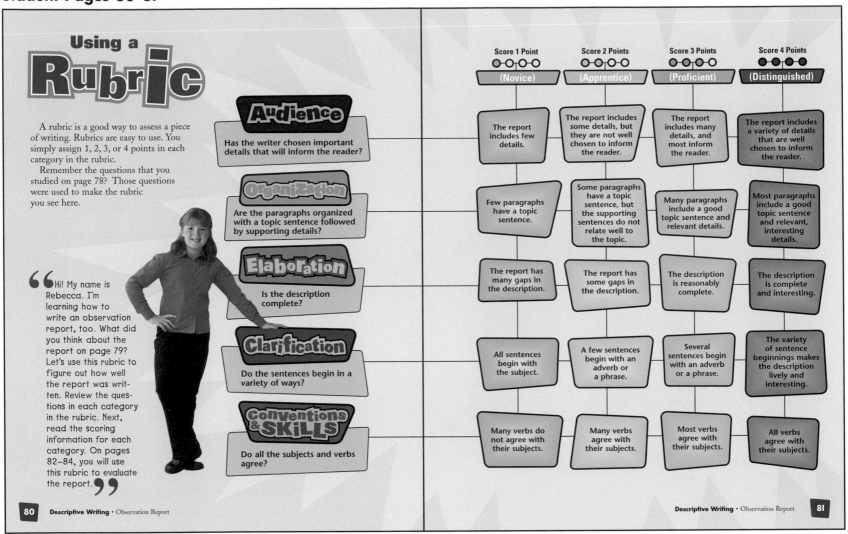

Using a Rubric

(Student Pages 80–81)

Use the text on Student Pages 82–84 to model the use of the rubric in evaluating a piece of writing. For more information on using a rubric, please see page T22.

Make Your Own Rubric

by Lee Bromberger, *Assessment Specialist*

Sometimes the best-designed rubric has shortcomings that are not revealed until the rubric is implemented with an assignment. It is important for the classroom teacher, therefore, to allow time to consider the assignment for which a rubric will be utilized. Doing so can lead to a rubric's improvement or the elimination of a rubric in favor of one that may work better next time. Since rubrics can be easily changed, teachers should be ready to revise rubrics. The best time to do so, with minimum effort, is immediately after a rubric's application to an assignment.

As teachers assess student work with the aid of a rubric, they should keep a set of notes regarding the strengths and weaknesses of the particular rubric itself. These notes could simply be placed under two columns—labeled "What Worked" and "What Failed"—on one sheet of paper. A brief annotation is often all that is needed. Once the classroom teacher has completed grading the assignment, the process of rubric reflection can begin. The result of this reflection would be changes to the rubric to make it more effective the next time it is used.

Teachers should consider sharing their perceptions about particular rubrics with colleagues, particularly if one team-teaches or utilizes a rubric previously applied by another teacher. These questions should be considered:

• Were the same rubric strengths and weaknesses noted?

• Have colleagues made changes that they found led to an improvement?

A team approach toward dissecting a rubric and improving its viability offers opportunities for confidence building and improved rubric designs for future assignments.

Most teachers learn through their early student teaching experiences that setting aside time to reflect on their various lessons is an integral step toward professional growth. As teachers orient themselves to rubric use and design and/or adapt a rubric for their assessment needs, teachers should continually evaluate the effectiveness of rubrics.

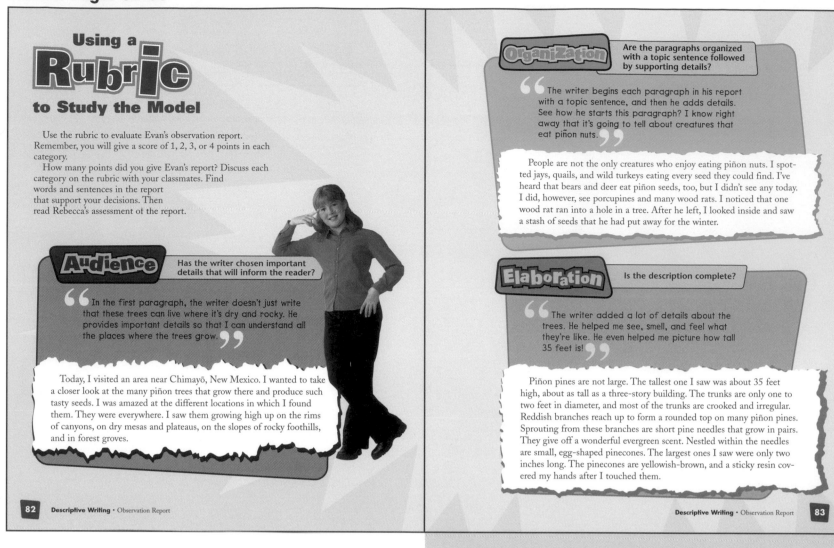

Using a Rubric to Study the Model

Use the rubric to evaluate Evan's observation report. Remember, you will give a score of 1, 2, 3, or 4 points in each category.

How many points did you give Evan's report? Discuss each category on the rubric with your classmates. Find words and sentences in the report that support your decisions. Then read Rebecca's assessment of the report.

Audience

Has the writer chosen important details that will inform the reader?

" In the first paragraph, the writer doesn't just write that these trees can live where it's dry and rocky. He provides important details so that I can understand all the places where the trees grow. "

Today, I visited an area near Chimayō, New Mexico. I wanted to take a closer look at the many piñon trees that grow there and produce such tasty seeds. I was amazed at the different locations in which I found them. They were everywhere. I saw them growing high up on the rims of canyons, on dry mesas and plateaus, on the slopes of rocky foothills, and in forest groves.

Organization

Are the paragraphs organized with a topic sentence followed by supporting details?

" The writer begins each paragraph in his report with a topic sentence, and then he adds details. See how he starts this paragraph? I know right away that it's going to tell about creatures that eat piñon nuts. "

People are not the only creatures who enjoy eating piñon nuts. I spotted jays, quails, and wild turkeys eating every seed they could find. I've heard that bears and deer eat piñon seeds, too, but I didn't see any today. I did, however, see porcupines and many wood rats. I noticed that one wood rat ran into a hole in a tree. After he left, I looked inside and saw a stash of seeds that he had put away for the winter.

Elaboration

Is the description complete?

" The writer added a lot of details about the trees. He helped me see, smell, and feel what they're like. He even helped me picture how tall 35 feet is! "

Piñon pines are not large. The tallest one I saw was about 35 feet high, about as tall as a three-story building. The trunks are only one to two feet in diameter, and most of the trunks are crooked and irregular. Reddish branches reach up to form a rounded top on many piñon pines. Sprouting from these branches are short pine needles that grow in pairs. They give off a wonderful evergreen scent. Nestled within the needles are small, egg-shaped pinecones. The largest ones I saw were only two inches long. The pinecones are yellowish-brown, and a sticky resin covered my hands after I touched them.

82 · **Descriptive Writing** · Observation Report

Descriptive Writing · Observation Report · 83

Using a Rubric to Study the Observation Report

(Student Pages 82–84)

Read the questions and answers on Student Pages 82–84. Discuss whether students agree or disagree with each point in Rebecca's assessment of the report. For example, do students agree that the writer varied the beginning of sentences? Can they think of a different and/or better way to begin any of the sentences?

Note on Conventions & Skills: Remind students that this rubric focuses on an important skill: making verbs agree with their subjects. However, students should always check their writing for errors in spelling, punctuation, and capitalization.

Make sure students have a good grasp of the basics of an observation report, as well as key aspects of the rubric.

Meeting Students' Needs:
Second Language Learners

The second language learner may encounter difficulty with the vocabulary words needed to write an observation report. Numerous books for primary readers provide picture references for vocabulary words. Additionally, "point and say" books written for travelers may be helpful. You may wish to provide or help students find books that can be used as vocabulary references.

Students Who Need Extra Help

Some students will need guidance in selecting the most relevant details for their network trees. Ask them to consider the following questions: "If you could only tell me three things about the [thing, place, or event] that you observed, what would they be?" and "What are the three most important details that you would like to share?" Guide students' responses toward the most significant details.

Gifted Students

Challenge students to create and keep an observation journal over an extended period of time. Arrange for them to meet periodically to share and discuss their journal entries. Encourage them to refine their observation skills.

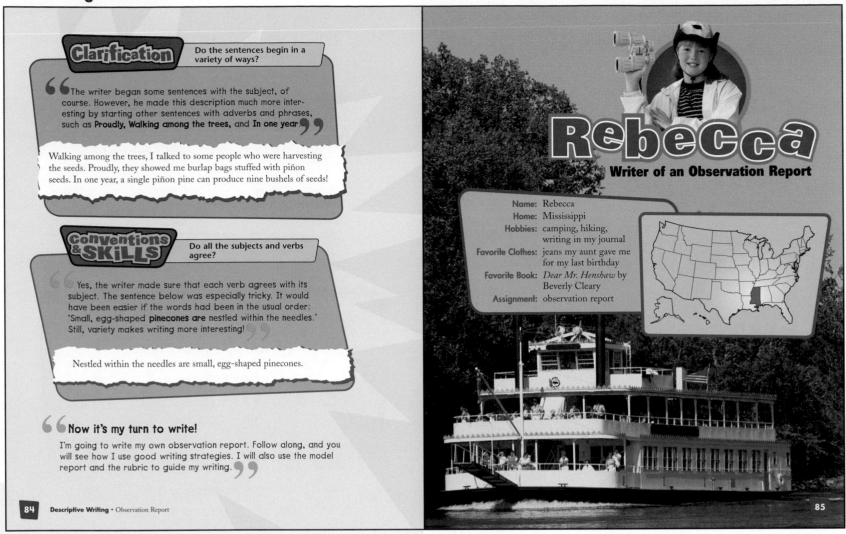

Clarification
Do the sentences begin in a variety of ways?

"The writer began some sentences with the subject, of course. However, he made this description much more interesting by starting other sentences with adverbs and phrases, such as **Proudly**, **Walking among the trees**, and **In one year.**"

Walking among the trees, I talked to some people who were harvesting the seeds. Proudly, they showed me burlap bags stuffed with piñon seeds. In one year, a single piñon pine can produce nine bushels of seeds!

Conventions & Skills
Do all the subjects and verbs agree?

"Yes, the writer made sure that each verb agrees with its subject. The sentence below was especially tricky. It would have been easier if the words had been in the usual order: 'Small, egg-shaped **pinecones are** nestled within the needles.' Still, variety makes writing more interesting!"

Nestled within the needles are small, egg-shaped pinecones.

"**Now it's my turn to write!**

I'm going to write my own observation report. Follow along, and you will see how I use good writing strategies. I will also use the model report and the rubric to guide my writing."

84 | **Descriptive Writing** · Observation Report

Rebecca
Writer of an Observation Report

Name:	Rebecca
Home:	Mississippi
Hobbies:	camping, hiking, writing in my journal
Favorite Clothes:	jeans my aunt gave me for my last birthday
Favorite Book:	*Dear Mr. Henshaw* by Beverly Cleary
Assignment:	observation report

85

Unlocking Text Structure:
Observation Report

The structure of any writing depends upon how information is organized. To help your students unlock the structure of the observation report, you may wish to use the graphic organizer in this unit. A network tree lends itself to writing an observation report. Emphasize that the details on a network tree should be arranged from most important to least important. You may wish to work with the students to create a network tree that plots the structure of the observation report on Student Page 79.

Rebecca:
Writer of an Observation Report

(Student Page 85)

Read the information about Rebecca.

Make sure students understand that she will write her own observation report in this chapter. Discuss what she might choose to write about. Check to see that student suggestions reflect an understanding of the descriptive mode of writing.

Point out that Rebecca will complete the steps in the writing process: Prewriting, Drafting, Revising, Editing, and Publishing. At each stage, she will demonstrate a good writing strategy and explain how she used it. Students should watch for key words, including **Gather, Organize, Write, Elaborate, Clarify, Proofread,** and **Share**.

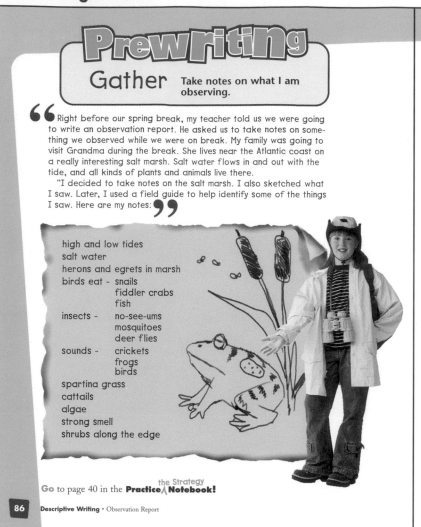

Prewriting
Gather — Take notes on what I am observing.

"Right before our spring break, my teacher told us we were going to write an observation report. He asked us to take notes on something we observed while we were on break. My family was going to visit Grandma during the break. She lives near the Atlantic coast on a really interesting salt marsh. Salt water flows in and out with the tide, and all kinds of plants and animals live there.

"I decided to take notes on the salt marsh. I also sketched what I saw. Later, I used a field guide to help identify some of the things I saw. Here are my notes:"

high and low tides
salt water
herons and egrets in marsh
birds eat - snails
          fiddler crabs
          fish
insects - no-see-ums
          mosquitoes
          deer flies
sounds - crickets
          frogs
          birds
spartina grass
cattails
algae
strong smell
shrubs along the edge

Go to page 40 in the Practice the Strategy Notebook!

86   Descriptive Writing • Observation Report

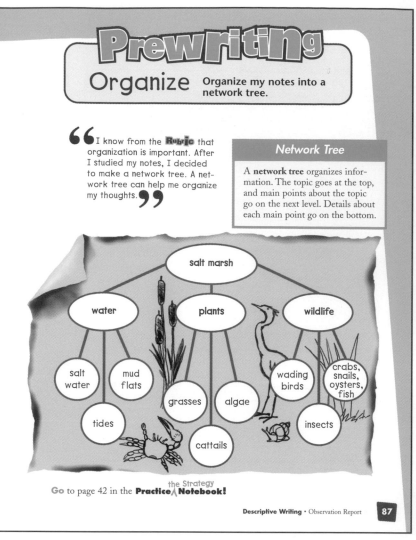

Prewriting
Organize — Organize my notes into a network tree.

"I know from the Rubric that organization is important. After I studied my notes, I decided to make a network tree. A network tree can help me organize my thoughts."

Network Tree

A **network tree** organizes information. The topic goes at the top, and main points about the topic go on the next level. Details about each main point go on the bottom.

salt marsh
- water
  - salt water
  - mud flats
  - tides
- plants
  - grasses
  - algae
  - cattails
- wildlife
  - wading birds
  - crabs, snails, oysters, fish
  - insects

Go to page 42 in the Practice the Strategy Notebook!

Descriptive Writing • Observation Report   87

Prewriting Gather

Strategy: Take notes on what I am observing.

(Student Page 86)

Read the text with students. Then study and discuss Rebecca's notes. Ask students to speculate about topics that Rebecca might write about in her observation report. [**Possible topics: plants and animals in and around the water, life in a salt marsh**]

Refer to the Rubric: The student spokesperson will refer to the rubric throughout the chapter. Remind students to get into the habit of referring back to the rubric so they fully understand its use as a tool for shaping their writing.

Practice the Strategy Notebook!

Assign pages 40–41 in the *Practice the Strategy Notebook*. (Your Own Writing sections should be used as time and students' abilities permit.) Explain that the students will practice this Gather strategy with a different topic.

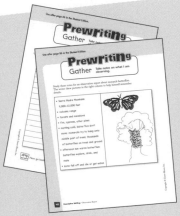

Prewriting Organize

Strategy: Organize my notes into a network tree.

(Student Page 87)

Explain that writing can be organized in many different ways. A graphic organizer is one way to organize information in preparation for writing.

Review the definition of a network tree. Then direct attention to Rebecca's network tree.

Practice the Strategy Notebook!

Assign pages 42–43 in the *Practice the Strategy Notebook*. Allow students plenty of time to complete this activity. If necessary, they can go back to the Gather step to find or generate more information for their network trees. Suggested responses for the *Practice the Strategy Notebook* appear in the Appendix at the back of this Teacher Edition.

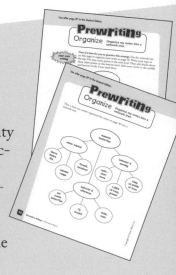

Drafting

Write

Strategy: Draft my report. For each main point in my network tree, write a topic sentence and add details.

(Student Pages 88–89)

Ask students what it means to write a rough draft. Help them understand that a draft is a temporary or "rough" form of a description. A draft will be changed and corrected several times before it is finished. Then ask a student to read Rebecca's words for the class, or read the words yourself.

Ask students why Rebecca is not overly concerned about making mistakes in spelling and grammar as she writes her draft. **[Possible response: She knows that spelling and grammar are important, but she is eager to put all the details she observed into writing at the drafting stage. She will check for errors later.]**

Practice the Strategy Notebook!

Assign pages 44–45 in the *Practice the Strategy Notebook*. Review the definitions of *topic sentence* and *detail sentence* with students. After they have completed their rough drafts, invite volunteers to share what they have written. Ask the class to identify each paragraph's topic sentence, to assess the relevance and importance of the detail sentences, and to determine whether each paragraph has been written in the first person.

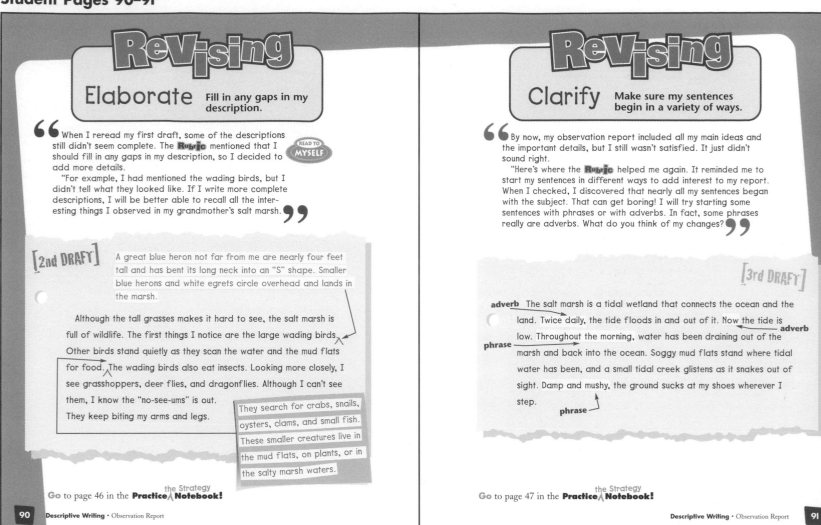

Revising Elaborate

Strategy: **Fill in any gaps in my description.**

(Student Page 90)

Ask a student to read Rebecca's words to the class.

Explain that one good way to help a reader understand an observation report is to fill in any gaps in the description. Guide students as they study the sample paragraph. Invite them to identify any remaining gaps. For instance, perhaps it should include more examples of wading birds.

Practice the Strategy Notebook!

Assign *Practice the Strategy Notebook* page 46. Ask volunteers to identify where they placed the details. Have them explain their reasoning.

Revising Clarify

Strategy: **Make sure my sentences begin in a variety of ways.**

(Student Page 91)

Ask a student to read Rebecca's words to the class. Next, have the class explain the different ways that she began her sentences. Point out that some phrases also function as adverbs. For example, *Throughout the morning* is both a phrase and an adverb (telling "when"). Do not be concerned about how students label the different beginnings. The goal is simply for them to begin their sentences in a variety of ways.

Practice the Strategy Notebook!

Assign *Practice the Strategy Notebook* page 47. Ask volunteers to share their revisions with the class.

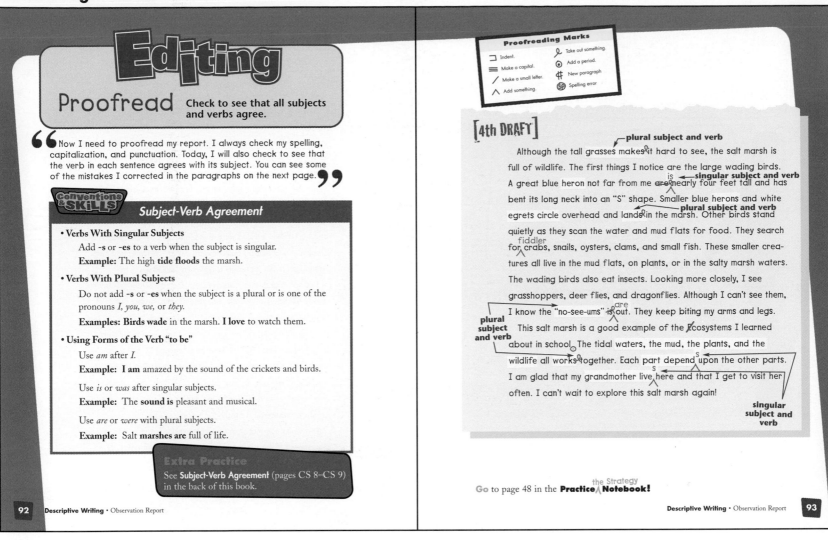

 Proofread

Strategy: Check to see that all subjects and verbs agree.
(Student Pages 92–93)

Discuss the difference between revising and editing. Help students understand that in the revising step they reread their draft to look for ways to improve its clarity and completeness. In the editing step, they look for errors in spelling, grammar, and punctuation.

Ask a volunteer to read Rebecca's words to the class. Remind students that good writers search for all kinds of spelling, punctuation, and grammar errors when they proofread. They also focus on specific skills that have given them problems in the past.

Practice the Strategy Notebook!

Assign *Practice the Strategy Notebook* pages 48–49. If necessary, review the proofreading marks and demonstrate their use on the chalkboard.

Extra Practice: Conventions & Skills Student Edition

If you did not use Student Pages CS 8–CS 9 as a pre-assessment tool, and your students need more practice in subject-verb agreement, you may wish to assign these pages now.

Conventions & Skills Practice

For more targeted practice related to this skill, see these lessons in the optional *Conventions & Skills Practice Book*:

Lesson 14: The Present Tense
Lesson 35: Making the Subject and Verb Agree
Lesson 36: Forms of *Be*

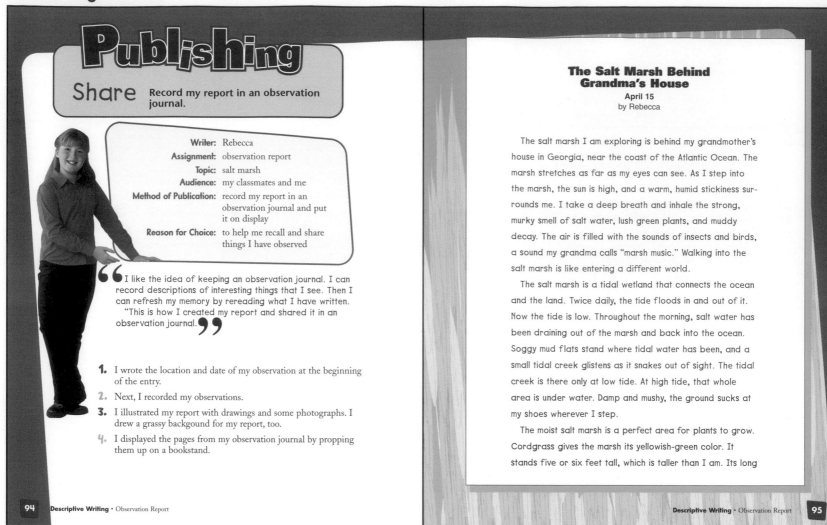

Publishing Share

Strategy: Record my report in an observation journal.

(Student Pages 94–97)

Challenge students to think of other ways Rebecca could share what she has written. Discuss whether they agree that this strategy was appropriate.

Using the Rubric

Ask students to work in pairs to use the rubric (reprinted on pages 50–51 of the *Practice the Strategy Notebook*) to evaluate Rebecca's paper. After each pair has developed its assessment, ask pairs to compare and discuss their decisions.

thin reeds sway in the breeze. Black needle rush reaches my waist, and the shorter spartina grass comes up to my knees. As I examine the standing water and tidal creeks, I can see colorful saltwater plankton and clumps of algae floating on the surface. Both are blooming, and they make the water thick and soupy. Along the edges of the marsh are cattails and shrubs. Salt myrtle and marsh elder are two shrubs I can identify.

Although the tall grasses make it hard to see what's here, the salt marsh is full of wildlife. The first things I notice are the large wading birds. A great blue heron not far from me

is nearly four feet tall and has bent its long neck into an "S" shape. Smaller blue herons and white egrets circle overhead and land in the marsh. Other birds stand quietly as they scan the water and mud flats for food. They search for fiddler crabs, snails, oysters, clams, and small fish. These smaller creatures live in the mud flats, on plants, or in the marsh waters. The wading birds also eat insects. Looking more closely, I see grasshoppers, deer flies, and dragon-flies. Although I can't see them, I know the "no-see-ums" are out. They keep biting my arms and legs!

This salt marsh is a good example of the ecosystems I learned about in school. The tidal waters, the mud, the plants, and the wildlife all work together. Each part depends on the other parts. These plants could not live here without the saltwater tide every day, and the wildlife would not be here at all if there were no plants. I am glad that my grandmother lives here and that I get to visit her often. I can't wait to explore this salt marsh again!

USING the Rubric for Assessment

Go to page 50 in the **Practice Notebook!** Use that rubric to assess Rebecca's paper. Try using the rubric to assess your own writing.
the Strategy

96   **Descriptive Writing** • Observation Report

Descriptive Writing • Observation Report   97

More Tips for the Writing Classroom

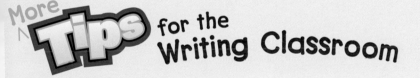

Establishing Criteria for Use During Tutorials

In order to make tutorial groups more student-friendly, give your students the opportunity to help establish criteria for evaluating the paper. It really does not matter what kind of paper your class is writing (narrative, descriptive, expository, etc.), but it does matter that the expectations are clear for everyone. The following are some suggestions for developing criteria for narrative or descriptive essays:

1. Ask your class what makes creative writing come alive. Guide them in a discussion that focuses on using specific words—nouns, adjectives, verbs, adverbs. Help them to understand similes, metaphors, and other forms of figurative language that may be appropriate for this grade level.

2. Ask your class for the key elements that make a story come alive. (Refer to stories you have read in class.) Guide them in a discussion that focuses on plot, setting, and theme.

3. Discuss how much effort is needed to produce good writing. Make sure students understand the importance of editing and revising drafts to final copy form.

4. Once papers are written to final copy form, take time to share and discuss some student works. Find places to publish and/or hang the works. Maybe just invite parents to come to an evening reading, or create your own classroom "book" that includes various forms of writings written throughout the year. Use your imagination.

your own
DESCRIPTIVE
writing
Science

Put the strategies you practiced in this unit to work to write your own descriptive essay, observation report, or both! You can:

- develop the writing you did in the Your Own Writing pages of the *Practice the Strategy Notebook*;

- pick an idea below and write something new;

- choose another idea of your own.

Be sure to follow the steps in the writing process. Use the rubrics in this unit to assess your writing.

Descriptive Essay	**Observation Report**
• a meteorologist who works at a local television station • a cave with stalactites and stalagmites • cirrus, cumulus, or nimbus clouds • a zoo keeper • the effect of a drought	• a science experiment • a chameleon changing colors • tadpoles changing into frogs • amoebas multiplying • an earthquake

portfolio

School–Home Connection

Keep a writing portfolio. Think about adding the activities from the *Practice the Strategy Notebook* to your writing portfolio. You may want to take your portfolio home to share.

Your Own Writing Descriptive Writing for Science

Assign either one or both genres to the students. Before they begin writing, review key information about each genre. Decide whether you wish students to:

- Choose one of the topics on this page in the Student Edition.

- Complete one of the pieces they partially drafted in the Your Own Writing pages in the *Practice the Strategy Notebook*.

- Generate a completely new idea.

Portfolio/School-Home Connection

Encourage the students to keep portfolios of their writing. You may also wish to duplicate and distribute the School-Home Letter included in this unit.

Work-in-Progress Portfolio

Remind students to review this portfolio often to revise existing pieces that have not been published. Encourage students to share pieces of their Work-in-Progress Portfolios with family members who can help in editing.

Published Portfolio

Encourage students to choose pieces from their Published Portfolios to share with family members.

Tips for the Writing Classroom

Tutorial Groups

Name of the student whose paper is being discussed _____

Date _____

Individual Comments

1. All members should read the same paper completely before making any corrections or comments. Then, without talking to any other member, write your comments on your copy of the paper.

Group Comments

2. Have one group member read the paper aloud one sentence at a time while other members make **oral** and **written** comments. Look for awkward sentences, sentence fragments, poor word choices, creative imagery or phrases, spelling, punctuation, etc. If the paper is a story, also look for logical plot development building to a climax, powerful character development, and a clear setting.

3. Make positive comments about the paper.

4. Give all papers/notes to the writer. **These notes must be placed in your notebook.**

All tutorial group members must sign below:

_____

_____

_____

_____

_____

Purpose: To facilitate tutorial group work. See page T64 for more information.
This page may be duplicated for classroom use.

Books on Teaching Writing

Atwell, Nancie, ed. *Coming to Know: Writing to Learn in the Intermediate Grades.* Portsmouth, NH: Heinemann, 1990.

This source focuses on content-area writing, especially the research report. Using narratives, it shows how to make good use of learning logs. The appendix lists 30 genres for report writing.

Fletcher, Ralph, and JoAnn Portalupi. *Craft Lessons: Teaching Writing K–8.* Portland, ME: Stenhouse, 1998.

Divided into chapters for K–2, 3–4, and 5–8, this book includes more than 25 one-page descriptions of strategies for aspects of all steps of the writing process. The book focuses on informative writing, with lessons specific to persuasion, comparison, how-to writing, and biography.

Calkins, Lucy McCormick. *The Art of Teaching Writing.* Portsmouth, NH: Heinemann, 1984.

This source offers invaluable insights on teaching writing, conferring with students, and working with different forms of writing. The author explains how children change as writers as they progress through the grades. One technique she explains is having students start with something they have noticed or wondered about and develop a story or idea from there.

Harvey, Stephanie. *Nonfiction Matters: Reading, Writing, and Research in Grades 3–8.* York, ME: Stenhouse, 1998.

This author discusses the nature of nonfiction writing, describing the selection of topics and the use of primary and secondary sources, including those on the Internet. The author also covers organizing information, revising drafts, creating oral presentations to accompany written reports, and designing rubrics with students' help.

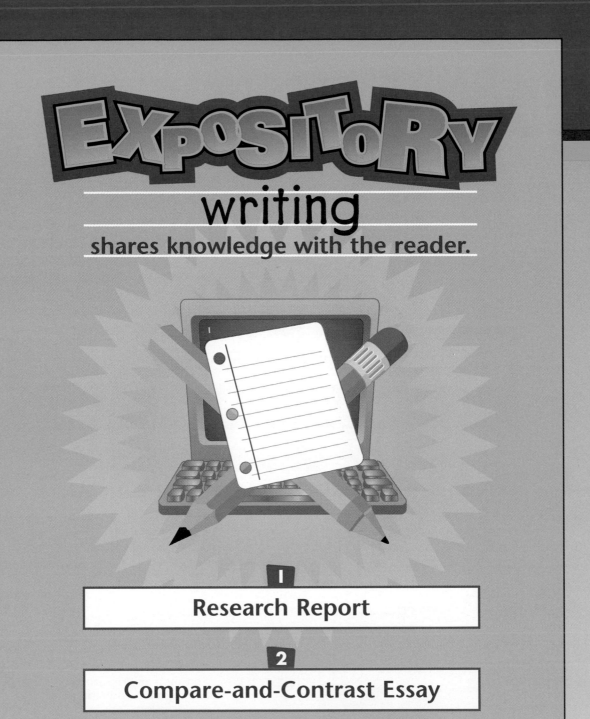

EXPOSITORY writing
shares knowledge with the reader.

1 Research Report

2 Compare-and-Contrast Essay

Defining Expository Writing

Begin this unit by having students examine some examples of expository writing, such as reports, business letters, e-mail, and factual articles from magazines and newspapers. Discuss what these examples have in common. Guide students to understand the following points:

- All are forms of nonfiction.
- All explain or discuss real objects, people, places, or events.
- All include facts, details, examples, definitions, and/or anecdotes.

Discuss why research reports, compare-and-contrast reports, and how-to essays are examples of expository writing, while fictional stories are not examples of expository writing.

Emphasize that the primary purpose of expository writing is to share factual information with the reader.

 **for the Writing Classroom**

by Ken Stewart, *Master Teacher*

Circle Discussions/Oral Communication

The importance of oral communication is multifaceted. Speaking and listening give students the opportunity to share and analyze ideas, interpret readings or writings, and understand that there are many sides when looking at problems or solutions. Students who are encouraged to participate in class discussions will become better writers because their knowledge and understanding of the topics being discussed will increase dramatically.

You can help your students realize that a discussion is an opportunity to be open with their personal (not private) thoughts about a topic. (**Note:** "Personal thoughts" are those that students can be comfortable sharing in group settings. "Private thoughts" are those that make a student very uneasy when discussed in a group setting.) Private thoughts are not appropriate for whole-class discussion. Make sure this distinction is clear before starting any kind of class discussions.

When the class is interpreting a piece of fiction, begin your discussions with the characters and plot. Have students focus on the relationship of the plot and characters to real-life situations. Then expand the discussion to the theme (the main lesson) the author wants the reader to learn. Finally, have students relate these lessons to personal opinions and experiences.

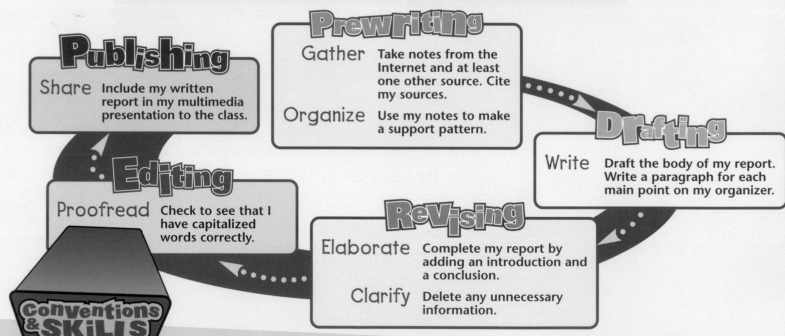

Before the students read the model on Student Page 101, you may wish to review the targeted **grammar, usage,** or **mechanics** convention. Remind students that proper nouns and proper adjectives name particular people, places, and things and must always be capitalized. Initials and abbreviations take the place of proper nouns. They, too, should be capitalized.

Examples: **America** is a democracy. (proper noun)
The **American** people enjoy many freedoms. (proper adjective)
Francis S. Key wrote the words for our national anthem. (proper nouns and initial)
We live in the **U.S.A.** (abbreviation)

Skill Assessment: To pre-assess your students' understanding of the targeted convention, you may wish to have them complete the corresponding lesson on Student Pages CS 10–CS 11 in the back of this book.

Skill Mini-Lesson: The Proofread activity in this chapter can be used as a mini-lesson on the targeted **grammar, usage,** or **mechanics** skill.

Once students begin sharing their viewpoints about problems, solutions, and themes, they will begin to understand and appreciate others' opinions. Encourage polite disagreement so students learn how to settle "arguments" in a civil manner. Your students will begin to see differing opinions as positive developments that encourage analytical and critical thought. These thought processes will transfer to meaningful writing.

To have successful circle discussions in the classroom:

1. Have students define what the word *discussion* really means. Make sure they realize that communicating orally demands that they speak clearly and listen carefully. Review good speaking and listening skills.

2. Make sure students know that inappropriate comments and "put downs" have no place in these discussions.

3. Act as a facilitator to get the discussion moving and to shift gears when the discussion begins to stall.

4. After a student has communicated his/her ideas, have him or her call on another student.

5. Encourage participation by setting up a recording method for bonus points that can be gained or lost.

For more information on listening skills, see "More Tips for the Writing Classroom" on page T92.

Time Management for This Chapter*

Session		Session		Session	
1	Discuss the research report genre; review the questions (Student Page 100). Read "Chief Joseph" (Student Page 101). Use the questions to analyze the report and use the rubric to assess it.	**6**	Read and discuss **DRAFTING: Write** (Student Pages 112–113).	**11**	Assign *Practice the Strategy Notebook* page 58. Encourage students to use the targeted strategy to revise a piece of their own writing.
2	Introduce Selena (Student Page 107) as a student-writer working on a research report. Read and discuss **PREWRITING: Gather** (Student Pages 108–109).	**7**	Assign *Practice the Strategy Notebook* page 56. Encourage students to use the targeted strategy in their own writing.	**12**	Read and discuss **EDITING: Proofread** (Student Pages 116–117).
3	Assign *Practice the Strategy Notebook* pages 52–53. Encourage students to use the targeted strategy in their own writing.	**8**	Read and discuss **REVISING: Elaborate** (Student Page 114).	**13**	Assign *Practice the Strategy Notebook* page 59. Encourage students to use the targeted strategy to edit their own writing.
4	Read and discuss **PREWRITING: Organize** (Student Pages 110–111). Discuss the purpose and mechanics of a support pattern and analyze Selena's support pattern.	**9**	Assign *Practice the Strategy Notebook* page 57. Encourage students to use the targeted strategy to revise a piece of their own writing.	**14**	Read and discuss **PUBLISHING: Share** (Student Pages 118–121). Discuss other ways Selena could share her research report.
5	Assign *Practice the Strategy Notebook* pages 54–55. Encourage students to use the targeted strategy in their own writing.	**10**	Read and discuss **REVISING: Clarify** (Student Page 115).	**15**	Review the rubric for this chapter (reprinted on *Practice the Strategy Notebook* pages 60–61). Ask pairs of students to use the rubric to discuss and evaluate Selena's report.

WRITER'S HANDBOOK

Remind students that they can refer to the Writer's Handbook in the back of the Student Edition for more information.

* To complete the chapter in fewer sessions, assign the *Practice the Strategy Notebook* pages on the same day the targeted strategy is introduced.

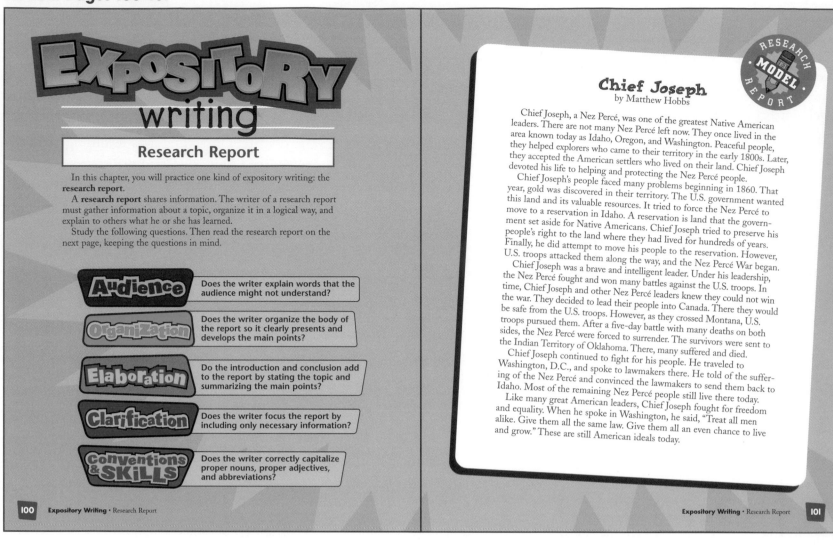

Introduce the Genre:
Research Report

Write *research* on the chalkboard. Explain that *re-* is a prefix meaning "again" and *search* means "to look." A *research report* is a type of expository writing. To write a research report, a writer "looks again" at things that have already been written about a topic. Emphasize that the writer of a research report should use multiple sources to learn about a topic.

Conclude by telling students that they are going to study and practice strategies for writing a research report.

Discuss the Questions

(Student Page 100)

Read the questions on Student Page 100 aloud. Point out the five categories and be sure students are clear on their meaning in the context of writing. Possible points to discuss:

Audience: The writer must keep his/her audience in mind and explain words that they might not understand.

Organization: Different types of writing lend themselves to different organizational strategies. A research report should clearly present and develop main points related to the topic.

Elaboration: A good writer fully explains a topic by elaborating. Adding an introduction and a conclusion to a report is one way to elaborate.

Clarification: A good writer includes only necessary information.

Conventions & Skills: Writers who observe conventions, such as the rules for capitalization, make their writing easier to read and understand.

Read the Model:
Research Report

(Student Page 101)

Read "Chief Joseph" aloud.

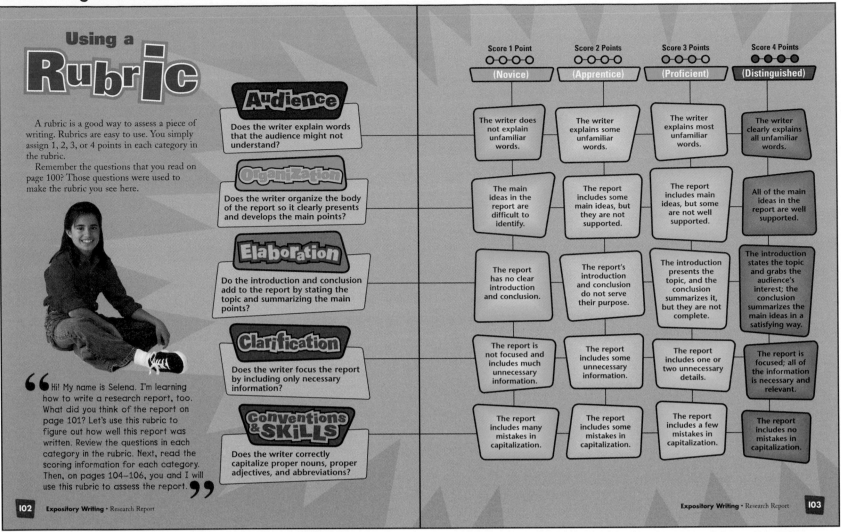

Using a Rubric

(Student Pages 102–103)

Use the text on Student Pages 104–106 to model the use of the rubric in evaluating a research report. For more information on using a rubric, please see page T22.

Developing Rubrics with Student Input

by Lee Bromberger, *Assessment Specialist*

Classroom teachers who use rubrics to evaluate student writing have invariably included the writing assignment objective(s) as part of the rubric's focus. Such objectives, combined with a teacher's experience in assessment, help focus the teacher's attention for that particular writing evaluation.

In such a common scenario, one significant voice is missing: the community of students. While many teachers can appropriately take pride in their invention, production, and assessment of student writing assignments, their failure to solicit student input as part of that process creates a significant void in the classroom. After all, students are writing the assignment and checking to see that they have met the objectives as defined by the assignment. In a sense, they are delivering the product that their teachers have "prepared" for them.

Allowing students to participate in the development of an assignment rubric yields the following "bonus" outcomes:

- **Students must review and reassess the objectives of the unit.** Asking students to determine the criteria of a particular assignment rubric places them in a position to consider what they have recently studied and what was of most value for them. Keep in mind that all students, especially younger ones, will need some guidance to help them think about what they learned. A class discussion (in which the teacher recaps main points of the instruction and helps students decide what was most helpful and least helpful to them) can help students debrief.

- **Students offer a "sounding board" for the teacher before beginning an assignment.** Teacher oversights or miscommunicated ideas can squash the best-developed writing assignment and rubric. Sometimes gathering students' perspectives will yield results that may surprise a teacher. Most writing teachers advise students to "cool off" or distance themselves from a writing assignment before they begin making revisions. Contributions from the student point of view can have the same effect for the teacher's development of assessments. The students will provide a cool voice or fresh perspective that can help derail any potential obstacles toward the writing assignment and its accompanying rubric.

- **Students will take ownership of the assignment.** Having contributed to the development of the assignment and the rubric, students will stake their claim to it as well.

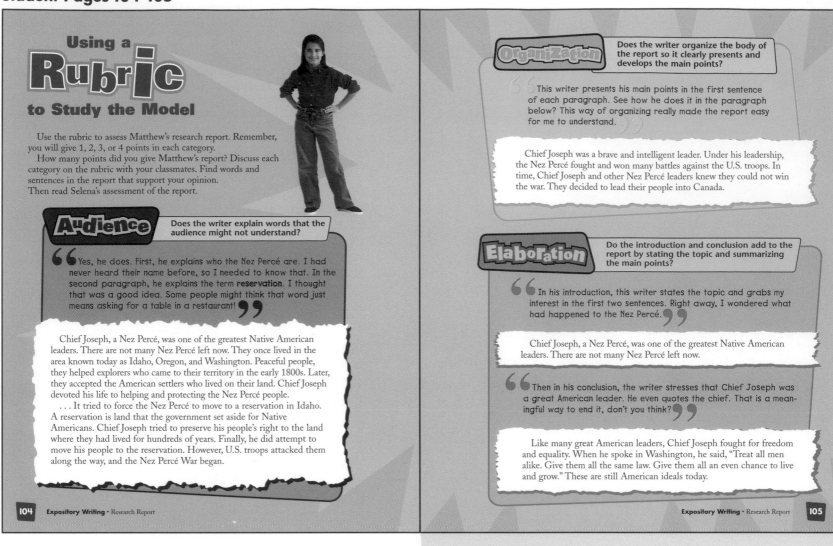

Using a **Rubric** to Study the Model

Use the rubric to assess Matthew's research report. Remember, you will give 1, 2, 3, or 4 points in each category.

How many points did you give Matthew's report? Discuss each category on the rubric with your classmates. Find words and sentences in the report that support your opinion. Then read Selena's assessment of the report.

Audience — Does the writer explain words that the audience might not understand?

❝ Yes, he does. First, he explains who the Nez Percé are. I had never heard their name before, so I needed to know that. In the second paragraph, he explains the term **reservation**. I thought that was a good idea. Some people might think that word just means asking for a table in a restaurant! ❞

Chief Joseph, a Nez Percé, was one of the greatest Native American leaders. There are not many Nez Percé left now. They once lived in the area known today as Idaho, Oregon, and Washington. Peaceful people, they helped explorers who came to their territory in the early 1800s. Later, they accepted the American settlers who lived on their land. Chief Joseph devoted his life to helping and protecting the Nez Percé people.

. . . It tried to force the Nez Percé to move to a reservation in Idaho. A reservation is land that the government set aside for Native Americans. Chief Joseph tried to preserve his people's right to the land where they had lived for hundreds of years. Finally, he did attempt to move his people to the reservation. However, U.S. troops attacked them along the way, and the Nez Percé War began.

Organization — Does the writer organize the body of the report so it clearly presents and develops the main points?

❝ This writer presents his main points in the first sentence of each paragraph. See how he does it in the paragraph below? This way of organizing really made the report easy for me to understand. ❞

Chief Joseph was a brave and intelligent leader. Under his leadership, the Nez Percé fought and won many battles against the U.S. troops. In time, Chief Joseph and other Nez Percé leaders knew they could not win the war. They decided to lead their people into Canada.

Elaboration — Do the introduction and conclusion add to the report by stating the topic and summarizing the main points?

❝ In his introduction, this writer states the topic and grabs my interest in the first two sentences. Right away, I wondered what had happened to the Nez Percé. ❞

Chief Joseph, a Nez Percé, was one of the greatest Native American leaders. There are not many Nez Percé left now.

❝ Then in his conclusion, the writer stresses that Chief Joseph was a great American leader. He even quotes the chief. That is a meaningful way to end it, don't you think? ❞

Like many great American leaders, Chief Joseph fought for freedom and equality. When he spoke in Washington, he said, "Treat all men alike. Give them all the same law. Give them all an even chance to live and grow." These are still American ideals today.

Using a Rubric to Study the Research Report
(Student Pages 104–106)

Read the questions and answers on Student Pages 104–106. You might point out that the ellipses on Student Page 104 indicate that part of the model report was omitted when it was presented here as an example.

Discuss whether students agree or disagree with each point in Selena's assessment of the report. For example, do they agree that the writer included only necessary information in the report? If not, ask students to point out any information that could be deleted and to explain why.

Note on Conventions & Skills: Remind students that this rubric focuses on an important skill: capitalizing words and abbreviations. However, students should also always check their writing for spelling and punctuation.

Make sure students have a good grasp of the features of a research report, as well as key aspects of the rubric.

Meeting Students' Needs:
Second Language Learners

The second language learner may encounter difficulty in reading and interpreting research materials. You may wish to help select research materials and to allow students to work in pairs. Because these learners tend to be adept at gleaning information from pictures, encourage students to watch videos and study pictures related to their topic.

Students Who Need Extra Help

Some students will need guidance in selecting appropriate sources of information. Enlist the aid of the school media specialist or set aside time to help students identify possible sources of information. You might ask them to share the sources they have selected with you before they begin taking notes.

Gifted Students

Challenge students to research other topics that interest them, perhaps related to current events, hobbies, or genealogy. Arrange for a media specialist to show students the research tools available at libraries. Encourage them to explore the (appropriate) available resources.

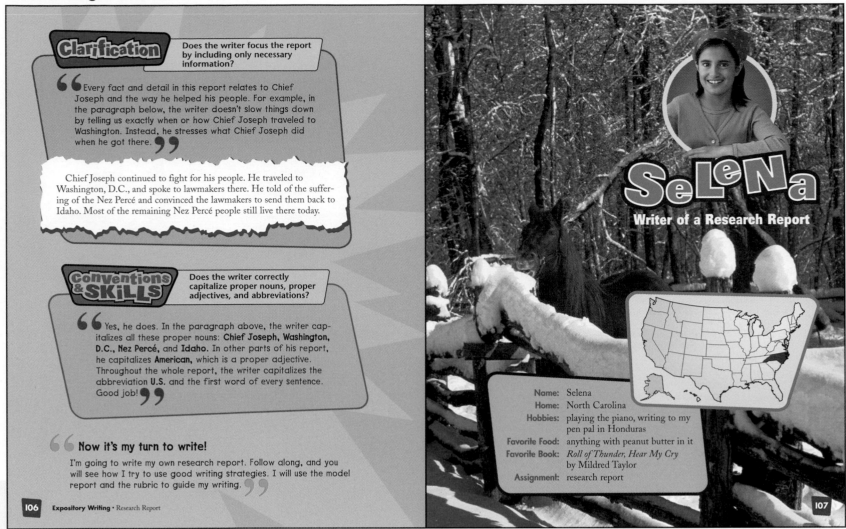

Clarification · Does the writer focus the report by including only necessary information?

❝ Every fact and detail in this report relates to Chief Joseph and the way he helped his people. For example, in the paragraph below, the writer doesn't slow things down by telling us exactly when or how Chief Joseph traveled to Washington. Instead, he stresses what Chief Joseph did when he got there. ❞

Chief Joseph continued to fight for his people. He traveled to Washington, D.C., and spoke to lawmakers there. He told of the suffering of the Nez Percé and convinced the lawmakers to send them back to Idaho. Most of the remaining Nez Percé people still live there today.

Conventions & Skills · Does the writer correctly capitalize proper nouns, proper adjectives, and abbreviations?

❝ Yes, he does. In the paragraph above, the writer capitalizes all these proper nouns: **Chief Joseph, Washington, D.C., Nez Percé,** and **Idaho.** In other parts of his report, he capitalizes **American,** which is a proper adjective. Throughout the whole report, the writer capitalizes the abbreviation **U.S.** and the first word of every sentence. Good job! ❞

❝ **Now it's my turn to write!**

I'm going to write my own research report. Follow along, and you will see how I try to use good writing strategies. I will use the model report and the rubric to guide my writing. ❞

106 · **Expository Writing** · Research Report

SeLeNa
Writer of a Research Report

Name:	Selena
Home:	North Carolina
Hobbies:	playing the piano, writing to my pen pal in Honduras
Favorite Food:	anything with peanut butter in it
Favorite Book:	*Roll of Thunder, Hear My Cry* by Mildred Taylor
Assignment:	research report

107

Unlocking Text Structure:
Research Report

The structure of any writing depends upon how information is organized. To help your students unlock the structure of the research report, you may wish to use the graphic organizer in this unit. The support pattern lends itself to writing a research report. In a research report, a topic is explained or "supported" by facts the writer gathers. A support pattern organizes these facts under the main points. Stress to students that supporting the topic is essential in writing a research report.

Selena:
Writer of a Research Report

(Student Page 107)

Read the information about Selena.

Make sure the students understand that she will write her own research report in this chapter. Discuss what Selena might choose to write about in her report. Check to see if student suggestions reflect an understanding of the expository mode of writing.

Point out that Selena will complete the steps in the writing process: Prewriting, Drafting, Revising, Editing, and Publishing. At each stage, she will demonstrate a good writing strategy and explain how she used it. Students should watch for key words, such as **Gather, Organize, Write, Elaborate, Clarify, Proofread,** and **Share.**

Gather — Take notes from the Internet and at least one other source. Cite my sources.

"My family is Mexican American, and many of my relatives have worked on farms. I grew up hearing about Cesar Chavez and all that he did to help farmworkers, especially Mexican Americans. When I found out we were going to write a research report, I decided to write about Cesar Chavez. I was eager to learn more about his life.

"I found a Web site about Cesar Chavez that was created by a person who admired him. However, my teacher asked me not to use it. She said it might have some incorrect information in it. Instead, she helped me find a Web site that was from a library on Latin American culture. I took notes from this Web site and from an interesting book about Cesar Chavez that I found at the library. My teacher reminded me to cite my sources as I took notes."

Citing Sources

When you **cite a source,** you tell readers where you found certain information. The examples below show how to present the information about a source. Pay attention to the order of the information and the use of commas, colons, and periods. Remember that the title of a book should be in italics or underlined. The title of an article should be in quotation marks.

To cite a book:
Author's last name, author's first name. *Book title.* City of publication: publisher, date of publication.

Example: Collins, David R. *Farmworker's Friend: The Story of Cesar Chavez.* Minneapolis: Carolrhoda Books, 1996.

To cite a Web site:
Author (if given), "Title of article." Sponsor of Web site. Date of article. Web site address.

Example: "The Story of Cesar Chavez." Latino Culture: U.S. 25 May 2001. http://latinoculture.about.com.

"Right away, I found interesting information for my report. My teacher had shown us how to put the information on note cards. Each fact or group of closely related facts gets its own note card. Here are three of my note cards. I added headings to my cards, too, so it would be easier to group them by topic later on."

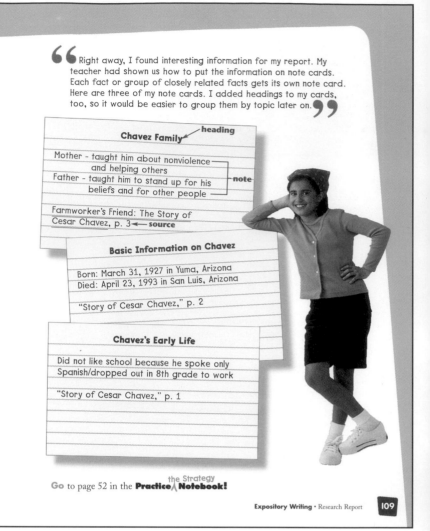

Chavez Family ← heading

Mother – taught him about nonviolence and helping others
Father – taught him to stand up for his beliefs and for other people ← note

Farmworker's Friend: The Story of Cesar Chavez, p. 3 ← source

Basic Information on Chavez

Born: March 31, 1927 in Yuma, Arizona
Died: April 23, 1993 in San Luis, Arizona

"Story of Cesar Chavez," p. 2

Chavez's Early Life

Did not like school because he spoke only Spanish/dropped out in 8th grade to work

"Story of Cesar Chavez," p. 1

Go to page 52 in the Practice the Strategy Notebook!

PreWriting Gather

Strategy: Take notes from the Internet and at least one other source. Cite my sources.

(Student Pages 108–109)

Read the text with students. Then discuss the notes from the book and Web site. Ask students to name other kinds of information that the writer should gather. **[Possible responses: information about why Chavez fought for farmworkers; his challenges and accomplishments]** Discuss other possible sources of information, such as encyclopedias, magazine articles, and interviews.

Refer to the Rubric: The student spokesperson will refer to the rubric throughout the chapter. Remind students to get into the habit of referring back to the rubric so they fully understand its use as a tool for shaping their writing.

Practice the Strategy Notebook!

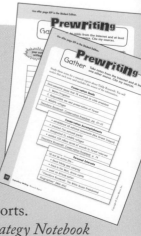

Assign pages 52–53 in the *Practice the Strategy Notebook.* (Your Own Writing sections should be used as time and students' abilities permit.) Explain that students will practice this Gather strategy with a different topic: Teddy Roosevelt. If you wish, have students choose their own topic and write their own research reports. Suggested responses for the *Practice the Strategy Notebook* appear in the Appendix at the back of this Teacher Edition.

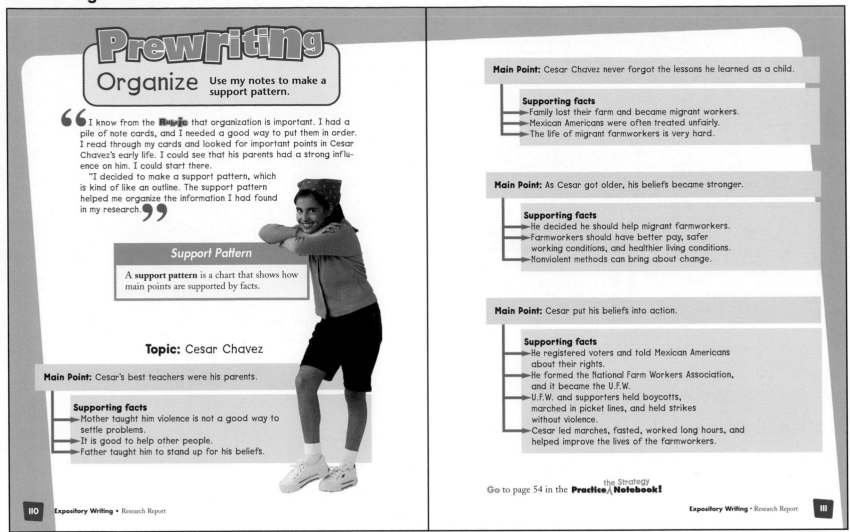

Prewriting
Organize
Use my notes to make a support pattern.

❝ I know from the **Rubric** that organization is important. I had a pile of note cards, and I needed a good way to put them in order. I read through my cards and looked for important points in Cesar Chavez's early life. I could see that his parents had a strong influence on him. I could start there.

"I decided to make a support pattern, which is kind of like an outline. The support pattern helped me organize the information I had found in my research. ❞

Support Pattern

A **support pattern** is a chart that shows how main points are supported by facts.

Topic: Cesar Chavez

Main Point: Cesar's best teachers were his parents.

Supporting facts
➤ Mother taught him violence is not a good way to settle problems.
➤ It is good to help other people.
➤ Father taught him to stand up for his beliefs.

Main Point: Cesar Chavez never forgot the lessons he learned as a child.

Supporting facts
➤ Family lost their farm and became migrant workers.
➤ Mexican Americans were often treated unfairly.
➤ The life of migrant farmworkers is very hard.

Main Point: As Cesar got older, his beliefs became stronger.

Supporting facts
➤ He decided he should help migrant farmworkers.
➤ Farmworkers should have better pay, safer working conditions, and healthier living conditions.
➤ Nonviolent methods can bring about change.

Main Point: Cesar put his beliefs into action.

Supporting facts
➤ He registered voters and told Mexican Americans about their rights.
➤ He formed the National Farm Workers Association, and it became the U.F.W.
➤ U.F.W. and supporters held boycotts, marched in picket lines, and held strikes without violence.
➤ Cesar led marches, fasted, worked long hours, and helped improve the lives of the farmworkers.

Go to page 54 in the **Practice the Strategy Notebook!**

Prewriting Organize

Strategy: Use my notes to make a support pattern.

(Student Pages 110–111)

Explain that writing can be organized in many ways. A graphic organizer is one way to organize information in preparation for writing. Review the definition of a support pattern. Then direct attention to Selena's support pattern. Point out how the facts and details are listed under the appropriate main point.

Practice the Strategy Notebook!

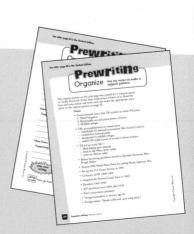

Assign pages 54–55 in the *Practice the Strategy Notebook.* Allow students sufficient time to complete this activity. If necessary, they can go back to the Gather step to find or generate more information for their support patterns.

Drafting

Write

Draft the body of my report. Write a paragraph for each main point on my organizer.

❝ I've done my research and organized my notes. Now I'm ready to draft the body of my report. I'll write a paragraph for every main point on my support pattern. I'll include supporting facts in each paragraph.

"The **Rubric** reminds me to think about my audience as I write. My classmates will be my audience. I will make sure to explain any words that they might not understand. I want to make it easy for them to learn about Cesar Chavez's life and work.

"You can read part of the body of my report on this page and the next page. Look for the main points. Did I explain any words that are new to you? ❞

Body

The **body** is the main part of a piece of writing. It comes between the introduction and the conclusion and explains the main ideas.

[1st DRAFT]

main point →

Cesar's best teachers were his parents. He was born in Yuma, Arizona, in 1927. He did not like his early school years, partly because Mexican American children were often treated unfairly. Cesar's mother taught him that violence was not the way to settle problems. She encouraged him to help other people. Cesar's father taught him to stand up for his beliefs.

main point

explain unfamiliar words

Cesar never forgot the lessons he learned as a child. When he was still a boy, his family was swindled, or cheated, out of their farm. They had to become migrant farmworkers in California. A migrant worker moves from place to place to pick crops. There Cesar discovered much more injustice. His family worked in the feilds for long hours and very little pay. They worked from Brawley to Oxnard. They often lived in one-room shacks without running water. His mother's name was Juana, and his father's name was Librado.

main point →

As Cesar got older, his beliefs became stronger. He joined the U.S. Navy at age 17. When he was 21, he married a woman named Helen Fabela. All during this time, Cesar believed that the farmworkers should recieve fair pay for their work. He believed that their working conditions should be safer. He knew that their living conditions should be healthier.

→ Cesar put his beliefs into action. He began by working to register mexican american voters. He told Mexican Americans about their rights in the u.s.a. In 1962, Cesar founded the National Farm Workers association. This union became the united farm workers, or the U.F.W. It used nonviolent ways to bring attention to the farmworkers' problems. u.f.w. members led boycotts, urging people not to buy products from companies that were unfair to migrant workers. Union Members also marched on picket lines and held strikes. Cesar led marches, held press conferences, and fasted (stopped eating). He worked long hours to help the workers get better pay and working conditions.

explain unfamiliar word

Go to page 56 in the **Practice the Strategy Notebook!**

Drafting Write

Strategy: Draft the body of my report. Write a paragraph for each main point on my organizer.

(Student Pages 112–113)

Review what it means to write a rough draft. Make sure students understand that a draft is a temporary or "rough" form of a report. A draft should be changed and corrected several times before it is finished. Then have a student read Selena's words for the class, or read the words yourself.

Ask students why Selena is not too concerned about making mistakes in spelling and grammar as she writes her draft. **[Possible response: She is eager to get all her information down on paper at the drafting stage. She will do her best with spelling and grammar and check for mistakes during the revising stage.]**

Practice the Strategy Notebook!

Assign page 56 in the *Practice the Strategy Notebook*. Allow sufficient time for students to complete their paragraphs. Ask volunteers to share their work. Ask students to identify the main idea they have developed in each of the paragraphs.

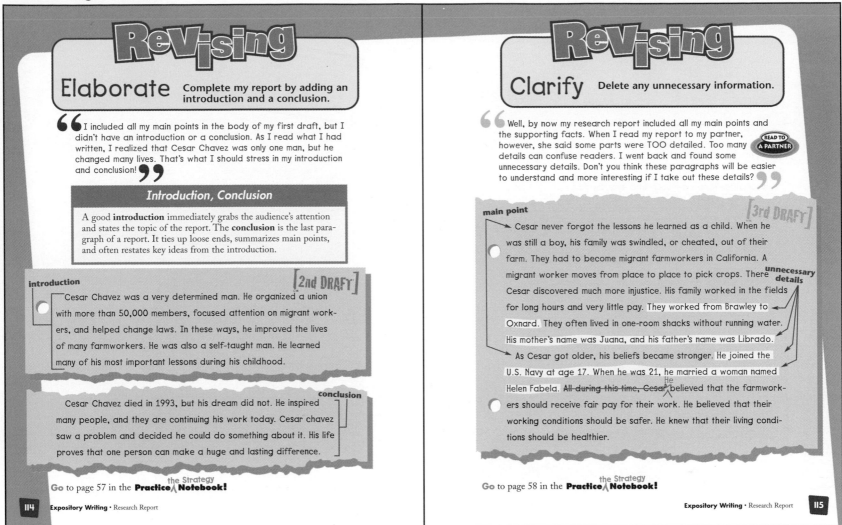

Revising — Elaborate

Strategy: Complete my report by adding an introduction and a conclusion.

(Student Page 114)

Ask a student to read Selena's words to the class.

Explain that a research report is not complete without an introduction that grabs the reader's attention and a conclusion that summarizes the main ideas. Review the definitions of *introduction* and *conclusion*. Then have students read the introduction and conclusion for the report on Cesar Chavez. Ask them to describe the strengths of these two paragraphs. [Possible responses: the introduction is interesting and states the topic of the report; the conclusion offers a satisfying ending.]

Practice the Strategy Notebook!

Assign *Practice the Strategy Notebook* page 57. Guide students as they compare the two introductions and conclusions for the report on Theodore Roosevelt.

Revising — Clarify

Strategy: Delete any unnecessary information.

(Student Page 115)

Ask a volunteer to read Selena's words to the class. Ask students why they think Selena chose the highlighted sentences to delete from her report. Help them recognize that these sentences add unnecessary and uninteresting details to her report. Acknowledge, though, that "unnecessary" is a subjective term. Everyone may not agree with Selena's choices.

Practice the Strategy Notebook!

Assign *Practice the Strategy Notebook* page 58. Ask volunteers to share their revisions with the class and explain their choices.

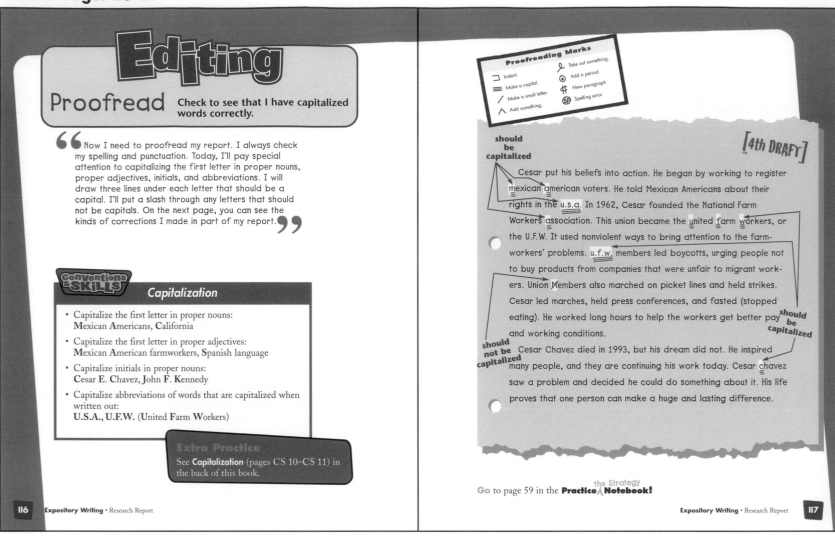

 Proofread

Strategy: **Check to see that I have capitalized words correctly.**

(Student Pages 116–117)

Discuss the difference between revising and editing. Guide students to understand that in the revising step, they look for ways to improve the completeness, organization, and clarity of their reports. In the editing step, they look for errors in spelling, punctuation, and grammar.

Ask a volunteer to read Selena's words to the class. Remind students that good writers search for all kinds of spelling, punctuation, and grammar errors when they proofread. They also focus on the kinds of skills they have had problems with in the past.

Extra Practice: Conventions & Skills Student Edition

If you did not use Student Pages CS 10–CS 11 as a pre-assessment tool, and your students need more practice in capitalization, you may wish to assign these pages now.

Conventions & Skills Practice

For more targeted practice related to this skill, see these lessons in the optional *Conventions & Skills Practice Book*:

Lesson 11: Common and Proper Nouns
Lesson 42: Proper Nouns and Proper Adjectives
Lesson 43: Initials and Abbreviations

Practice the Strategy Notebook!

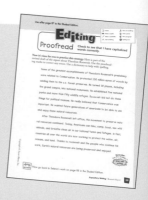

Assign *Practice the Strategy Notebook* page 59. If necessary, review the proofreading marks and demonstrate their use on the chalkboard.

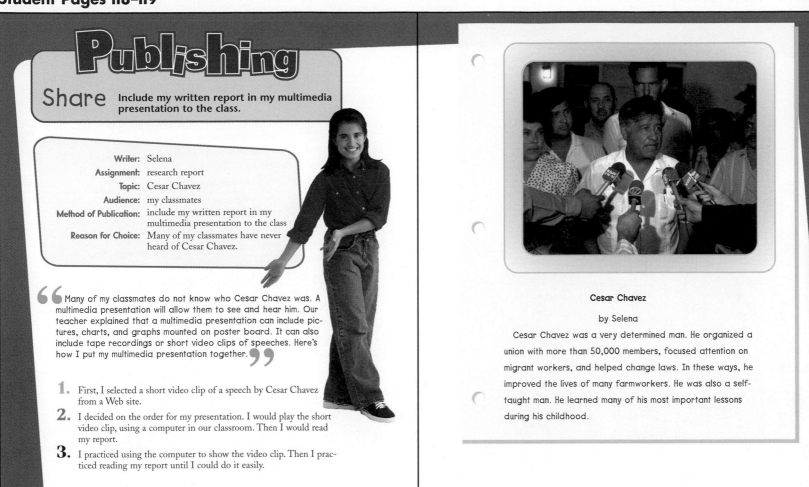

Publishing

Share
Include my written report in my multimedia presentation to the class.

Writer: Selena
Assignment: research report
Topic: Cesar Chavez
Audience: my classmates
Method of Publication: include my written report in my multimedia presentation to the class
Reason for Choice: Many of my classmates have never heard of Cesar Chavez.

" Many of my classmates do not know who Cesar Chavez was. A multimedia presentation will allow them to see and hear him. Our teacher explained that a multimedia presentation can include pictures, charts, and graphs mounted on poster board. It can also include tape recordings or short video clips of speeches. Here's how I put my multimedia presentation together. "

1. First, I selected a short video clip of a speech by Cesar Chavez from a Web site.
2. I decided on the order for my presentation. I would play the short video clip, using a computer in our classroom. Then I would read my report.
3. I practiced using the computer to show the video clip. Then I practiced reading my report until I could do it easily.

Cesar Chavez

by Selena

Cesar Chavez was a very determined man. He organized a union with more than 50,000 members, focused attention on migrant workers, and helped change laws. In these ways, he improved the lives of many farmworkers. He was also a self-taught man. He learned many of his most important lessons during his childhood.

Publishing Share

Strategy: Include my written report in my multimedia presentation to the class.

(Student Pages 118–121)

Challenge students to think of other ways Selena could share her research report. Discuss whether they agree that this strategy was appropriate.

Using the Rubric

Ask students to work in pairs to use the rubric (reprinted on pages 60–61 of the *Practice the Strategy Notebook*) to evaluate Selena's paper. After each pair has developed its assessment, ask students to compare and discuss their decisions.

Cesar's best teachers were his parents. He was born in Yuma, Arizona, in 1927. He did not like his early school years, partly because Mexican American children were often treated unfairly. Cesar's mother taught him that violence was not the way to settle problems. She encouraged him to help other people. Cesar's father taught him to stand up for his beliefs.

Cesar never forgot the lessons he learned as a child. When he was still a boy, his family was swindled, or cheated, out of their farm. They had to become migrant farmworkers in California. A migrant worker moves from place to place to pick crops. There Cesar discovered much more injustice. His family worked in the fields for long hours and very little pay. They often lived in one-room shacks without running water.

As Cesar got older, his beliefs became stronger. He believed that the farmworkers should receive fair pay for their work. He believed that their working conditions should be safer. He knew that their living conditions should be healthier.

Cesar put his beliefs into action. He began by working to register Mexican American voters. He told Mexican Americans about their rights in the U.S.A. In 1962, Cesar founded the

National Farm Workers Association. This union became the United Farm Workers, or the U.F.W. It used nonviolent ways to bring attention to the farmworkers' problems. U.F.W. members led boycotts, urging people not to buy products from companies that were unfair to migrant workers. Union members also marched on picket lines and held strikes. Cesar led marches, held press conferences, and fasted (stopped eating). He worked long hours to help the workers get better pay and working conditions.

Cesar Chavez died in 1993, but his dream did not. He inspired many people, and they are continuing his work today. Cesar Chavez saw a problem and decided he could do something about it. His life proves that one person can make a huge and lasting difference.

Sources

Collins, David R. Farmworker's Friend: The Story of Cesar Chavez. Minneapolis: Carolrhoda Books, 1996.

"The Story of Cesar Chavez." Latino Culture: U.S. 25 May 2001. http://latinoculture.about.com.

USING the Rubric for Assessment

Go to pages 60–61 in the **Practice Notebook!** Use that the Strategy rubric to assess Selena's paper. Try using the rubric to assess your own writing.

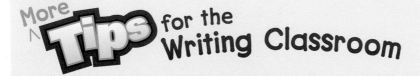

More Tips for the Writing Classroom

Listening Skills

When introducing the significance of communicating effectively, emphasize to your students the importance of developing good listening skills. They must understand that attentive listening is just as important as clearly voicing their ideas. In the classroom most educators constantly have their students respond to direct questioning or give their opinions about a particular topic. Since listening is at least fifty percent of effective oral communication, then it is imperative that you establish good listening skills in your classroom.

With your guidance, have your class discuss the rules of good listening. Use the following questions to guide the discussion:

1. How important is listening?

2. What are some rules about listening we should observe in our classroom?

List responses on the board/overhead projector and transfer them to a poster board to be displayed and referred to throughout the year.

Note: Rules should include remaining silent while another person speaks; looking at the speaker; nodding or smiling to show understanding; asking for clarification when necessary; and restating what you heard or think you heard.

STRATEGIES for Writers

School–Home Connection

Dear Family,

As your child learns and practices different kinds of writing, he or she will be working with a very important writing device—a graphic organizer. Graphic organizers are the charts, webs, tables, and other visual tools we use to help us make sense of information for our writing projects. This year, your child will be using the following graphic organizers:

- A Storyboard—plots the events in a story in the order in which they happen.

- A Sequence Chain—shows steps or events in the order in which they happen.

- A Spider Map—organizes information about one topic. The topic is written in the center of the "spider." Details related to the topic are written on the spider's "legs."

- A Network Tree—organizes information about a topic. The topic goes at the top. Main ideas related to the topic go on the next level. Details relating to each main idea go on the bottom level.

- A Support Pattern—shows main ideas relating to a topic and how each main idea is supported by facts and details.

- An Attribute Chart—organizes information about how two things are alike or different. An attribute is a quality of something.

- A Cause-and-Effect Chain—shows the reasons (causes) for specific events or results (effects).

- A Story Map—shows the beginning, middle, and end of a story.

- A Pros and Cons Chart—shows the positive points (pros) and negative points (cons) about a topic or issue.

- An Outline—shows how a topic is supported by main points and sub-points.

There are many kinds of graphic organizers. Your child may show a preference for one kind over another. It doesn't matter what kind he or she uses, as long as the organizer helps your child arrange information in a logical order and improve his or her writing.

You may wish to copy the letter above and send it home with your students.

 for the **Writing Classroom**

by Ken Stewart, *Master Teacher*

Flexibility and Student Input

The words *writing process* convey to our students that writing (no matter which genre) is a process. We want our students to follow the logical orderly steps of prewriting, drafting, revising, editing, and publishing. Since writing is a process, we must allow for individual differences and build flexibility and choice into our learning structure. Too often, we give writing assignments and expect everyone to finish them at the same time. Many times, however, we should be engag-ing the students in discussions as to what they think are fair time estimates to complete the task at a high level. If we allow ourselves to "think outside of the box" (a concept that may be difficult due to our own experiences in school), we will begin to see that expecting everyone to finish a process assignment at the same time is unrealistic and may be harmful to real learning.

Try the following suggestions and see how your students react:

1. Establish clear and concise criteria for the writing assign-ment and share these criteria with your class.

2. Let your students know how long you think the assignment should take to complete. (Include time for peer tutorials.)

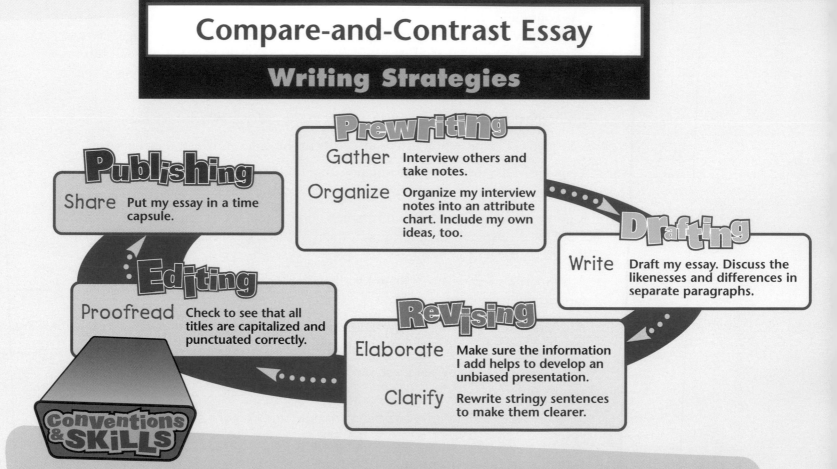

Before the students read the model on Student Page 123, you may wish to review the targeted **grammar, usage,** or **mechanics** convention. Remind students that titles must be punctuated and capitalized follow-ing these rules:

> **Capitalize** the first word, last word, and all other words except articles, short prepositions, and conjunctions.
>
> **Underline** the titles of books, movies, and television series.
>
> Use **quotation mark**s around the titles of songs, poems, stories, and television episodes.

Skill Assessment: To pre-assess your students' understanding of how to handle titles, you may wish to have them complete the corresponding lesson on Student Pages CS 12–CS 13 in the back of the Student Edition.

Skill Mini-Lesson: The Proofread activity in this chapter can be used as a mini-lesson on the targeted **grammar, usage,** or **mechanics** skill.

3. Ask your students how long they think the assignment will take to complete.

4. Come to consensus. (Discuss what *consensus* means.)

5. After the class decides on a due date, make the assignment due over the course of that week. (For example, if the original due date was on Tuesday, October 2, make the due date the week of October 1 through October 5.)

6. Have your students record the due dates. (Then follow your established policy on handling late assignments.)

7. It is suggested that you encourage your students to turn their revised "final" paper in at the beginning of the week (Monday/Tuesday) in order to get it back within a day or two with your comments so they may make corrections.

Although this process will not eliminate late work, it will greatly reduce the number of late papers. You have given students input and ownership in the decision-making process. You have made a significant choice in sharing some of your power with your students. This is just one of the small steps that will lead to a classroom structure where your students will, with your guidance, plan their own lessons and evaluate the quality of their own work.

(For more information about week-long due dates and student input, see page T104.)

Time Management for This Chapter*

Session		Session		Session	
1	Discuss the compare-and-contrast genre; review the questions (Student Page 122). Read "Television Goes to the Movies" (Student Page 123). Use the questions to analyze the essay and use the rubric to assess it.	**6**	Read and discuss **DRAFTING: Write** (Student Pages 132–133).	**11**	Assign *Practice the Strategy Notebook* page 68. Encourage students to use the targeted strategy to revise a piece of their own writing.
2	Introduce Henry (Student Page 129) as a student-writer working on a compare-and-contrast essay. Read and discuss **PREWRITING: Gather** (Student Page 130).	**7**	Assign *Practice the Strategy Notebook* pages 65–66. Encourage students to use the targeted strategy in their own writing.	**12**	Read and discuss **EDITING: Proofread** (Student Pages 136–137).
3	Assign *Practice the Strategy Notebook* pages 62–63. Encourage students to use the targeted strategy in their own writing.	**8**	Read and discuss **REVISING: Elaborate** (Student Page 134).	**13**	Assign *Practice the Strategy Notebook* page 69. Encourage students to use the targeted strategy to edit a piece of their own writing.
4	Read and discuss **PREWRITING: Organize** (Student Page 131). Discuss the purpose and mechanics of an attribute chart and analyze Henry's chart.	**9**	Assign *Practice the Strategy Notebook* page 67. Encourage students to use the targeted strategy to revise a piece of their own writing.	**14**	Read and discuss **PUBLISHING: Share** (Student Pages 138–139). Discuss other ways Henry could share his essay.
5	Assign *Practice the Strategy Notebook* page 64. Encourage students to use the targeted strategy in their own writing.	**10**	Read and discuss **REVISING: Clarify** (Student Page 135).	**15**	Review the rubric for this chapter (reprinted on *Practice the Strategy Notebook* pages 70–71). Ask pairs of students to use the rubric to discuss and evaluate Henry's essay.

WRITER'S HANDBOOK

Remind students that they can refer to the Writer's Handbook in the back of the Student Edition for more information.

* To complete the chapter in fewer sessions, assign the *Practice the Strategy Notebook* pages on the same day the targeted strategy is introduced.

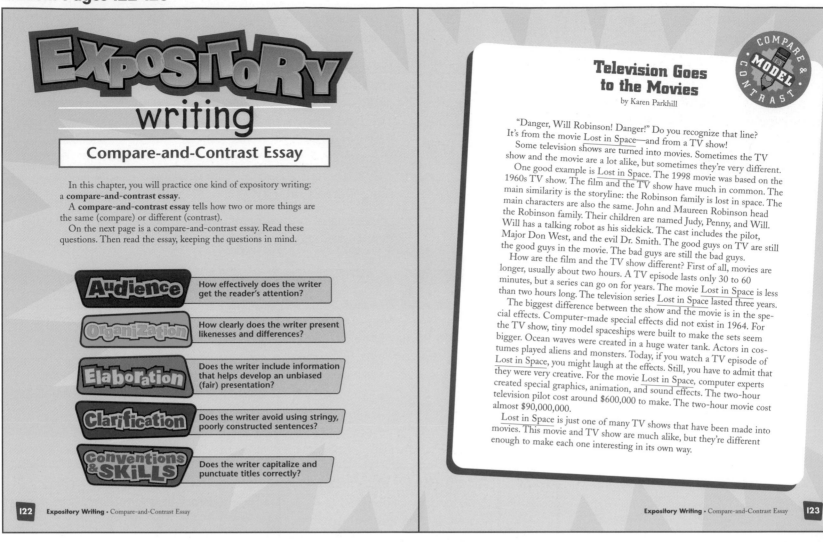

EXPOSITORY writing

Compare-and-Contrast Essay

In this chapter, you will practice one kind of expository writing: a **compare-and-contrast essay**.

A **compare-and-contrast essay** tells how two or more things are the same (compare) or different (contrast).

On the next page is a compare-and-contrast essay. Read these questions. Then read the essay, keeping the questions in mind.

Audience How effectively does the writer get the reader's attention?

Organization How clearly does the writer present likenesses and differences?

Elaboration Does the writer include information that helps develop an unbiased (fair) presentation?

Clarification Does the writer avoid using stringy, poorly constructed sentences?

Conventions & Skills Does the writer capitalize and punctuate titles correctly?

122 Expository Writing • Compare-and-Contrast Essay

Television Goes to the Movies
by Karen Parkhill

COMPARE & CONTRAST MODEL

"Danger, Will Robinson! Danger!" Do you recognize that line? It's from the movie Lost in Space—and from a TV show!

Some television shows are turned into movies. Sometimes the TV show and the movie are a lot alike, but sometimes they're very different.

One good example is Lost in Space. The 1998 movie was based on the 1960s TV show. The film and the TV show have much in common. The main similarity is the storyline: the Robinson family is lost in space. The main characters are also the same. John and Maureen Robinson head the Robinson family. Their children are named Judy, Penny, and Will. Will has a talking robot as his sidekick. The cast includes the pilot, Major Don West, and the evil Dr. Smith. The good guys on TV are still the good guys in the movie. The bad guys are still the bad guys.

How are the film and the TV show different? First of all, movies are longer, usually about two hours. A TV episode lasts only 30 to 60 minutes, but a series can go on for years. The movie Lost in Space is less than two hours long. The television series Lost in Space lasted three years.

The biggest difference between the show and the movie is in the special effects. Computer-made special effects did not exist in 1964. For the TV show, tiny model spaceships were built to make the sets seem bigger. Ocean waves were created in a huge water tank. Actors in costumes played aliens and monsters. Today, if you watch a TV episode of Lost in Space, you might laugh at the effects. Still, you have to admit that they were very creative. For the movie Lost in Space, computer experts created special graphics, animation, and sound effects. The two-hour television pilot cost around $600,000 to make. The two-hour movie cost almost $90,000,000.

Lost in Space is just one of many TV shows that have been made into movies. This movie and TV show are much alike, but they're different enough to make each one interesting in its own way.

Expository Writing • Compare-and-Contrast Essay 123

Introduce the Genre:
Compare-and-Contrast Essay

Choose two objects in the room, such as a window and a door. Ask students to call out ways the two objects are alike. [**Possible response: Both are flat; both will open and close.**] and different [**Possible response: The door is bigger.**]

Tell students they are comparing and contrasting. One type of expository writing is the *compare-and-contrast essay*. In this type of expository writing, the author explains how two or more things are alike and different.

Explain to students that they are going to study and practice strategies for writing a compare-and-contrast essay.

Discuss the Questions

(Student Page 122)

Read the questions on Student Page 122 aloud. Point out the five categories and make sure students are clear on their meaning in the context of writing. Here are some possible points to discuss:

Audience: To interest the audience, the writer should provide an attention-grabbing opening.

Organization: Different kinds of writing lend themselves to different organizational styles. A compare-and-contrast essay should clearly describe the similarities and differences of two or more topics.

Elaboration: In expository writing, the writer must remain unbiased, reporting only factual information.

Clarification: Good writers present information in well-constructed sentences that do not go on forever.

Conventions & Skills: Good writers punctuate titles correctly to help make their writing easy to read and understand.

Read the Model:
Compare-and-Contrast Essay

(Student Page 123)

Read "Television Goes to the Movies" aloud.

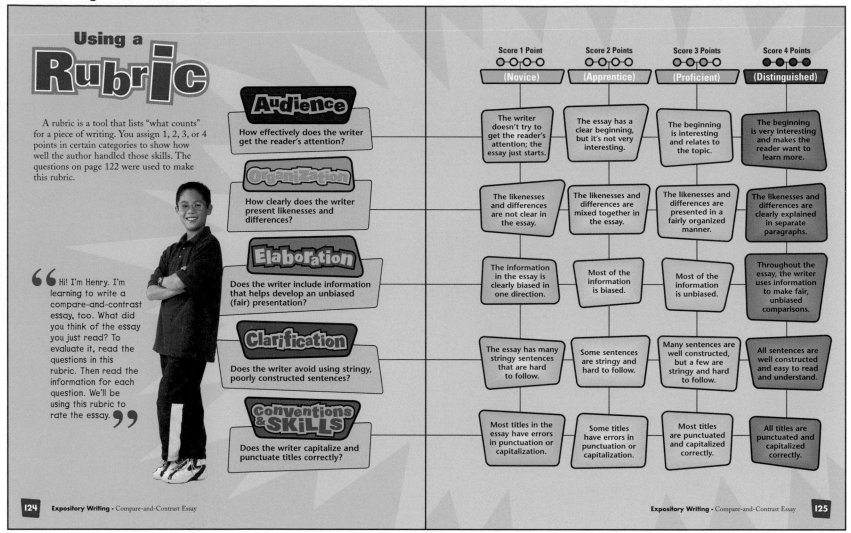

Using a Rubric

(Student Pages 124–125)

Use the text on Student Pages 126–128 to model the use of the rubric in evaluating a piece of writing. For more information on using a rubric, please see page T22.

Internet Sources Related to Rubrics

The Internet provides a variety of information about understanding, developing, and using rubrics. The following Web sites may prove helpful. (**Note:** Web sites are subject to change at any time.)

http://www.interactiveclassroom.com This site contains information about various forms of assessment, as well as tips for using rubrics and some rubric templates.

http://www.middleweb.com/rubricsHG.html This site explains rubrics and how to use them. It also provides templates for some unusual rubrics, including rubrics to evaluate an "invention report" and a scrapbook, along with more conventional rubrics for evaluating a persuasive essay and a book report.

http://www.odyssey.on.ca/~elaine.coxon/rubrics.htm This site provides a multitude of rubric templates for every imaginable field of study and content area. Every content area—from traditional writing rubrics to dance, mathematics, science, physical education, and thinking skills—is represented.

http://intranet.cps.k12.il.us/Assessments/Ideas_and_Rubrics/ideas_and_rubrics.html This site, presented by the Chicago Public Schools, offers rubric tutorials, along with lessons and templates.

http://www.bham.wednet.edu/online/volcano/daily.htm This site offers a very good rubric to evaluate daily student performance in a small group setting.

http://www.calpress.com/rubric.html This site provides a unique rubric to help assess holistic critical thinking. It includes guidelines for assessing these cognitive skills: analysis, interpretation, evaluation, inference, explanation, and self-regulation.

http://www.ncsu.edu/midlink/ho.html This site offers many resources related to rubrics, including several multimedia rubrics.

http://www.bham.wednet.edu/mod8cyl.htm This site contains a rubric for evaluating how well students perform at various points in the research cycle.

http://www.stedwards.edu/cte/grub.htm This site contains a good rubric for evaluating students' participation in a group. It helps assess such areas as how equally members of the group participate and how well they cooperate.

http://pegasus.cc.ucf.edu/~jmorris/rubric.htm This site contains an extensive list of Web resources for rubrics.

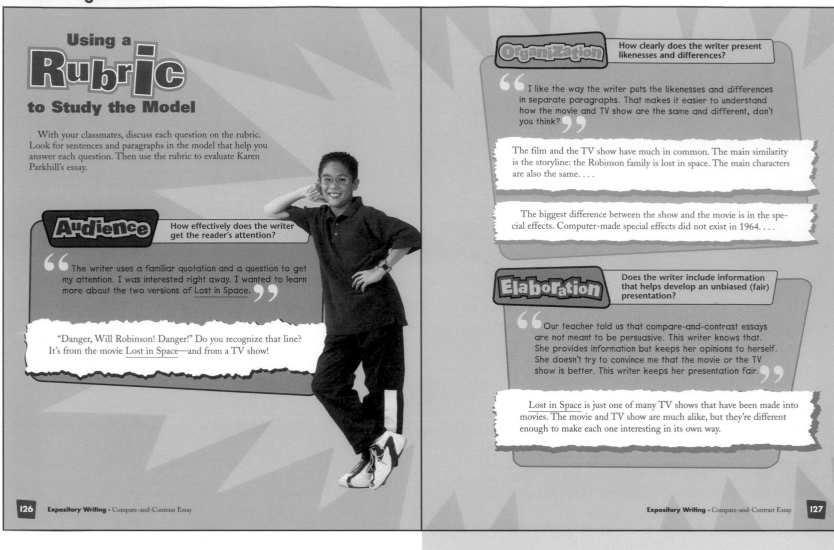

Using a **Rubric** to Study the Model

With your classmates, discuss each question on the rubric. Look for sentences and paragraphs in the model that help you answer each question. Then use the rubric to evaluate Karen Parkhill's essay.

Audience — How effectively does the writer get the reader's attention?

❝ The writer uses a familiar quotation and a question to get my attention. I was interested right away. I wanted to learn more about the two versions of Lost in Space. ❞

"Danger, Will Robinson! Danger!" Do you recognize that line? It's from the movie Lost in Space—and from a TV show!

Organization — How clearly does the writer present likenesses and differences?

❝ I like the way the writer puts the likenesses and differences in separate paragraphs. That makes it easier to understand how the movie and TV show are the same and different, don't you think? ❞

The film and the TV show have much in common. The main similarity is the storyline: the Robinson family is lost in space. The main characters are also the same. . . .

The biggest difference between the show and the movie is in the special effects. Computer-made special effects did not exist in 1964. . . .

Elaboration — Does the writer include information that helps develop an unbiased (fair) presentation?

❝ Our teacher told us that compare-and-contrast essays are not meant to be persuasive. This writer knows that. She provides information but keeps her opinions to herself. She doesn't try to convince me that the movie or the TV show is better. This writer keeps her presentation fair. ❞

Lost in Space is just one of many TV shows that have been made into movies. The movie and TV show are much alike, but they're different enough to make each one interesting in its own way.

Using a Rubric to Study the Model

(Student Pages 126–128)

Read the questions and answers on Student Pages 126–128. Discuss whether students agree with Henry's assessment of the essay at each point. For example, do they think the writer presented unbiased information throughout her essay? What would they have changed, added, or eliminated?

Note on Conventions & Skills: Remind students that this rubric focuses on using correct capitalization and punctuation in titles. However, they should always check their writing for correct spelling and other punctuation and capitalization.

Make sure students have a good grasp of the features of a compare-and-contrast essay, as well as key aspects of the rubric.

Meeting Students' Needs:
Second Language Learners

Review the definitions of *alike* and *different* and *compare* and *contrast*. Help students understand that when they compare two objects or topics, they look for things about them that are alike. When they contrast, they look for ways that the objects or topics are different.

Students Who Need Extra Help

Choose two objects in the room—maybe the door and window again—and ask students to describe them. Then have them explain ways the two objects are different. Finally, have them explain ways the two objects are alike. If necessary, repeat the exercise with other pairs of objects.

Gifted Students

Tell students that compare-and-contrast essays can also be written by using a sequential compare-and-contrast structure, describing one entire topic first and then the other. For example, Karen Parkhill could have described *Lost in Space* (the TV show) and then compared certain points, such as its special effects, with *Lost in Space* (the movie). Have students compare and contrast the two styles. Some may want to try using both forms.

Clarification — Does the writer avoid using stringy, poorly constructed sentences?

" I didn't see any stringy sentences in this essay. The writer keeps most of her sentences rather short and to the point. Even her longer sentences are easy to read and understand. They are well organized and have only one main idea. "

The main characters are also the same. John and Maureen Robinson head the Robinson family. Their children are named Judy, Penny, and Will. Will has a talking robot as his sidekick. The cast includes the pilot, Major Don West, and the evil Dr. Smith. The good guys on TV are still the good guys in the movie. The bad guys are still the bad guys.

Conventions & Skills — Does the writer capitalize and punctuate titles correctly?

" The writer remembered to underline Lost in Space and capitalize the important words in it. She even knew that the titles of movies and television series are treated the same way. "

The movie Lost in Space is less than two hours long. The television series Lost in Space lasted three years.

" **Now it's my turn to write!**
I'm going to write my own compare-and-contrast essay. Follow along to see how I do my best to use good writing strategies. I'm going to use the model and the rubric to help me. "

128   Expository Writing • Compare-and-Contrast Essay

HeNRY
Writer of a Compare-and-Contrast Essay

Name: Henry
Home: Massachusetts
Hobbies: baseball, learning about American history
Favorite Teacher: Ms. Lillard, history teacher
Favorite Book: *Baseball's Greatest Games* by Dan Gutman
Assignment: compare-and-contrast essay

129

Unlocking Text Structure:
Compare-and-Contrast Essay

The structure of any writing depends on how the information in it is organized. To help your students unlock the structure of their compare-and-contrast essays, you may wish to use the graphic organizer in this chapter. The attribute chart lends itself to two kinds of text structure—*parallel* compare-and-contrast and *sequential* compare-and-contrast.

This chapter focuses on parallel structure—comparing similar attributes and then contrasting different attributes. You may also want to tell students about sequential structure—describing one entire topic and then describing the second one and examining the similarities and differences between them. Both structures can be used in a compare-and-contrast essay.

Henry:
Writer of a Compare-and-Contrast Essay

(Student Page 129)

Read the information about Henry. Explain that Boston is steeped in American history. It is also the home of the Boston Red Sox and Fenway Park.

Make sure students understand that Henry will write his own compare-and-contrast essay in this chapter. Discuss what he might choose to write about. Check to see that student suggestions reflect an understanding of the expository mode of writing.

Point out that Henry will complete the steps in the writing process: Prewriting, Drafting, Revising, Editing, and Publishing. At each stage, he will demonstrate a good writing strategy and explain how he used it. Students should watch for key words, including **Gather, Organize, Write, Elaborate, Clarify, Proofread,** and **Share**.

Prewriting

Gather Interview others and take notes.

"I love baseball. I love to watch it, play it, talk about it, and read about it. Lucky for me, we have a professional baseball team right here in Boston.

"When my teacher asked us to write a compare-and-contrast essay, I thought about the Red Sox game I went to last month. I knew my friend Eli had watched the same game on television. I thought about how seeing it at the stadium was different from seeing it on TV. I decided to interview Eli and get his thoughts about it. Here are some of the questions I asked him and the notes I took on his answers."

Interview

An **interview** is a way to gather information. In an interview, you ask someone prepared questions and record his or her thoughts or opinions.

Questions for Eli

Q: What's the best thing about watching a ball game on TV?
  announcers give history, tell stories
  stats are always on screen
  close-up shots and instant replays
  always have a good view
Q: Have you been to a game at the ballpark?
  Yes
Q: Is there anything you miss about the stadium when you watch at home?
  yes, the crowd
  fun to be with other fans
  smell of popcorn, peanuts, and hot dogs

Go to page 62 in the Practice the Strategy Notebook!

Prewriting

Organize Organize my interview notes into an attribute chart. Include my own ideas, too.

"I know from the **Rubric** that organization is important. I looked at my notes from my interview with Eli and thought about my own experiences at the park. I needed a way to organize my notes and ideas. I decided to make a chart."

Attribute Chart

An attribute is a quality of something. An **attribute chart** can help organize information about how two things are alike and different.

Game on TV	Attribute	Game at the Stadium
walk to couch	Getting There	take a car or bus, find a parking space
close-ups, instant replays, stats on screen	What You See	whole field, stats on scoreboard
announcers giving history, stories; crowd cheering in the distance	What You Hear	crowd cheering all around you; announcer naming players and so on
no crowds, no waiting in lines, no interruptions	Surroundings	lots of people, have to wait in lines, fun to share experience
always comfortable	How You Feel	could be hot, cold, soaked in a rainstorm

Go to page 64 in the Practice the Strategy Notebook!

Prewriting Gather

Strategy: Interview others and take notes.

(Student Page 130)

Read Henry's words aloud. Discuss why his topic choice is a good one. [**Possible response: It is something he knows about and is interested in.**] Have a volunteer read Henry's interview questions. What do students notice about these questions? [**Possible responses: They are specific and relevant; they ask about watching a game on television and from the stands.**]

Practice the Strategy Notebook!

Assign pages 62–63 in the *Practice the Strategy Notebook*. (Your Own Writing sections should be used as time and students' abilities permit.) Explain that students will practice this Gather strategy with another topic. Suggested responses for the *Practice the Strategy Notebook* appear in the Appendix at the back of this Teacher Edition.

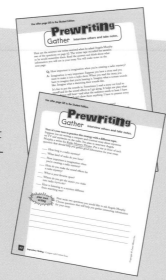

Prewriting Organize

Strategy: Organize my interview notes into an attribute chart. Include my own ideas, too.

(Student Page 131)

Tell students that a graphic organizer, such as an attribute chart, is one way to organize information in preparation for writing. Review the definition of an *attribute chart*. Then direct attention to Henry's chart. Review the categories on his chart (Getting There, What You See, etc.). Discuss how Henry may have determined these categories. Encourage students to suggest notes that he might add to his chart.

Practice the Strategy Notebook!

Assign page 64 in the *Practice the Strategy Notebook*. Allow students plenty of time to complete this activity. Discuss how students implemented this Organize strategy.

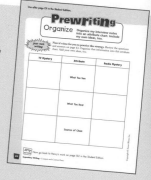

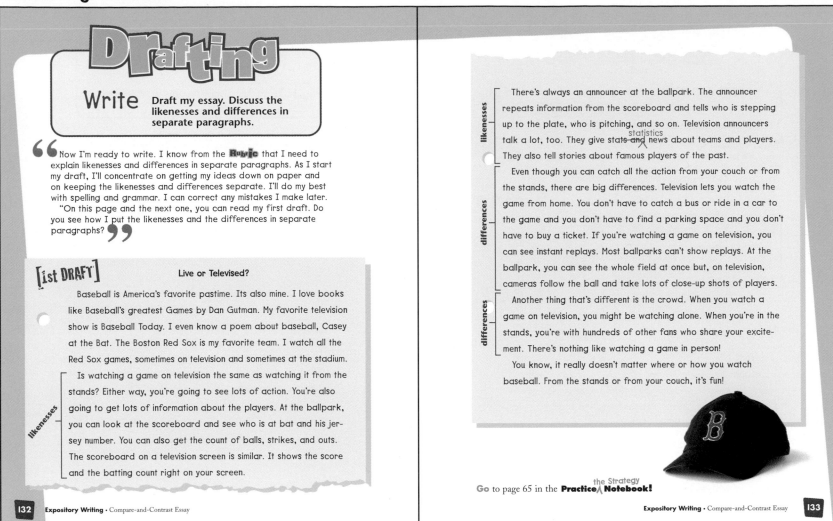

Drafting

Write

Draft my essay. Discuss the likenesses and differences in separate paragraphs.

" Now I'm ready to write. I know from the **Rubric** that I need to explain likenesses and differences in separate paragraphs. As I start my draft, I'll concentrate on getting my ideas down on paper and on keeping the likenesses and differences separate. I'll do my best with spelling and grammar. I can correct any mistakes I make later.

"On this page and the next one, you can read my first draft. Do you see how I put the likenesses and the differences in separate paragraphs? "

[1st DRAFT]

Live or Televised?

Baseball is America's favorite pastime. Its also mine. I love books like Baseball's greatest Games by Dan Gutman. My favorite television show is Baseball Today. I even know a poem about baseball, Casey at the Bat. The Boston Red Sox is my favorite team. I watch all the Red Sox games, sometimes on television and sometimes at the stadium.

likenesses Is watching a game on television the same as watching it from the stands? Either way, you're going to see lots of action. You're also going to get lots of information about the players. At the ballpark, you can look at the scoreboard and see who is at bat and his jersey number. You can also get the count of balls, strikes, and outs. The scoreboard on a television screen is similar. It shows the score and the batting count right on your screen.

likenesses There's always an announcer at the ballpark. The announcer repeats information from the scoreboard and tells who is stepping up to the plate, who is pitching, and so on. Television announcers talk a lot, too. They give stats~~and~~ statistics news about teams and players. They also tell stories about famous players of the past.

differences Even though you can catch all the action from your couch or from the stands, there are big differences. Television lets you watch the game from home. You don't have to catch a bus or ride in a car to the game and you don't have to find a parking space and you don't have to buy a ticket. If you're watching a game on television, you can see instant replays. Most ballparks can't show replays. At the ballpark, you can see the whole field at once but, on television, cameras follow the ball and take lots of close-up shots of players.

differences Another thing that's different is the crowd. When you watch a game on television, you might be watching alone. When you're in the stands, you're with hundreds of other fans who share your excitement. There's nothing like watching a game in person!

You know, it really doesn't matter where or how you watch baseball. From the stands or from your couch, it's fun!

Go to page 65 in the **Practice** the Strategy **Notebook!**

Drafting Write

Strategy: Draft my essay. Discuss the likenesses and differences in separate paragraphs.

(Student Pages 132–133)

Make sure students understand that a draft is a temporary or "rough" form of an essay. It will be corrected and changed several times before it is finished. Then have a volunteer read Henry's words for the class, or read them aloud yourself.

Ask which strategy Henry intends to use in his first draft. **[Response: Discuss the likenesses and differences in separate paragraphs.]** Refer back to Henry's attribute chart. Discuss how he turned the points on his chart into paragraphs.

Refer to the Rubric: The student spokesperson will refer to the rubric throughout the chapter. Remind students to get into the habit of referring back to the rubric so they fully understand its use as a tool for shaping their writing.

Practice the Strategy Notebook!

Assign pages 65–66 in the *Practice the Strategy Notebook*. After students have written their paragraphs, have volunteers read their work aloud. Ask the rest of the class to comment on whether each paragraph discusses likenesses or differences.

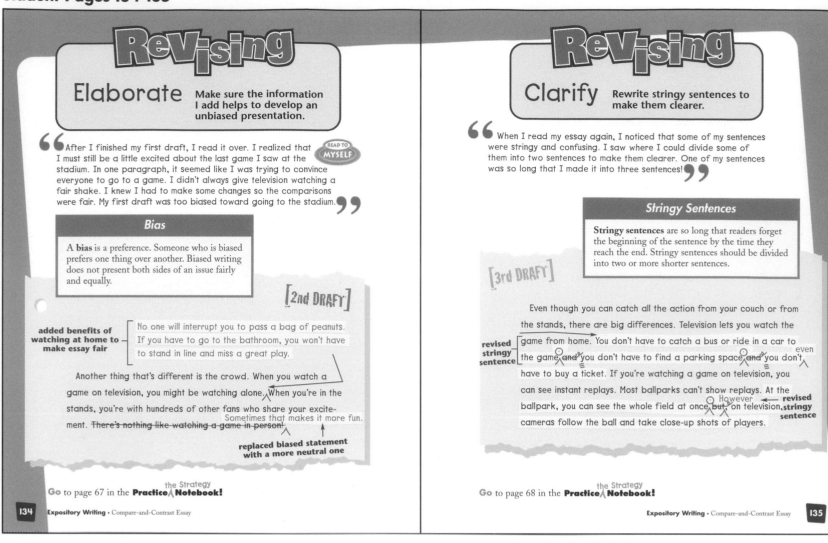

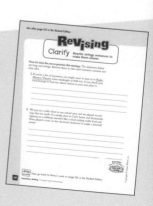

Revising Elaborate

Strategy: **Make sure the information I add helps to develop an unbiased presentation.**

(Student Page 134)

Have a volunteer read Henry's words aloud. Tell students that reading a first draft aloud can help them determine whether it is unbiased. Point out the definition of *bias,* and have students discuss how Henry's additions and deletions improved his paragraph. [**Possible response: They made his paper fairer and less biased.**]

Practice the Strategy Notebook!

Assign *Practice the Strategy Notebook* page 67. Have volunteers tell which sentences they selected as being biased and ask them to read their revisions. Discuss whether the rewritten sentences are now unbiased.

Revising Clarify

Strategy: **Rewrite stringy sentences to make them clearer.**

(Student Page 135)

Review the definition of *stringy sentences.* Remind students that good sentences are clear and concise. Ask a volunteer to read Henry's words to the class. Have a volunteer read the paragraph aloud as Henry first wrote it and as he revised it.

Practice the Strategy Notebook!

Assign *Practice the Strategy Notebook* page 68. Call on students to read their revised sentences aloud. Discuss the different ways that students improved the stringy sentences and stress that there are often several effective ways to rewrite a stringy sentence.

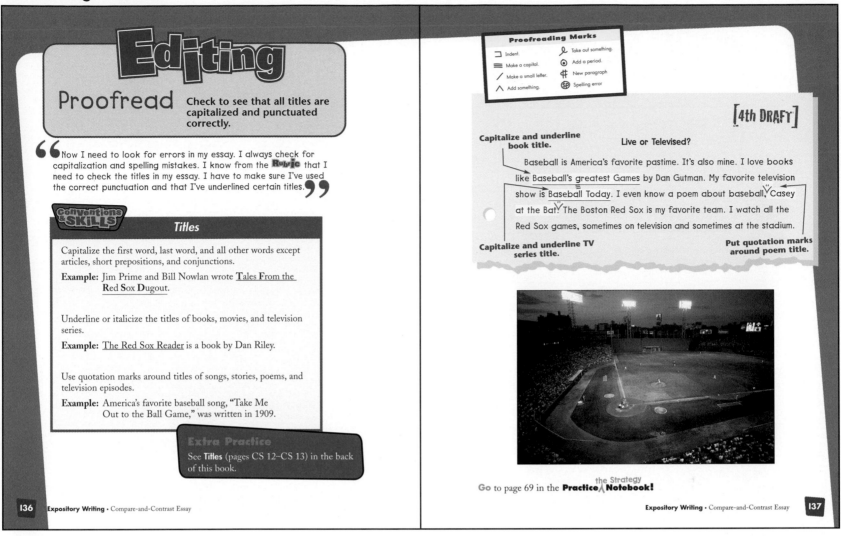

Editing · Proofread

Strategy: Check to see that all titles are capitalized and punctuated correctly.

(Student Pages 136–137)

Review the difference between revising and editing. Make sure students understand that revising involves making changes that will improve clarity, organization, and completeness. During editing, the writer corrects errors in spelling, punctuation, and capitalization. Explain that the strategy in this lesson is to check titles, but Henry will be marking other errors in his essay as well.

Read the information on titles and how to write them correctly. Have volunteers point out the places where Henry corrected errors in his essay.

Extra Practice: Conventions & Skills Student Edition

If you did not use Student Pages CS 12–CS 13 as a pre-assessment tool, and your students need more practice in writing titles correctly, you may wish to assign these pages now.

Conventions & Skills Practice

For more targeted practice related to this skill, see this lesson in the optional *Conventions & Skills Practice Book*:

Lesson 44: Titles

Practice the Strategy Notebook!

Assign *Practice the Strategy Notebook* page 69. If necessary, review the proofreading marks and demonstrate their use on the chalkboard.

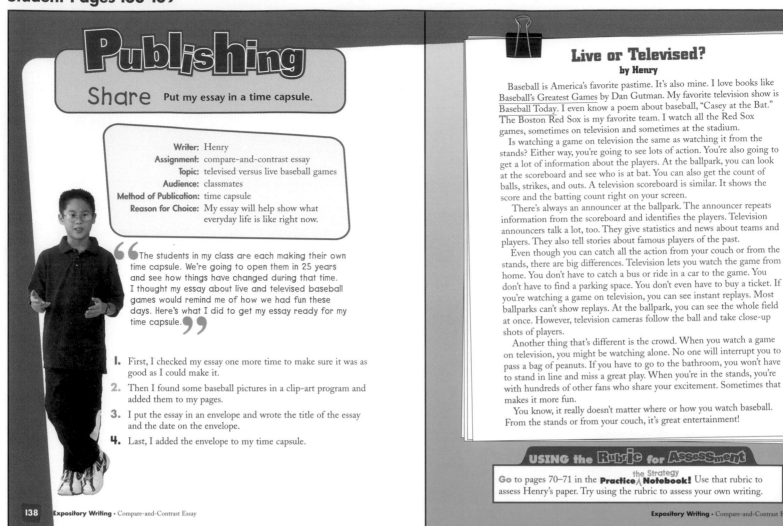

Publishing

Share Put my essay in a time capsule.

Writer: Henry
Assignment: compare-and-contrast essay
Topic: televised versus live baseball games
Audience: classmates
Method of Publication: time capsule
Reason for Choice: My essay will help show what everyday life is like right now.

"The students in my class are each making their own time capsule. We're going to open them in 25 years and see how things have changed during that time. I thought my essay about live and televised baseball games would remind me of how we had fun these days. Here's what I did to get my essay ready for my time capsule."

1. First, I checked my essay one more time to make sure it was as good as I could make it.

2. Then I found some baseball pictures in a clip-art program and added them to my pages.

3. I put the essay in an envelope and wrote the title of the essay and the date on the envelope.

4. Last, I added the envelope to my time capsule.

138 **Expository Writing** • Compare-and-Contrast Essay

Live or Televised?
by Henry

Baseball is America's favorite pastime. It's also mine. I love books like Baseball's Greatest Games by Dan Gutman. My favorite television show is Baseball Today. I even know a poem about baseball, "Casey at the Bat." The Boston Red Sox is my favorite team. I watch all the Red Sox games, sometimes on television and sometimes at the stadium.

Is watching a game on television the same as watching it from the stands? Either way, you're going to see lots of action. You're also going to get a lot of information about the players. At the ballpark, you can look at the scoreboard and see who is at bat. You can also get the count of balls, strikes, and outs. A television scoreboard is similar. It shows the score and the batting count right on your screen.

There's always an announcer at the ballpark. The announcer repeats information from the scoreboard and identifies the players. Television announcers talk a lot, too. They give statistics and news about teams and players. They also tell stories about famous players of the past.

Even though you can catch all the action from your couch or from the stands, there are big differences. Television lets you watch the game from home. You don't have to catch a bus or ride in a car to the game. You don't have to find a parking space. You don't even have to buy a ticket. If you're watching a game on television, you can see instant replays. Most ballparks can't show replays. At the ballpark, you can see the whole field at once. However, television cameras follow the ball and take close-up shots of players.

Another thing that's different is the crowd. When you watch a game on television, you might be watching alone. No one will interrupt you to pass a bag of peanuts. If you have to go to the bathroom, you won't have to stand in line and miss a great play. When you're in the stands, you're with hundreds of other fans who share your excitement. Sometimes that makes it more fun.

You know, it really doesn't matter where or how you watch baseball. From the stands or from your couch, it's great entertainment!

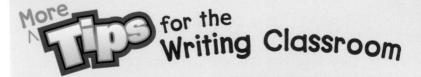

USING the Rubric for Assessment

Go to pages 70-71 in the **Practice the Strategy Notebook!** Use that rubric to assess Henry's paper. Try using the rubric to assess your own writing.

139 **Expository Writing** • Compare-and-Contrast Essay

Publishing Share

Strategy: Put my essay in a time capsule.

(Student Pages 138–139)

Challenge students to think of other ways Henry could share his essay. Discuss whether they think his method was appropriate.

Using the Rubric

Ask students to work in pairs to use the rubric (reprinted on pages 70–71 of the *Practice the Strategy Notebook)* to evaluate Henry's paper. After each pair has reached its decision, have pairs compare and discuss their evaluations.

More Tips for the Writing Classroom

Week-Long Due Dates and Student Input

By allowing your students the flexibility of turning in major writing assignments over a range of due dates, you may feel that you are creating more work for yourself by re-grading papers turned in early. However, you are really not grading the entire piece over. Ask the students to return the graded draft(s) with their corrected final copy. Then only check the sections you had marked for improvement on the draft.

In addition to using flexible deadlines, you may wish to use the Tell Me What You Think blackline master on page T106 to encourage student input in the development of assignments. Set the tone by reminding students that the goal of every assignment is increased understanding and that they will not gain that understanding with frivolous or silly assignments. Be sure you have specific learning goals in mind before sharing the blackline master with the class. Discuss the blackline master as a class before allowing students to work in small groups.

your own EXPOSITORY writing
Social Studies

Put the strategies you practiced in this unit to work to write your own compare-and-contrast essay, research report, or both! You can:

- develop the writing you did in the Your Own Writing pages of the *Practice the Strategy Notebook*;
- pick an idea below and write something new;
- choose another idea of your own.

Be sure to follow the steps in the writing process. Use the rubrics in this unit to assess your writing.

Research Report

- how immigrants enter the United States
- how the Secret Service protects the president of the United States
- how volunteering affects our community
- how a certain service organization helps people during disasters

Compare-and-Contrast Essay

- the climate in two states
- the Declaration of Independence and the Constitution
- lifestyles in the United States and another country
- the South Pole and the North Pole

 portfolio  School-Home Connection

Keep a writing portfolio. Think about adding the activities from the *Practice the Strategy Notebook* to your writing portfolio. You may want to take your portfolio home to share.

Your Own Writing Expository Writing for Social Studies

Assign either one or both genres to the students. Before they begin writing, review key information about each genre. Decide whether you wish students to:

- Choose one of the topics on this page in the Student Edition.
- Complete one of the pieces they partially drafted in the Your Own Writing pages in the *Practice the Strategy Notebook*.
- Generate a completely new idea.

Portfolio/School-Home Connection

Encourage the students to keep portfolios of their writing. You may also wish to duplicate and distribute the School-Home Letter included in this unit.

Work-in-Progress Portfolio

Remind students to review this portfolio often to revise existing pieces that have not been published. Encourage students to share pieces of their Work-in-Progress Portfolios with family members who can help in editing.

Published Portfolio

Encourage students to choose pieces from their Published Portfolios to share with family members.

 for the
Writing Classroom

Tell Me What You Think

Many times your teacher may ask you to write a paper, read a story, or complete any number of assignments. Then your teacher may tell you what he/she wants you to learn. For example, you may be instructed to read a short story and to make a record of the main characters, setting, plot, etc. However, you and your classmates may find that you would rather act out a scene, design a book cover, take a survey, chat on line, etc. How would you like to help your teacher decide what "things" should be learned and how long (within reason) you should take to learn the material? Well, this is your chance. Be serious, make good suggestions, and work together.

Name _____

Date _____

1. Your teacher will give you the important points in the lesson he/she expects you to know. Write them here.

    a. _____

    b. _____

    c. _____

2. After class discussion, record additional important points that were suggested.

    a. _____

    b. _____

    c. _____

3. Write the assignment your group developed here.

    _____

    _____

4. Assignment starting date: _____ Assignment due date: _____
Place this paper in your class binder/folder and refer to it often.

Purpose: To gain student input on assignments. See page T104 for more information. This page may be duplicated for classroom use.

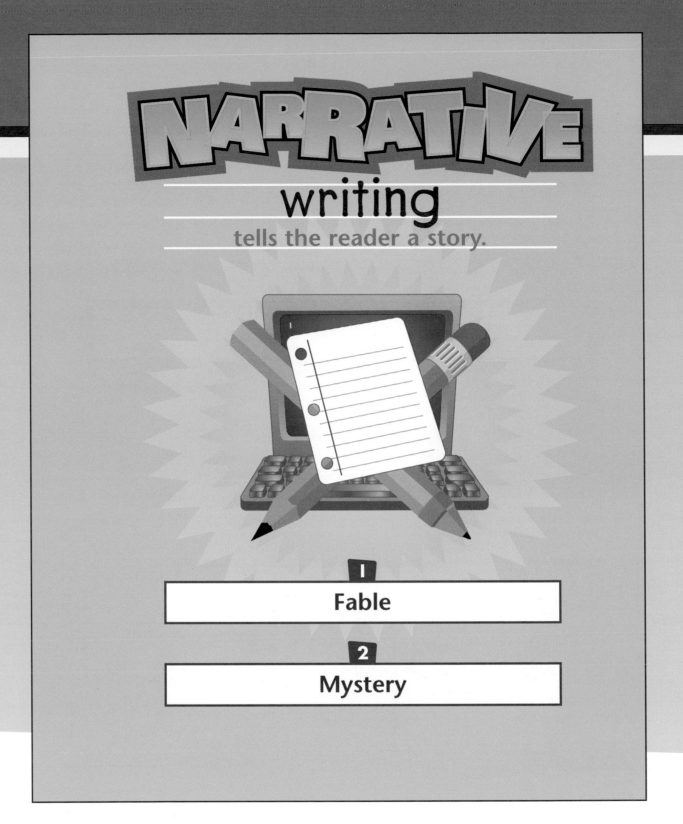

NARRATIVE

writing

tells the reader a story.

1
Fable

2
Mystery

Defining Narrative Writing

Begin by having students help you create spider maps on the chalkboard. Make one for narrative writing, one for descriptive writing, and one for expository writing. Have students suggest characteristics and examples of each kind of writing to add to the maps. Review what they have learned about each kind of writing from previous units. Conclude this activity by saying that they are now going to learn about a special kind of narrative writing.

Read the unit opener (Student Page 141) with students. Discuss the difference between narrative writing that is nonfiction, which they addressed in Unit 1, and narrative writing that is fiction. Ask for or provide examples of both kinds of narrative writing. [**Nonfiction examples: personal narrative, eyewitness account; fiction examples: fable, mystery, other stories**]

 **for the Writing Classroom**

by Ken Stewart, *Master Teacher*

Creating Personal Journals

Journal writing can be fun! Then why do so many students seem to abhor the idea of putting their thoughts down into a journal? How can the teacher make this an enjoyable activity?

One thing that seems to "turn off" students is the fact that many educators want them to journal on a daily basis. Although this is an admirable concept, it is probably an unrealistic practice for most students. To many of your stu-

dents, it will become a monotonous, forced task over time. Why not have fewer purposeful journaling times and, at the same time, encourage free (anytime) personal journaling?

Make a distinction between "purposeful journaling" and "free personal" journaling. Purposeful journaling occurs when the teacher gives a prompt or direction on what to write about. Free journaling takes place when the student writes about personal (not private) experiences. These entries, although personal, can be shared with the teacher or other classmates whenever necessary.

No matter what type of journal writing is being explored, it is a time for students to work on developing their own

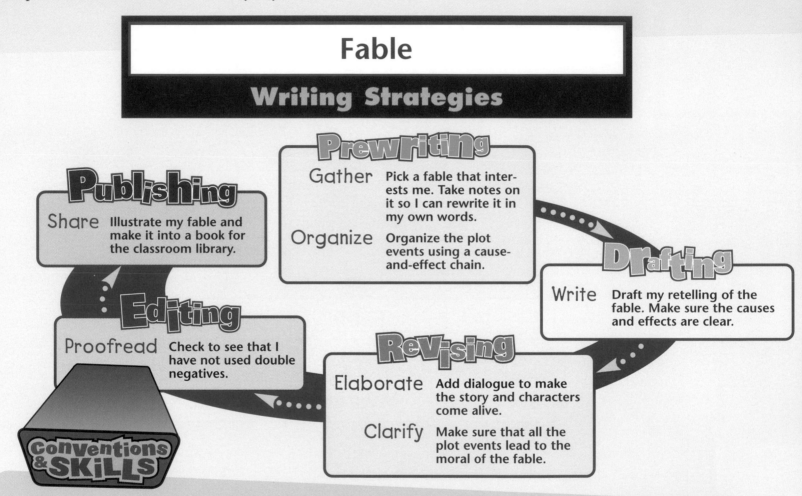

Fable

Writing Strategies

Publishing

Share — Illustrate my fable and make it into a book for the classroom library.

Prewriting

Gather — Pick a fable that interests me. Take notes on it so I can rewrite it in my own words.

Organize — Organize the plot events using a cause-and-effect chain.

Drafting

Write — Draft my retelling of the fable. Make sure the causes and effects are clear.

Editing

Proofread — Check to see that I have not used double negatives.

Conventions & Skills

Revising

Elaborate — Add dialogue to make the story and characters come alive.

Clarify — Make sure that all the plot events lead to the moral of the fable.

Before the students read the model on Student Page 143, you may wish to review the targeted **grammar** convention. Explain that negatives are words such as *no, not, none, nothing, nobody, no one, nowhere, hardly, barely, neither,* and *never.* Writers should use no more than one negative word in a sentence. You might mention that a sentence with two independent clauses can have a negative word in each clause.

Examples: **Correct:** Alicia saw **nothing** when she opened the door. (one negative: *nothing*)

Incorrect: Alicia **didn't** see **nothing** when she opened the door. (two negatives: *didn't* and *nothing*)

Skill Assessment: To pre-assess your students' understanding of double negatives, you may wish to have them complete the corresponding lesson on Student Pages CS 14–CS 15 in the back of the Student Edition.

Skill Mini-Lesson: The Proofread activity in this chapter can be used as a mini-lesson on the targeted **grammar, usage,** or **mechanics** skill.

"voice." For this reason, it is recommended that you not grade student journals as you would regular assignments. You could, however, consider including student journals as part of a class grade or extra credit.

To further personalize journals, ask your students to create their own journals and design their own covers. (Zaner-Bloser has excellent blank journals for this activity.) Also, encourage your students to draw, cut or paste, put in pockets, and add photographs to the pages to express themselves in other ways. The goal is to make the journal an interactive record that truly displays your students' feelings.

Here are four easy steps to good journal writing:
1. Define purposeful and personal journaling.
2. Journal with a purpose only once or twice a week.
3. Encourage personal journaling as often as students want.
4. Establish (ideally with the class) how the journals will be evaluated.

(See "More Tips for the Writing Classroom: Purposeful Journal Writing," page T119.)

Time Management for This Chapter*

Session 1	Discuss the definition of narrative writing and the fable genre; review the questions (Student Page 142). Read "The Fox and the Crow" (Student Page 143). Use the questions to analyze the fable, and use the rubric to assess it.	**Session 6**	Read and discuss **DRAFTING: Write** (Student Pages 152–153).	**Session 11**	Assign *Practice the Strategy Notebook* page 78. Encourage students to use the targeted strategy to revise a piece of their own writing.
2	Introduce Brian (Student Page 149) as a student-writer working on a fable. Read and discuss **PREWRITING: Gather** (Student Page 150).	**7**	Assign *Practice the Strategy Notebook* pages 75–76. Encourage students to use the targeted strategy in their own writing.	**12**	Read and discuss **EDITING: Proofread** (Student Pages 156–157).
3	Assign *Practice the Strategy Notebook* pages 72–73. Encourage students to use the targeted strategy in their own writing.	**8**	Read and discuss **REVISING: Elaborate** (Student Page 154).	**13**	Assign *Practice the Strategy Notebook* page 79. Encourage students to use the targeted strategy to edit a piece of their own writing.
4	Read and discuss **PREWRITING: Organize** (Student Page 151). Discuss the purpose and mechanics of a cause-and-effect chain and analyze Brian's chain.	**9**	Assign *Practice the Strategy Notebook* page 77. Encourage students to use the targeted strategy to revise a piece of their own writing.	**14**	Read and discuss **PUBLISHING: Share** (Student Pages 158–161). Discuss other ways Brian could share his fable.
5	Assign *Practice the Strategy Notebook* page 74. Encourage students to use the targeted strategy in their own writing.	**10**	Read and discuss **REVISING: Clarify** (Student Page 155).	**15**	Review the rubric for this chapter (reprinted on *Practice the Strategy Notebook* pages 80–81). Ask pairs of students to use the rubric to discuss and evaluate Brian's fable.

WRITER'S HANDBOOK

*To complete the chapter in fewer sessions, assign the *Practice the Strategy Notebook* pages on the same day the targeted strategy is introduced.

Remind students that they can refer to the Writer's Handbook in the back of the Student Edition for more information.

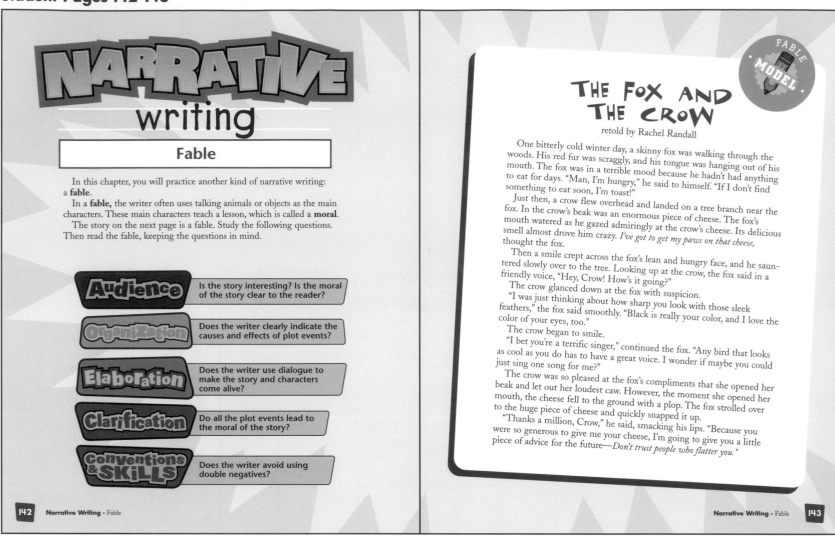

NARRATIVE writing

Fable

In this chapter, you will practice another kind of narrative writing: a **fable**.

In a **fable**, the writer often uses talking animals or objects as the main characters. These main characters teach a lesson, which is called a **moral**.

The story on the next page is a fable. Study the following questions. Then read the fable, keeping the questions in mind.

Audience — Is the story interesting? Is the moral of the story clear to the reader?

Organization — Does the writer clearly indicate the causes and effects of plot events?

Elaboration — Does the writer use dialogue to make the story and characters come alive?

Clarification — Do all the plot events lead to the moral of the story?

Conventions & Skills — Does the writer avoid using double negatives?

142   Narrative Writing • Fable

THE FOX AND THE CROW
retold by Rachel Randall

One bitterly cold winter day, a skinny fox was walking through the woods. His red fur was scraggly, and his tongue was hanging out of his mouth. The fox was in a terrible mood because he hadn't had anything to eat for days. "Man, I'm hungry," he said to himself. "If I don't find something to eat soon, I'm toast!"

Just then, a crow flew overhead and landed on a tree branch near the fox. In the crow's beak was an enormous piece of cheese. The fox's mouth watered as he gazed admiringly at the crow's cheese. Its delicious smell almost drove him crazy. *I've got to get my paws on that cheese,* thought the fox.

Then a smile crept across the fox's lean and hungry face, and he sauntered slowly over to the tree. Looking up at the crow, the fox said in a friendly voice, "Hey, Crow! How's it going?"

The crow glanced down at the fox with suspicion.

"I was just thinking about how sharp you look with those sleek feathers," the fox said smoothly. "Black is really your color, and I love the color of your eyes, too."

The crow began to smile.

"I bet you're a terrific singer," continued the fox. "Any bird that looks as cool as you do has to have a great voice. I wonder if maybe you could just sing one song for me?"

The crow was so pleased at the fox's compliments that she opened her beak and let out her loudest caw. However, the moment she opened her mouth, the cheese fell to the ground with a plop. The fox strolled over to the huge piece of cheese and quickly snapped it up.

"Thanks a million, Crow," he said, smacking his lips. "Because you were so generous to give me your cheese, I'm going to give you a little piece of advice for the future—*Don't trust people who flatter you.*"

Narrative Writing • Fable   143

Introduce the Genre:
Fable

Ask students to read the description of a *fable* on Student Page 142. Have them identify the two important parts that most fables include. **[Response: talking animals or objects; a lesson or moral]** Then ask volunteers to retell a fable they know. Have other students supply the moral. Discuss how the different elements of the fable, such as plot, characters, and setting, help teach the moral.

Conclude by telling students that they are going to study and practice strategies for rewriting a fable in their own words.

Discuss the Questions

(Student Page 142)

Read the questions on Student Page 142 aloud. Explain the importance of the five areas in creating a good piece of writing. Possible guidelines for this discussion are:

Audience: The writer must make sure the fable is interesting and the moral of the fable is clear to the audience.

Organization: In a fable, the causes and effects must be easy to identify.

Elaboration: Dialogue adds life to a story; it also helps the reader learn about the characters.

Clarification: All the parts of a fable must lead to the moral.

Conventions & Skills: Good writers always avoid double negatives; this kind of grammatical mistake can confuse the reader.

Read the Model:
Fable

(Student Page 143)

Read "The Fox and the Crow" aloud.

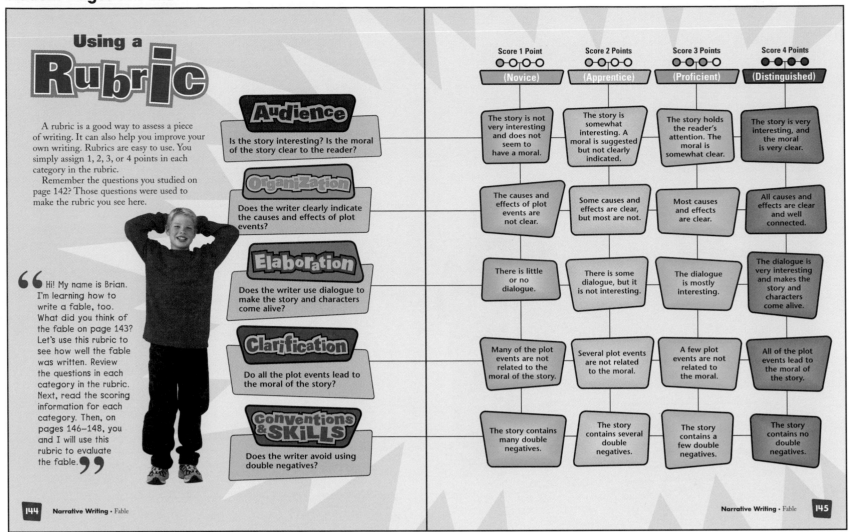

Using a Rubric

A rubric is a good way to assess a piece of writing. It can also help you improve your own writing. Rubrics are easy to use. You simply assign 1, 2, 3, or 4 points in each category in the rubric.

Remember the questions you studied on page 142? Those questions were used to make the rubric you see here.

Hi! My name is Brian. I'm learning how to write a fable, too. What did you think of the fable on page 143? Let's use this rubric to see how well the fable was written. Review the questions in each category in the rubric. Next, read the scoring information for each category. Then, on pages 146–148, you and I will use this rubric to evaluate the fable.

Audience
Is the story interesting? Is the moral of the story clear to the reader?

Organization
Does the writer clearly indicate the causes and effects of plot events?

Elaboration
Does the writer use dialogue to make the story and characters come alive?

Clarification
Do all the plot events lead to the moral of the story?

Conventions & Skills
Does the writer avoid using double negatives?

Score 1 Point (Novice)	Score 2 Points (Apprentice)	Score 3 Points (Proficient)	Score 4 Points (Distinguished)
The story is not very interesting and does not seem to have a moral.	The story is somewhat interesting. A moral is suggested but not clearly indicated.	The story holds the reader's attention. The moral is somewhat clear.	The story is very interesting, and the moral is very clear.
The causes and effects of plot events are not clear.	Some causes and effects are clear, but most are not.	Most causes and effects are clear.	All causes and effects are clear and well connected.
There is little or no dialogue.	There is some dialogue, but it is not interesting.	The dialogue is mostly interesting.	The dialogue is very interesting and makes the story and characters come alive.
Many of the plot events are not related to the moral of the story.	Several plot events are not related to the moral.	A few plot events are not related to the moral.	All of the plot events lead to the moral of the story.
The story contains many double negatives.	The story contains several double negatives.	The story contains a few double negatives.	The story contains no double negatives.

Using a Rubric

(Student Pages 144–145)

Use the text on Student Pages 146–148 to model the use of the rubric in evaluating a fable. If you need more information on using a rubric with your students, please see "Using a Rubric" on page T22.

Helping Students Create Rubrics for Self-Assessment

by Lee Bromberger, *Assessment Specialist*

Here is a recipe for a creating a rubric in which students can contribute their own criteria to the teacher's criteria. The result provides an instrument for effective student self-evaluation of their writing.

- **Complement the objective of the writing assignment.** Is the writing descriptive, narrative, or persuasive? Choose the appropriate writing genre and include it as part of the rubric.
- **Include a weakness from a previous writing assignment.** Where did the student struggle on the last evaluated writing: comma usage, paragraph unity, tone? Make this a highlighted focus of the self-assessment rubric. **Note:** Some students may need assistance from the classroom teacher to complete this step.

- **Choose a writing strength.** Focusing on a facet of writing on which a student can succeed builds confidence and motivates students to tackle the new writing assignment as they know they will be assessed for a part of their writing that they do well. Once again, the classroom teacher may need to guide students in their choice of a writing strength.
- **Select two other writing areas.** Avoiding overlap (and depending on the grade level), choose at least two of the following traditional writing skills: ideas/content; organization; style and word choice; mechanics; and publishing/manuscript conventions.

Observing these four guidelines will produce a rubric of at least five focus areas for the writing. Teachers should be aware that a rubric-building process like this one has the following strengths: student ownership, meaningful flexibility, and a long-term view of the writing program.

Its weaknesses include the fact that it is time-consuming and difficult for some students. Students also may have difficulty adjusting to their new role, and some goals chosen by students may be too easy or unrealistic.

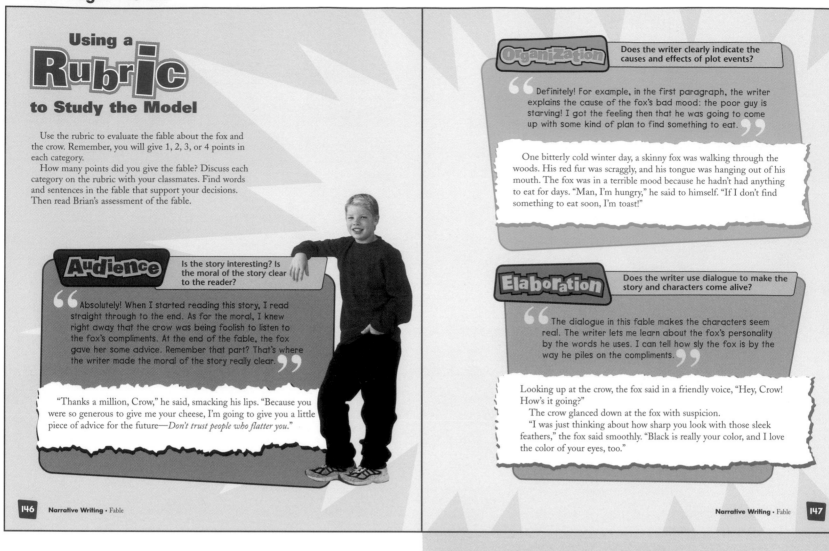

Using a **Rubric** to Study the Model

Use the rubric to evaluate the fable about the fox and the crow. Remember, you will give 1, 2, 3, or 4 points in each category.

How many points did you give the fable? Discuss each category on the rubric with your classmates. Find words and sentences in the fable that support your decisions. Then read Brian's assessment of the fable.

Audience — Is the story interesting? Is the moral of the story clear to the reader?

"Absolutely! When I started reading this story, I read straight through to the end. As for the moral, I knew right away that the crow was being foolish to listen to the fox's compliments. At the end of the fable, the fox gave her some advice. Remember that part? That's where the writer made the moral of the story really clear."

"Thanks a million, Crow," he said, smacking his lips. "Because you were so generous to give me your cheese, I'm going to give you a little piece of advice for the future—*Don't trust people who flatter you.*"

Organization — Does the writer clearly indicate the causes and effects of plot events?

"Definitely! For example, in the first paragraph, the writer explains the cause of the fox's bad mood: the poor guy is starving! I got the feeling then that he was going to come up with some kind of plan to find something to eat."

One bitterly cold winter day, a skinny fox was walking through the woods. His red fur was scraggly, and his tongue was hanging out of his mouth. The fox was in a terrible mood because he hadn't had anything to eat for days. "Man, I'm hungry," he said to himself. "If I don't find something to eat soon, I'm toast!"

Elaboration — Does the writer use dialogue to make the story and characters come alive?

"The dialogue in this fable makes the characters seem real. The writer lets me learn about the fox's personality by the words he uses. I can tell how sly the fox is by the way he piles on the compliments."

Looking up at the crow, the fox said in a friendly voice, "Hey, Crow! How's it going?"

The crow glanced down at the fox with suspicion.

"I was just thinking about how sharp you look with those sleek feathers," the fox said smoothly. "Black is really your color, and I love the color of your eyes, too."

Using a Rubric to Study the Model

(Student Pages 146–148)

Read the questions and answers on Student Pages 146–148. Discuss whether students agree with Brian's assessment of the fable. For example, do they agree that the writer uses dialogue to help communicate the fox's personality? What did they learn about the fox from the dialogue?

Note on Conventions & Skills: Remind students that they should always check their writing for correct spelling, punctuation, and capitalization. In addition, this lesson will help them focus on avoiding double negatives.

Meeting Students' Needs:
Second Language Learners

Have pairs of students take turns retelling in their own words a fable from their cultural background. Then have them ask each other questions about the fable and its moral.

Students Who Need Extra Help

Ask students to create a web for the fox and a web for the crow. Have them list words and phrases from the fable and supply their own to describe each character.

Gifted Students

Have students create a set of illustrations for this fable. Ask volunteers to share their illustrations with the class and describe how they decided which scenes to illustrate and how they dealt with any special challenges in illustrating them.

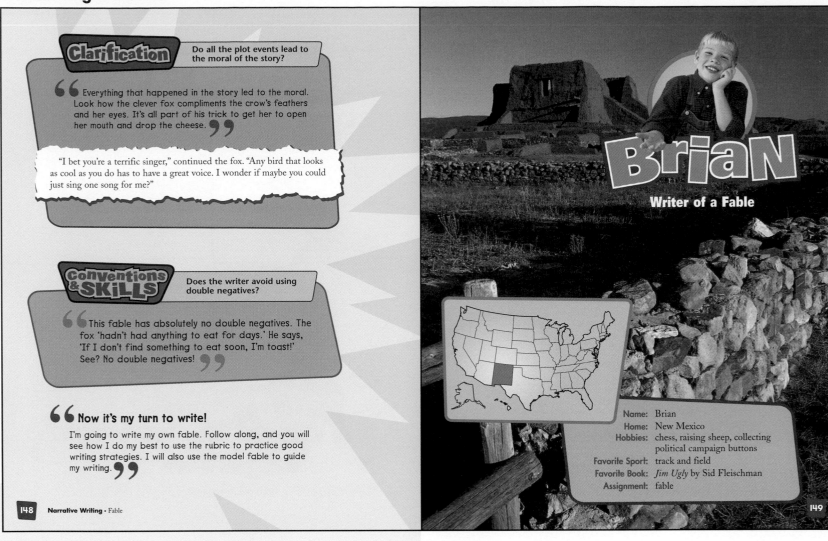

Clarification — Do all the plot events lead to the moral of the story?

66 Everything that happened in the story led to the moral. Look how the clever fox compliments the crow's feathers and her eyes. It's all part of his trick to get her to open her mouth and drop the cheese. 99

"I bet you're a terrific singer," continued the fox. "Any bird that looks as cool as you do has to have a great voice. I wonder if maybe you could just sing one song for me?"

Conventions & SKiLLS — Does the writer avoid using double negatives?

66 This fable has absolutely no double negatives. The fox 'hadn't had anything to eat for days.' He says, 'If I don't find something to eat soon, I'm toast!' See? No double negatives! 99

66 **Now it's my turn to write!**

I'm going to write my own fable. Follow along, and you will see how I do my best to use the rubric to practice good writing strategies. I will also use the model fable to guide my writing. 99

148   Narrative Writing · Fable

BriaN
Writer of a Fable

Name: Brian
Home: New Mexico
Hobbies: chess, raising sheep, collecting political campaign buttons
Favorite Sport: track and field
Favorite Book: *Jim Ugly* by Sid Fleischman
Assignment: fable

149

Unlocking Text Structure:
Fable

The structure of a piece of writing depends on how the information it contains is organized. To help students unlock the structure of the fable, you may want to refer them to the graphic organizer in this chapter, a cause-and-effect chain. This type of organizer is appropriate for narrative writing because it establishes two types of text structure: chronological and causative. Help students understand that in any story, the writer must determine both the order in which events happen and why they happen. The chain will help students see that events cause—and are caused by—other events.

Brian:
Writer of a Fable

(Student Page 149)

Read the information about Brian.

Make sure students understand that he is going to rewrite a fable in his own words. Ask them to speculate on fables he might choose. Do they know any fables that are related to his hobbies, home, or favorite sport?

Point out that Brian will complete the steps in the writing process: Prewriting, Drafting, Revising, Editing, and Publishing. At each stage, he will demonstrate a good writing strategy and explain how he used it. Students should watch for these key words: **Gather, Organize, Write, Elaborate, Clarify, Proofread,** and **Share**.

Prewriting

Gather
Pick a fable that interests me. Take notes on it so I can rewrite it in my own words.

> I help raise the sheep and lambs on our family's ranch in New Mexico. When I looked through a book of fables, the one that caught my eye was **The Boy Who Cried Wolf**. I've never actually had to protect my lambs from a wolf, but I do have to chase away the neighbors' dogs sometimes!

Fable, Moral

A **fable** is a short story that often uses talking animals or objects as the main characters. It teaches a moral. A **moral** is a lesson taught through a fable. For example, the moral of *The Fox and the Crow* is "Don't trust flatterers."

> When our teacher asked us to rewrite a fable, I started thinking about how I could rewrite **The Boy Who Cried Wolf** with a kid like me as the main character. The original fable was set in ancient times, but mine could take place now, in New Mexico. Here are some notes I took about the plot of the fable.

The Boy Who Cried Wolf

- A boy got bored watching the sheep.
- He decided it would be funny to cry wolf and trick the villagers into running out to the pasture.
- His trick worked several times—all the people came running and the boy laughed.
- Then a real wolf came.
- When the boy cried wolf this time, nobody came.
- Moral: nobody will believe someone who lies all the time, even when he's telling the truth.

Go to page 72 in the **Practice the Strategy Notebook!**

Prewriting

Organize
Organize the plot events using a cause-and-effect chain.

> I know from the **Rubric** that organization is important. I decided to use my notes about the fable to make a cause-and-effect chain that will show how one thing leads to another. You can see the first part of my chain on this page. When I finish my chain, I'll have the whole plot in it. This will help me make sure my own fable is well organized.

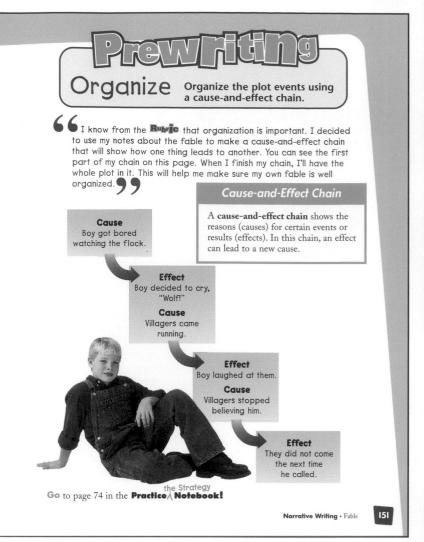

Cause-and-Effect Chain

A **cause-and-effect chain** shows the reasons (causes) for certain events or results (effects). In this chain, an effect can lead to a new cause.

Cause
Boy got bored watching the flock.

Effect
Boy decided to cry, "Wolf!"

Cause
Villagers came running.

Effect
Boy laughed at them.

Cause
Villagers stopped believing him.

Effect
They did not come the next time he called.

Go to page 74 in the **Practice the Strategy Notebook!**

Prewriting Gather

Strategy: Pick a fable that interests me. Take notes on it so I can rewrite it in my own words.

(Student Page 150)

Read Brian's words aloud. Then discuss his notes on the fable he chose. Ask students to comment on how the items are listed and connected. [**Possible responses: The list is organized chronologically; the events all lead to the moral.**]

Practice the Strategy Notebook!

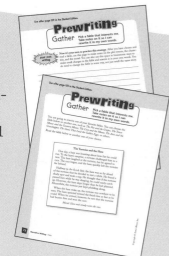

Assign pages 72–73 in the *Practice the Strategy Notebook*. (Your Own Writing sections should be used as time and students' abilities permit.) Students will rewrite their own fables. See page T121 for collections of fables. Suggested responses for the *Practice the Strategy Notebook* appear in the Appendix in the back of this Teacher Edition.

Prewriting Organize

Strategy: Organize the plot events using a cause-and-effect chain.

(Student Page 151)

Explain that writing can be organized in many different ways. A graphic organizer called a cause-and-effect chain is one way to organize information in preparation for writing.

Ask students to read the definition of a cause-and-effect chain. Then have them study Brian's chain and describe how the events are connected.

Practice the Strategy Notebook!

Assign page 74 in the *Practice the Strategy Notebook*. Have students share the cause-and-effect chains they created for their own fables.

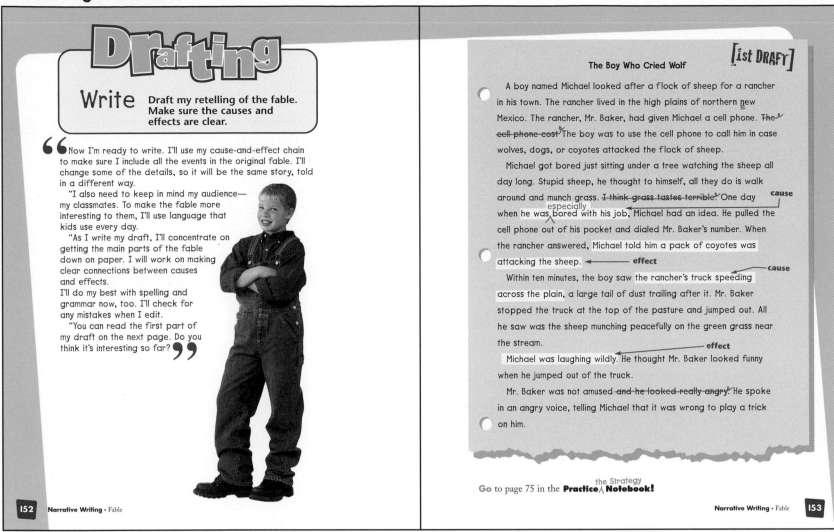

The Boy Who Cried Wolf [1st DRAFT]

A boy named Michael looked after a flock of sheep for a rancher in his town. The rancher lived in the high plains of northern new Mexico. The rancher, Mr. Baker, had given Michael a cell phone. ~~The cell phone cost~~ The boy was to use the cell phone to call him in case wolves, dogs, or coyotes attacked the flock of sheep.

Michael got bored just sitting under a tree watching the sheep all day long. Stupid sheep, he thought to himself, all they do is walk around and munch grass. ~~I think grass tastes terrible.~~ One day when he was bored with his job, Michael had an idea. He pulled the cell phone out of his pocket and dialed Mr. Baker's number. When the rancher answered, Michael told him a pack of coyotes was attacking the sheep.

Within ten minutes, the boy saw the rancher's truck speeding across the plain, a large tail of dust trailing after it. Mr. Baker stopped the truck at the top of the pasture and jumped out. All he saw was the sheep munching peacefully on the green grass near the stream.

Michael was laughing wildly. He thought Mr. Baker looked funny when he jumped out of the truck.

Mr. Baker was not amused ~~and he looked really angry.~~ He spoke in an angry voice, telling Michael that it was wrong to play a trick on him.

Go to page 75 in the Practice the Strategy Notebook!

Drafting Write

Strategy: **Draft my retelling of the fable. Make sure the causes and effects are clear.**

(Student Pages 152–153)

Review what it means to draft a piece of writing. Make sure all students understand that a draft is a temporary or "rough" form of a fable or other piece of writing. Remind them that a draft will have to be changed and corrected, perhaps several times, before the piece of writing is finished. Ask for a volunteer to read Brian's words aloud for the class.

Ask students what Brian will keep in mind as he writes his draft. [**Possible responses: He will refer to his cause-and-effect chain; he wants to use everyday language that will appeal to his audience; he will do his best with spelling and grammar and correct his mistakes later.**]

Refer to the Rubric: The student spokesperson will refer to the rubric throughout the chapter. Remind students to get into the habit of referring back to the rubric so they fully understand its use as a tool for shaping their writing.

Practice the Strategy Notebook!

Assign pages 75–76 in the *Practice the Strategy Notebook.* Allow students time to draft their own fables.

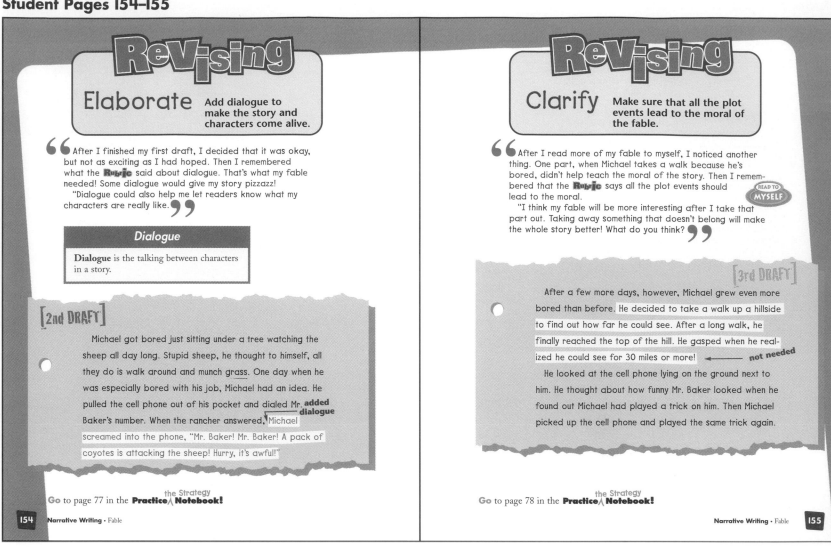

Revising

Elaborate
Add dialogue to make the story and characters come alive.

❝ After I finished my first draft, I decided that it was okay, but not as exciting as I had hoped. Then I remembered what the **Rubric** said about dialogue. That's what my fable needed! Some dialogue would give my story pizzazz!

"Dialogue could also help me let readers know what my characters are really like." ❞

Dialogue

Dialogue is the talking between characters in a story.

[2nd DRAFT]

Michael got bored just sitting under a tree watching the sheep all day long. Stupid sheep, he thought to himself, all they do is walk around and munch grass. One day when he was especially bored with his job, Michael had an idea. He pulled the cell phone out of his pocket and dialed Mr. Baker's number. When the rancher answered, *Michael screamed into the phone, "Mr. Baker! Mr. Baker! A pack of coyotes is attacking the sheep! Hurry, it's awful!"* ← **added dialogue**

Go to page 77 in the **Practice the Strategy Notebook!**

154   **Narrative Writing** · Fable

Revising

Clarify
Make sure that all the plot events lead to the moral of the fable.

❝ After I read more of my fable to myself, I noticed another thing. One part, when Michael takes a walk because he's bored, didn't help teach the moral of the story. Then I remembered that the **Rubric** says all the plot events should lead to the moral.

"I think my fable will be more interesting after I take that part out. Taking away something that doesn't belong will make the whole story better! What do you think? ❞

READ TO MYSELF

[3rd DRAFT]

After a few more days, however, Michael grew even more bored than before. ~~He decided to take a walk up a hillside to find out how far he could see. After a long walk, he finally reached the top of the hill. He gasped when he realized he could see for 30 miles or more!~~ ← **not needed**

He looked at the cell phone lying on the ground next to him. He thought about how funny Mr. Baker looked when he found out Michael had played a trick on him. Then Michael picked up the cell phone and played the same trick again.

Go to page 78 in the **Practice the Strategy Notebook!**

Narrative Writing · Fable   155

Revising Elaborate

Strategy: Add dialogue to make the story and characters come alive.

(Student Page 154)

Ask a student to read Brian's words to the class.

Explain that dialogue can make a story more interesting. Hearing a character talk allows the reader to get to know that character and notice differences between characters. Point out how Brian elaborates on the way Michael speaks. Ask students to find a word in the excerpt that tells how Michael is speaking. **[Response: *screamed*]**

Practice the Strategy Notebook!

Assign page 77 in the *Practice the Strategy Notebook.* Have students read the dialogue they wrote. Stress that there are many different ways to write the same dialogue.

Revising Clarify

Strategy: Make sure that all the plot events lead to the moral of the fable.

(Student Page 155)

Ask a student to read Brian's words to the class.

Ask students whether they agree that Brian's change improved his fable. Have them decide how to make sure that all the parts of a piece of writing add something and are really necessary. Then ask them to check other excerpts from Brian's fable and see if all the parts that he included are necessary.

Practice the Strategy Notebook!

Assign page 78 the *Practice the Strategy Notebook.* Discuss which parts of the paragraph students think should be crossed out and why.

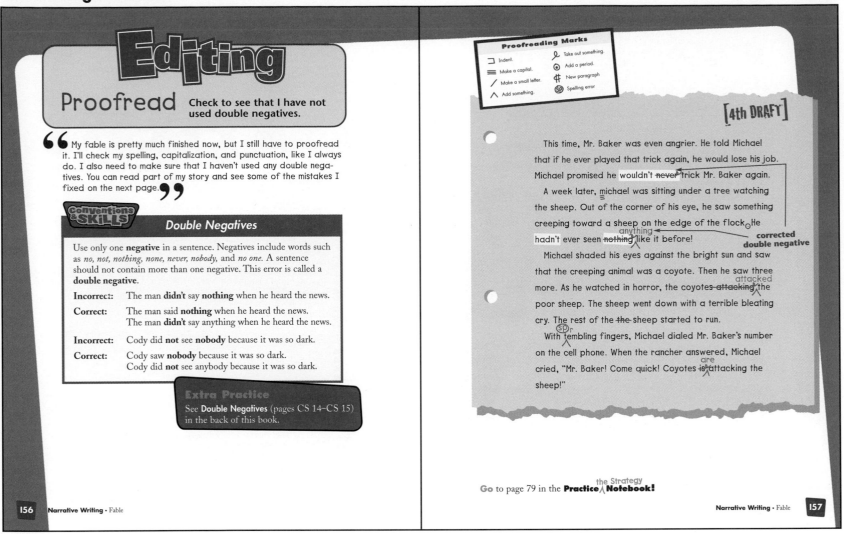

Editing

Proofread

Check to see that I have not used double negatives.

"My fable is pretty much finished now, but I still have to proofread it. I'll check my spelling, capitalization, and punctuation, like I always do. I also need to make sure that I haven't used any double negatives. You can read part of my story and see some of the mistakes I fixed on the next page."

Conventions & SKILLS

Double Negatives

Use only one **negative** in a sentence. Negatives include words such as *no, not, nothing, none, never, nobody,* and *no one.* A sentence should not contain more than one negative. This error is called a **double negative.**

Incorrect:	The man **didn't** say **nothing** when he heard the news.
Correct:	The man said **nothing** when he heard the news. The man **didn't** say **anything** when he heard the news.
Incorrect:	Cody did **not** see **nobody** because it was so dark.
Correct:	Cody saw **nobody** because it was so dark. Cody did **not** see **anybody** because it was so dark.

Extra Practice
See **Double Negatives** (pages CS 14–CS 15) in the back of this book.

156 | Narrative Writing • Fable

Proofreading Marks

⊐ Indent.　　　　　✎ Take out something.
≡ Make a capital.　　⊙ Add a period.
/ Make a small letter.　⌗ New paragraph
∧ Add something.　　　SP Spelling error

[4th DRAFT]

This time, Mr. Baker was even angrier. He told Michael that if he ever played that trick again, he would lose his job. Michael promised he wouldn't ~~never~~ trick Mr. Baker again.

A week later, michael was sitting under a tree watching the sheep. Out of the corner of his eye, he saw something creeping toward a sheep on the edge of the flock. He hadn't ever seen ~~nothing~~ anything like it before! ← **corrected double negative**

Michael shaded his eyes against the bright sun and saw that the creeping animal was a coyote. Then he saw three more. As he watched in horror, the coyotes ~~attacking~~ attacked the poor sheep. The sheep went down with a terrible bleating cry. The rest of the ~~the~~ sheep started to run.

With tembling fingers, Michael dialed Mr. Baker's number on the cell phone. When the rancher answered, Michael cried, "Mr. Baker! Come quick! Coyotes ~~is~~ are attacking the sheep!"

Go to page 79 in the **Practice the Strategy Notebook!**

Narrative Writing • Fable | 157

Editing　Proofread

Strategy: Check to see that I have not used double negatives.

(Student Pages 156–157)

Discuss the difference between revising and editing. Make sure that students understand that in the revising step they reread their draft to look for ways to make it clearer, more interesting, or better organized. In the editing step, they look for mistakes in spelling, grammar, and punctuation.

Ask a volunteer to read Brian's words to the class. Remind students that good writers search for all kinds of spelling, punctuation, and grammar errors when they proofread. They also focus on the kinds of skills they have had problems with in the past.

Extra Practice: Conventions & Skills
Student Edition

If you did not use Student Pages CS 14–CS 15 as a pre-assessment, you may wish to assign those pages now.

Conventions & Skills Practice

For more targeted practice related to this skill, see this lesson in the optional *Conventions & Skills Practice Book*:

Lesson 38: Negatives

Practice the Strategy Notebook!

Assign page 79 in the *Practice the Strategy Notebook.* Discuss the edits that students think are necessary.

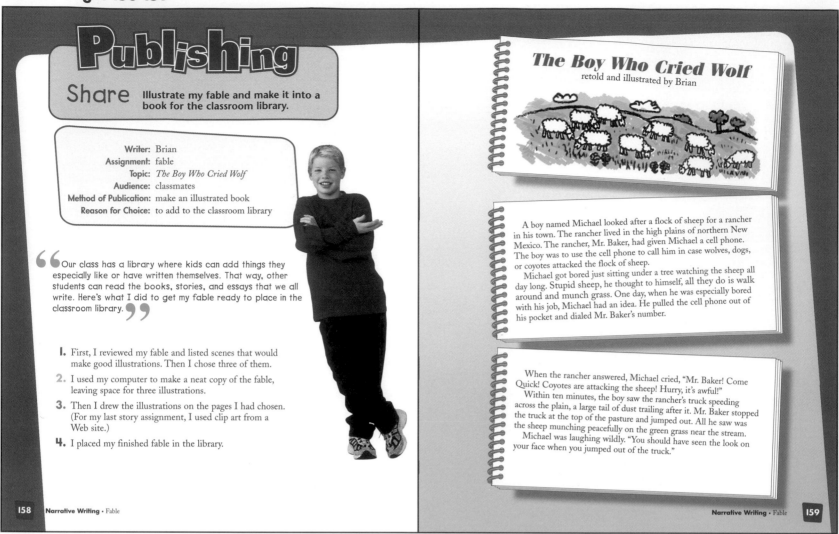

Publishing

Share

Illustrate my fable and make it into a book for the classroom library.

Writer: Brian
Assignment: fable
Topic: *The Boy Who Cried Wolf*
Audience: classmates
Method of Publication: make an illustrated book
Reason for Choice: to add to the classroom library

"Our class has a library where kids can add things they especially like or have written themselves. That way, other students can read the books, stories, and essays that we all write. Here's what I did to get my fable ready to place in the classroom library."

1. First, I reviewed my fable and listed scenes that would make good illustrations. Then I chose three of them.
2. I used my computer to make a neat copy of the fable, leaving space for three illustrations.
3. Then I drew the illustrations on the pages I had chosen. (For my last story assignment, I used clip art from a Web site.)
4. I placed my finished fable in the library.

158 Narrative Writing · Fable

The Boy Who Cried Wolf
retold and illustrated by Brian

A boy named Michael looked after a flock of sheep for a rancher in his town. The rancher lived in the high plains of northern New Mexico. The rancher, Mr. Baker, had given Michael a cell phone. The boy was to use the cell phone to call him in case wolves, dogs, or coyotes attacked the flock of sheep.

Michael got bored just sitting under a tree watching the sheep all day long. Stupid sheep, he thought to himself, all they do is walk around and munch grass. One day, when he was especially bored with his job, Michael had an idea. He pulled the cell phone out of his pocket and dialed Mr. Baker's number.

When the rancher answered, Michael cried, "Mr. Baker! Come Quick! Coyotes are attacking the sheep! Hurry, it's awful!"

Within ten minutes, the boy saw the rancher's truck speeding across the plain, a large tail of dust trailing after it. Mr. Baker stopped the truck at the top of the pasture and jumped out. All he saw was the sheep munching peacefully on the green grass near the stream.

Michael was laughing wildly. "You should have seen the look on your face when you jumped out of the truck."

Narrative Writing · Fable **159**

Publishing Share

Strategy: Illustrate my fable and make it into a book for the classroom library.

(Student Pages 158–161)

Ask students to think of other ways that Brian could share his fable. Discuss whether they agree that this method was a suitable one.

Using the Rubric

Ask students to work in pairs to use the rubric (reprinted on pages 80–81 of the *Practice the Strategy Notebook*) to evaluate Brian's fable. After each pair has finished its evaluation, ask volunteers to provide reasons for their decisions.

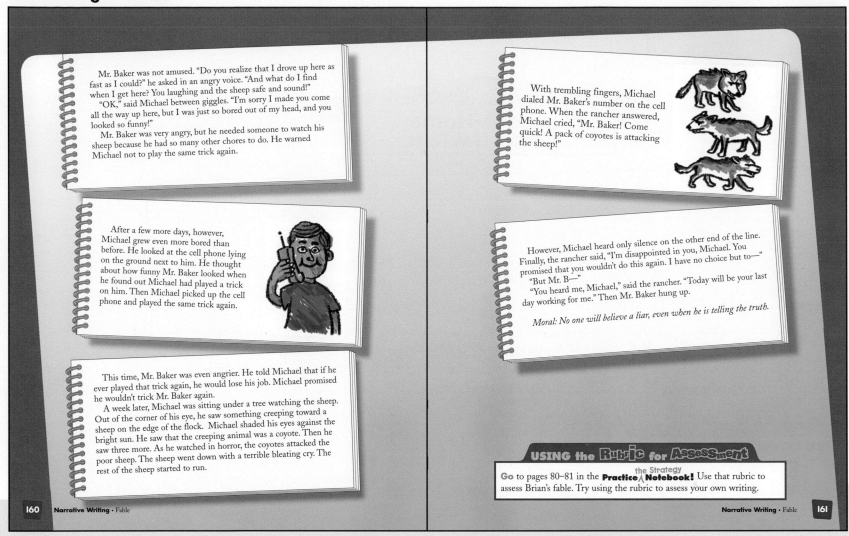

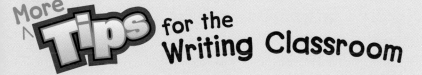

Purposeful Journal Writing

For student journal writing to be a worthwhile activity, your students must be totally engaged in the subject matter. First, it is your responsibility, as the teacher, to provide a variety of inspirational activities that stimulate the imagination. These activities might include:

1. engaging the students in meaningful service learning, such as working with the elderly, protecting the environment, sharing with the mentally challenged, or helping the homeless.

2. inviting noteworthy people from the community to speak on such topics as overcoming obstacles, their jobs, their hobbies, and so on.

3. planning special events that involve family members, such as having parents in for a picnic lunch, setting up after-school sessions for sharing writing, or sponsoring a grandparents' day. Activities like these provide much material for the students' journals.

Secondly, it is the role of the teacher to help every student develop his/her writing voice. Encourage your students to write from not only the head, but also the heart. Allow them to make spelling, punctuation, and grammatical errors in their initial journal entries. Later, if the writing is expressive and significant, give your students an opportunity to make corrections.

School–Home Connection

Dear Family,

Your child has been learning and practicing many kinds of writing. It's been an exciting adventure, as we have explored many ways of expressing our thoughts, feelings, and observations in writing. You can help your child continue to develop a love of writing by encouraging him or her to make writing a part of everyday life.

Here are some easy ways you can help to make writing a part of your child's daily life.

- Help your child establish a regular correspondence with a pen pal. This person could be a relative or friend who lives in another area. It could be someone your child meets during a vacation or at camp. It could even be a classmate or another child in your neighborhood. The correspondence can be on paper or by e-mail. For safety and security reasons, be sure you know who your child's pen pal is, and monitor this activity as closely as possible.

- Encourage your child to do a daily writing activity, such as writing in a diary or keeping a journal. Explain to him or her that this kind of writing is especially helpful because it gives a person an outlet for his or her thoughts and feelings. It's also a great way of recording a kind of personal history. Years later, your child will be able to read his or her entries and remember things that might otherwise be forgotten.

- Help your child to develop real-life application skills by encouraging him or her to do some organizational writing, such as writing lists or schedules. This is a great activity for developing organizational skills and goal setting skills. It's also an easy writing activity.

- Help your child to nurture his or her creativity by encouraging him or her to write poetry or song lyrics, descriptions, or short stories.

Writing is not just for the classroom. Encourage your child to use writing in everyday situations to help develop skills and habits that will last a lifetime.

You may wish to copy the letter above and send it home with your students.

Books on Teaching Writing

Harris, Karen R., and Steven Graham. *Making the Writing Process Work: Strategies for Composition and Self-Regulation.* Cambridge, MA: Brookline, 1996.

Emphasizing "strategy instruction," the authors offer teachers of grades 4–8 explicit instruction in the areas of generating content, planning, writing, and revising. The focus is on the narrative genre, but the approach applies to other areas as well, including report writing.

Stewig, John Warren. *Read to Write: Using Children's Literature as a Springboard for Teaching Writing.* 3rd ed. Katonah, NY: Richard Owen, 1990.

This source for teachers of grades 3–8 offers strategies for using characterization, point of view, setting, and plot and conflict to help build a story. The author also focuses on editing strategies that students can use to improve their stories.

Fable Collections:

Lessie, Pat. *Fablesauce.* Athol, MA: Haley's, 1999.

Pinkney, Jerry. *Aesop's Fables.* New York: SeaStar Books, 2000.

Rosenthal, Paul. *Yo, Aesop! Get a Load of These Fables.* New York: Simon & Schuster, 1998.

Scieszka, Jon. *Squids Will be Squids: Fresh Morals, Beastly Fables.* New York: Viking, 1998.

Buss, Kathleen, and Lee Karnowski. *Reading and Writing Literary Genres.* Newark, DE: IRA, 2000.

The author discusses in detail six fiction genres: realistic, mysteries, traditional folk tales, pourquoi stories and fables, modern folk tales, and fantasy. This source includes examples of each genre, an extensive bibliography, and many graphic organizers.

 **Tips** for the **Writing Classroom**

by Ken Stewart, *Master Teacher*

Quality Versus Quantity

Assigning more work does not necessarily mean that more learning is taking place. In fact, it could mean just the opposite. Too often, when we teach writing, we have a tendency to belabor a technique or point so much that we lose sight of the big picture. As educated adults, we want, and often demand, variety in our lives. We should offer nothing less to our students. After you are comfortable with the quality and level of learning that has taken place in a lesson, move on. It does not matter that there may be (according to the textbook) a few more points to be discussed, more questions to be answered, or more activities to be completed.

Involve your students in determining when it is time to move on, and encourage them to help students who are having trouble meeting the established criteria. The following suggestions should help you.

1. When giving an assignment, clearly write the criteria into your lesson plans.
2. While introducing the lesson, make sure students thoroughly understand your criteria.

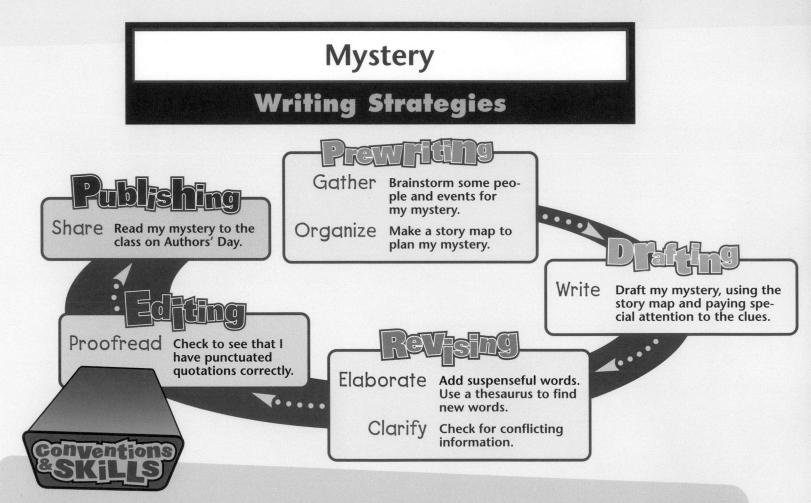

Mystery

Writing Strategies

Prewriting

Gather — Brainstorm some people and events for my mystery.

Organize — Make a story map to plan my mystery.

Drafting

Write — Draft my mystery, using the story map and paying special attention to the clues.

Revising

Elaborate — Add suspenseful words. Use a thesaurus to find new words.

Clarify — Check for conflicting information.

Editing

Proofread — Check to see that I have punctuated quotations correctly.

Conventions & Skills

Publishing

Share — Read my mystery to the class on Authors' Day.

Before the students read the model on Student Pages 163–165, you may wish to review the targeted **mechanics** convention. Explain that a **direct quotation** is a speaker's exact words. An **indirect quotation** retells a speaker's words. Direct quotations require quotation marks around the beginning and end of the speaker's words. A comma should separate the speaker's words from the rest of the sentence. A direct quotation begins with a capital letter. The end punctuation is added before the last quotation mark.

Examples: **Direct Quotation:** Ms. Singh whispered, "Even Sherlock Holmes couldn't solve this mystery."

Indirect Quotation: Ms. Singh said that even Sherlock Holmes couldn't solve this mystery.

Skill Assessment: To pre-assess your students' understanding of the targeted convention, you may wish to have them complete the corresponding lesson on Student Pages CS 16–CS 17 in the back of the Student Edition.

Skill Mini-Lesson: The Proofread activity in this chapter can be used as a mini-lesson on the targeted **grammar, usage,** or **mechanics** skill.

3. After the lesson has been taught, determine if students have achieved the criteria at an acceptable level.

4. If most of your students are having problems with a lesson, you may need to adjust your expectations/criteria or method of presenting the information. You may meet with the students who are displaying competency to ascertain what techniques they are using to learn the material or process.

5. You might also give students who are achieving competency the opportunity, with your supervision, to work with the class or groups to explain and teach the material or process.

6. Re-evaluate and move on. If some students are still having problems, let them know that there will be future lessons (applications) that will allow them to gain a better understanding of the material or process.

7. Keep a record of students who may be having problems with the lesson so that you may work with them individually or in small groups later.

(See "More Tips for the Writing Classroom: Alternatives for Assessing Understanding of a Novel or Story," page T134.)

Time Management for This Chapter*

Session		Session		Session	
1	Discuss the definitions of narrative writing and the mystery genre; review the questions (Student Page 162). Read "The Case of the Disappearing Soccer Shirt" (Student Pages 163–165). Use the questions to analyze the mystery. Use the rubric to assess it.	**6**	Read and discuss **DRAFTING: Write** (Student Pages 174–175).	**11**	Assign *Practice the Strategy Notebook* page 89. Encourage students to use the targeted strategy to revise a piece of their own writing.
2	Introduce Tia (Student Page 171) as a student-writer working on a mystery. Read and discuss **PREWRITING: Gather** (Student Page 172).	**7**	Assign *Practice the Strategy Notebook* pages 86–87. Encourage students to use the targeted strategy in their own writing.	**12**	Read and discuss **EDITING: Proofread** (Student Pages 178–179).
3	Assign *Practice the Strategy Notebook* pages 82–83. Encourage students to use the targeted strategy in their own writing.	**8**	Read and discuss **REVISING: Elaborate** (Student Page 176).	**13**	Assign *Practice the Strategy Notebook* pages 90–91. Encourage students to use the targeted strategy in their own writing.
4	Read and discuss **PREWRITING: Organize** (Student Page 173). Discuss the purpose and mechanics of a story map and analyze Tia's chart.	**9**	Assign *Practice the Strategy Notebook* page 88. Encourage students to use the targeted strategy to revise a piece of their own writing.	**14**	Read and discuss **PUBLISHING: Share** (Student Pages 180–183). Discuss other ways Tia could share her mystery.
5	Assign *Practice the Strategy Notebook* pages 84–85. Encourage students to use the targeted strategy in their own writing.	**10**	Read and discuss **REVISING: Clarify** (Student Page 177).	**15**	Review the rubric for this chapter (reprinted on *Practice the Strategy Notebook* pages 92–93). Ask pairs of students to use the rubric to evaluate Tia's mystery.

WRITER'S HANDBOOK

* To complete the chapter in fewer sessions, assign the *Practice the Strategy Notebook* pages on the same day the targeted strategy is introduced.

Remind students that they can refer to the Writer's Handbook in the back of the Student Edition for more information.

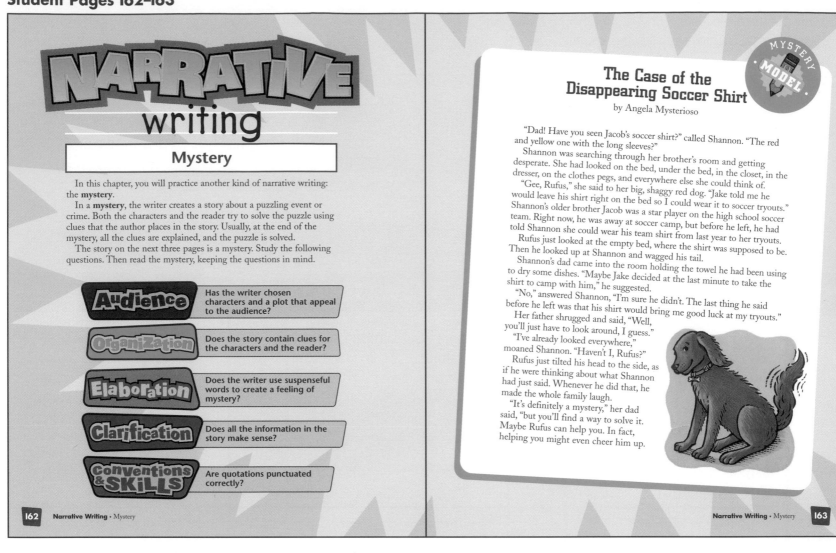

Introduce the Genre:
Mystery

Ask students to read the description of a *mystery* on Student Page 162. Discuss how writers of mysteries use clues. **[Response: Both the characters and the reader try to solve the puzzle using clues that the writer places in the story. The reader learns about the clues at the same time the characters do. Usually, at the end of the mystery, all the clues are explained and the puzzle is solved.]** Then ask volunteers to summarize mysteries they have read. Discuss how the elements of the mystery, such as plot, characters, setting, and clues, help make mysteries fun to read.

Conclude by telling students that they are going to study and practice strategies for writing a mystery.

Discuss the Questions

(Student Page 162)

Read the questions on Student Page 162 aloud. Discuss the category above each question. Explain the importance of each category in creating a good piece of writing. Here are possible guidelines for this discussion:

Audience: The writer must always try to appeal to his or her audience. In this genre, writers use characters and plot to appeal to readers.

Organization: In mysteries, writers cleverly insert clues for the characters and the reader.

Elaboration: Mystery authors try to use suspenseful words to create a feeling of mystery.

Clarification: Mysteries often have complicated plots, so writers must make sure that all the information in the story makes sense and does not conflict.

Conventions & Skills: Good writers make sure a speaker's exact words are enclosed in quotation marks and punctuated correctly. They also punctuate indirect quotations correctly.

Read the Model:
Mystery

(Student Pages 163–165)

Read "The Case of the Disappearing Soccer Shirt" aloud.

I've noticed that he's been pretty unhappy since Jake went to soccer camp. All he does is hide behind the couch. I wonder why."

Shannon glanced down at her shaggy dog. "Rufus will be a huge help, I'm sure," she said with a smile. She used both hands to pull Rufus's long, tangled fur out of his eyes. "There," she said, "can you see better now? Are you ready to help me find Jake's shirt, old boy?"

"Why don't you ask Lizzie to help you, too?" Dad suggested. Lizzie was Shannon's younger sister.

"All right," answered Shannon, "but I'm not sure she'll be much help either."

A few minutes later, Lizzie eagerly joined her sister in the search for the missing shirt. Lizzie looked in the basement, poked in and around the washer and dryer, and burrowed through all the closets. Meanwhile, Shannon scoured the car and garage. She also ransacked her room, Lizzie's room, and Jake's room—again! Rufus did not offer much assistance. Mostly, he lay in a lump on the living room rug or hid behind the couch.

"I have to find that shirt really soon," Shannon reminded Lizzie. "Soccer tryouts start in three hours. If I don't find that shirt, I'll have to wear something else. I really want to wear Jake's shirt because I need all the good luck I can get at the tryouts. That shirt has got to be around here somewhere!"

Then Lizzie's eyes got big and round. "Maybe someone stole Jake's shirt!" she whispered. "I bet someone snuck in here and took it while we weren't looking!"

Shannon grinned and shook her head. "I don't think so, Lizzie, but I have to admit I don't have any better ideas right now. Anyway, Rufus would bark if a stranger came into our house." Then she spotted his tail sticking out from behind the couch. "But maybe not."

An hour later, Shannon had given up hope of locating the missing shirt. She was slouched on a kitchen chair, slowly helping her dad peel potatoes for their dinner.

Lizzie had gotten tired of searching, too, and was watching TV in the family room. She was lying on the couch, petting Rufus with her

stockinged foot as she watched her favorite cartoons. "You really miss Jacob, don't you, boy?" Lizzie mumbled to the unhappy dog. "I bet that's why you didn't even notice when someone came in and stole his shirt."

Rufus got up slowly and sheepishly squeezed himself back behind the couch. After a while, Lizzie wondered how he was doing and peeped over the back of the couch. Then she let out a scream!

"Shannon! Dad! I found the thief!"

As Shannon and their dad rushed into the family room, Lizzie reached behind the couch, where Rufus was hiding. As the others watched in suspense, she pulled out the red and yellow shirt. Then Rufus crawled out from behind the couch and lay on the rug with his head on his front paws.

"Rufus had the shirt all along!" Shannon said with a sigh of relief. "Why would he take Jacob's shirt?"

"I think I know," said Dad. "Rufus really misses Jake, and dogs have a strong sense of smell. To Rufus, the shirt smells like Jake, so he pulled the shirt off the bed and carried it to his hideaway behind the couch. It probably made him feel as if Jake were nearby."

Shannon gave Rufus a warm hug, and the dog licked her face and wagged his tail. "Sorry, boy, but I need that shirt more than you do right now," she explained. "I'll give it back to you as soon as tryouts are over—I promise!"

Dad reached down and patted Rufus's head. "Why don't we take him with us to the tryouts? That way, he can keep a close watch over his favorite shirt!"

"It's everyone's favorite shirt today!" Shannon added.

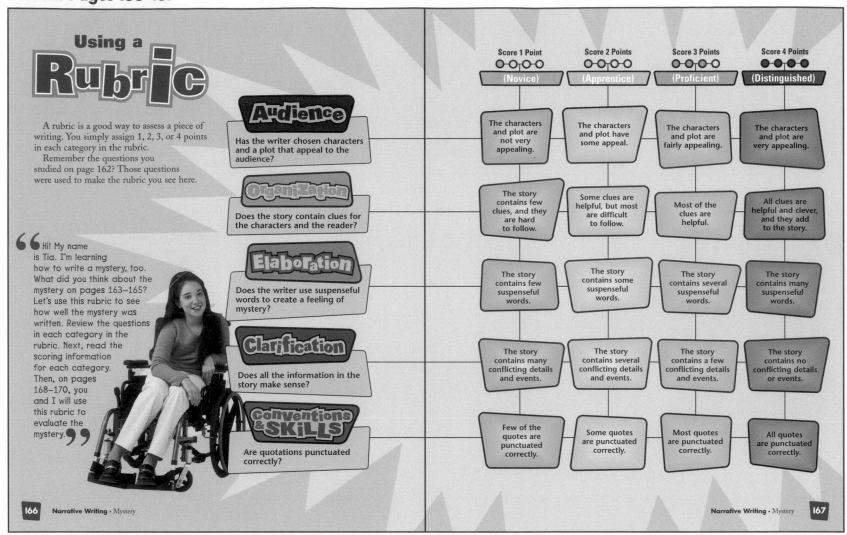

Using a Rubric

(Student Pages 166–167)

Use the text on Student Pages 168–170 to model how to use the rubric to assess a mystery. If you need more information on using a rubric, please see page T22.

Differentiating 3, 4, and 5 Point Rubrics: Which Choice Is Right for Me?

by Lee Bromberger, *Assessment Specialist*

How many performance quality levels should a rubric have? The following are some thoughts on rubrics with different point values.

A **three-point rubric** may be best to use with young students who are first becoming exposed to rubric evaluation. Modern Americans (even children!) have been educated by marketers to think in terms of three's: *good, better,* and *best* choices dominate the consumer landscape. Such a familiarity can be helpful when youngsters are first learning to use rubrics.

The **five-point rubric** offers teachers an opportunity to extend the levels of expectation for a particular assignment. As a result, five-point rubrics tend to be more exhaustive and comprehensive. This tendency can result in too much hair splitting for the teacher. The teacher is now under pressure to work efficiently and accurately while achieving a grading uniformity among the other evaluators.

The significant detraction to the three- and five-point rubric scales is the natural tendency of the assessor to choose the middle score. The "middle" point scale, afforded by the odd number of points on the rubric, becomes the safe choice. Extensive training is necessary to teach assessors to avoid the temptation of the middle choice.

A **four-point rubric** (employed throughout Grades 3–8 of *Strategies for Writers*) provides a better alternative to the problems posed by the three- and five-point rubrics. The use of four separate point divisions allows rubric developers ample breadth to measure content without the sometimes overwhelming choices of the five-point scale. The important advantage of the four-point rubric is its lack of "middle." Assessors are forced to make a sometimes difficult decision between assigning two points or three points, based on the merits of the writing. Understanding the considerations that need to be made in such an instance is the key to employing an effective four-point rubric scale.

Falling upon simplicity is often the best choice when determining which rubric scale to employ. The four-point scale, while potentially more difficult to develop because of its lack of a middle and "safe" point scale, yields a more accurate measure of student achievement and a valid rubric assessment.

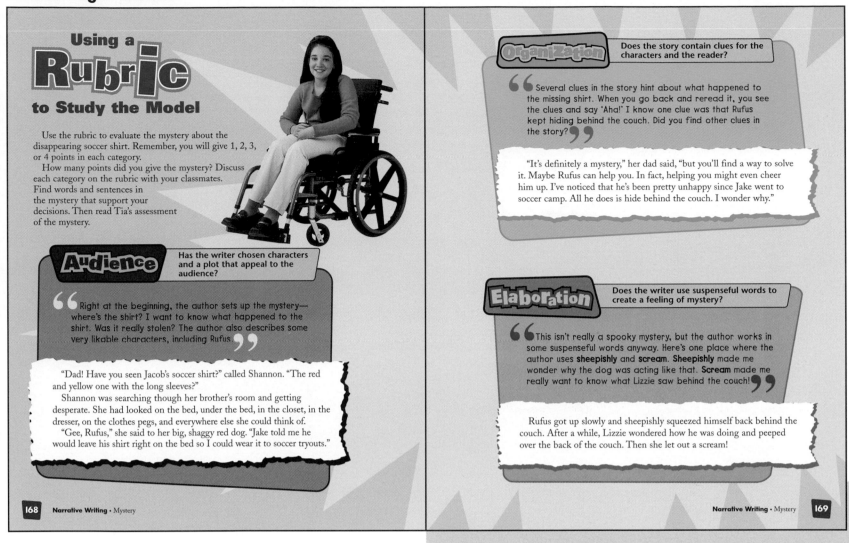

Using a Rubric to Study the Model

(Student Pages 168–170)

Read the questions and answers on Student Pages 168–170. Discuss whether students agree or disagree with Tia's assessment of the mystery. For example, do students agree that the writer planted clues effectively in this story? Were the clues too easy to figure out? Were they too difficult?

Note on Conventions & Skills: Remind students that they should always check their writing for correct spelling, punctuation, and capitalization. In addition, this lesson will focus on the mechanics of direct and indirect quotations.

Meeting Students' Needs:
Second Language Learners

Have pairs of students take turns retelling a mystery story they have read, including the clues. Have the listening partner try to guess the outcome of the mystery and explain how the clues helped him or her solve it.

Students Who Need Extra Help

Ask students to identify all the clues in "The Case of the Disappearing Soccer Shirt." Also have them identify the "red herrings": false clues meant to lead the characters and readers away from the truth. One red herring is the suggestion that the shirt was stolen.

Gifted Students

Have a group of students act out "The Case of the Disappearing Soccer Shirt." Have them assign roles, write a script, find props, and present their play to the rest of the class.

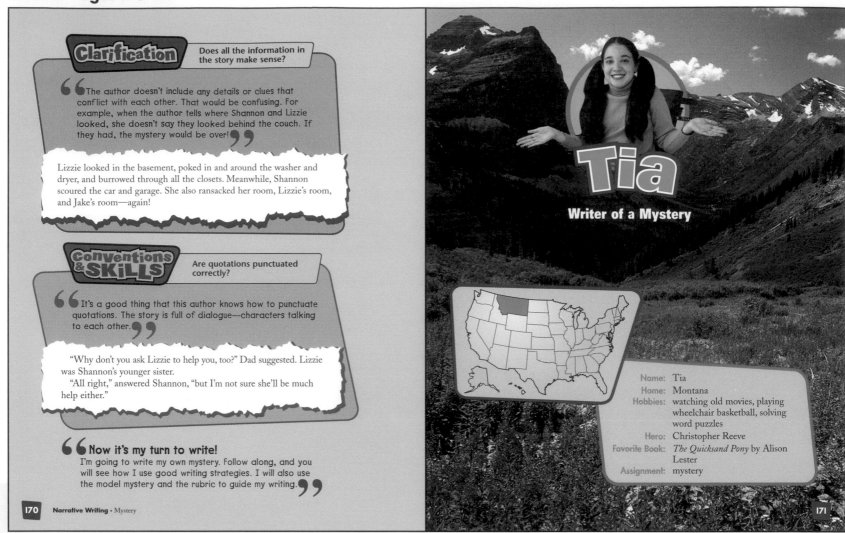

Unlocking Text Structure:
Mystery

The structure of a piece of writing depends on how the information it contains is organized. To help students unlock the structure of the mystery, you may want to refer them to the graphic organizer in this chapter, a story map. The story map is a favorite of narrative writers because it helps establish the important elements of a story: setting, characters, plot/problem, main events, and outcome.

A story map helps establish both a *causative* and a *chronological* text structure, showing the causes of the main events and the order in which the events occur. Make sure students grasp that in a mystery, the writer must clearly establish all of these elements as a framework for adding the clues that readers will need to solve the puzzle.

Tia:
Writer of a Mystery

(Student Page 171)

Read the information about Tia.

Make sure students understand that she is going to write her own mystery. Have them speculate about what she might choose as a topic. Which of Tia's hobbies could she use in her mystery?

Point out that Tia will complete the steps in the writing process: Prewriting, Drafting, Revising, Editing, and Publishing. At each stage, she will demonstrate a good writing strategy and explain how she used it. Students should watch for key words, including **Gather, Organize, Write, Elaborate, Clarify, Proofread,** and **Share**.

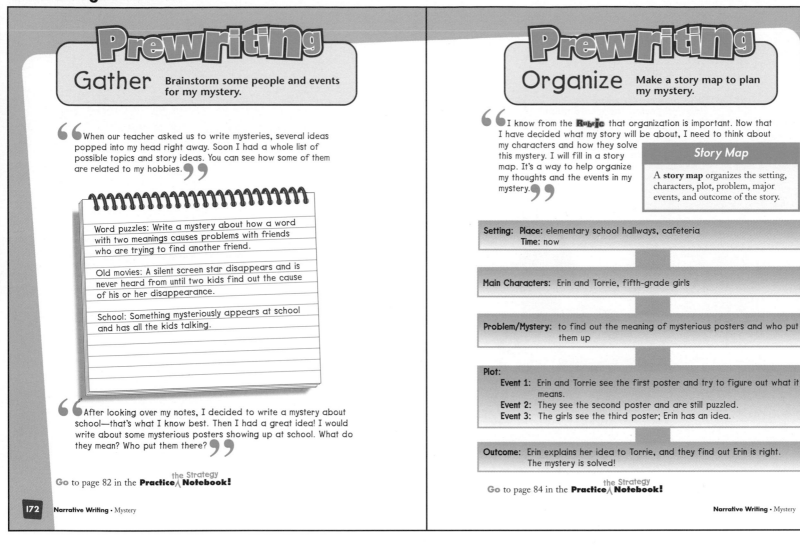

Prewriting

Gather
Brainstorm some people and events for my mystery.

"When our teacher asked us to write mysteries, several ideas popped into my head right away. Soon I had a whole list of possible topics and story ideas. You can see how some of them are related to my hobbies."

Word puzzles: Write a mystery about how a word with two meanings causes problems with friends who are trying to find another friend.

Old movies: A silent screen star disappears and is never heard from until two kids find out the cause of his or her disappearance.

School: Something mysteriously appears at school and has all the kids talking.

"After looking over my notes, I decided to write a mystery about school—that's what I know best. Then I had a great idea! I would write about some mysterious posters showing up at school. What do they mean? Who put them there?"

Go to page 82 in the Practice the Strategy Notebook!

Prewriting

Organize
Make a story map to plan my mystery.

"I know from the Rubric that organization is important. Now that I have decided what my story will be about, I need to think about my characters and how they solve this mystery. I will fill in a story map. It's a way to help organize my thoughts and the events in my mystery."

Story Map
A **story map** organizes the setting, characters, plot, problem, major events, and outcome of the story.

Setting: Place: elementary school hallways, cafeteria
Time: now

Main Characters: Erin and Torrie, fifth-grade girls

Problem/Mystery: to find out the meaning of mysterious posters and who put them up

Plot:
Event 1: Erin and Torrie see the first poster and try to figure out what it means.
Event 2: They see the second poster and are still puzzled.
Event 3: The girls see the third poster; Erin has an idea.

Outcome: Erin explains her idea to Torrie, and they find out Erin is right. The mystery is solved!

Go to page 84 in the Practice the Strategy Notebook!

Prewriting Gather

Strategy: Brainstorm some people and events for my mystery.

(Student Page 172)

Read Tia's words aloud. Ask students to suggest other questions relating to her statements. [**Possible responses: Strange posters appear in the hallways. (What do they say?); The posters make confusing statements and are in different colors. (Why are they in different colors?)**]

Refer to the Rubric: The student spokesperson will refer to the rubric throughout the chapter. Remind students to get into the habit of referring back to the rubric so they fully understand its use as a tool for shaping their writing.

Practice the Strategy Notebook!

Assign pages 82–83 in the *Practice the Strategy Notebook*. (Your Own Writing sections should be used as time and students' abilities permit.) Explain that the student will practice this Gather strategy with a different topic.

Prewriting Organize

Strategy: Make a story map to plan my mystery.

(Student Page 173)

Explain that writing can be organized in many ways. A graphic organizer, such as a story map, is one way to organize information in preparation for writing.

Review the definition and mechanics of a story map. Then have students study Tia's story map and note how it creates a "road map" for her to follow as she writes.

Practice the Strategy Notebook!

Assign pages 84–85 in the *Practice the Strategy Notebook*. Encourage volunteers to share the story maps they created. Suggested responses for the *Practice the Strategy Notebook* appear in the Appendix at the back of this Teacher Edition.

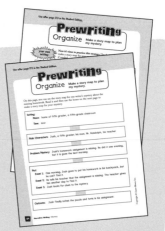

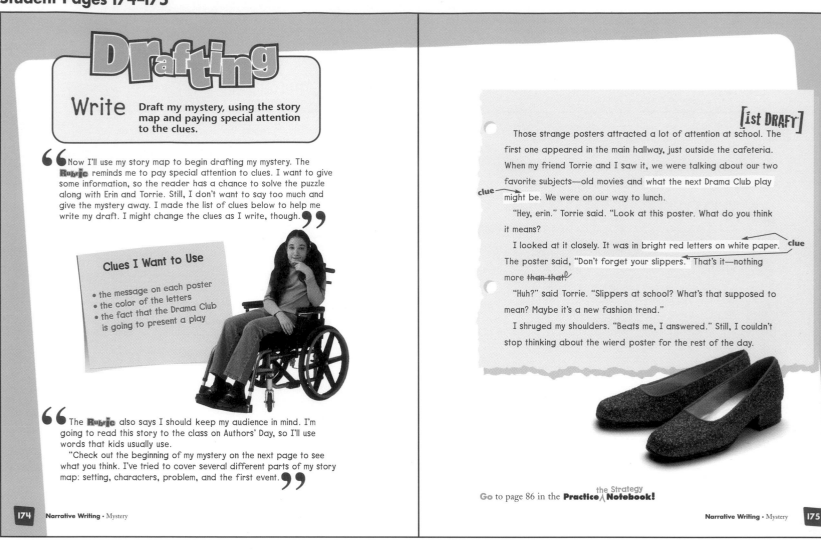

Drafting

Write — Draft my mystery, using the story map and paying special attention to the clues.

" Now I'll use my story map to begin drafting my mystery. The **Rubric** reminds me to pay special attention to clues. I want to give some information, so the reader has a chance to solve the puzzle along with Erin and Torrie. Still, I don't want to say too much and give the mystery away. I made the list of clues below to help me write my draft. I might change the clues as I write, though. "

Clues I Want to Use

- the message on each poster
- the color of the letters
- the fact that the Drama Club is going to present a play

" The **Rubric** also says I should keep my audience in mind. I'm going to read this story to the class on Authors' Day, so I'll use words that kids usually use.

"Check out the beginning of my mystery on the next page to see what you think. I've tried to cover several different parts of my story map: setting, characters, problem, and the first event. "

[1st DRAFT]

Those strange posters attracted a lot of attention at school. The first one appeared in the main hallway, just outside the cafeteria. When my friend Torrie and I saw it, we were talking about our two favorite subjects—old movies and what the next Drama Club play might be. We were on our way to lunch. — clue

"Hey, erin." Torrie said. "Look at this poster. What do you think it means?"

I looked at it closely. It was in bright red letters on white paper. — clue The poster said, "Don't forget your slippers." That's it—nothing more ~~than that~~.

"Huh?" said Torrie. "Slippers at school? What's that supposed to mean? Maybe it's a new fashion trend."

I shrugged my shoulders. "Beats me, I answered." Still, I couldn't stop thinking about the wierd poster for the rest of the day.

Go to page 86 in the **Practice the Strategy Notebook!**

Drafting Write

Strategy: Draft my mystery, using the story map and paying special attention to the clues.

(Student Pages 174–175)

Review what it means to draft a piece of writing. Remind students that a draft is a temporary or "rough" form of a mystery or other piece of writing. It should be changed and corrected several times before the piece of writing is finished. Ask a volunteer to read Tia's words aloud for the class.

Ask students what special element of a mystery Tia will keep in mind as she writes her draft. [**Possible response: She must pay special attention to planting clues for the characters and reader.**]

Practice the Strategy Notebook!

Assign pages 86–87 in the *Practice the Strategy Notebook*. Encourage students to read their rough drafts to their partners. The partners will check to see whether their drafts followed their story maps.

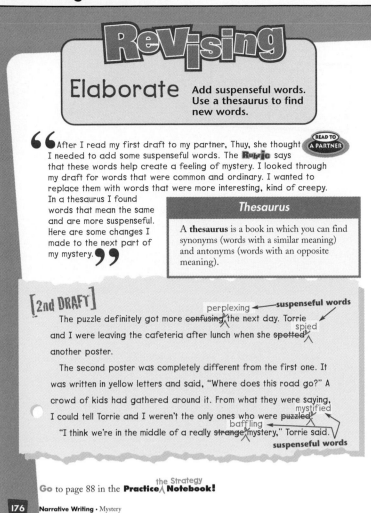

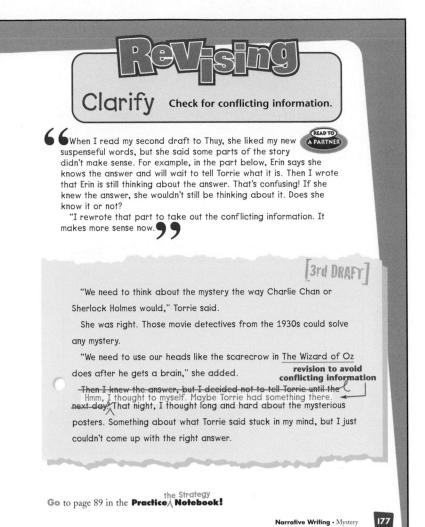

Revising Elaborate

Strategy: Add suspenseful words. Use a thesaurus to find new words.

(Student Page 176)

Ask a student to read Tia's words to the class.

Explain that mysteries benefit from the use of suspenseful words. Ask students to define *suspenseful.* Then have them list some synonyms and near-synonyms for *suspenseful.* **[Possible answers: mysterious, eerie, creepy, weird]** If necessary, have students practice using a thesaurus to find synonyms. Then discuss how the words inserted on Student Page 176 add suspense to the story. Have students suggest other suspenseful words and phrases Tia could have used.

Revising Clarify

Strategy: Check for conflicting information.

(Student Page 177)

Ask a student to read Tia's words to the class.

Ask students whether they think Tia's change made her mystery less confusing. Discuss the difference between inserting clues and adding conflicting information. **[Possible response: Clues help readers, but conflicting information confuses them.]**

Practice the Strategy Notebook!

Assign page 88 in the *Practice the Strategy Notebook.* Have students share the suspenseful words they added to the sentences.

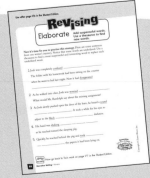

Practice the Strategy Notebook!

Assign page 89 in the *Practice the Strategy Notebook.* Have students suggest revisions to the sample paragraph and explain the reasons for them.

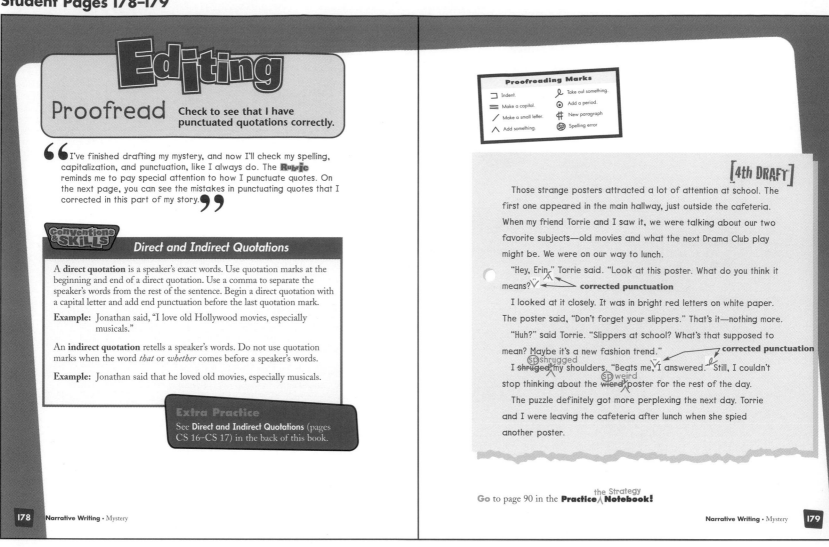

 Proofread

Strategy: Check to see that I have punctuated quotations correctly.

(Student Pages 178–179)

Review the difference between revising and editing. Remind students that in the revising step, they reread their drafts to look for ways to make them clearer and more interesting. In the editing step, they look for mistakes in grammar, punctuation, and capitalization.

Ask a volunteer to read Tia's words to the class. Remind students that good writers search for all kinds of spelling, punctuation, and grammar errors when they proofread. They also focus on the kinds of skills they have had problems with in the past.

Extra Practice: Conventions & Skills Student Edition

If you did not use Student Pages CS 16–CS 17 as a pre-assessment, you may wish to assign those pages now.

Conventions & Skills Practice

For more targeted practice related to this skill, see this lesson in the optional *Conventions & Skills Practice Book:*

Lesson 49: Direct and Indirect Quotations

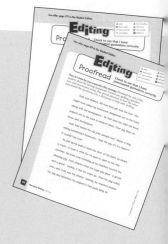

the Strategy
Practice ∧ Notebook!

Assign pages 90–91 in the *Practice the Strategy Notebook.* Have students point out direct and indirect quotations in the writing sample. Discuss how each kind of quotation should be punctuated.

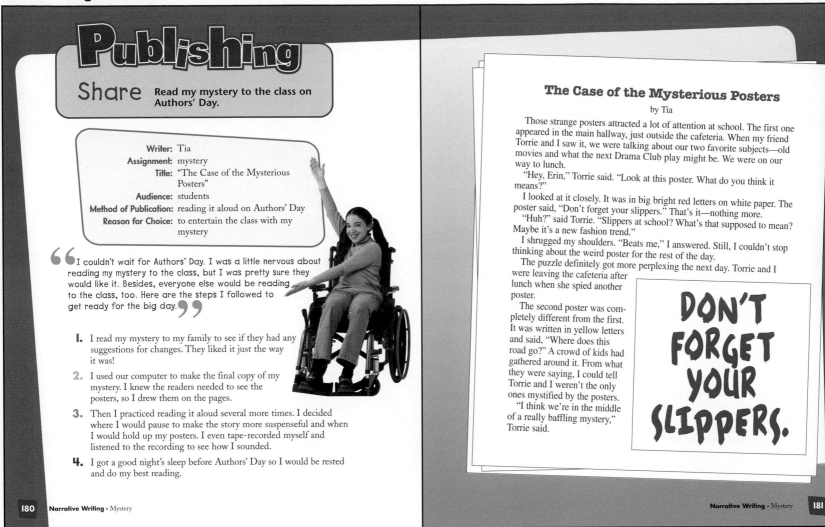

Publishing Share

Strategy: Read my mystery to the class on Authors' Day.

(Student Pages 180–183)

Ask students to think of other ways that Tia could have shared her mystery. Discuss whether they agree that this method was suitable.

Using the Rubric

Ask students to work in pairs to use the rubric (reprinted on pages 92–93 of the *Practice the Strategy Notebook*) to evaluate Tia's mystery. After each pair has made its evaluation, ask volunteers to explain the reasons for their decisions.

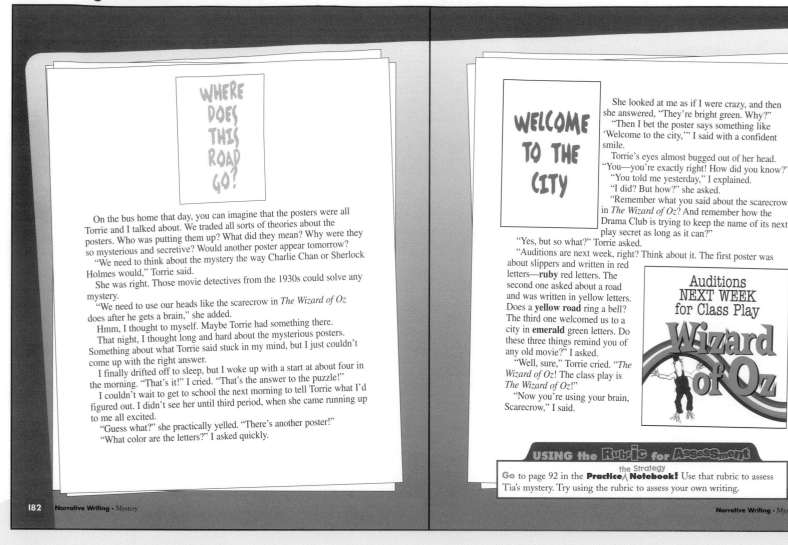

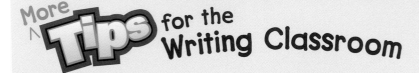

for the Writing Classroom

Alternatives for Assessing Understanding of a Novel or Story

TEST! TEST! TEST! Hopefully you will become comfortable with evaluating the quality of your students' work without always "testing." Here are some suggestions for using student writing, in lieu of testing, to evaluate students' understanding of a novel or story. Fit the activity to your criteria and try a few.

1. Have your students write to the author of a novel or story that they discussed in class. Choose an author who is living, find an address (or e-mail address), and mail the letter.

2. Have your students design a book cover depicting the theme, plot, characters, or setting of a novel or story. On the inside of the cover, ask students to write about the theme, plot, characters, or setting they depicted. Take time to share student work in class.

3. Invite colleagues or parents to speak to your class about novels or stories you are reading with your class. Have your students prepare questions for the speaker in advance. Encourage students to write an article for the school or local newspaper focusing on the speaker's presentation.

4. Have your students research a topic of interest from the novel or story, design a bookmark, and write important information on the back of the bookmark. Laminate the bookmarks and have students use them as they read their novels. These bookmarks make great hall passes.

Challenge yourself to design other unique and exciting writing experiences to evaluate the extent of your students' learning. You might also have your students design their own test, using the Make a Test blackline master on page T136.

your own NARRATIVE writing
Social Studies

Put the strategies you practiced in this unit to work to write your own fable, mystery, or both! You can:

- develop the writing you did in the Your Own Writing pages of the *Practice the Strategy Notebook*;

- pick an idea below and write something new;

- choose another idea of your own.

Be sure to follow the steps in the writing process. Use the rubrics in this unit to assess your writing.

Fable
• a fable set in another country
• a fable set in another time period
• a fable about an important event in United States history
• a fable about an important event in your state

Mystery
• a mystery involving a famous person
• a mystery about a famous place in the world
• a mystery about traveling back in history
• a mystery about an event in history

portfolio

School–Home Connection

Keep a writing portfolio. Think about adding the activities from the *Practice the Strategy Notebook* to your writing portfolio. You may want to take your portfolio home to share.

Your Own Writing Narrative Writing for Social Studies

Assign either one or both genres to the students. Before they begin writing, review key information about each genre. Decide whether you wish students to:

- Choose one of the topics on this page in the Student Edition.
- Complete one of the pieces they partially drafted in the Your Own Writing pages in the *Practice the Strategy Notebook*.
- Generate a completely new idea.

Portfolio/School-Home Connection

Encourage the students to keep portfolios of their writing. You may also wish to duplicate and distribute the School-Home Letter included in this unit.

Work-in-Progress Portfolio

Remind students to review this portfolio often to revise existing pieces that have not been published. Encourage students to share pieces of their Work-in-Progress Portfolios with family members who can help in editing.

Published Portfolio

Encourage students to choose pieces from their Published Portfolios to share with family members.

Name _____

for the **Writing Classroom**

Make a Test

Hey! Are you tired of taking tests designed by your teacher? Wouldn't you like to know the questions and answers ahead of time? Then do something about it! Design your own test and answer key with your classmates. Make sure you include important points and clearly state your questions and answers.

Name _____ Date _____

1. **Discuss important points of the lesson(s).** Your teacher will discuss the important points of the lesson(s). You need to include questions about these points on your test. Take good notes below.

   _____

   _____

   _____

   _____

2. **Assign team roles:** Leader, Recorder, Attender

   One person should be the **leader.** The leader makes sure everyone is on task.

   Two people should be the **recorders.** The recorders take notes and should be good writers.

   One person should be the **attender.** The attender makes sure everyone participates, is positive, and uses a 12-inch voice.

3. **Decide what type(s) of questions you want on your test**—matching, true/false, etc. Your teacher may instruct you to include an essay question. Essay-question answers are good ways to show off your writing skills.

4. **Make the test.** At the top of your test, write the names of all team members and the title of your test.

   • Now, with your team choose the questions you want on the test.

   • On one piece of paper, record the questions. On another piece of paper, write the answers. Make sure the numbers of the questions and answers match.

   • When your team has completed the test, collect everyone's notes and staple them to the back of your test and answer key.

   • Turn in all work to your teacher.

Purpose: To gain student input in designing assignments. See page T134 for more information.
This page may be duplicated for classroom use.

PERSUASIVE writing

tries to convince the reader of something.

1 Book Review

2 Letter to the Editor

Defining Persuasive Writing

Begin by writing on the chalkboard the following sentences:

- A golden retriever is a large, furry dog known for its friendly personality.

- I want to tell you about the time Archie, my golden retriever, went on a camping trip with our family.

- Golden retrievers often serve as guide dogs for blind people, while collies and beagles usually do not.

Then have students review the definition of *persuasive writing* on Student Page 185. Point out that two sentences on the board are informative and one is narrative, suggesting that the writer is about to tell a story. None is persuasive. Have students suggest some persuasive sentences on the same subject. Add them to the board. [**Possible example: There are many reasons why the golden retriever is the best breed of dog in the world.**]

Discuss with students how the sentences differ and how they are alike. Conclude by saying that students will learn and practice two forms of persuasive writing: a book review and a letter to the editor.

Read the unit opener (Student Page 185) with students. Ask for or provide other examples of persuasive writing.

 **for the Writing Classroom**

by Ken Stewart, *Master Teacher*

Interdisciplinary Units and Meaningful Writing

In an interdisciplinary unit, two or more educational disciplines are connected to improve and reinforce student learning. The more educational disciplines that are connected, the more meaningful the learning becomes. Students need to understand that information in one classroom is valuable not only in all classrooms but also in the world outside school. For this reason, your interdisciplinary units should attempt to include as many subject areas as possible and must include a segment that connects all of the learning to "real" life.

Too often in classrooms, opportunities to connect what we are reading and writing about slip by. We fail to bridge the gap between "classroom learning" (i.e., learning that our students do not take beyond the classroom) and "meaningful learning" (i.e., learning that our students retain).

Once we begin to tie every lesson together within our own classroom, it naturally follows to look for links outside the

Book Review

Writing Strategies

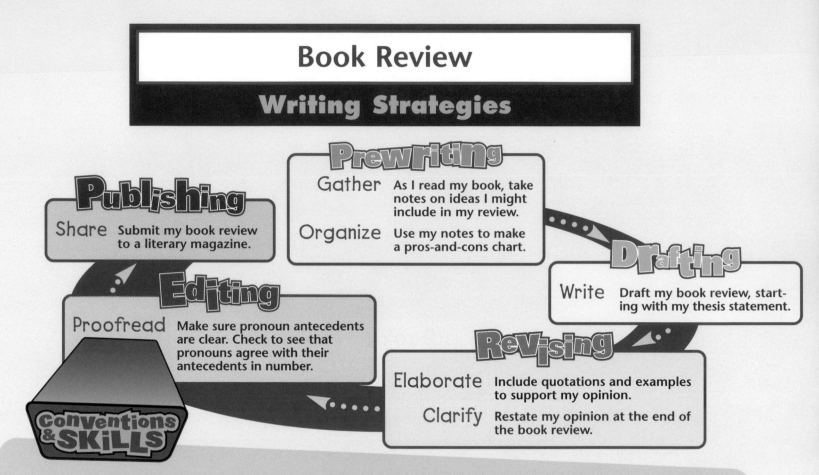

Prewriting

Gather — As I read my book, take notes on ideas I might include in my review.

Organize — Use my notes to make a pros-and-cons chart.

Publishing

Share — Submit my book review to a literary magazine.

Drafting

Write — Draft my book review, starting with my thesis statement.

Editing

Proofread — Make sure pronoun antecedents are clear. Check to see that pronouns agree with their antecedents in number.

Revising

Elaborate — Include quotations and examples to support my opinion.

Clarify — Restate my opinion at the end of the book review.

Conventions & SKILLS

Before the students read the model on Student Page 187, you may wish to review the targeted grammar convention. Remind students that an **antecedent** is the word or phrase a **pronoun** replaces. The antecedent of a pronoun must be clear and must agree with the pronoun in number. That is, a singular antecedent requires a singular pronoun. A plural antecedent must have a plural pronoun.

Examples: **Unclear Antecedent: Julie** told **Cheryl** that **she** had made the team. (Does *she* refer to *Julie* or *Cheryl*?)

Clear Antecedent: Julie said that **she** had made the team. (*She* clearly refers to *Julie.*)

Incorrect: A blind **person** learns to work with **their** guide dogs. (*Person* is singular, but *their* is plural.)

Correct: Blind **people** learn to work with **their** guide dogs. (*People* and *their* are both plural.)

Skill Assessment: To pre-assess your students' understanding of pronouns and antecedents, you may wish to have them complete the corresponding lesson on Student Pages CS 18–CS 19 in the back of the Student Edition.

Skill Mini-Lesson: The Proofread activity in this chapter can be used as a mini-lesson on the targeted **grammar, usage,** or **mechanics** skill.

classroom in order to construct interdisciplinary units. For example, when teaching about a story or novel, teachers need to provide avenues that allow students to connect in-class learning to real-life situations. Encourage your students to:

1. see the connection between the elements that make a story or novel effective and those that will improve their own creative or narrative writing.

2. discuss themes and relate them to their personal lives or to events in society in order to consciously see a relationship.

3. take this knowledge and apply it in other subject areas and in real-life situations.

4. analyze and debate, from different points of view, numerous solutions to problems or how to accomplish tasks.

5. evaluate their decisions and/or products for effectiveness or quality.

Every lesson should be planned so your students see that what is being taught is worthwhile and beneficial to them. When your students accept the idea that nothing is taught or learned in isolation, they will want to learn and will become more engaged in the whole process of planning and evaluating lessons. Learning becomes a life-long, meaningful experience.

(See "More Tips for the Writing Classroom: Designing an Interdisciplinary Project," page T149.)

Time Management for This Chapter*

Session		Session		Session	
1	Discuss the book review genre, and review the questions (Student Page 186). Read the review of *And Now Miguel* (Student Page 187). Use the questions to analyze the book review and use the rubric to assess it.	**6**	Read and discuss **DRAFTING: Write** (Student Pages 196–197).	**11**	Assign *Practice the Strategy Notebook* page 100. Encourage students to use the targeted strategy to revise a piece of their own writing.
2	Introduce Jared (Student Page 193) as a student-writer working on a book review. Read and discuss **PREWRITING: Gather** (Student Page 194).	**7**	Assign *Practice the Strategy Notebook* page 98. Encourage students to use the targeted strategy in their own writing.	**12**	Read and discuss **EDITING: Proofread** (Student Pages 200–201).
3	Assign *Practice the Strategy Notebook* pages 94–95. Encourage students to use the targeted strategy in their own writing.	**8**	Read and discuss **REVISING: Elaborate** (Student Page 198).	**13**	Assign *Practice the Strategy Notebook* page 101. Encourage students to use the targeted strategy to edit a piece of their own writing.
4	Read and discuss **PREWRITING: Organize** (Student Page 195). Discuss the purpose and mechanics of a pros-and-cons chart and analyze Jared's chart.	**9**	Assign *Practice the Strategy Notebook* page 99. Encourage students to use the targeted strategy to revise a piece of their own writing.	**14**	Read and discuss **PUBLISHING: Share** (Student Pages 202–205). Discuss other ways Jared could share his book review.
5	Assign *Practice the Strategy Notebook* pages 96–97. Encourage students to use the targeted strategy in their own writing.	**10**	Read and discuss **REVISING: Clarify** (Student Page 199).	**15**	Review the rubric for this chapter (reprinted on *Practice the Strategy Notebook* pages 102–103). Ask pairs of students to use the rubric to discuss and evaluate Jared's book review.

WRITER'S HANDBOOK

Remind students that they can refer to the Writer's Handbook in the back of the Student Edition for more information.

*To complete the chapter in fewer sessions, assign the *Practice the Strategy Notebook* pages on the same day the targeted strategy is introduced.

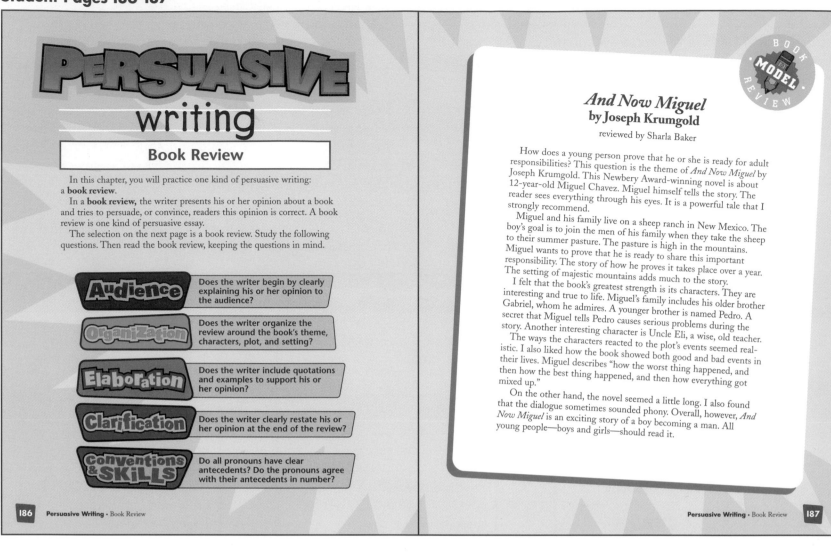

PERSUASIVE writing

Book Review

In this chapter, you will practice one kind of persuasive writing: a **book review**.

In a **book review,** the writer presents his or her opinion about a book and tries to persuade, or convince, readers this opinion is correct. A book review is one kind of persuasive essay.

The selection on the next page is a book review. Study the following questions. Then read the book review, keeping the questions in mind.

Audience Does the writer begin by clearly explaining his or her opinion to the audience?

Organization Does the writer organize the review around the book's theme, characters, plot, and setting?

Elaboration Does the writer include quotations and examples to support his or her opinion?

Clarification Does the writer clearly restate his or her opinion at the end of the review?

Conventions & Skills Do all pronouns have clear antecedents? Do the pronouns agree with their antecedents in number?

186   **Persuasive Writing** · Book Review

And Now Miguel
by Joseph Krumgold

reviewed by Sharla Baker

How does a young person prove that he or she is ready for adult responsibilities? This question is the theme of *And Now Miguel* by Joseph Krumgold. This Newbery Award-winning novel is about 12-year-old Miguel Chavez. Miguel himself tells the story. The reader sees everything through his eyes. It is a powerful tale that I strongly recommend.

Miguel and his family live on a sheep ranch in New Mexico. The boy's goal is to join the men of his family when they take the sheep to their summer pasture. The pasture is high in the mountains. Miguel wants to prove that he is ready to share this important responsibility. The story of how he proves it takes place over a year. The setting of majestic mountains adds much to the story.

I felt that the book's greatest strength is its characters. They are interesting and true to life. Miguel's family includes his older brother Gabriel, whom he admires. A younger brother is named Pedro. A secret that Miguel tells Pedro causes serious problems during the story. Another interesting character is Uncle Eli, a wise, old teacher.

The ways the characters reacted to the plot's events seemed realistic. I also liked how the book showed both good and bad events in their lives. Miguel describes "how the worst thing happened, and then how the best thing happened, and then how everything got mixed up."

On the other hand, the novel seemed a little long. I also found that the dialogue sometimes sounded phony. Overall, however, *And Now Miguel* is an exciting story of a boy becoming a man. All young people—boys and girls—should read it.

Persuasive Writing · Book Review   187

Introduce the Genre:
Book Review

Ask students to read the description of a book review on Student Page 186. Have them identify the purpose of a book review, which is one kind of persuasive writing. [**Response: It gives an opinion about a book and tries to persuade readers that this opinion is correct.**] Then ask students what kinds of information they would like to get from a book review. [**Possible responses: whether a book is worth reading, whether they might like it, what the book's strengths and weaknesses are, what books it is similar to**]

Conclude by telling students that they are going to study and practice strategies for writing a book review.

Discuss the Questions

(Student Page 186)

Read the questions on Student Page 186 aloud. Explain the importance of each category in creating a good piece of writing. Here are possible guidelines for this discussion:

Audience: In this genre, the writer's goal is to explain his or her opinion clearly and then convince the audience that this opinion is correct.

Organization: Most reviews mention the book's theme, characters, plot, and setting, but they might emphasize one of these more than the others.

Elaboration: The audience will be more likely to accept the writer's opinion if the opinion is supported with quotations and examples.

Clarification: Good writers make their opinions clear by restating them at the end of the review.

Conventions & Skills: Good writers always make sure that pronouns and their antecedents are clearly linked and agree in number.

Read the Model:
Book Review

(Student Page 187)

Read the book review of *And Now Miguel* aloud.

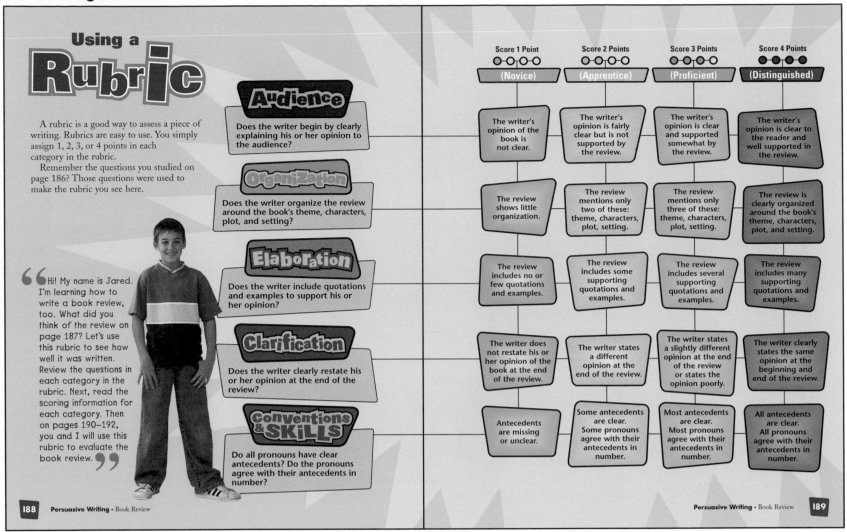

Using a Rubric

(Student Pages 188–189)

Use the text on Student Pages 190–192 to model how to use the rubric to assess the book review. If you need more general information about using a rubric, please see page T22.

Raising Rubric Awareness

by Lee Bromberger, *Assessment Specialist*

As teachers work hard to incorporate rubrics into their classroom routine, they must also recognize the need to continue to promote their rubric assessments outside the classroom.

With each assignment utilizing a new rubric, teachers should consider forwarding a copy of the rubric to the students' homes. (In *Strategies for Writers*, a copy of the rubric for each chapter is in the *Practice the Strategy Notebook*. This copy may be duplicated and sent home.) Teachers may also wish to include an explanatory letter with the rubric. As the level of expectation for student work increases, students' families should be made aware of the new standards and the ways in which they will be implemented through rubric assessment. Teachers may also wish to include an explanation of these changes, as well as the role (if appropriate) students played in developing the new rubric.

Another effective technique teachers can use to raise rubric awareness outside the classroom is to appear before a

parent-teacher organization meeting. One or more teachers could present rubrics to parents and perhaps even demonstrate using a rubric to evaluate a piece of writing. Such appearances educate parents while also establishing an appropriate focus on grade-level curriculum.

Internally, efforts can also be made to increase rubric awareness. For example, collecting rubrics from other resources, including non-educational venues such as supermarkets or restaurants, will help other educators focus on rubrics. Teachers can study these other rubrics and find the means by which to improve rubrics already in use, as well as further insight as they develop new rubrics.

Setting aside model writings and their accompanying rubrics throughout an entire school year can establish a rubric reference guide. These papers, which should fall across the rubric scale from "Novice" to "Distinguished," may be assembled into a binder for teacher reference in the future. These *anchor papers* will offer benchmarks by which teachers can gauge their own effectiveness as they become comfortable with implementing rubrics in their classrooms. In addition, other faculty members can use these papers on staff curriculum (i.e., in-service) work days.

Increasing awareness of rubrics can be as important as the development and implementation of the rubrics themselves. Notification, publication, and discussion of rubrics outside the classroom can go a long way to help assert the validity of rubric evaluation within the classroom.

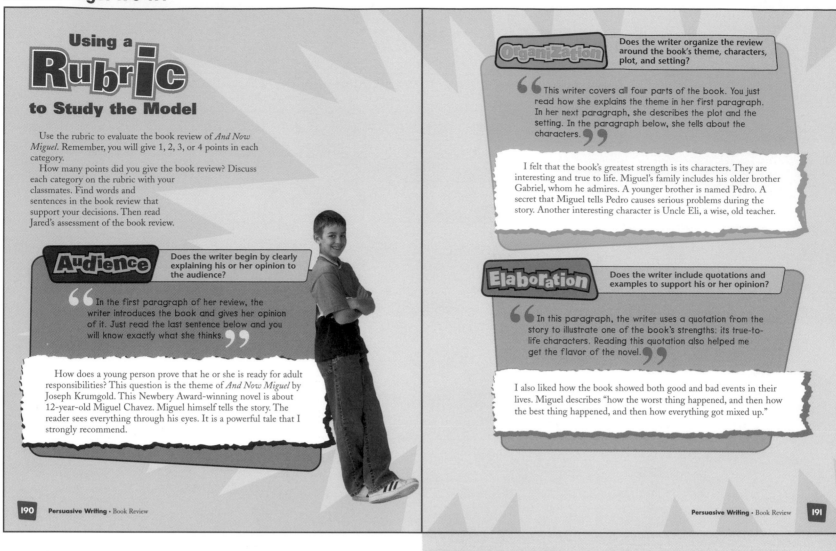

Using a Rubric to Study the Model

Use the rubric to evaluate the book review of *And Now Miguel*. Remember, you will give 1, 2, 3, or 4 points in each category.

How many points did you give the book review? Discuss each category on the rubric with your classmates. Find words and sentences in the book review that support your decisions. Then read Jared's assessment of the book review.

Audience

Does the writer begin by clearly explaining his or her opinion to the audience?

" In the first paragraph of her review, the writer introduces the book and gives her opinion of it. Just read the last sentence below and you will know exactly what she thinks. "

How does a young person prove that he or she is ready for adult responsibilities? This question is the theme of *And Now Miguel* by Joseph Krumgold. This Newbery Award-winning novel is about 12-year-old Miguel Chavez. Miguel himself tells the story. The reader sees everything through his eyes. It is a powerful tale that I strongly recommend.

Organization

Does the writer organize the review around the book's theme, characters, plot, and setting?

" This writer covers all four parts of the book. You just read how she explains the theme in her first paragraph. In her next paragraph, she describes the plot and the setting. In the paragraph below, she tells about the characters. "

I felt that the book's greatest strength is its characters. They are interesting and true to life. Miguel's family includes his older brother Gabriel, whom he admires. A younger brother is named Pedro. A secret that Miguel tells Pedro causes serious problems during the story. Another interesting character is Uncle Eli, a wise, old teacher.

Elaboration

Does the writer include quotations and examples to support his or her opinion?

" In this paragraph, the writer uses a quotation from the story to illustrate one of the book's strengths: its true-to-life characters. Reading this quotation also helped me get the flavor of the novel. "

I also liked how the book showed both good and bad events in their lives. Miguel describes "how the worst thing happened, and then how the best thing happened, and then how everything got mixed up."

Using a Rubric to Study the Model

(Student Pages 190–192)

Read the questions and answers on Student Pages 190–192. Discuss whether students agree or disagree with Jared's assessment of the book review. For example, do students agree that the writer reviewed the plot, theme, characters, and setting of *And Now Miguel*? Would they have organized this discussion differently? How?

Note on Conventions & Skills: Remind students that they should always check their writing for spelling, punctuation, and capitalization. In addition, this lesson will help them focus on matching pronouns and their antecedents.

Meeting Students' Needs:
Second Language Learners

Have pairs of students read book reviews from an appropriate source. Have them list words they do not understand and then take turns looking them up in a dictionary. Have all pairs then share their new words in a group discussion.

Students Who Need Extra Help

Ask students to access the reader book reviews of amazon.com or another on-line bookstore. Ask them to read the reviews of five books. Then have them use the reviews to rank the books from the one they would most like to read to the one they would least like to read. Have students explain how the book reviews helped them make their decisions.

Gifted Students

Have students find a published review of a book they have read. Perhaps the school or community librarian can help them locate one. Then have them present a critique of the review to the class, explaining ways that they agree and disagree with the reviewer.

Clarification — Does the writer clearly restate his or her opinion at the end of the review?

"In the last paragraph, the writer mentions two weaknesses of the book but still urges people to read it. There is no doubt that she liked this story. After reading her review, I think I would, too."

On the other hand, the novel seemed a little long. I also found that the dialogue sometimes sounded phony. Overall, however, *And Now Miguel* is an exciting story of a boy becoming a man. All young people—boys and girls—should read it.

Conventions & Skills — Do all pronouns have clear antecedents? Do the pronouns agree with their antecedents in number?

"The writer made sure that all pronouns agree with their antecedents in number. In the very first paragraph, for example, she is careful with a tricky antecedent. Because a **young person** is singular, the writer has to use **he** or **she** as the pronoun, not **they**."

How does a young person prove that he or she is ready for adult responsibilities? This question is the theme of *And Now Miguel* by Joseph Krumgold.

"Now it's my turn to write!

I'm going to write my own book review. Follow along, and you will see how I use good writing strategies. I will also use the model book review and the rubric to guide my writing."

192 **Persuasive Writing** · Book Review

Jared
Writer of a Book Review

Name:	Jared
Home:	California
Hobbies:	reading about history, mountain biking, camping
Favorite Food:	anything cooked over a campfire!
Assignment:	book review

193

Unlocking Text Structure:
Book Review

The structure of a piece of writing depends on how the information it contains is organized. To help students unlock the structure of the book review, you may want to refer them to the graphic organizer in this chapter, a pros-and-cons chart. This kind of chart is appropriate for persuasive writing because it establishes both a *parallel* text structure and an *analytical* one. Help students understand that in a book review, the writer may choose to present a strength and then a weakness (parallel structure) or first discuss strengths and then weaknesses (a kind of analytical structure). Ask students to determine which kind of structure Jared's review uses. **[analytical]**

Jared:
Writer of a Book Review

(Student Page 193)

Read the information about Jared.

Remind students that he is going to write his own book review. Ask them to speculate on what book Jared might choose to write about. Do they know any specific books that are related to his interests?

Point out that Jared will complete the steps in the writing process: Prewriting, Drafting, Revising, Editing, and Publishing. At each stage, he will demonstrate a good writing strategy and explain how he used it. Students should watch for key words, including **Gather, Organize, Write, Elaborate, Clarify, Proofread,** and **Share**.

Prewriting

Gather
As I read my book, take notes on ideas I might include in my review.

"After my teacher, Mrs. Summers, asked us to write a book review, I just couldn't find a book that seemed interesting. Then Mrs. Summers suggested The Arrow Over the Door by Joseph Bruchac. One of the main characters is a Quaker. I had mentioned in class one day that I am a Quaker, and Mrs. Summers remembered!

"The book is based on a real event that happened during the American Revolution. After I read the jacket copy, I really wanted to read the book. As I read, I took notes about ideas I might want to use in my review."

Notes on The Arrow Over the Door
by Joseph Bruchac

- Story takes place in 1777 during the Revolutionary War near Saratoga, (upstate) NY.
- Samuel Russell is young Quaker boy.
- Stands Straight is Abenaki Indian boy.
- Story is told from each boy's point of view.
- Theme: each boy learns about himself, his own strengths, and his people's beliefs.
- Plot follows Quakers and Indians until they finally meet.
- Story contains much interesting information about Quaker and Abenaki traditions and beliefs.

Go to page 94 in the **Practice the Strategy Notebook!**

Prewriting

Organize
Use my notes to make a pros-and-cons chart.

"After reviewing my notes, I decided to make a pros-and-cons chart. It will help me figure out what I liked and disliked about The Arrow Over the Door. A pros-and-cons chart can also help me make sure I cover the book's theme, characters, plot, and setting, like the **Rubric** suggests."

Pros-and-Cons Chart

A **pros-and-cons chart** shows the positive points (pros) and negative points (cons) about a topic or issue.

	Pros (what I liked)	Cons (what I disliked)
Plot	Two people tell a story, and the stories come together at the end.	Book ended too soon; I wanted to know what the boys did as the war continued.
Theme	Each boy questions his own beliefs but comes to understand them better.	
Setting	The author uses the setting—upstate New York—to show the loneliness but also the friendliness of the wilderness.	
Characters	I learned how the two boys are similar and different.	
Language	The author made the Abenaki and Quaker speech different.	
Other	I learned interesting details about Quakers and Abenakis; the author himself is Abenaki.	Author could have told more about some of the other characters.

Go to page 96 in the **Practice the Strategy Notebook!**

Prewriting Gather

Strategy: As I read my book, take notes on ideas I might include in my review.

(Student Page 194)

Read Jared's words aloud. Ask students how he organized his notes. [**Possible response: The list is organized by plot, setting, characters, and theme.**]

Refer to the Rubric: The student spokesperson will refer to the rubric throughout the chapter. Remind students to get into the habit of referring back to the rubric so they fully understand its use as a tool for shaping their writing.

Practice the Strategy Notebook!

Assign pages 94–95 in the *Practice the Strategy Notebook.* (Your Own Writing sections should be used as time and students' abilities permit.) Explain that the students will practice this Gather strategy with a book of their own choosing.

Prewriting Organize

Strategy: Use my notes to make a pros-and-cons chart.

(Student Page 195)

Explain that a graphic organizer such as a pros-and-cons chart is one way to organize information in preparation for writing. Review the attributes of a pros-and-cons chart. Then have students examine and comment on Jared's chart.

Practice the Strategy Notebook!

Assign pages 96–97 in the *Practice the Strategy Notebook.* If you wish, have students share with their partners the pros-and-cons charts they create. Suggested responses for the *Practice the Strategy Notebook* appear in the Appendix in the back of this Teacher Edition.

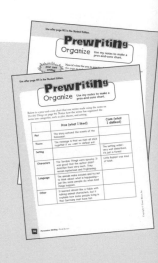

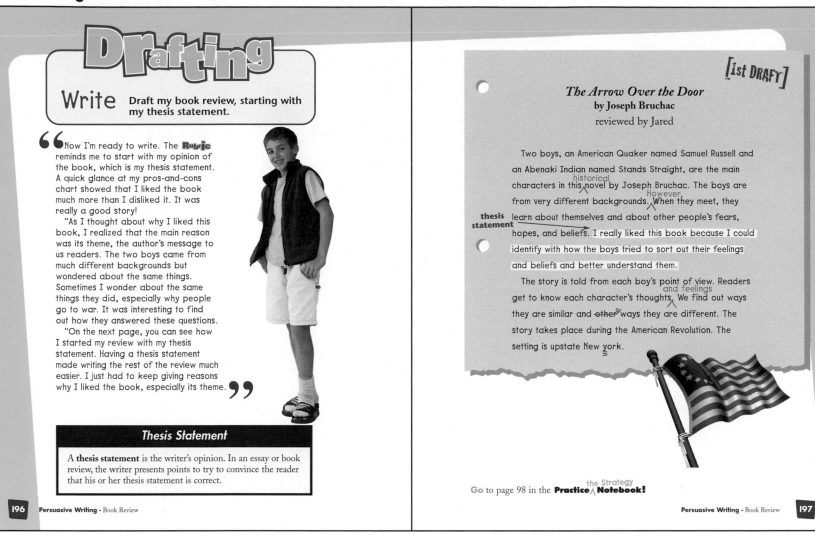

Drafting

Write — Draft my book review, starting with my thesis statement.

❝Now I'm ready to write. The **Rubric** reminds me to start with my opinion of the book, which is my thesis statement. A quick glance at my pros-and-cons chart showed that I liked the book much more than I disliked it. It was really a good story!

"As I thought about why I liked this book, I realized that the main reason was its theme, the author's message to us readers. The two boys came from much different backgrounds but wondered about the same things. Sometimes I wonder about the same things they did, especially why people go to war. It was interesting to find out how they answered these questions.

"On the next page, you can see how I started my review with my thesis statement. Having a thesis statement made writing the rest of the review much easier. I just had to keep giving reasons why I liked the book, especially its theme.❞

Thesis Statement

A **thesis statement** is the writer's opinion. In an essay or book review, the writer presents points to try to convince the reader that his or her thesis statement is correct.

[1st DRAFT]

The Arrow Over the Door
by Joseph Bruchac
reviewed by Jared

Two boys, an American Quaker named Samuel Russell and an Abenaki Indian named Stands Straight, are the main characters in this historical novel by Joseph Bruchac. The boys are from very different backgrounds. However, When they meet, they learn about themselves and about other people's fears, hopes, and beliefs. I really liked this book because I could identify with how the boys tried to sort out their feelings and beliefs and better understand them.

The story is told from each boy's point of view. Readers get to know each character's thoughts and feelings. We find out ways they are similar and other ways they are different. The story takes place during the American Revolution. The setting is upstate New york.

Go to page 98 in the **Practice the Strategy Notebook!**

Drafting Write

Strategy: Draft my book review, starting with my thesis statement.

(Student Pages 196–197)

Briefly review what it means to draft a piece of writing. Remind students that a draft will be changed and corrected several times before the piece of writing is finished. Ask a volunteer to read Jared's words aloud for the class.

Ask students what Jared will keep in mind as he writes his draft. [**Possible responses: He will refer to his pros-and-cons chart; he will write a thesis statement and keep rereading it to make sure his review supports it; he will do his best with spelling and grammar right now and concentrate on getting his ideas down.**]

Have students review the definition of a thesis statement. Have someone read aloud Jared's thesis statement in his draft.

Practice the Strategy Notebook!

Assign page 98 in the *Practice the Strategy Notebook*. Invite volunteers to read the opening paragraphs of their reviews. Have the class try to identify the thesis statement in each writer's paragraph.

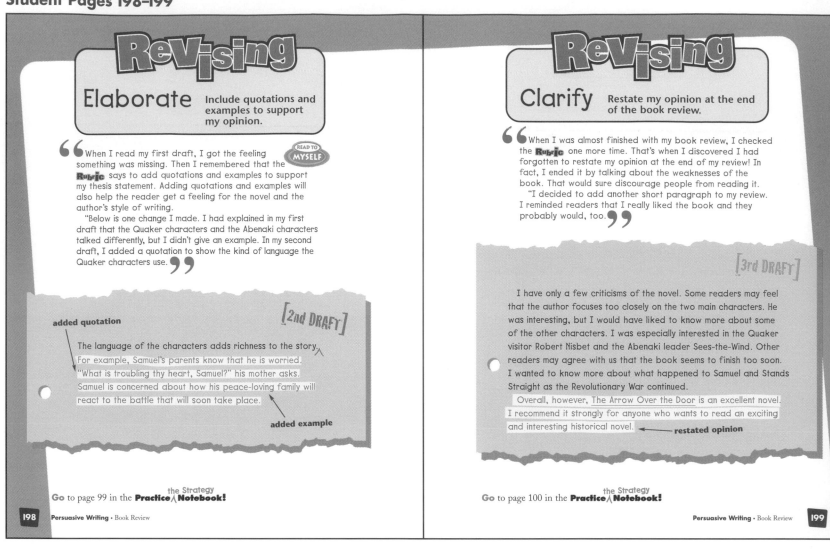

Revising Elaborate

Strategy: Include quotations and examples to support my opinion.

(Student Page 198)

Ask a student to read Jared's words to the class.

Discuss how quotations and examples add to a book review. **[Possible response: They support the writer's opinion, clarify it, and add interest.]** If you wish, ask students to write a statement about a book they have read. Then have them add an example or quotation that elaborates on the statement, following the model of Jared's review of *The Arrow Over the Door*.

Practice the Strategy Notebook!

Assign page 99 in the *Practice the Strategy Notebook*. Discuss where students think Jared needs to add examples or quotations. What kinds of information should he add?

Revising Clarify

Strategy: Restate my opinion at the end of the book review.

(Student Page 199)

Ask a student to read Jared's words to the class. Discuss how restating the writer's opinion strengthens and clarifies a book review. **[Possible responses: It reminds readers of your opinion and reinforces it; it helps make the book review convincing.]**

Practice the Strategy Notebook!

Assign page 100 in the *Practice the Strategy Notebook*. Have students discuss their reactions to each of the three conclusions and explain how they determined which was the best one.

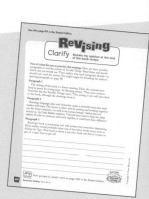

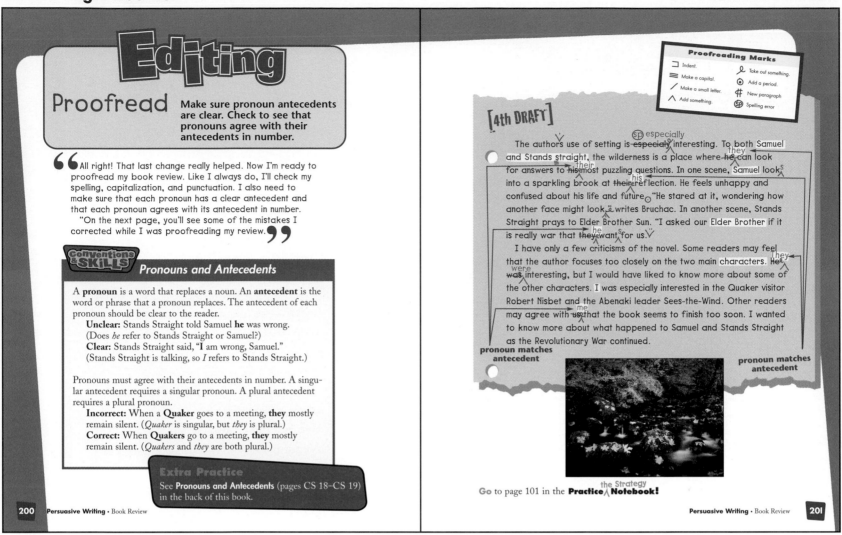

Editing

Proofread

Strategy: **Make sure pronoun antecedents are clear. Check to see that pronouns agree with their antecedents in number.**

(Student Pages 200–201)

Remind students that in the revising step they reread their drafts to look for ways to make them better organized, clearer, and more convincing. In the editing step, they look for mistakes in spelling, grammar, and punctuation.

Ask a volunteer to read Jared's words to the class. You might also discuss the fact that pronouns should agree with their antecedents in gender. *He* and *his* should refer to singular male nouns; *she* and *her* should refer to singular female nouns. Point out that students can avoid some problems by using plural nouns whenever possible: Good **writers** take **their** work seriously.

Extra Practice: Conventions & Skills Student Edition

If you did not use Student Pages CS 18–CS 19 as a pre-assessment, you may wish to assign those pages now.

Conventions & Skills Practice

For more targeted practice related to pronouns, see this lesson in the optional *Conventions & Skills Practice Book*:

Lesson 34: Pronoun Antecedents

the Strategy
Practice ∧ Notebook!

Assign page 101 in the *Practice the Strategy Notebook*. Have students point out the pronoun errors they corrected.

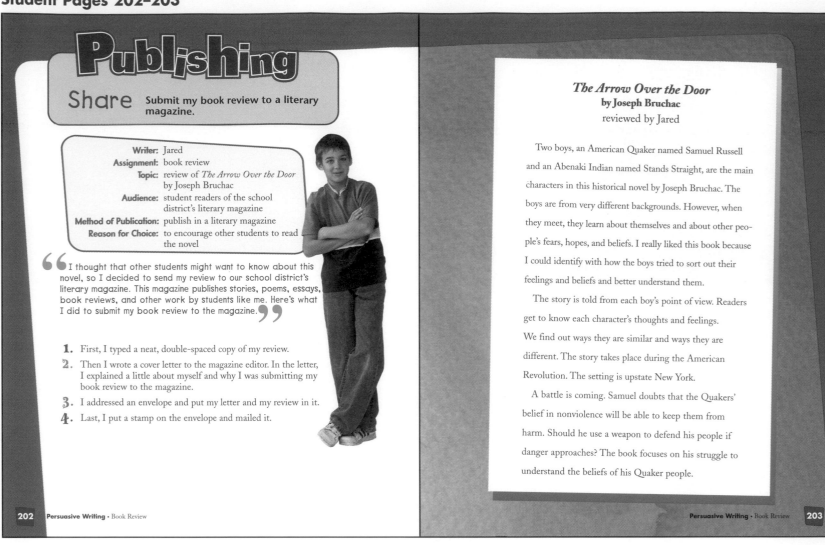

Publishing Share

Strategy: Submit my book review to a literary magazine.

(Student Pages 202–205)

Ask students to think of other ways that Jared could have shared his book review. Discuss whether they agree that this method was a suitable one.

Using the Rubric

Ask students to work in pairs to use the rubric (reprinted on pages 102–103 of the *Practice the Strategy Notebook*) to evaluate Jared's book review. After each pair has reached its decision, ask volunteers to share their evaluations.

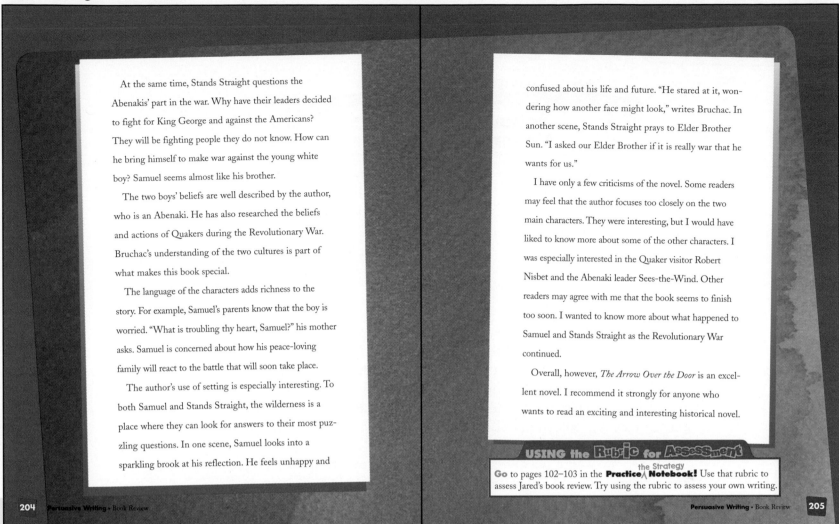

At the same time, Stands Straight questions the Abenakis' part in the war. Why have their leaders decided to fight for King George and against the Americans? They will be fighting people they do not know. How can he bring himself to make war against the young white boy? Samuel seems almost like his brother.

The two boys' beliefs are well described by the author, who is an Abenaki. He has also researched the beliefs and actions of Quakers during the Revolutionary War. Bruchac's understanding of the two cultures is part of what makes this book special.

The language of the characters adds richness to the story. For example, Samuel's parents know that the boy is worried. "What is troubling thy heart, Samuel?" his mother asks. Samuel is concerned about how his peace-loving family will react to the battle that will soon take place.

The author's use of setting is especially interesting. To both Samuel and Stands Straight, the wilderness is a place where they can look for answers to their most puzzling questions. In one scene, Samuel looks into a sparkling brook at his reflection. He feels unhappy and

confused about his life and future. "He stared at it, wondering how another face might look," writes Bruchac. In another scene, Stands Straight prays to Elder Brother Sun. "I asked our Elder Brother if it is really war that he wants for us."

I have only a few criticisms of the novel. Some readers may feel that the author focuses too closely on the two main characters. They were interesting, but I would have liked to know more about some of the other characters. I was especially interested in the Quaker visitor Robert Nisbet and the Abenaki leader Sees-the-Wind. Other readers may agree with me that the book seems to finish too soon. I wanted to know more about what happened to Samuel and Stands Straight as the Revolutionary War continued.

Overall, however, *The Arrow Over the Door* is an excellent novel. I recommend it strongly for anyone who wants to read an exciting and interesting historical novel.

USING the Rubic for Assessment

Go to pages 102–103 in the **Practice Notebook!** Use that rubric to assess Jared's book review. Try using the rubric to assess your own writing.

204 Persuasive Writing • Book Review

205 Persuasive Writing • Book Review

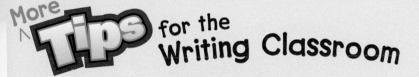

More Tips for the Writing Classroom

More Tips for the Writing Classroom: Designing an Interdisciplinary Project

Remember that in an interdisciplinary unit, two or more educational disciplines are connected to improve and reinforce student learning. With this in mind, always look for natural connections in all subject areas: math, science, language arts, social studies, foreign language, art, music, physical education and health, family and consumer sciences, and technology. As teachers, we can find connections with other disciplines and create units that show students that what they are learning is meaningful.

When planning an interdisciplinary project, follow these helpful hints:

1. Decide on an appropriate theme or topic for your grade level.

2. Establish your goals and objectives.

3. Decide how many disciplines the unit will encompass.

4. Meet with other teachers involved to get a general understanding of their goals and objectives.

5. Write out detailed lesson plans (with dates) including a culminating event that brings all disciplines together. (Each teacher must do this.)

6. Meet a second time with everyone involved to discuss specific plans and assignments.

7. Decide on your evaluation methods.

8. Present the unit to your students and ask for their suggestions.

School–Home Connection

Dear Family,

Our class is learning and practicing many different kinds of writing. Writing is an opportunity for people to express their thoughts and feelings, as well as a chance to communicate information to others.

Encourage your child to think of himself or herself as a writer. Every piece of written material your child produces brings him or her one step closer to being a good communicator and a person who thinks creatively. Your support and encouragement mean a great deal.

Celebrate your child's writing. Here are some easy and fun ways you can encourage your child to write.

- Create a quiet place for your child to write. Set aside a small space where your child can daydream, take notes, doodle, whatever. It doesn't have to be anything fancy—just a spot where your child can go that's just for writing.
- Participate in your child's writing efforts. Offer to be interviewed for a writing assignment. Your memories or experiences may prove very valuable to your young writer.
- Post your child's writing in a special place at home. A refrigerator door is a great place to publish your child's work. Another great idea is a simple bulletin board.
- Finally, encourage your child to read. It doesn't matter what topic interests your child. Whatever it is, there are books about it. Try your public library for a great selection of books on any topic. People who love to read often become people who love to write.

Try these simple but effective ways to help your child become a better writer. You'll be surprised at how well they work!

You may wish to copy the letter above and send it home with your students.

Books on Teaching Writing

Tompkins, Gail E. *Teaching Writing: Balancing Process and Product*. Upper Saddle River, NJ: Merrill, 2000.

This college textbook contains strong chapters on strategies and genres, including journal writing, letter writing, biographical writing, and poetry, along with expository, narrative, and persuasive writing. The ideas are presented as a writing workshop for teachers and include student samples.

Brusko, Mike. *Writing Rules!: Teaching Kids to Write for Life, Grades 4–8*. Portsmouth, NH: Heinemann, 1999.

The author focuses on the writing skills that students need in their everyday lives. He pays special attention to clarifying the purpose for writing and getting the readers' attention. This second skill is especially useful in persuasive writing.

Bromley, Karen, Linda Irwin-De Vitis, and Marcia Modlo. *Graphic Organizers: Visual Strategies for Active Learning*. New York: Scholastic, 1995.

The authors provide tips on using graphic organizers in teaching across the curriculum. They also describe organizing techniques that students can use to plan their writing in the content areas, including various genres of persuasive writing.

Lane, Barry. *After the End: Teaching and Learning Creative Revision*. Portsmouth, NH: Heinemann, 1993.

This author stresses the importance of helping students take charge of their own writing. This "idea book" for upper elementary through high school contains two parts: "Creating a Language of Craft" and "The Writer's Struggle." It guides teachers in using revision techniques as part of the writing process and in dealing with specific revision problems. This source is loaded with writing examples and techniques for stimulating students' writing and revising.

 **for the Writing Classroom**

by Ken Stewart, *Master Teacher*

Using Videos to Inspire Student Writing

We all enjoy watching movies, and your students are no different. If used correctly, videos can inspire student writing and lead to real learning. As you know, we live in a visually oriented world. Students grow up watching commercials, MTV, movies, and computer screens and playing video games. You can tap into the visual medium as a way of teaching your students that there is more to the world than these

visual electronics. Your students will accept the learning if it is not forced; let it flow naturally. Let them enjoy the show and see that learning can be fun.

To be successful, you must have a clear understanding of your objectives. Choose a "fun" video that fits what you want to teach. For example, if you want your students to understand the literary elements that make a story or novel interesting, focus your video lesson plans on character development, setting, plot, and climax. Then when your students read novels or stories, point out the relationship between the story elements in printed literature and in video "literature." Eventually, relate this learning to your students' creative writings.

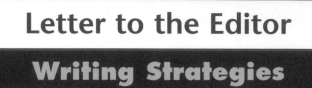

Letter to the Editor

Writing Strategies

Prewriting

Gather — Use what I read and learn from others to form an opinion about a topic.

Organize — Make an outline to focus and support my opinion.

Drafting

Write — Draft my letter to the editor. State my opinion, support it, and sum up my argument.

Revising

Elaborate — Add reasons and facts to support my opinion.

Clarify — Add signal words to clarify my ideas.

Editing

Proofread — Check that I have written all six parts of a business letter correctly and that there are no sentence fragments.

Conventions & SKILLS

Publishing

Share — Submit my essay to a newspaper or magazine.

Before the students read the model on Student Page 207, you may wish to review the targeted **grammar, usage,** or **mechanics** convention. Remind students that every complete sentence has a subject and a verb and states a complete thought.

A **sentence fragment** is a group of words that begins with a capital letter and ends with a period or other end punctuation but does not state a complete thought. It might be missing a subject or a verb.

Example: **Sentence fragment:** Are performing an important service. (has a verb but no subject)

Complete sentence: By recycling, people are performing an important service. (has a subject and a verb and is a complete thought)

Skill Assessment: To pre-assess your students' understanding of the targeted convention, you may wish to have them complete the corresponding lesson on Student Pages CS 20–CS 21 in the back of the Student Edition.

Skill Mini-Lesson: The Proofread activity in this chapter can be used as a mini-lesson on the targeted **grammar, usage,** or **mechanics** skill.

When students better understand story elements, they will develop exciting characters that their readers will care about. Their plots will be better developed with interesting conflicts and cliff-hanging climaxes that lead to unique solutions, and they will develop settings that paint colorful, detailed pictures for their readers.

Remember to choose videos that can help you teach curriculum objectives. Use videos to help improve students' vocabulary, understanding of literary terms, note-taking skills, outlining skills, journal writing, etc. Videos can become powerful learning tools if you plan effectively.

Note: Make sure you do not overuse videos in the classroom. (See "More Tips for the Writing Classroom: Journal Writing Using Videos," page T162.)

Time Management for This Chapter*

Session		Session		Session	
1	Discuss persuasive writing and the letter to the editor genre; review the questions (Student Page 206). Read the letter to the editor about recycling (Student Page 207). Use the questions to analyze the letter, and use the rubric to assess it.	**6**	Read and discuss **DRAFTING: Write** (Student Pages 216–217).	**11**	Assign *Practice the Strategy Notebook* page 111. Encourage students to use the targeted strategy to revise a piece of their own writing.
2	Introduce Halle (Student Page 213) as a student-writer working on a letter to the editor. Read and discuss **PREWRITING: Gather** (Student Page 214).	**7**	Assign *Practice the Strategy Notebook* pages 108–109. Encourage students to use the targeted strategy in their own writing.	**12**	Read and discuss **EDITING: Proofread** (Student Pages 220–221).
3	Assign *Practice the Strategy Notebook* pages 104–105. Encourage students to use the targeted strategy in their own writing.	**8**	Read and discuss **REVISING: Elaborate** (Student Page 218).	**13**	Assign *Practice the Strategy Notebook* pages 112–113. Encourage students to use the targeted strategy to edit a piece of their own writing.
4	Read and discuss **PREWRITING: Organize** (Student Page 215). Discuss the purpose and mechanics of an outline and analyze Halle's outline.	**9**	Assign *Practice the Strategy Notebook* page 110. Encourage students to use the targeted strategy to revise a piece of their own writing.	**14**	Read and discuss **PUBLISHING: Share** (Student Pages 222–223). Discuss other ways Halle could share her letter.
5	Assign *Practice the Strategy Notebook* pages 106–107. Encourage students to use the targeted strategy in their own writing.	**10**	Read and discuss **REVISING: Clarify** (Student Page 219).	**15**	Review the rubric for this chapter (reprinted on *Practice the Strategy Notebook* pages 114–115). Ask pairs of students to use the rubric to discuss and evaluate Halle's letter to the editor.

WRITER'S HANDBOOK

Remind students that they can refer to the Writer's Handbook in the back of the Student Edition for more information.

*To complete the chapter in fewer sessions, assign the *Practice the Strategy Notebook* pages on the same day the targeted strategy is introduced.

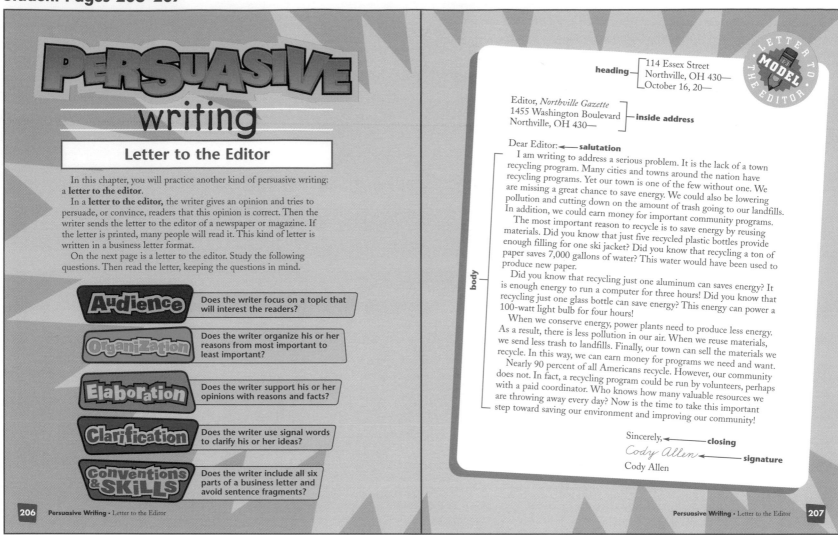

Introduce the Genre:
Letter to the Editor

Ask students to read the description of a letter to the editor on Student Page 206. Have them explain the purpose of a letter to the editor. [**Response: to present an opinion and persuade readers that it is correct**] Then ask volunteers to help you list subjects that would be appropriate for a letter to the editor. Have students brainstorm what a writer might say in a letter on several of the listed topics, as well as the kind of facts and reasons the writer could include to support his or her opinion.

Conclude by telling students that they are going to study and practice strategies for writing a letter to the editor.

Discuss the Questions

(Student Page 206)

Read the questions on Student Page 206 aloud. Here are some guidelines for this discussion:

Audience: In this genre, writers try to choose a topic they know will interest certain readers and send it to a newspaper or magazine that these people often read.

Organization: Organizing reasons from most important to least important places the reason with the most impact at the beginning of the letter. By doing this, writers increase their chances of persuading readers.

Elaboration: Writers should try to provide reasons and facts that the readers will find persuasive. Writers want to build on their readers' knowledge and interests.

Clarification: Signal words act as road signs to help readers follow the writer's explanations.

Conventions & Skills: Writers of effective letters to the editor include all six parts of a business letter and avoid sentence fragments.

Read the Model:
Letter to the Editor

(Student Page 207)

Read the letter about recycling aloud.

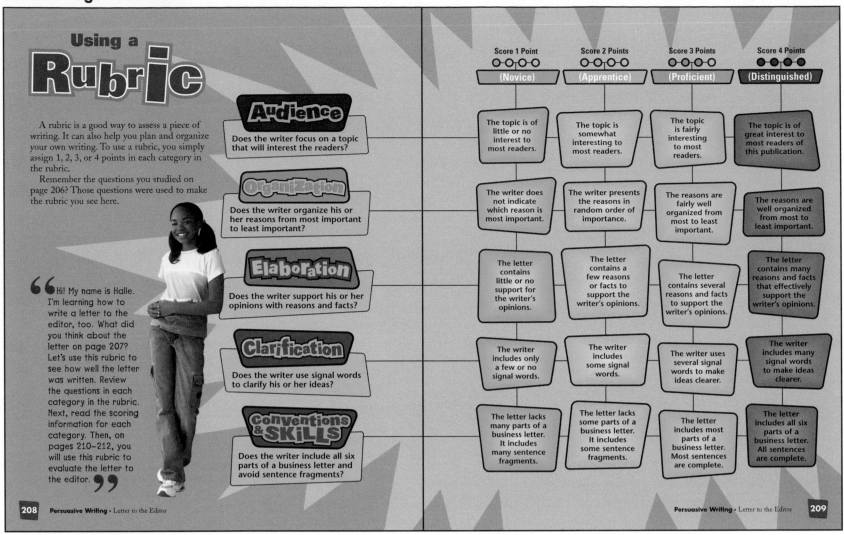

Using a Rubric

(Student Pages 208–209)

Use the text on Student Pages 210–212 to model how to use the rubric to assess the model letter to the editor. If you need more information about using a rubric, please see page T22.

Avoiding Rubric Pitfalls

by Lee Bromberger, *Assessment Specialist*

Avoiding the following pitfalls will help ensure the successful use of rubrics in any curriculum.

- **Pitfall:** Developing rubrics having an odd number of evaluative scales.

  Using rubrics based on a three- or a five-point scale only serves to encourage a middle choice, i.e., a "2" on a three-point scale or a "3" on a five-point scale. Choose even-numbered rubrics, such as the four-point rubric scale.

- **Pitfall:** Using rubric criteria that lack specificity and clarity.

  Failure to make clear distinctions when developing the rubric criteria leads to assessment difficulties. For example, classifying homophone errors as spelling errors and not usage errors could penalize a student for spelling and for usage, based on the same homophone error. Similarly, vague rubric criteria (e.g., "The paper is good.") are difficult to implement.

- **Pitfall:** Failing to review all rubrics with students before the rubric is used to assess student work.

  Students need to know the assignment expectations.

- **Pitfall:** Failing to train staff to utilize rubrics.

  When rubrics are implemented throughout a school, they lead to uniformity of assessment and consensus building among the teachers. Implementation should include training, evaluation, and discussion of rubrics and sample assessments.

- **Pitfall:** Failing to consistently implement rubrics and establish them as a routine element of the class.

  Students need to see the role that rubrics will play in the class curriculum. If rubrics become a once-in-a-while diversion, as opposed to a staple of assessment, students will fail to consider them as invaluable assets to help them improve the quality of their work.

- **Pitfall:** Failing to publicize rubric implementation.

  Positive publicity for your program gains the support of parents, administrators, school board members, and community members. Let everyone know the success of your new approach to student and curriculum assessment.

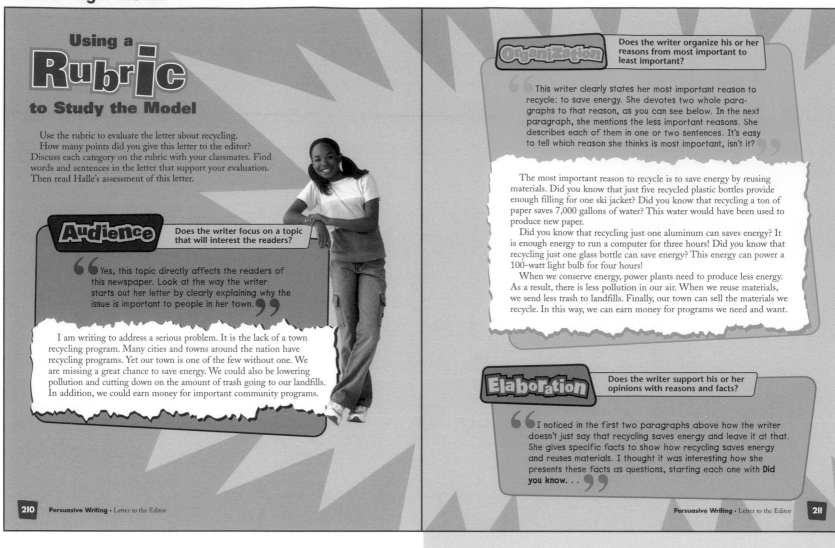

Using a Rubric to Study the Model

Use the rubric to evaluate the letter about recycling. How many points did you give this letter to the editor? Discuss each category on the rubric with your classmates. Find words and sentences in the letter that support your evaluation. Then read Halle's assessment of this letter.

Audience
Does the writer focus on a topic that will interest the readers?

Yes, this topic directly affects the readers of this newspaper. Look at the way the writer starts out her letter by clearly explaining why the issue is important to people in her town.

I am writing to address a serious problem. It is the lack of a town recycling program. Many cities and towns around the nation have recycling programs. Yet our town is one of the few without one. We are missing a great chance to save energy. We could also be lowering pollution and cutting down on the amount of trash going to our landfills. In addition, we could earn money for important community programs.

Organization
Does the writer organize his or her reasons from most important to least important?

This writer clearly states her most important reason to recycle: to save energy. She devotes two whole paragraphs to that reason, as you can see below. In the next paragraph, she mentions the less important reasons. She describes each of them in one or two sentences. It's easy to tell which reason she thinks is most important, isn't it?

The most important reason to recycle is to save energy by reusing materials. Did you know that just five recycled plastic bottles provide enough filling for one ski jacket? Did you know that recycling a ton of paper saves 7,000 gallons of water? This water would have been used to produce new paper.

Did you know that recycling just one aluminum can saves energy? It is enough energy to run a computer for three hours! Did you know that recycling just one glass bottle can save energy? This energy can power a 100-watt light bulb for four hours!

When we conserve energy, power plants need to produce less energy. As a result, there is less pollution in our air. When we reuse materials, we send less trash to landfills. Finally, our town can sell the materials we recycle. In this way, we can earn money for programs we need and want.

Elaboration
Does the writer support his or her opinions with reasons and facts?

I noticed in the first two paragraphs above how the writer doesn't just say that recycling saves energy and leave it at that. She gives specific facts to show how recycling saves energy and reuses materials. I thought it was interesting how she presents these facts as questions, starting each one with **Did you know. . .**

210   **Persuasive Writing** • Letter to the Editor

Persuasive Writing • Letter to the Editor   211

Using a Rubric to Study the Model

(Student Pages 210–212)

Read the questions and answers on Student Pages 210–212. Discuss whether students agree or disagree with Halle's assessment of the letter to the editor. For example, are the reasons for supporting recycling ranked from most important to least important? Does the letter provide the kinds of facts and reasons that are likely to persuade readers?

Note on Conventions & Skills: Remind students that they should always check their writing for correct spelling, punctuation, and capitalization. In addition, this lesson will focus on avoiding sentence fragments.

Meeting Students' Needs:
Second Language Learners

Have students bring to class a letter to the editor from your local newspaper. Have pairs of them read their letters together and explain in their own words the writer's opinion and supporting facts and reasons. Then have them discuss whether the writer of each letter followed the rubric guidelines for writing an effective letter to the editor.

Students Who Need Extra Help

Have students complete the activity above for Second Language Learners. Then have them rewrite the letters, adding elements they think the original writer has left out. Encourage them to make up details, if necessary.

Gifted Students

Have each student research and write a letter to the editor from a famous person in history about an important issue of his or her time. For example, students might pretend to be Abraham Lincoln and write about slavery or the Civil War, or they could be Mother Teresa and write about helping poor people. Have students share their letters with the class.

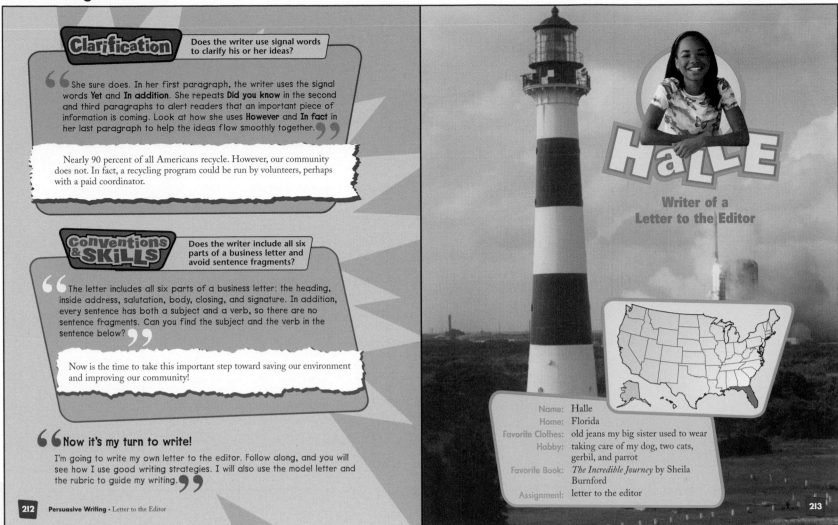

Unlocking Text Structure:
Letter to the Editor

The structure of a piece of writing depends on how the information it contains is organized. To help students unlock the structure of the letter to the editor, you may want to refer them to the graphic organizer in this chapter, an outline.

An outline is well suited to persuasive writing, such as a letter to the editor, because it helps to organize the reasons and facts that support the writer's opinion. It also helps the writer put the reasons and facts in order, from most to least important. The arrangement of information in an outline can often be transferred with little change to a letter.

Halle:
Writer of a Letter to the Editor

(Student Page 213)

Read the information about Halle.

Remind students that she is going to write her own letter to the editor. Ask students to speculate on the topic Halle might choose. Can they find a clue in her hobbies that might suggest something she could write about in her letter to the editor?

Point out that Halle will complete the steps in the writing process: Prewriting, Drafting, Revising, Editing, and Publishing. At each stage, she will demonstrate a good writing strategy and explain how she used it. Students should watch for key words, including **Gather, Organize, Write, Elaborate, Clarify, Proofread,** and **Share**.

PreWriting
Gather — Use what I read and learn from others to form an opinion about a topic.

" I love pets! That's why I got so upset when I learned that our local animal shelter is in big trouble. The people who work and volunteer there have way too much to do. The staff really cares about animals—like I do—but they don't get enough money or help. I decided something had to be done!

"First, I wanted to learn as much as I could about animal shelters. I found some good newspaper and magazine articles at the library. The librarian helped me find some information on the Internet, and I talked to people at the local shelter. Here are some of the notes I took on what I learned. "

Opinion

An **opinion** is a belief, often strong, that cannot be proven to be true.

My Notes About the Local Animal Shelter

- The shelter finds homes for animals, provides shelter for strays, helps people find lost pets, educates people about owning pets, helps control rabies and other diseases, and investigates pet abuse and neglect.
- The shelter is understaffed. Cages get cleaned only once a week. Animals get little time outside their cages.
- The shelter needs volunteers to care for and play with the animals, help get animals ready for adoption, clean cages and play areas, raise money, talk to school classes about the shelter, answer telephones, and do many other tasks.

Go to page 104 in the **Practice the Strategy Notebook!**

214 · **Persuasive Writing** · Letter to the Editor

PreWriting
Organize — Make an outline to focus and support my opinion.

" After reading over my notes on the animal shelter, I decided to write a letter to the editor of our local newspaper. I will encourage the people in our town, especially the kids, to volunteer at the shelter and help make it a great place for animals and people.

"The **Rubric** reminds me to organize my reasons from most important to least important. I decided to use an outline to do that. I've got three main points. They'll be the Roman numerals I., II., and III. I'll make I. my most important reason. "

I. The shelter provides important services.
   A. It finds homes for animals.
   B. It helps people find lost pets.
   C. It helps control rabies and other diseases.
   D. The staff investigates pet abuse and neglect.
II. Staff is working hard, but there aren't enough people.
   A. There is only one staff person for every 40 animals.
   B. Cages get cleaned only once a week.
   C. Animals do not get much play time.
III. Community is not helping enough with money.
   A. Shelter needs more equipment and supplies.
   B. Our town spends more on holiday decorations than on the animal shelter.

Outline

An **outline** shows the main points or reasons and supporting details or facts in a piece of writing. Each main point or reason should have a Roman numeral. Each supporting detail should have a capital letter. An outline can be written in sentences or phrases—but not a combination of both.

Go to page 106 in the **Practice the Strategy Notebook!**

Persuasive Writing · Letter to the Editor · 215

PreWriting Gather

Strategy: Use what I read and learn from others to form an opinion about a topic.

(Student Page 214)

Read Halle's words aloud. Ask students to review the notes she took for her letter. Has Halle included facts and reasons that are likely to appeal to her audience? Can students think of other kinds of information she might have included? **[Possible responses: Shelters are mostly supported by donations; it is fun to volunteer at a shelter; how many dogs and cats are served at the local shelter and shelters nationwide.]**

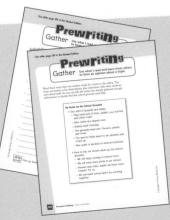

Practice the Strategy Notebook!

Assign pages 104–105 in the *Practice the Strategy Notebook*. (Your Own Writing sections should be used as time and students' abilities permit.) Help students identify reliable and appropriate Internet sites, if necessary.

PreWriting Organize

Strategy: Make an outline to focus and support my opinion.

(Student Page 215)

Review the mechanics of an outline, including the use of Roman numerals, capital letters, and numbers to organize main points and details.

Then note that Halle organized only her reasons in her outline. Her letter will also need an introduction that states her opinion and a conclusion that sums up her argument.

Practice the Strategy Notebook!

Assign pages 106–107 in the *Practice the Strategy Notebook*. Have pairs of students share the outlines they create. Suggested responses for the *Practice the Strategy Notebook* appear in the Appendix at the back of this Teacher Edition.

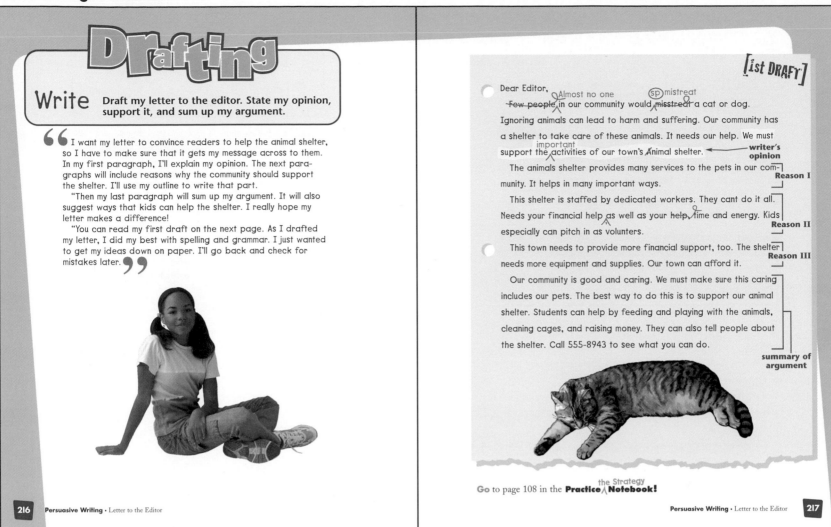

Drafting

Write
Draft my letter to the editor. State my opinion, support it, and sum up my argument.

"I want my letter to convince readers to help the animal shelter, so I have to make sure that it gets my message across to them. In my first paragraph, I'll explain my opinion. The next paragraphs will include reasons why the community should support the shelter. I'll use my outline to write that part.

"Then my last paragraph will sum up my argument. It will also suggest ways that kids can help the shelter. I really hope my letter makes a difference!

"You can read my first draft on the next page. As I drafted my letter, I did my best with spelling and grammar. I just wanted to get my ideas down on paper. I'll go back and check for mistakes later."

216 **Persuasive Writing** · Letter to the Editor

[1st DRAFT]

Dear Editor,

Almost no one   (sp) mistreat

~~Few people~~ in our community would ~~mistreat~~ a cat or dog. Ignoring animals can lead to harm and suffering. Our community has a shelter to take care of these animals. It needs our help. We must support the activities of our town's Animal shelter. ← **writer's opinion**

The animals shelter provides many services to the pets in our community. It helps in many important ways. } **Reason I**

This shelter is staffed by dedicated workers. They cant do it all. Needs your financial help as well as your help, time and energy. Kids especially can pitch in as volunters. } **Reason II**

This town needs to provide more financial support, too. The shelter needs more equipment and supplies. Our town can afford it. } **Reason III**

Our community is good and caring. We must make sure this caring includes our pets. The best way to do this is to support our animal shelter. Students can help by feeding and playing with the animals, cleaning cages, and raising money. They can also tell people about the shelter. Call 555-8943 to see what you can do. } **summary of argument**

Go to page 108 in the **Practice the Strategy Notebook!**

Persuasive Writing · Letter to the Editor 217

Drafting Write

Strategy: Draft my letter to the editor. State my opinion, support it, and sum up my argument.

(Student Pages 216–217)

If you wish, review what it means to draft a piece of writing. Then ask a volunteer to read Halle's words aloud for the class.

Ask students what purposes Halle has assigned to each paragraph in her letter. **[Response: Her first paragraph will explain her opinion, her second and perhaps third paragraphs will include supporting facts and reasons, and her last paragraph will sum up her argument.]**

Ask students what information Halle is planning to include for students. **[Response: She wants to encourage other students to get involved in the shelter, so she will include information about what they can do and how they can get started.]**

Refer to the Rubric: The student spokesperson will refer to the rubric throughout the chapter. Remind students to get into the habit of referring back to the rubric so they fully understand its use as a tool for shaping their writing.

Practice the Strategy Notebook!

Assign pages 108–109 in the *Practice the Strategy Notebook*. Give students time to draft their own letters to the editor, based on their outlines.

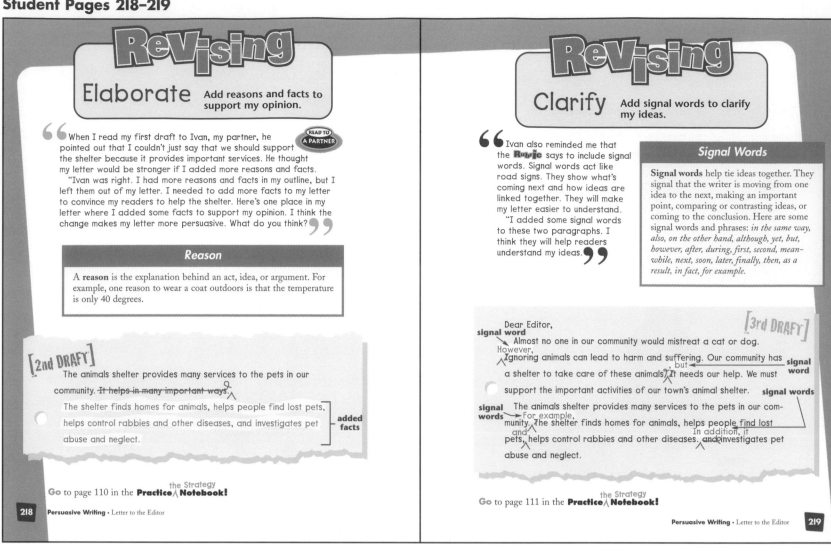

ReViSing Elaborate

Strategy: Add reasons and facts to support my opinion.

(Student Page 218)

Ask a student to read Halle's words to the class.

Then explain that including supporting reasons and facts is always important, especially in persuasive writing. Ask students how they would respond to persuasive writing that presented only the writer's feelings and opinions, without backing them up with facts or reasons. **[Possible response: Such writing would probably not persuade readers of anything.]** Finally, have students explain how the change Halle made to her letter made it more persuasive. Have them suggest other facts and reasons Halle might have added to her letter.

Practice the Strategy Notebook!

Assign page 110 in the *Practice the Strategy Notebook*. Encourage the students to explain the kinds of changes they would make in the writing sample.

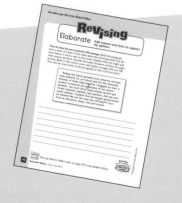

ReViSing Clarify

Strategy: Add signal words to clarify my ideas.

(Student Page 219)

Ask a student to read Halle's words to the class.

Have students review Halle's changes. Ask if they would have used signal words in different places than she put them. Point out that signal words, especially *however,* can often be placed in different positions in a sentence. In addition, different signal words can serve the same purpose, such as using *but* or *however* to show contrast.

Practice the Strategy Notebook!

Assign page 111 in the *Practice the Strategy Notebook*. Ask pairs of students to share where they inserted signal words in the writing sample. Then discuss the sample as a class.

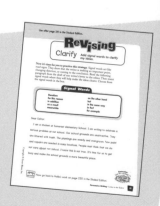

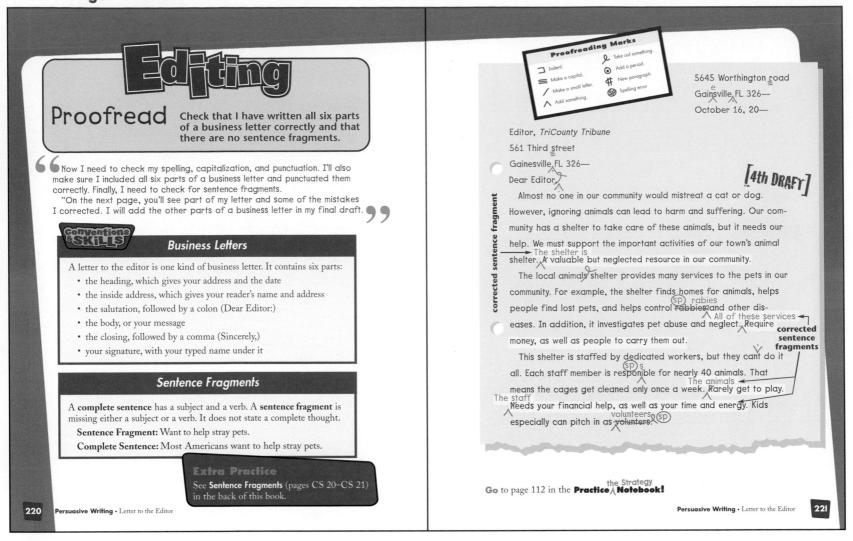

Editing Proofread

Strategy: Check that I have written all six parts of a business letter correctly and that there are no sentence fragments.

(Student Pages 220–221)

If you wish, review the difference between revising and editing. (Revising refers to looking for ways to make a draft better organized, more complete, or more persuasive. Editing involves looking for errors in spelling, punctuation, and grammar.)

Ask a volunteer to read Halle's words to the class. If necessary, review the definitions of dependent and independent clauses and ask students to suggest examples.

Extra Practice: Conventions & Skills
Student Edition

If you did not use Student Pages CS 20–CS 21 as a pre-assessment, you may wish to assign those pages now.

Conventions & Skills Practice

For more targeted practice related to this skill, see these lessons in the optional *Conventions & Skills Practice Book*:

Lesson 9: Dependent and Independent Clauses
Lesson 10: Avoiding Fragments, Run-ons, Comma Splices

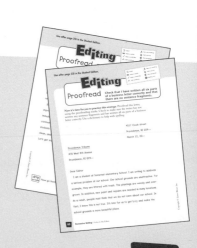

the Strategy
Practice Notebook!

Assign pages 112–113 in the *Practice the Strategy Notebook*. Encourage the students to point out the errors they found and corrected.

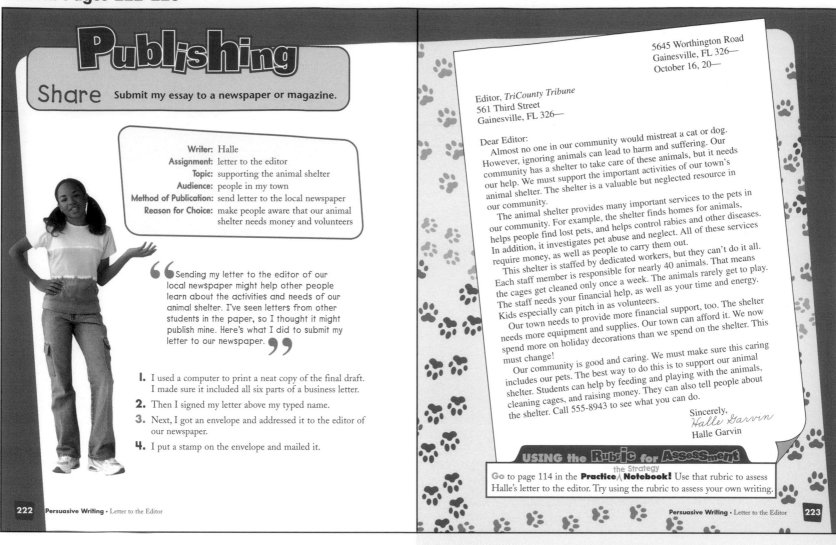

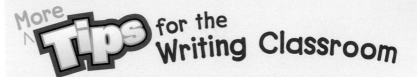

Publishing   Share

Strategy: Submit my essay to a newspaper or magazine.

(Student Pages 222–223)

Ask students to think of other ways that Halle could have shared her letter to the editor. Do they agree that this choice was an appropriate one?

Using the Rubric

Ask students to work in pairs to use the rubric (reprinted on pages 114–115 of the *Practice the Strategy Notebook*) to evaluate Halle's letter to the editor. After each pair has reached its decision, ask volunteers to provide reasons for their evaluations.

More Tips for the Writing Classroom

Journal Writing Using Videos

One classroom activity to use when watching a movie is journal writing. (The blackline master on page T164 provides a good way to recap the movie once students have completed their journal entries. You may want to have students share their responses in a group.)

First, choose a movie that follows a theme you have been studying in class and watch the movie in sections (20–30 minutes). Then have your students journal their thoughts for five to ten minutes. Encourage your students to write about how they felt about the story and to avoid simply retelling the events of the story. Ask them to relate an event in the video to their own real-life experiences. By the time they finish viewing the movie, your students should have three to four journal entries.

Ask your students to choose their best journal entry and revise it to final form. The students should then turn in all their entries with the best one on top. This will save you grading time because you will grade only the top copy for your established criteria. The other copies will be checked only for a "completion" grade.

your own PERSUASIVE writing
Responding to Literature

Put the strategies you practiced in this unit to work to write your own book review, letter to the editor, or both! You can:

- develop the writing you did in the Your Own Writing pages of the *Practice the Strategy Notebook*;

- pick an idea below and write something new;

- choose another idea of your own.

Be sure to follow the steps in the writing process. Use the rubrics in this unit to assess your writing.

Book Review	Letter to the Editor
• of *Hatchet* by Gary Paulsen, *Ramona Quimby* by Beverly Cleary, *My Side of the Mountain* by Jean Craighead George, or another novel • of a poem or collection of poems • of a biography, such as *Journey to Topaz* by Yoshiko Uchida	• about a community issue discussed in a nonfiction book you have read • about how a problem in your community was faced by a character in a novel • about a biography you read that will interest your readers

portfolio

School–Home Connection

Keep a writing portfolio. Think about adding the activities from the *Practice the Strategy Notebook* to your writing portfolio. You may want to take your portfolio home to share.

Your Own Writing
Persuasive Writing for Responding to Literature

Assign either one or both genres to the students. Before they begin writing, review key information about each genre. Decide whether you wish students to:
- Choose one of the topics on this page in the Student Edition.
- Complete one of the pieces they partially drafted in the Your Own Writing pages in the *Practice the Strategy Notebook*.
- Generate a completely new idea.

Portfolio/School-Home Connection

Encourage the students to keep portfolios of their writing. You may also wish to duplicate and distribute the School-Home Letter included in this unit.

Work-in-Progress Portfolio

Remind students to review this portfolio often to revise existing pieces that have not been published. Encourage students to share pieces of their Work-in-Progress Portfolios with family members who can help in editing.

Published Portfolio

Encourage students to choose pieces from their Published Portfolios to share with family members.

Name _____

 for the
Writing Classroom

Journal Writing Using Videos

Yahoo! Let's watch a movie. Did you know that you can learn about life by watching a movie? Well, you can. Movies have the same elements as stories or novels. A good movie has well-developed characters, a setting(s), and a plot (conflict/solutions). In order to write meaningful journal entries, you must take good notes to keep the facts straight. Then write journal entries that express your **personal** views about specific characters and/or the story.

Movie Notes

Important characters and personality traits:

1. _____

2. _____

3. _____

Setting(s):

_____

Main plot:

_____

_____

_____

Working with your teacher and your classmates, list specific events leading up to the climax.

_____

_____

After you have watched the entire movie:

- On another sheet of paper, write 1–2 paragraphs explaining why you liked or disliked the story (plot) or certain characters in the video.
- Have one of your classmates read and edit your paragraph(s).
- Make revisions and write a final draft.
- Staple all notes to the back of your favorite journal entry and give everything to your teacher.

Purpose: To help students use movies as a vehicle for writing instruction. See page T162 for more information.
This page may be duplicated for classroom use.

TEST writing

A writing test measures how well you can organize your ideas on an assigned topic.

Test Writing

Test Writing
- ☑ starts with a writing prompt.
- ☑ may not let writers use outside sources.
- ☑ may have a time limit.
- ☑ may not allow writers to recopy.

Test Writing

Tell students that every time they write, they do so for one of two reasons: they want to write or they need to write. Point out that one student may decide to write an adventure story or describe a scene because she enjoys writing and wants to share her ideas. Later that day, she may need to write directions to her house for a new friend or write a letter to explain a problem with a CD and ask for a refund.

Challenge students to name some other times when people have to write. **[Possible responses: job application letters; thank-you notes; minutes of a meeting; reports for school]**

Conclude by telling students that this type of writing is sometimes called *writing on demand*. One type of writing on demand is the writing test. In this test students are given a topic, called a *writing prompt,* and a certain amount of time in which to write. The writing is then evaluated, just like any other test.

Emphasize that there is no reason to be concerned about writing tests. Many of the steps and strategies that students have learned in the first five chapters can be applied to tests of writing.

Note: The strategies presented in this chapter can be applied to any test writing situation.

 for the **Writing Classroom**

by Ken Stewart, *Master Teacher*

Student-Generated Lesson Plans

Our main goal as educators should be to guide students to take responsibility for their own learning. There is no better way to do this than to give them more ownership of their learning. By allowing students (from start to finish) to help decide what their lessons will look like and how they will evaluate their learning, you encourage them to become more engaged and internalize what is being taught. More importantly, your students will show that they understand the

process necessary to complete a task at a quality level. These skills, once mastered, will help your students for the rest of their lives.

To help students learn effectively on their own (or with other students), we need to give them

- opportunities to make their own decisions,
- freedom to create their own product,
- responsibility to evaluate their learning, and
- a chance to succeed or to fail.

When students fail, it is important that they understand why they failed. It is also important for you to remember that learning is taking place even when students are not successful.

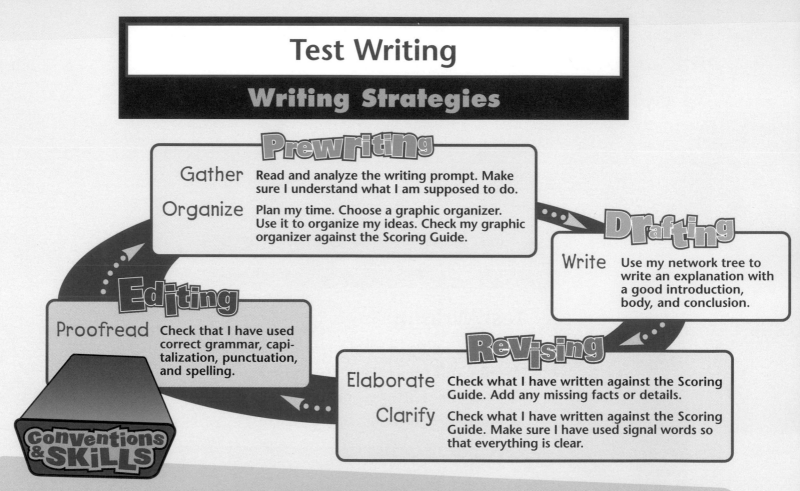

Test Writing

Writing Strategies

Prewriting

Gather — Read and analyze the writing prompt. Make sure I understand what I am supposed to do.

Organize — Plan my time. Choose a graphic organizer. Use it to organize my ideas. Check my graphic organizer against the Scoring Guide.

Drafting

Write — Use my network tree to write an explanation with a good introduction, body, and conclusion.

Editing

Proofread — Check that I have used correct grammar, capitalization, punctuation, and spelling.

Conventions & Skills

Revising

Elaborate — Check what I have written against the Scoring Guide. Add any missing facts or details.

Clarify — Check what I have written against the Scoring Guide. Make sure I have used signal words so that everything is clear.

This chapter is a general review of key skills. Before students read the model on Student Page 229, you may wish to review one or more key **grammar, usage,** or **mechanics** conventions. The following conventions are particularly important in writing tests:

Compound Sentences	Student Pages CS 2–CS 3
Pronouns	Student Pages CS 4–CS 5 and CS 18–CS 19
Subject and Verb Agreement	Student Pages CS 8–CS 9
Sentence Completeness	Student Pages CS 20–CS 21

Skill Assessment: To pre-assess your students' understanding of the key conventions being reviewed, you may wish to have them complete the corresponding lesson on Student Pages CS 22–CS 23 in the back of the Student Edition.

Skill Mini-Lesson: The Proofread activity in this chapter can be used as a mini-lesson to review **grammar, usage,** and **mechanics** skills.

As educators, we must be willing to reverse the roles in the classroom. As the year progresses, give your students increasing amounts of responsibility to construct their own lesson plans. Your role will be similar to that of an employer or supervisor. You need to establish specific criteria that must be met to complete the task (job) at a quality level, and you need to set a due date(s) for the project. You will also oversee the process, assist when your students (employees) need help, and determine whether the product meets quality standards.

Having students generate their own lesson plans should occur toward the end of the year. You are asking your students to put into practice the knowledge and skills they have developed over the school year. Give it a try. You will be quite pleased with the results.

(See "More Tips for the Writing Classroom: Structuring Student-Generated Lesson Plans" on page T178.)

Time Management for This Chapter

Session 1	Introduce the concept of writing on demand (Student Page 225). Discuss the writing prompt. Study the three parts of the prompt (Student Pages 226–227).	Session 6	Read and discuss **PREWRITING: Gather** (Student Pages 234–235). Assign *Practice the Strategy Notebook* page 116.	Session 11	Read and discuss **REVISING: Clarify** (Student Page 243). Assign *Practice the Strategy Notebook* page 121.
2	Explain the role of the student guide and discuss the Scoring Guide (Student Page 228).	7	Read and discuss **PREWRITING: Organize** (Student Page 236) and **PREWRITING: Gather and Organize** (Student Page 237).	12	Read and discuss **EDITING: Proofread** (Student Pages 244–246).
3	Read and discuss the test writing model, "Tell Me a Story!" (Student Page 229).	8	Read and discuss **PREWRITING: Organize** (Student Pages 238–239). Assign *Practice the Strategy Notebook* page 117.	13	Assign *Practice the Strategy Notebook* pages 122–123.
4	Apply and discuss the Audience, Organization, and Elaboration elements of the Scoring Guide for "Tell Me a Story!" (Student Pages 230–231).	9	Read and discuss **DRAFTING: Write** (Student Pages 240–241). Assign *Practice the Strategy Notebook* pages 118–119.	14	Review the Test Tips (Student Page 247).
5	Apply and discuss the Clarification and Conventions & Skills elements of the Scoring Guide for "Tell Me a Story!" (Student Page 232). Reintroduce Phanna as a student-guide taking a writing test (Student Page 233).	10	Read and discuss **REVISING: Elaborate** (Student Page 242). Assign *Practice the Strategy Notebook* page 120.	15	Assign the trial test (Student Page 248).

WRITER'S HANDBOOK

Remind students that they can refer to the Writer's Handbook in the back of the Student Edition for more information.

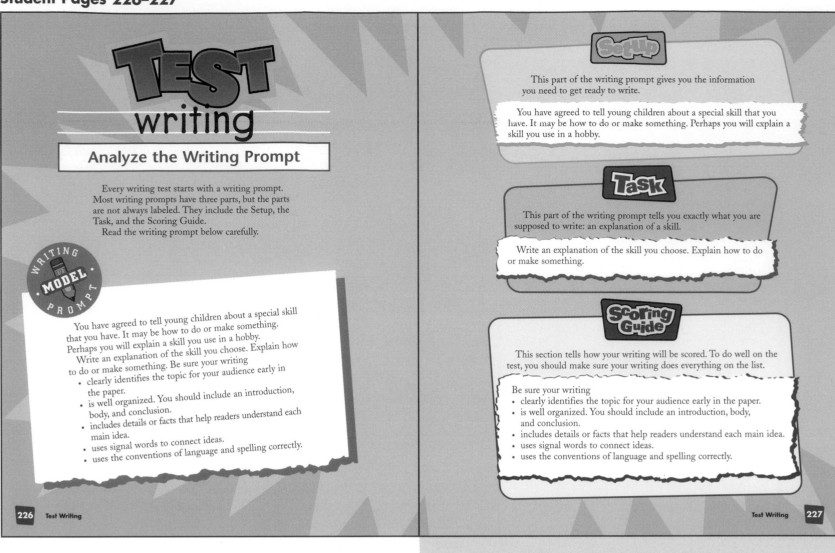

Introduce the Writing Prompt:
Expository Writing

Before students turn to Student Page 226, write the word *prompt* on the chalkboard. Ask what it means to be prompt. [**Possible response: on time**] Then ask if anyone knows other meanings for *prompt*. Explain that one meaning for *prompt* is "to cause." When an actor in a play forgets his or her lines, someone offstage will whisper the first few words. This usually causes the actor to recall his or her lines. These few words are called a prompt. Ask a volunteer to explain why an assigned writing topic is called a writing prompt. [**Possible response: It causes someone to write on a particular subject.**]

Discuss the Writing Prompt

Read the writing prompt on Student Page 226 aloud. Ask students to listen carefully for the three parts of the prompt. Read the writing prompt a second time, pausing between parts. Then have students open their books to pages 226–227.

Discuss the purpose of each part of the writing prompt. Stress that these parts are often not labeled in tests. Students will have to find them by themselves. Ask if they can think of a word they have used in other chapters that means the same as *Scoring Guide.* [**Possible response: rubric**]

Meeting Students' Needs:
Second Language Learners

Explain that *Setup* is a compound word, made by joining two smaller words: *set* and *up*. In a writing prompt, Setup means "a description of the situation." Have students name other compound words, such as *playground* and *sidewalk*. Also discuss synonyms for the word *Task*, such as *job* and *assignment*.

Students Who Need Extra Help

Help students understand that the Setup part of the writing prompt provides background information. It describes the situation they will write about or pretend to be experiencing. The Task is the actual assignment, what they will write. The Task often includes a word that tells the kind of writing they should do, such as *explain*, *describe*, *convince*, or *persuade*.

Gifted Students

Have students work with partners to practice writing the Setup and Task parts of their own writing prompts. Then have pairs exchange their work and provide feedback on the clarity of each other's work.

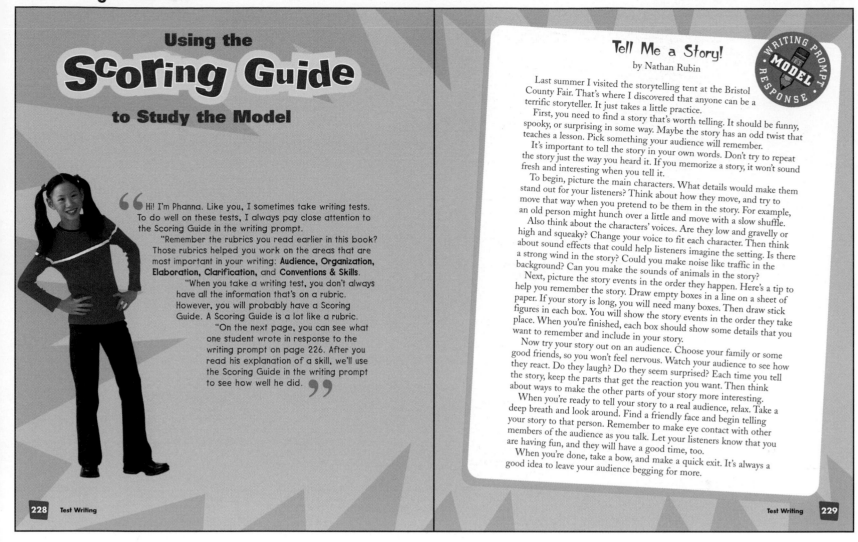

228 Test Writing

Using the Scoring Guide to Study the Model

Hi! I'm Phanna. Like you, I sometimes take writing tests. To do well on these tests, I always pay close attention to the Scoring Guide in the writing prompt.

"Remember the rubrics you read earlier in this book? Those rubrics helped you work on the areas that are most important in your writing: **Audience, Organization, Elaboration, Clarification,** and **Conventions & Skills**.

"When you take a writing test, you don't always have all the information that's on a rubric. However, you will probably have a Scoring Guide. A Scoring Guide is a lot like a rubric.

"On the next page, you can see what one student wrote in response to the writing prompt on page 226. After you read his explanation of a skill, we'll use the Scoring Guide in the writing prompt to see how well he did."

Tell Me a Story!
by Nathan Rubin

Last summer I visited the storytelling tent at the Bristol County Fair. That's where I discovered that anyone can be a terrific storyteller. It just takes a little practice.

First, you need to find a story that's worth telling. It should be funny, spooky, or surprising in some way. Maybe the story has an odd twist that teaches a lesson. Pick something your audience will remember.

It's important to tell the story in your own words. Don't try to repeat the story just the way you heard it. If you memorize a story, it won't sound fresh and interesting when you tell it.

To begin, picture the main characters. What details would make them stand out for your listeners? Think about how they move, and try to move that way when you pretend to be them in the story. For example, an old person might hunch over a little and move with a slow shuffle.

Also think about the characters' voices. Are they low and gravelly or high and squeaky? Change your voice to fit each character. Then think about sound effects that could help listeners imagine the setting. Is there a strong wind in the story? Could you make noise like traffic in the background? Can you make the sounds of animals in the story?

Next, picture the story events in the order they happen. Here's a tip to help you remember the story. Draw empty boxes in a line on a sheet of paper. If your story is long, you will need many boxes. Then draw stick figures in each box. You will show the story events in the order they take place. When you're finished, each box should show some details that you want to remember and include in your story.

Now try your story out on an audience. Choose your family or some good friends, so you won't feel nervous. Watch your audience to see how they react. Do they laugh? Do they seem surprised? Each time you tell the story, keep the parts that get the reaction you want. Then think about ways to make the other parts of your story more interesting.

When you're ready to tell your story to a real audience, relax. Take a deep breath and look around. Find a friendly face and begin telling your story to that person. Remember to make eye contact with other members of the audience as you talk. Let your listeners know that you are having fun, and they will have a good time, too.

When you're done, take a bow, and make a quick exit. It's always a good idea to leave your audience begging for more.

Test Writing 229

Using the Scoring Guide to Study the Model
(Student Page 228)

Have a volunteer read Phanna's words aloud. Review the meaning and function of a rubric. You may wish to have students review a rubric in an earlier chapter. Be sure they understand the similarities and differences between a rubric and the Scoring Guide. Students should understand that although the Scoring Guides found in writing prompts do not include the criteria for various levels of accomplishment, they do provide guidance in the five key areas of assessment: **Audience, Organization, Elaboration, Clarification,** and **Conventions & Skills**. (If you wish, have students review the rubric for the Scoring Guide on pages 124–125 of the *Practice the Strategy Notebook*.)

Read the Model:
Writing Prompt Response
(Student Page 229)

Read "Tell Me a Story!" aloud as students follow along in their books.

Discuss the Model

(Student Pages 230–232)

Read Phanna's words aloud or have a volunteer read them. Make sure students understand that the highlighted statements were taken from the Scoring Guide in the writing prompt.

Briefly discuss the importance of each of the five areas in responding to the prompt. Have students decide if they agree or disagree with Phanna's assessment of the model. The questions below may help promote discussion.

Audience: Why is it important to tell the reader your topic early in the paper? Does the first paragraph of Nathan's essay make you want to read further?

Organization: Was it easy to follow the essay? How does the word *First* help the reader?

Elaboration: Which details do you think are most helpful for the reader? Is there anything else the writer could have included?

Clarification: What is a signal word? Which ones did the writer use? What other signal words can you name?

Conventions & Skills: What does the term *conventions* mean? Why is it important that we all agree to use certain conventions in writing? Which conventions did the writer use in her response to the prompt?

Incorporating Rubrics Into the Classroom

by Lee Bromberger, *Assessment Specialist*

Beyond soliciting student input and teaching students how rubrics will be implemented with assignments, teachers can introduce other measures to make rubrics a consistent part of the classroom routine. Following are some suggestions:

- Provide each student with a copy of the rubric when new assignments are introduced to the class. Review these new materials with the students.

- Practice using rubrics with students to evaluate actual student writings. (Always obtain the writers' permission before using any student writing publicly.)

- Solicit student input when developing a new rubric. Students' input will become more plentiful—and more helpful—the more students work with rubrics.

- As students become familiar with rubrics, hold a rubric-designing contest. Allow students to choose the winner.

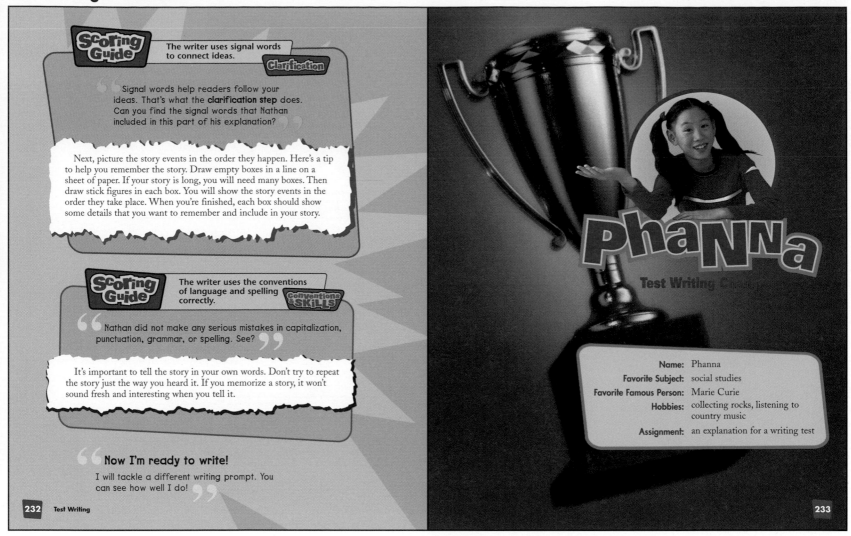

Scoring Guide The writer uses signal words to connect ideas.

Clarification

" Signal words help readers follow your ideas. That's what the **clarification step** does. Can you find the signal words that Nathan included in this part of his explanation?

Next, picture the story events in the order they happen. Here's a tip to help you remember the story. Draw empty boxes in a line on a sheet of paper. If your story is long, you will need many boxes. Then draw stick figures in each box. You will show the story events in the order they take place. When you're finished, each box should show some details that you want to remember and include in your story.

Scoring Guide The writer uses the conventions of language and spelling correctly.

Conventions & Skills

" Nathan did not make any serious mistakes in capitalization, punctuation, grammar, or spelling. See? "

It's important to tell the story in your own words. Don't try to repeat the story just the way you heard it. If you memorize a story, it won't sound fresh and interesting when you tell it.

" **Now I'm ready to write!**
I will tackle a different writing prompt. You can see how well I do! "

232 Test Writing

Phanna

Test Writing Champ

Name:	Phanna
Favorite Subject:	social studies
Favorite Famous Person:	Marie Curie
Hobbies:	collecting rocks, listening to country music
Assignment:	an explanation for a writing test

233

- If a rubric is adapted for several assignments, enlarge the rubric and post it in the classroom as a visual reminder.
- Develop a writing contest at the school. Distribute the rubric that will be used to judge the submissions for the contest.
- Place student writings and their accompanying rubrics into a writing folder for each student. Review the strengths and weaknesses of previous writings when meeting with students in writing centers or writing workshop classes.

As teachers incorporate these and other measures, students will gain an increasing comfort with rubric assessment. In time, this comfort can lead to improved writing performance, a decrease in time needed to assess student writing, and an acceptance of rubric evaluation as an integral part of the class curriculum.

Phanna:
Test Writing Champ

(Student Page 233)

Read the information about Phanna. Explain that she will be writing a response to a test prompt. She will take students through each step in the process and demonstrate good writing strategies that will help them do well when they write for almost any test. Emphasize that the steps and strategies are similar to the ones they have studied earlier.

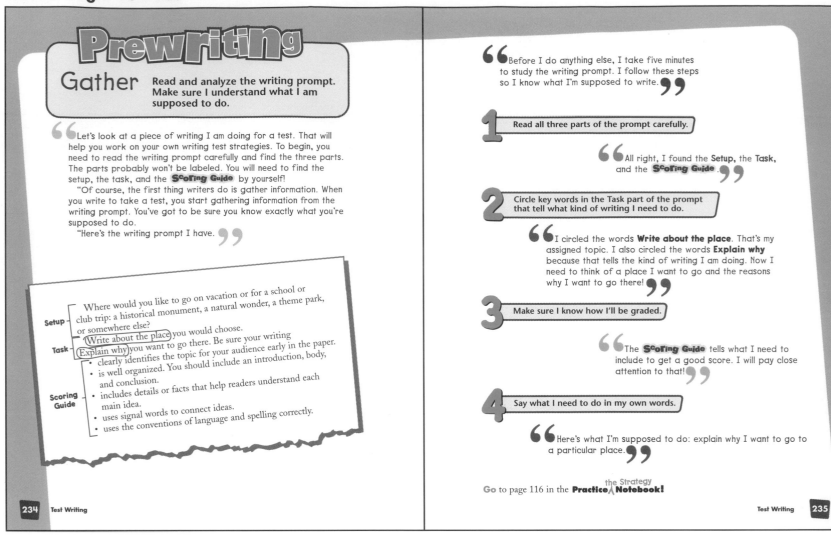

Prewriting Gather

Strategy: Read and analyze the writing prompt. Make sure I understand what I am supposed to do.

(Student Pages 234–235)

Read Phanna's words aloud or ask a volunteer to read them to the class. Emphasize the importance of knowing exactly what a prompt asks you to do. Even if you wrote a really exciting story, it would not receive a good score if the prompt asked for an explanation.

Point out the three parts of the prompt. Ask which part tells them what to do. **[the Task]** Review the four steps for analyzing a prompt. Pay close attention to Step 2, the Task. Review the differences between an explanation, which is a form of expository writing, and other types of writing, such as narrative and persuasive writing.

Point out that being able to describe the Task in one's own words (Step 4) helps ensure that students understand what the prompt requires.

Practice the Strategy Notebook!

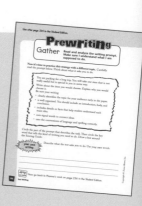

Assign page 116 in the *Practice the Strategy Notebook*. (Your Own Writing sections should be used as time and students' abilities permit.) Explain that students will practice this Gather strategy with another writing prompt. Suggested responses for the *Practice the Strategy Notebook* appear in the Appendix in the back of this Teacher Edition.

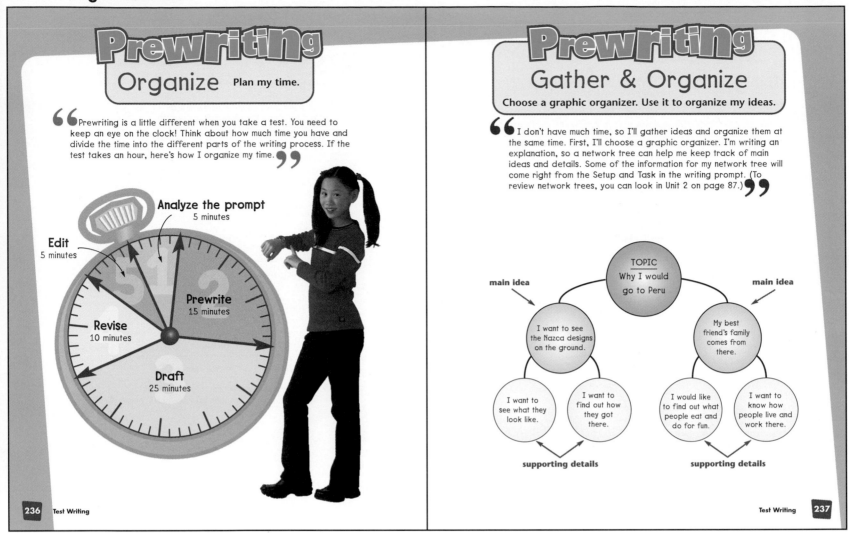

Prewriting Organize

Strategy: Plan my time.

(Student Page 236)

Explain that students writing for a test must organize their time, as well as their notes and ideas. The time allotted for writing tests will vary. Here are some guidelines for various testing periods:

Total Test Minutes:	60	90	120
1. Analyze the prompt	5	7	10
2. Prewrite	15	24	30
3. Draft	25	37	50
4. Revise	10	15	20
5. Edit	5	7	10

Point out that drafting constitutes less than half of the allotted time for the entire test. Explain that many students do poorly on writing tests because they begin writing before they have a plan and continue writing until they run out of time.

Prewriting Gather & Organize

Strategy: Choose a graphic organizer. Use it to organize my ideas.

(Student Page 237)

Remind students that earlier Phanna circled the words *Write about the place* and *Explain why*. Using a network tree as a graphic organizer helps her "see" the parts and list possible details. Ask if students think Phanna has a good plan for writing.

Discuss other graphic organizers that might make sense for this assignment. Point out that this step combines the strategies of Gather and Organize to save time as students write for a test.

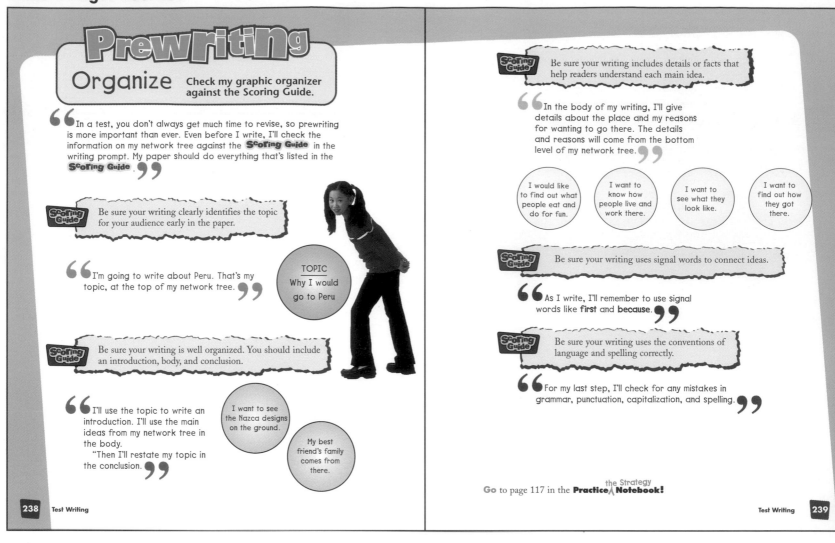

Prewriting Organize

Strategy: Check my graphic organizer against the Scoring Guide.

(Student Pages 238–239)

Make sure students understand that the Scoring Guide is taken from the writing prompt. If necessary, turn back to Student Page 226 to point out the source. Guide students to recognize how the network tree supports the Scoring Guide. Point out that the topic is written at the top of the tree.

Explain that the graphic organizer may be adjusted to meet the requirements of the Scoring Guide. Students might also decide to use a different graphic organizer, as long as it lends itself to an explanation. Possibilities include an outline, sequence chain, or support pattern.

Point out that the conventions of language and spelling are addressed at the editing step.

Practice the Strategy Notebook!

Assign page 117 in the *Practice the Strategy Notebook*. You may wish to have volunteers share their graphic organizers with the class.

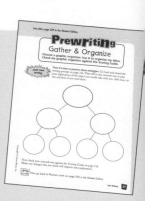

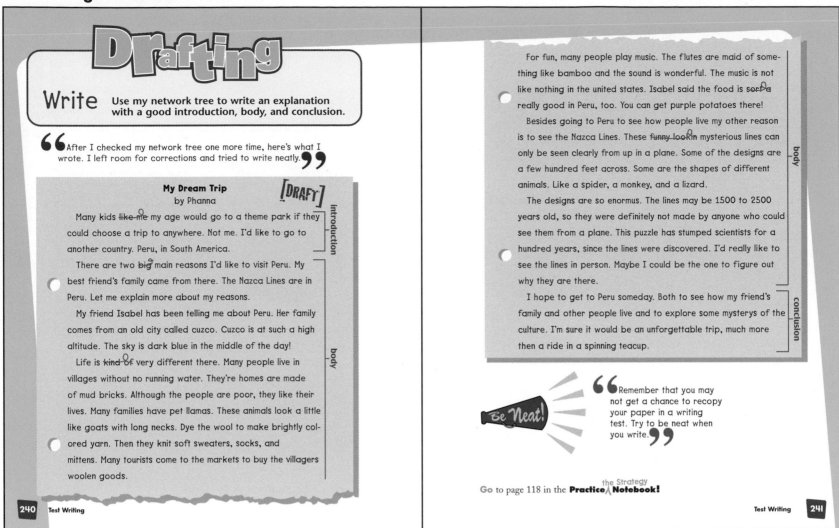

Drafting

Write

Use my network tree to write an explanation with a good introduction, body, and conclusion.

"After I checked my network tree one more time, here's what I wrote. I left room for corrections and tried to write neatly."

My Dream Trip
by Phanna   [DRAFT]

introduction

Many kids ~~like me~~ my age would go to a theme park if they could choose a trip to anywhere. Not me. I'd like to go to another country. Peru, in South America.

body

There are two ~~big~~ main reasons I'd like to visit Peru. My best friend's family came from there. The Nazca Lines are in Peru. Let me explain more about my reasons.

My friend Isabel has been telling me about Peru. Her family comes from an old city called cuzco. Cuzco is at such a high altitude. The sky is dark blue in the middle of the day!

Life is ~~kind of~~ very different there. Many people live in villages without no running water. They're homes are made of mud bricks. Although the people are poor, they like their lives. Many families have pet llamas. These animals look a little like goats with long necks. Dye the wool to make brightly colored yarn. Then they knit soft sweaters, socks, and mittens. Many tourists come to the markets to buy the villagers woolen goods.

body

For fun, many people play music. The flutes are maid of something like bamboo and the sound is wonderful. The music is not like nothing in the united states. Isabel said the food is sorta really good in Peru, too. You can get purple potatoes there!

Besides going to Peru to see how people live my other reason is to see the Nazca Lines. These ~~funny lookin~~ mysterious lines can only be seen clearly from up in a plane. Some of the designs are a few hundred feet across. Some are the shapes of different animals. Like a spider, a monkey, and a lizard.

The designs are so enormus. The lines may be 1500 to 2500 years old, so they were definitely not made by anyone who could see them from a plane. This puzzle has stumped scientists for a hundred years, since the lines were discovered. I'd really like to see the lines in person. Maybe I could be the one to figure out why they are there.

conclusion

I hope to get to Peru someday. Both to see how my friend's family and other people live and to explore some mysterys of the culture. I'm sure it would be an unforgettable trip, much more then a ride in a spinning teacup.

Be Neat!

"Remember that you may not get a chance to recopy your paper in a writing test. Try to be neat when you write."

Go to page 118 in the **Practice the Strategy Notebook!**

Drafting Write

Strategy: Use my network tree to write an explanation with a good introduction, body, and conclusion.

(Student Pages 240–241)

Point out that when writing for a test, students may not have time to recopy their drafts. In some testing situations, they will be provided with an answer booklet. These, too, restrict a student's ability to recopy.

Encourage students to leave room between the lines when writing a draft in a testing situation. This allows them to make corrections or add and delete text as they revise and proofread. Although neatness is not technically a factor in evaluation, urge students to write neatly so evaluators do not misread what they have written.

Discuss Phanna's draft. Ask students to identify parts that they like or parts that could be improved. Ask if the topic is clear. Remind students that Phanna is not too worried about making errors in spelling and grammar now. She will do her best in these areas and correct any errors later.

Practice the Strategy Notebook!

Assign pages 118–119 in the *Practice the Strategy Notebook.* Invite volunteers to read all or part of their drafts to the class.

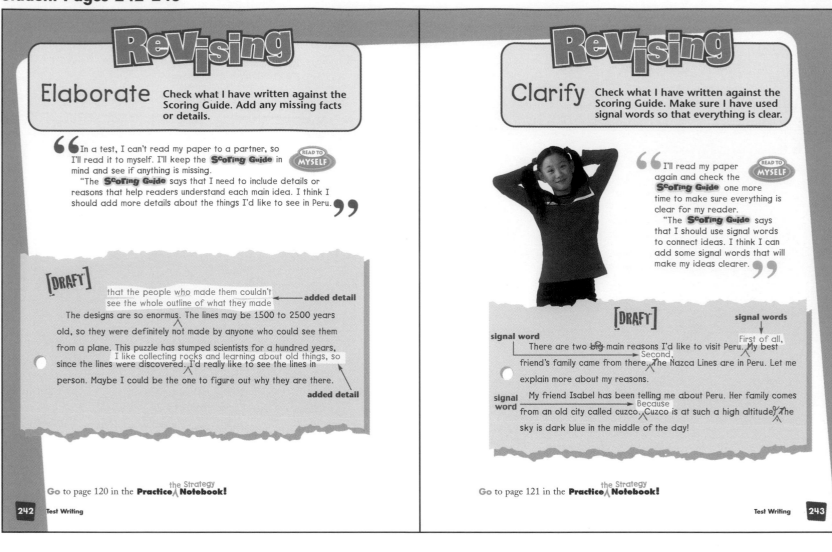

Revising Elaborate

Strategy: **Check what I have written against the Scoring Guide. Add any missing facts or details.**

(Student Page 242)

Discuss Phanna's revision. Ask students if her additions help them understand her explanation. Have students point out other places in the draft where information might be added.

Practice the Strategy Notebook!

Assign page 120 in the *Practice the Strategy Notebook*. This might be used as a class activity.

Revising Clarify

Strategy: **Check what I have written against the Scoring Guide. Make sure I have used signal words so that everything is clear.**

(Student Page 243)

Have a volunteer read Phanna's words aloud. Have students note the changes she made and explain how they make her draft clearer.

Practice the Strategy Notebook!

Assign page 121 in the *Practice the Strategy Notebook*. You might challenge students to name other signal words the writer could have used.

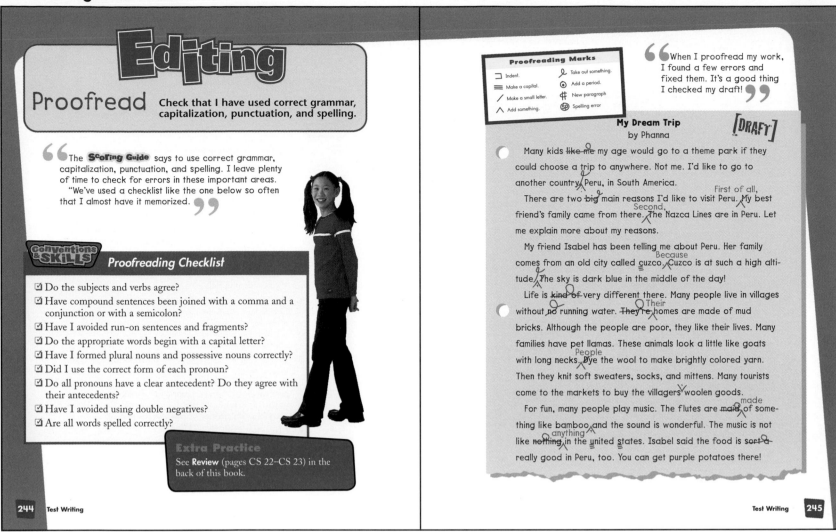

Editing Proofread

Strategy: Check that I have used correct grammar, capitalization, punctuation, and spelling.

(Student Pages 244–246)

Emphasize the importance of allowing time for editing and proofreading. One common mistake students make in writing tests is using all of the allotted time to write, with no time left to proofread.

Advise students to look for any errors as they proofread. However, point out that basic errors in sentence completeness, punctuation, and spelling will likely affect their scores more than minor errors.

Note: Because this is a testing situation, spelling corrections are shown in the student model without the "sp" notation.

Review the proofreading checklist with students. Refer to the appropriate Extra Practice pages, including pages CS 22–CS 23, if they need additional practice. The following lessons in the *Conventions & Skills Practice Book* may be helpful:

Lesson 8: Compound Sentences
Lesson 10: Avoiding Fragments, Run-ons, Comma Splices
Lesson 12: Plural and Possessive Nouns
Lesson 13: Personal and Possessive Pronouns
Lesson 31: Subject and Object Pronouns
Lesson 34: Pronoun Antecedents
Lesson 35: Making the Subject and Verb Agree
Lesson 41: Writing Sentences Correctly

Practice the Strategy Notebook!

Assign pages 122–123 in the *Practice the Strategy Notebook*. Have students refer to the Scoring Guide to assess Phanna's work.

that the people who made them couldn't see the whole outline of what they made

Besides going to Peru to see how people live, my other reason is to see the Nazca Lines. These ~~funny lookin~~ mysterious lines can only be seen clearly from up in a plane. Some of the designs are a few hundred feet across. Some are the shapes of different animals, like a spider, a monkey, and a lizard.

The designs are so enormus! The lines may be 1500 to 2500 years old, so they were definitely not made by anyone who could see them from a plane. This puzzle has stumped scientists *I like collecting rocks and learning about old things, so* for a hundred years, since the lines were discovered. I'd really like to see the lines in person. Maybe I could be the one to figure out why they are there.

I hope to get to Peru someday, Both to see how my friend's family and other people live and to explore some mysterys of the culture. I'm sure it would be an unforgettable trip, much more ~~then~~ *than* a ride in a spinning teacup.

Go to page 122 in the **Practice** *the Strategy* **Notebook!**

We're finished! That wasn't so bad! The main thing to remember is that when you write for a test, you use the writing process. It's just a little different from other writing. Remember these important steps when you write for a test.

test tips

1. **Analyze the writing prompt before you start to write.**
   Remember, most writing prompts have three parts: the Setup, the Task, and the Scoring Guide. The parts will probably not be labeled, so you have to figure them out yourself.

2. **Make sure you understand the task before you start to write. Remember to**
   • Read all three parts of the prompt carefully.
   • Circle key words in the Task part of the prompt that tell what kind of writing you need to do. The Task might also identify your audience.
   • Make sure you know how you will be graded.
   • Describe the assignment in your own words to make sure you understand it.

3. **Keep an eye on the clock.**
   Decide how much time you are going to spend on each part of the writing process and try to stick to your schedule. Do not spend so much time on prewriting that you do not have any time left to write!

4. **Reread your writing. Check it against the Scoring Guide at least twice.**
   Remember the rubrics we have used all year? A Scoring Guide on a writing test is like a rubric. It can help you keep what is important in mind. That way, you can make sure you have done everything the Scoring Guide asks you to do.

5. **Plan, plan, plan!**
   You do not get much time to revise during a test, so planning is more important than ever.

6. **Write neatly.**
   Remember, if the people who score your test cannot read your writing, it does not matter how good your paper is!

More Tips for the Writing Classroom

Structuring Student–Generated Lesson Plans

Giving your students opportunities to create, organize, and write their own lesson plans is vital to evaluate whether "real" learning has taken place throughout the school year. The following suggestions will help you and your students structure student-generated lessons:

1. Create or have your students create teams.

2. Choose a general theme or topic, such as acceptance and appreciation of differences.

3. Establish specific criteria you want your students to achieve.

4. Have students use their imaginations in teaching the subject matter. For example, they might write lessons that require the class to

   • read a story or novel related to the theme or topic.

   • write a critique or keep journal entries.

   • find a way to show how their vocabulary has improved.

   • create a visual that depicts a topic or theme (i.e., diorama, poster, play, video, computer program, etc.).

5. Establish a due date for the lessons and have students write detailed daily lesson plans. (Provide them with a calendar on which to write their plans.)

6. Have all members of the team sign the lesson plan and submit it for your approval.

7. Provide time for the team to present its approved lesson.

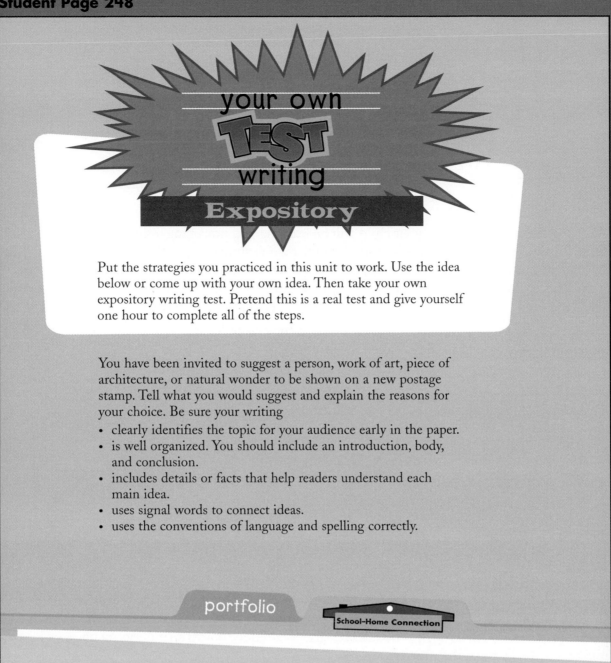

your own

TEST

writing

Expository

Put the strategies you practiced in this unit to work. Use the idea below or come up with your own idea. Then take your own expository writing test. Pretend this is a real test and give yourself one hour to complete all of the steps.

You have been invited to suggest a person, work of art, piece of architecture, or natural wonder to be shown on a new postage stamp. Tell what you would suggest and explain the reasons for your choice. Be sure your writing

- clearly identifies the topic for your audience early in the paper.
- is well organized. You should include an introduction, body, and conclusion.
- includes details or facts that help readers understand each main idea.
- uses signal words to connect ideas.
- uses the conventions of language and spelling correctly.

portfolio

School–Home Connection

Keep a writing portfolio. Think about adding the activities from the *Practice the Strategy Notebook* to your writing portfolio. You may want to take your portfolio home to share.

248 Test Writing

Your Own Writing
Test Writing

Assign the writing prompt to the students. Before they begin writing, review key information about writing on demand.

Note: A rubric is not provided for students in a testing situation in all states. For that reason, this chapter includes a Scoring Guide instead of a rubric. This Scoring Guide appears as a fully developed rubric on pages 124–125 in the *Practice the Strategy Notebook*. You may wish to have students use this rubric to assess their response to the writing prompt.

Portfolio/School-Home Connection

Encourage the students to keep portfolios of their writing. You may also wish to duplicate and distribute the School-Home Letter included in this unit.

Work-in-Progress Portfolio

Remind students to review this portfolio often to revise existing pieces that have not been published. Encourage students to share pieces of their Work-in-Progress Portfolios with family members who can help in editing.

Published Portfolio

Encourage students to choose pieces from their Published Portfolios to share with family members.

School–Home Connection

Dear Family,

During the next few weeks, your child will be learning and practicing a different kind of writing—writing for a test. Many kinds of tests now require students to write essay-style answers to questions. Standardized tests, such as proficiency and achievement tests, increasingly require students to write essays. That's why we are taking time during the school year to help your child learn and practice some specific skills that will help him or her write for a test.

Students must remember six basic things when they write for a test. They are outlined in the chapter of *Strategies for Writers* called Test Writing.

1. Analyze the writing prompt before you start to write.

   The writing prompt is the assignment your child is given for a test. It includes the Setup, the Task, and the Scoring Guide.

   - The Setup gives the background for the writing assignment.
   - The Task tells exactly what the writer is supposed to do.
   - The Scoring Guide tells how the writing will be evaluated.

2. Make sure you understand the task before you start to write.

   This strategy reminds the child to read the prompt carefully, circle key words in the Task, understand the grading, and explain the task in his or her own words.

3. Keep an eye on the clock.

   This is a reminder to the child that writing for a test often must be done in a limited amount of time. The child must decide how much time to spend on each part of the writing process and stick to the schedule. It's also a reminder not to spend too much time on any one part of the process.

4. Reread your writing. Check it against the Scoring Guide at least twice.

   The Scoring Guide is much like the rubrics your child has been using all year to organize and evaluate his or her writing projects. Using the Scoring Guide will help your child focus on what's important in writing for a test.

5. Plan, plan, plan!

   There's not much time to revise during a test, so planning is very important. This strategy reminds your child to pay special attention to the Prewriting part of the writing process.

6. Write neatly.

   The people who will grade the test need to be able to read it easily. This is a reminder for your child to make sure his or her writing is clear and understandable.

   Help your child prepare for writing tests by following these simple steps. Writing for a test doesn't have to be stressful. With the right tools and good writing habits, your child can feel good about writing for a test.

You may wish to copy the letter above and send it home with your students.

Conventions & Skills

The activities on the following pages provide additional practice in the grammar, usage, and mechanics skills you worked with throughout this book. Use the activities to get extra practice in these skills. Complete each activity on a separate sheet of paper.

Table of Contents

 Forming Compound Sentences

When two sentences are joined together correctly, they become a **compound sentence**. When they are joined incorrectly, they become a **run-on**.

Review the Rule

- Compound sentences can be formed by placing a **comma** and a **coordinating conjunction** between two related sentences. The words *and*, *but*, and *or* are coordinating conjunctions.

  Run-on: Swimming is fun but it can be dangerous.
  Correct: Swimming is fun, but it can be dangerous.

- Compound sentences can also be formed by placing a **semicolon** (;) between two related sentences.

  Run-on: Everyone should learn how to swim this skill can save a life.
  Correct: Everyone should learn how to swim; this skill can save a life.

Practice

Correct each run-on below by rewriting it as a compound sentence. Number a separate sheet of paper 1.–15. You can choose whether to join the sentences with a comma and a conjunction or with a semicolon.

1. You should always swim with a friend it is dangerous to swim alone.
2. It is fun to swim in the sunshine but the sun can burn your skin.
3. Sunscreen protects your skin but you must apply it often.
4. There are often numbers on the side of a swimming pool they show the depth of the water.
5. You can swim in the shallow end but you should never dive into shallow water.
6. The deep end of a pool can be dangerous only good swimmers go there.

7. Many beaches and pools have lifeguards they are ready to help in emergencies.
8. Lifeguards must earn lifesaving certificates and they must also have first-aid certificates.
9. Lifeguards must be alert they save many lives each year.
10. Most pools and beaches have rules and swimmers must obey the rules at all times.
11. You should never push someone into the water and you should always watch out for other swimmers.
12. You must be careful on a water slide or you might hurt yourself or another swimmer.
13. You must not swim near the diving boards or someone might land on top of you.
14. Diving can be fun but you must learn how to dive safely.
15. Always wait quietly for your turn on the diving board divers need to concentrate.

Apply

On another sheet of paper, rewrite this paragraph, correcting any compound sentences that have been formed incorrectly.

I love to go to the pool with my friends but I don't know how to swim. My mother tried to teach me my uncle tried, too. Some people were just not meant to be fish you can enjoy the water without swimming in it. I am going to scout camp next week. Maybe I will learn to swim there but please don't count on it!

Possible answers appear below.

Practice

1. You should always swim with a friend; it is dangerous to swim alone.
2. It is fun to swim in the sunshine, but the sun can burn your skin.
3. Sunscreen protects your skin, but you must apply it often.
4. There are often numbers on the side of a swimming pool; they show the depth of the water.
5. You can swim in the shallow end, but you should never dive into shallow water.
6. The deep end of a pool can be dangerous; only good swimmers should go there.
7. Many beaches and pools have lifeguards; they are ready to help in emergencies.
8. Lifeguards must earn lifesaving certificates, and they must also have first-aid certificates.
9. Lifeguards must be alert; they save many lives each year.
10. Most pools and beaches have rules, and swimmers must obey the rules at all times.
11. You should never push someone into the water, and you should always watch out for other swimmers.
12. You must be careful on a water slide, or you might hurt yourself or another swimmer.
13. You must not swim near the diving boards, or someone might land on top of you.
14. Diving can be fun, but you must learn how to dive safely.
15. Always wait quietly for your turn on the diving board; divers need to concentrate.

Apply

I love to go to the pool with my friends, but I don't know how to swim. My mother tried to teach me; my uncle tried, too. Some people were just not meant to be fish. **You** can enjoy the water without swimming in it. I am going to scout camp next week. Maybe I will learn to swim there, but please don't count on it!

 Forms of Pronouns

Pronouns are words that take the place of nouns.

Review the Rule

1. The **subject pronouns** are *I, he, she, we,* and *they.* Subject pronouns are used when the pronoun is the subject of a sentence.

2. The **object pronouns** are *me, him, her, us,* and *them.* Object pronouns are used when the pronoun is a direct object or the object of a preposition.

3. The words **you** and **it** can be used as subject and object pronouns.

4. **Possessive pronouns,** including *my, your, his, her, its,* and *their,* show ownership.

5. When you write about yourself and another person, always name the other person first.

    Incorrect: I and Kim are in the same group.
    Correct: Kim and I are in the same group.

Practice

Number your paper from 1.–15. Choose the correct form of each pronoun and write it on your paper. Then write the number of the rule above that applies.

1. When (I and my family/my family and I/my family and me) went to Alaska, we got to see the northern lights.

2. A French scientist named Pierre Gassendi saw the northern lights in 1621; (he/him/his) named (they/them/their) the aurora borealis.

3. Aurora was a character from Roman mythology; (she/her) was the goddess of the dawn.

4. Boreas was also a character from mythology; the Romans called (he/him) the god of the north wind.

5. The lights begin late at night, and (they/them) continue until dawn.

6. Sometimes the northern lights were very bright; (my brother and me/me and my brother/my brother and I) could read without any other light.

7. (I and my dad/My dad and I/Me and my dad) looked up the best viewing times.

8. If strong moonlight hits (they/them), the lights look blue.

9. (My family and I/I and my family/My family and me) drove far away from the city to see the northern lights.

10. Another tourist told (me and my brother/my brother and me/my brother and I) that near midnight is the best viewing time.

11. When people first saw these lights long ago, (they/them) could not figure out what was happening.

12. An Alaskan girl told (me and Mom/Mom and me/Mom and I) that she never whistles at the northern lights.

13. According to a legend, whistling makes the lights come close to people and snatch (them/they) away.

14. When (my brother and I/me and my brother/my brother and me) saw the aurora borealis, we took many pictures.

15. Watching the aurora borealis always makes (my mom and me/me and my mom/my mom and I) happy.

Apply

Read this part of a draft about the northern lights. On your paper, rewrite the paragraph, correcting the pronoun errors. Underline the correct pronouns. You should find and correct seven errors.

> Him and I stood quietly watching the northern lights. Them hypnotized we. At times, it seemed as if us could reach out and touch they. We knew that wasn't possible, though. A glowing arc suddenly appeared in front of me and him. The arc stretched high into the sky, and then it disappeared from us sight. We stared into the night, wondering what would happen next.

Answers appear below.

Practice

1. my family and I; Rules 1 and 5

2. he; Rule 1   them; Rule 2

3. she; Rule 1

4. him; Rule 2

5. they; Rule 1

6. my brother and I; Rules 1 and 5

7. My dad and I; Rules 1 and 5

8. them; Rule 2

9. My family and I; Rules 1 and 5

10. my brother and me; Rules 2 and 5

11. they; Rule 1

12. Mom and me; Rules 2 and 5

13. them; Rule 2

14. my brother and I; Rules 1 and 5

15. my mom and me; Rules 2 and 5

Apply

He and I stood quietly watching the northern lights. They hypnotized us. At times, it seemed as if we could reach out and touch them. We knew that wasn't possible, though. A glowing arc suddenly appeared in front of him and me. The arc stretched high into the sky, and then it disappeared from our sight. We stared into the night, wondering what would happen next.

 Plural and Possessive Nouns

A **plural noun** names more than one person, place, or thing. Regular plural nouns are formed by adding **-s** and **-es**. Irregular plural nouns have many different spellings. A **possessive noun** shows ownership. Plural nouns and possessive nouns are sometimes confused because both often end in **s**.

Review the Rule

Plural Nouns

- Add *-s* or *-es* to form the plural of most nouns.

  Examples: building ⟶ buildings; bench ⟶ benches

- Change *y* to *i* and add *-es* to form the plural of some nouns ending in *y*.

  Example: story ⟶ stories

- Change *f* to *v* and add *-es* to form the plural of some nouns ending in *f*.

  Example: wife ⟶ wives

- Some nouns change their spelling or remain unchanged in their plural form.

  Examples: goose ⟶ geese; deer ⟶ deer

Possessive Nouns

- Add an **apostrophe** and *-s* to form the possessive of singular and plural nouns that do not end in *s*.

  Examples: the woman's car; the women's cars

- Add only an apostrophe to form the possessive of plural nouns that end in *s*.

  Example: the Mohawks' traditions

Practice

Let's practice the rules for forming plural and possessive nouns. On your paper, number 1.–15. Then find the error in each sentence below and write the correct plural or possessive noun form. Label it **PL** for plural or **POSS** for possessive.

1. Zookeepers care for animals at zoos, especially the babys.
2. Most peoples become zookeepers because they love animals.
3. They take time to answer childrens questions.
4. They tell the children not to give candys to the animals.
5. Zookeepers may care for everything from sheeps to sharks.
6. They must know what leafs and other foods each animal eats.
7. Some animals eat tomatos and other vegetables.
8. Other animals, such as wolfs, eat only meat.
9. Zookeepers have a powerful influence on the animals lives.
10. They must know when an animal needs a veterinarians help.
11. Veterinarians are sometimes heros at the zoo.
12. They protect animals from many varietys of disease.
13. They can diagnose an illness just by looking at an animals eyes.
14. A zookeepers life is a busy one.
15. Many zoos success depends on the keepers' skill.

Apply

On your paper, rewrite this part of a descriptive essay. Correct four mistakes in plural and possessive nouns. Underline the nouns you have corrected, and label them **PL** for plural or **POSS** for possessive.

Crystal is currently working in the zoos nursery. She takes care of orphaned baby gorillas and treats them like childs. The little gorilla's often rush to sit in Crystals lap.

Answers appear below.

Practice

1. **babies (PL)**
2. **people (PL)**
3. **children's (PL POSS)**
4. **candies (PL)**
5. **sheep (PL)**
6. **leaves (PL)**
7. **tomatoes (PL)**
8. **wolves (PL)**
9. **animals' (PL POSS)**
10. **veterinarian's (POSS)**
11. **heroes (PL)**
12. **varieties (PL)**
13. **animal's (POSS)**
14. **zookeeper's (POSS)**
15. **zoos' (PL POSS)**

Apply

Crystal is currently working in the <u>zoo's</u> (POSS) nursery. She takes care of orphaned baby gorillas and treats them like <u>children</u> (PL). The little <u>gorillas</u> (PL) often rush to sit in <u>Crystal's</u> (POSS) lap.

 **Subject-Verb Agreement**

Singular subjects take **singular verbs. Plural subjects** take **plural verbs.** If you learn the following rules, you will always know how to make subjects and verbs agree.

Review the Rule

- **Verbs With Singular Subjects**

  Add **-s** or **-es** to a verb when the subject is singular.

  Examples: A carnivorous **plant eats** animals.

  It needs the animal's nitrogen.

- **Verbs With Plural Subjects**

  Do not add **-s** or **-es** when the subject is a plural noun or is one of the pronouns *I, you, we,* or *they.*

  Examples: **Venus flytraps** grow in bogs.

  They trap insects.

- **Using Forms of the Verb "to be"**

  Use *am* after *I.*

  Example: **I am** interested in carnivorous plants.

  Use *is* or *was* after singular subjects.

  Example: My Venus flytrap **plant is** very healthy.

  Use *are* or *were* with plural subjects.

  Example: Carnivorous **plants are** rare.

CS 8   **Conventions & Skills** · Subject-Verb Agreement

Practice

Number your paper 1.–15. Write the subject and verb in each sentence. If they do not agree, write the whole sentence, correcting the error.

1. Venus flytraps grow in the bogs of North and South Carolina.
2. They sprout in very wet ground.
3. They eats flies, bees, and ants.
4. The Venus flytrap leaf lies on the ground.
5. A bright red color on the leaf attract insects.
6. A sweet liquid is on the edge of the leaf.
7. This sweet liquid also lure insects onto the leaf.
8. Then the two sections of the leaf snaps together quickly.
9. Only small insects escapes between the sharp points.
10. After a while, the leaf closes tightly.
11. The Venus flytrap surround the body with liquid.
12. The decomposing insect give the plant its nitrogen.
13. Bees pollinate the flowers safely.
14. I put my finger inside a Venus flytrap.
15. It were actually painless.

Apply

In this paragraph, some of the subjects and verbs do not agree. Rewrite the paragraph on your paper, correcting the errors.

Two flies darts around the Venus flytrap. Finally one comes to the edge of the leaf and lick the sweet-smelling liquid. It steps farther onto the leaf. Suddenly, the plant snap shut! The fly struggles. The trap tightens, and the fly disappear.

Conventions & Skills · Subject-Verb Agreement   CS 9

Answers appear below.

Practice

1. flytraps grow
2. They sprout
3. They **eat** flies, bees, and ants.
4. leaf lies
5. A bright red color on the leaf **attracts** insects.
6. liquid is
7. This sweet liquid also **lures** insects onto the leaf.
8. Then the two sections of the leaf **snap** together quickly.
9. Only small insects **escape** between the sharp points.
10. leaf closes
11. The Venus flytrap **surrounds** the body with liquid.
12. The decomposing insect **gives** the plant its nitrogen.
13. Bees pollinate
14. I put
15. It **was** actually painless.

Apply

Two flies **dart** around the Venus flytrap. Finally one comes to the edge of the leaf and **licks** the sweet-smelling liquid. It steps farther onto the leaf. Suddenly, the plant **snaps** shut! The fly struggles. The trap tightens, and the fly **disappears**.

Capitalization

Proper nouns name a particular person, place, or thing. They are also used to form proper adjectives. Proper nouns can include initials, and they can be used in abbreviations. The first letter in all of these forms of proper nouns should be capitalized.

Review the Rule

1. Capitalize the first letter in proper nouns:
   Missouri River, **S**acajawea

2. Capitalize the first letter in proper adjectives:
   Native **A**merican legend, **S**hoshoni chief

3. Capitalize the initials in proper nouns:
   Ben **N.** Campbell, **W.C.** Wyeth

4. Capitalize abbreviations of words that are capitalized when written out: **U.S.** (**U**nited **S**tates), **N.D.** (**N**orth **D**akota)

Practice

Let's put the rules for capitalization to work. Number your paper 1.–15. Find words and abbreviations in each sentence that have errors in capitalization. Write them correctly. Also write the number of the rule you applied.

1. The story of Sacajawea has become an american folk legend.

2. sacajawea means "bird woman" in the Shoshoni language.

3. Sacajawea was born in the 1780s, and her father was a shoshoni chief.

4. She grew up in the area of the United States that became montana and utah.

5. Sacajawea's husband was a french-Canadian fur trader named Toussaint Charbonneau.

6. Meriwether Lewis and william clark hired Charbonneau as an interpreter.

7. Lewis and Clark let charbonneau bring Sacajawea with him.

8. The expedition traveled through Shoshoni territory in the rocky mountains.

9. The american explorers stopped in the village where Sacajawea had been born.

10. The Villagers wanted to kill the explorers.

11. Sacajawea helped save the Explorers' lives.

12. Lewis and Clark reached the Pacific Ocean in november of 1805.

13. W. c. Wyeth painted a famous picture of Sacajawea guiding Lewis and Clark.

14. The united states congress decided to issue a coin honoring Sacajawea.

15. The new u.s. dollar has her image on it.

Apply

Read this paragraph from a research report about Sacajawea. Rewrite the paragraph on your paper, correcting all errors in capitalization.

> Although a stone on the wind river reservation marks the grave of sacajawea, no one really knows when or how she died. One legend says that sacajawea died in 1812 when she was only 25 years old. Other legends tell of a shoshoni woman who lived to be 100 years old and died at fort washakie in wyoming. This woman claimed to be sacajawea and knew many details about the u.s. expedition led by meriwether lewis and william clark.

Answers appear below.

Practice

1. **American**; Rule 2

2. **Sacajawea**; Rule 1

3. **Shoshoni**; Rule 2

4. **Montana, Utah**; Rule 1

5. **French**; Rule 2

6. **William Clark**; Rule 1

7. **Charbonneau**; Rule 1

8. **Rocky Mountains**; Rule 1

9. **American**; Rule 2

10. **villagers**; Rule 1

11. **explorers'**; Rule 2

12. **November**; Rule 1

13. **C.**; Rule 3

14. **United States Congress**; Rules 1 and 2

15. **U.S.**; Rule 4

Apply

Although a stone on the **Wind River Reservation** marks the grave of **Sacajawea**, no one really knows when or how she died. One legend says that **Sacajawea** died in 1812 when she was only 25 years old. Other legends tell of a **Shoshoni** woman who lived to be 100 years old and died at **Fort Washakie** in **Wyoming**. This woman claimed to be **Sacajawea** and knew many details about the **U.S.** expedition led by **Meriwether Lewis** and **William Clark**.

 Titles

Titles are the names of books, movies, poems, songs, stories, and television series and episodes.

ReView the Rule

1. For all titles, capitalize the first word, last word, and all other words except articles, short prepositions, and conjunctions.

2. Underline or italicize the titles of books, movies, and television series.

3. Use quotation marks around titles of songs, stories, poems, and television episodes.

Practice

Now let's use what you have learned. Number your paper 1.–15. Rewrite each incorrect title correctly. Add the number of the rule above that applies. If the title in the sentence is correct, write **Correct**.

1. When you were younger, you probably watched sesame street on television.

2. Did you know that Sesame Street has won more Emmy awards than any other children's program?

3. Young children love to sing Elmo's Song.

4. Older children are more likely to watch shows such as Bill Nye, the science Guy and Nick News.

5. Many people watch reruns of The Addams Family and the munsters.

6. The Munsters was first shown on TV in 1964.

7. The first episode was titled My Fair Munster.

8. Maybe you enjoy National Geographic Special and other programs that take you around the world.

9. National geographic special has been nominated for Emmy awards nearly 100 times.

10. My favorite episode was called Air Force One.

11. My brother has watched an episode called Leopards of Zanzibar three times.

12. National Geographic also contributed to the movie pearl harbor.

13. ABC's Wide World of Sports has won more awards than any other sports show.

14. In 2001, wide world of sports celebrated its fortieth anniversary.

15. Wide World of Sports also publishes books, such as Race Across America.

Apply

Read this paragraph about television's Emmy Awards. Rewrite the paragraph on your paper, correcting the errors in capitalization, underlining, and punctuation.

The Emmy Awards go to actors, writers, and others who work in television. Each year, TV series such as The west wing and frasier are nominated as best shows in different categories. Will any series ever catch up to "The Mary Tyler Moore Show"? It won 29 Emmy Awards.

Answers appear below.

Practice

1. <u>Sesame Street</u>; Rule 1

2. <u>Sesame Street</u>; Rule 2
   Emmy Awards; Rule 1

3. "Elmo's Song"; Rule 3

4. <u>Bill Nye, the Science Guy</u> and <u>Nick News</u>; Rules 1 and 2

5. <u>The Munsters</u>; Rule 1

6. <u>The Munsters</u>; Rule 2

7. "My Fair Munster"; Rule 3

8. Correct

9. <u>National Geographic Special</u>; Rules 1 and 2
   Emmy Awards; Rule 1

10. "Air Force One"; Rule 3

11. "Leopards of Zanzibar"; Rule 3

12. <u>Pearl Harbor</u>; Rules 1 and 2

13. Correct

14. <u>Wide World of Sports</u>; Rules 1 and 2

15. <u>Wide World of Sports</u>; Rule 2
    <u>Race Across America</u>; Rule 2

Apply

The Emmy Awards go to actors, writers, and others who work in television. Each year, TV series such as **<u>The West Wing</u>** and **<u>Frasier</u>** are nominated as best shows in different categories. Will any series ever catch up to **<u>The Mary Tyler Moore Show</u>**? It won 29 Emmy Awards.

 Double Negatives

Negatives include words such as *no, not, none, nothing, nobody, no one, nowhere, hardly, barely, neither,* and *never.*

Review the Rule

Use only one **negative** in a sentence. If you use two of these words in a sentence, you are using a **double negative,** which is a grammar error.

Incorrect: There **wasn't no** one on the playground.

Correct: There was **no** one on the playground.
There **wasn't** anyone on the playground.

Practice

Now let's practice avoiding double negatives. Number your paper 1.–15. Read each sentence. If it is correct, write **Correct** on your paper. If the sentence contains a double negative, rewrite the sentence correctly. Remember that you often can correct a double negative in more than one way.

1. Everyone has read fables, which usually feature talking animals.
2. Some readers have not never heard of Aesop.
3. Historians do not know nothing about his life.
4. Most experts believe that he was not a real person.
5. Aesop's fables are not hardly the only popular fables.
6. Another famous writer of fables was the French author Jean de La Fontaine.
7. La Fontaine first followed the pattern set by Aesop, but later he focused on political topics.
8. Many lovers of fables believe that La Fontaine cannot be surpassed by no one as a storyteller.

9. Nobody can't forget his clever story of The Fox and the Crow.
10. No one can leave Lewis Carroll out when listing modern fable writers.
11. To many readers, his story Alice in Wonderland doesn't have no equals.
12. Fable fans must not forget Joel Chandler Harris or Beatrix Potter neither.
13. Joel Chandler Harris wrote the Bre'r Rabbit tales, fables set in the American South.
14. Some readers feel that there has not never been a better fable than Beatrix Potter's Peter Rabbit.
15. J.R.R. Tolkien's Hobbit is a fable, but his imaginary creatures are not no real animals.

Apply

Some sentences in this fable contain double negatives. Rewrite the fable to correct the errors.

 A peacock went to Juno, the queen of the gods. "There isn't nothing I would like better than to have a pretty singing voice like the other birds," he explained.

Juno replied, "You're not no good singer, but you do have a beautiful tail."

"But what about my ugly voice?" the peacock said.

Juno frowned. "Go away and don't never complain no more. If I gave you a beautiful voice, you would just find some other reason to be unhappy!"

Possible answers appear below.

Practice

1. Correct
2. Some readers have never heard of Aesop.
3. Historians know nothing about his life. (*or* Historians do not know anything about his life.)
4. Correct
5. Aesop's fables are not the only popular fables. (*or* Aesop's fables are hardly the only popular fables.)
6. Correct
7. Correct
8. Many lovers of fables believe that La Fontaine cannot be surpassed by anyone as a storyteller. (*or* Many lovers of fables believe that La Fontaine can be surpassed by no one as a storyteller.)
9. Nobody can forget his clever story of The Fox and the Crow.
10. Correct
11. To many readers, his story Alice in Wonderland doesn't have any equals. (*or* To many readers, his story Alice in Wonderland has no equals.)
12. Fable fans must not forget Joel Chandler Harris or Beatrix Potter either.

13. Correct
14. Some readers feel that there has never been a better fable than Beatrix Potter's Peter Rabbit. (*or* Some readers feel that there has not ever been a better fable than Beatrix Potter's Peter Rabbit.)
15. J.R.R. Tolkien's Hobbit is a fable, but his imaginary creatures are not real animals.

Apply

A peacock went to Juno, the queen of the gods. "There isn't anything I would like better than to have a pretty singing voice like the other birds," he explained.

Juno replied, "You're not a good singer, but you do have a beautiful tail."

"But what about my ugly voice?" the peacock said.

Juno frowned. "Go away and don't ever complain any more. If I gave you a beautiful voice, you would just find some other reason to be unhappy!"

 Direct and Indirect Quotations

A **direct quotation** is a speaker's exact words. An **indirect quotation** retells a speaker's words.

Review the Rule

For a **direct quotation**, use quotation marks at the beginning and end of the speaker's exact words. Use a comma to separate the speaker's exact words from the rest of the sentence. Begin a direct quotation with a capital letter and add end punctuation before the last quotation mark.

Example: Cora said, "I think mysteries are both fun and interesting."

An **indirect quotation** is not placed in quotation marks. It often begins with the word *that* or *whether*.

Example: Cora said that she thinks mysteries are both fun and interesting.

Practice

Now let's practice what you've learned about direct and indirect quotations. Number your paper 1.–15. Read each sentence. If the sentence is a direct quotation, write **D** on your paper. Then rewrite the sentence as an *indirect* quotation. If the sentence is an indirect quotation, write **I** on your paper. Then rewrite the sentence as a *direct* quotation.

1. Professor Holman announced to us that her talk would be about the history of mystery stories.
2. "Many readers consider Edgar Allan Poe to be the inventor of the modern mystery story," she said.
3. The professor explained that Poe's mysteries thrilled readers.
4. "Another early detective novel was *The Moonstone* by Wilkie Collins," she continued.
5. She added, "Collins was a good friend of Charles Dickens, another famous novelist."

6. I whispered to my mother that I had read a story by Wilkie Collins.
7. The professor said, "In 1887, the world's most famous literary detective appeared."
8. She explained that the detective was Sherlock Holmes.
9. She added that Holmes became an instant hit with readers.
10. "Is there anyone who does not recognize the tall, thin detective with the pipe and famous hat?" she asked.
11. "The Sherlock Holmes stories are told by his friend, Dr. Watson," she continued.
12. She added that *The Hound of the Baskervilles* is her favorite Holmes tale.
13. "Another interesting English detective was Father Brown," said the professor.
14. Then she asked whether the audience had a favorite Agatha Christie character.
15. "This English author is the creator of Miss Marple," she said.

Apply

This section of a mystery contains both direct and indirect quotations. Rewrite it on your paper, correcting the punctuation errors.

> As they entered the creepy old house, Robert and Jenny held their breath. Robert told Jenny that "he hoped the staircase was strong enough to hold them".
> "I hope so, too. Jenny replied in a whisper.
> As he put his hand on the stair railing, Robert heard "a strange, moaning sound."
> There's something behind that door! "Jenny screamed."

Possible answers appear below.

Practice

1. **I;** Professor Holman announced, "My talk will be about the history of mystery stories."
2. **D;** She said that many readers consider Edgar Allan Poe to be the inventor of the modern mystery story.
3. **I;** The professor explained, "Poe's mysteries thrilled readers."
4. **D;** She said that another early detective novel was *The Moonstone* by Wilkie Collins.
5. **D;** She added that Collins was a good friend of Charles Dickens, another famous novelist.
6. **I;** I whispered to my mother, "I read a story by Wilkie Collins."
7. **D;** The professor said that in 1887, the world's most famous literary detective appeared.
8. **I;** She explained, "The detective was Sherlock Holmes."
9. **I;** She added, "Holmes became an instant hit with readers."
10. **D;** She asked if there was anyone who did not recognize the tall, thin detective with the pipe and famous hat.
11. **D;** She explained that the Sherlock Holmes stories are told by his friend, Dr. Watson.
12. **I;** She added, "*The Hound of the Baskervilles* is my favorite Holmes tale."

13. **D;** The professor said that another interesting English detective was Father Brown.
14. **I;** Then she asked, "Do you have a favorite Agatha Christie character?"
15. **D;** She said that this English author was the creator of Miss Marple.

Apply

As they entered the creepy old house, Robert and Jenny held their breath. Robert told Jenny that he hoped the staircase was strong enough to hold them.

"I hope so, too," Jenny replied in a whisper.

As he put his hand on the stair railing, Robert heard a strange, moaning sound.

"There's something behind that door!" Jenny screamed.

 Pronouns and Antecedents

A **pronoun** is a word that replaces a noun. An **antecedent** is the word or phrase that a pronoun replaces. The antecedent of each pronoun should be clear. Pronouns must also agree with their antecedents in number.

Review the Rule

- The **antecedent** of a pronoun should be clear.

   Unclear: She checked the books and the reviews and is pleased with **them**. (Does *them* refer to books or reviews?)

   Clear: She checked the book reviews and is pleased with **them**. (The antecedent of *them* has to be *reviews*.)

- A **singular antecedent** requires a **singular pronoun**.

   Incorrect: A good **reviewer** tries to give the pros and cons of the novel **they** choose. (*Reviewer* is singular, but *they* is plural.)

   Correct: A good **reviewer** tries to give the pros and cons of the novel **she** chooses. (*Reviewer* and *she* are both singular.)

- A **plural antecedent** requires a **plural pronoun**.

   Incorrect: The book **reviewers** selected **his** book carefully. (*Reviewers* is plural, but *his* is singular.)

   Correct: The book **reviewers** selected **their** books carefully. (*Reviewers* and *their* are both plural.)

Practice

Number a separate sheet of paper 1.–10. If the pronoun and its antecedent agree, write them both. If the pronoun and its antecedent do not agree, write the whole sentence, correcting the error.

1. Quakers are a small group of people, but they have had a strong influence on world history.
2. Quakers consider George Fox to be the founder of her religion, the Society of Friends.
3. Early Quakers faced many challenges. Most English people were suspicious of him.
4. The Quakers refused to remove their hats when an important person passed.
5. Friends also used the words *thee* and *thou* instead of *you*. Some of them still use these words today.
6. Early Quakers also dressed in plain, simple clothes. They were mostly black or gray.
7. A Quaker today does not wear unusual clothes. Many of them, however, try to live a simple life.
8. Friends have helped people around the world for many years. For example, it has helped war refugees.
9. Quakers believe that they have a special mission to work for peace.
10. Some people confuse Quakers with Amish people. He is very different, however.

Apply

In this paragraph from a book review, two pronouns and their antecedents do not agree in number. Another antecedent is unclear. Rewrite the paragraph on your paper, correcting the errors.

In this book, Sheila Penrose describes groups such as the Mohawk, Seneca, and Abenaki. It used to live in the Northeast. She also includes beautiful color illustrations of clothing, homes, and artwork. It is breathtaking, with many fine details. Any reader interested in Native Americans should make this book their first choice!

Possible answers appear below.

Practice

1. **Quakers, they**
2. **Quakers consider George Fox to be the founder of their religion, the Society of Friends.**
3. **Early Quakers faced many challenges. Most English people were suspicious of them.**
4. **Quakers, their**
5. **Friends, them**
6. **clothes, They**
7. **Quakers today do not wear unusual clothes. Many of them, however, try to live a simple life.**
8. **Friends have helped people around the world for many years. For example, they have helped war refugees.**
9. **Quakers, they**
10. **Some people confuse Quakers with Amish people. They are very different, however.**

Apply

   In this book, Sheila Penrose describes groups such as the Mohawk, Seneca, and Abenaki. **They** used to live in the Northeast. She also includes beautiful color illustrations of clothing, homes, and artwork. **The clothing** is breathtaking, with many fine details. **Readers** interested in Native Americans should make this book their first choice!

 Sentence Fragments

A **sentence fragment** is a group of words that is punctuated like a sentence but is missing either a subject or a verb.

Review the Rule

A **complete sentence** has both a subject and a verb and expresses a complete thought. If a group of words is punctuated like a sentence but lacks either a subject or a verb, it is a **sentence fragment**.

Examples:

Sentence Fragment: Shelters in many communities throughout the state. (a subject without a verb)

Sentence Fragment: Are working hard to come up with new ideas. (a verb without a subject)

Complete Sentence: Many **experts have** ideas for solving the problem of stray animals. (a complete sentence with both a subject and a verb)

Practice

Number a separate sheet of paper 1.–15. Read the sentences below. If a sentence is complete, write **Correct**. If the words are a sentence fragment, rewrite the sentence and correct the error. Write **S** if you added a subject or **V** if you added a verb.

1. The Humane Society of the United States is the world's largest animal protection organization.
2. Has millions of supporters around the country.
3. Was founded in 1954.
4. Its staff includes veterinarians, scientists, and lawyers.
5. The Society's focus on companion animals, such as dogs and cats.
6. The Humane Society is also concerned with farm, circus, and zoo animals.
7. Pet overpopulation, a serious nationwide problem.
8. In 27 states, pets adopted from shelters must be spayed or neutered.
9. Helps to prevent pet overpopulation.
10. Helps to train animal shelter workers.
11. Work with police and judges to prevent animal abuse.
12. Opposes cruel methods of hunting and trapping.
13. Humane Society International is a worldwide organization.
14. Also supports a youth education division.
15. The group's encouragement of respect for and kindness toward animals.

Apply

Here is the body of a short letter to the director of an animal shelter. Rewrite it, adding the missing parts of a business letter. Make up information, if necessary. Also, correct any sentence fragments you find.

Our class would like to visit your shelter. We would like to know when would be a good time. Don't want to get in the way. One teacher, one parent, and about 23 students. We are eager to see the animals and find out how we can help. Please reply by February 4, if possible.

Possible answers appear below.

Practice

1. Correct
2. The Humane Society has millions of supporters around the country. S
3. The organization was founded in 1954. S
4. Correct
5. The Society's focus is on companion animals, such as dogs and cats. V
6. Correct
7. Pet overpopulation continues to be a serious nationwide problem. V
8. Correct
9. Spaying helps to prevent pet overpopulation. S
10. The Humane Society helps to train animal shelter workers. S
11. The Society's members work with police and judges to prevent animal abuse. S
12. The Humane Society opposes cruel methods of hunting and trapping. S
13. Correct
14. The organization also supports a youth education division. S
15. The group's encouragement of respect for and kindness toward animals is well known. V

Apply

1234 Redsail Drive
Orsville, KY 402––
January 4, 20––

Sheila Henderson, Director
Humane Society Animal Shelter
24 Roanoke Drive
Orsville, KY 402––

Dear Ms. Henderson:

Our class would like to visit your shelter. We would like to know when would be a good time. We don't want to get in the way. Our group will include one teacher, one parent, and about 23 students. We are eager to see the animals and find out how we can help. Please reply by February 4, if possible.

Sincerely,

Ben Joseph

Ben Joseph

 Review

Proofreading Checklist

☑ Do the subjects and verbs agree?
☑ Have compound sentences been joined with a comma and a conjunction or with a semicolon?
☑ Have I avoided run-on sentences and fragments?
☑ Do the appropriate words begin with a capital letter?
☑ Have I formed plural nouns and possessive nouns correctly?
☑ Did I use the correct form of each pronoun?
☑ Do all pronouns have a clear antecedent? Do they agree with their antecedents?
☑ Have I avoided using double negatives?
☑ Are all words spelled correctly?

Practice

Number a sheet of paper 1.–20. Rewrite each sentence, correcting any errors in grammar, capitalization, punctuation, or spelling. Use the checklist to help you.

1. Our class take a trip to a historic place every year.
2. Last year the class voted to visit boston, massachusetts.
3. The Freedom trail is a great way to see everything and it is free.
4. The trail through the streets begin on the Boston Common.
5. The place where British soldiers drilled.
6. As we past the graves of Samuel adams and John Hancock, I remembered reading about him.
7. Next we visited a bilding called the old south meeting house.
8. The famous Boston Tea Party began their.
9. The trail then took us to Paul Reveres house.
10. It was completed in 1677, it's the oldest house in Boston.
11. The Old North church with its steeple were just a few blocks away.
12. This is where two lantern's warned that the british were coming.
13. Our guide took a picture of Katrina and I.
14. What is that Monument on the hill!
15. It honors the heros of the Battle of Bunker hill.
16. The USS *Constitution* is docked in Boston Harbor but it is usually called "Old Ironsides."
17. The ship was closed for the day we were not able to see nothing.
18. We rested on benches that were put there for tourists' to use.
19. Near the Boston common were another well-know memorial.
20. It honors the african american soldiers who fought in the Civil War.

Apply

Copy the following travel brochure on your paper. Correct any mistakes.

Visit New England Now!
• Fall is the best time to see vermont.
• The summers noisy crouds have all gone home.
• Trees are turning colors and the air is cool and fresh.
• Everyones favorite time of year.
• Give we a chance to show you a good time.

Possible answers appear below.

Practice

1. Our class **takes** a trip to a historic place every year.
2. Last year the class voted to visit **Boston, Massachusetts.**
3. The Freedom **Trail** is a great way to see everything, and it is free.
4. The trail through the streets **begins** on the Boston Common.
5. **This is** the place where British soldiers drilled.
6. As we **passed** the graves of Samuel **Adams** and John Hancock, I remembered reading about **them.**
7. Next we visited a **building** called the **Old South Meeting House.**
8. The famous Boston Tea Party began **there.**
9. The trail then took us to Paul Revere's house.
10. It was completed in 1677; it's the oldest house in Boston.
11. The Old North **Church** with its steeple **was** just a few blocks away.
12. This is where two **lanterns** warned that the **British** were coming.
13. Our guide took a picture of Katrina and **me.**
14. What is that **monument** on the hill**?**
15. It honors the **heroes** of the Battle of Bunker **Hill.**
16. The USS *Constitution* is docked in Boston Harbor, but it is usually called "Old Ironsides."
17. The ship was closed for the day; we were not able to see **anything.**
18. We rested on benches that were put there for **tourists** to use.
19. Near the Boston **Common was** another **well-known** memorial.
20. It honors the **African American** soldiers who fought in the Civil War.

Apply

Visit New England Now!
• Fall is the best time to see **Vermont.**
• The summer's noisy **crowds** have all gone home.
• Trees are turning colors, and the air is cool and fresh.
• **This is** everyone's favorite time of year.
• Give **us** a chance to show you a good time.

Writer's HandBook

The Writer's Handbook is designed to give you more help as well as some great hints for making your writing the best it can be. It uses the Gather, Organize, Write, Elaborate, Clarify, Proofread, and Share categories you have become familiar with during the course of this book. Use the Writer's Handbook any time you have more questions or just need a little extra help.

Table of Contents

Writer's Handbook   HB 1

Research

Research is an important part of writing. When you look for information about a topic, you are doing research. It's important to use good sources.

A **source** is anything or anyone with information. **Primary sources** include books or people that are closest to the information. Diaries, journals, and other writings of people who lived during the described events are considered primary sources. **Secondary sources** are books or people who use other books or people to get information. Primary and secondary sources fit into three categories—**printed, electronic,** and **personal**.

Use a variety of primary and secondary sources from different categories when you do research. That way you can make sure the information is accurate and you will have lots of it to choose from. Talk to your teacher about how many sources and what kinds of sources to use for different writing projects.

- **Printed sources** include books, magazines, newspapers, letters, journals and diaries, and reference materials such as encyclopedias and dictionaries.
- **Electronic sources** include the Internet, television, radio, and videos.
- **Personal sources** include people you interview or observe and your own experiences and memories.

When doing research, keep these points in mind:

- When you use sources, be sure they are **credible** ones. Credible means that the source can be trusted to have accurate information. Generally, books, magazines, and reference materials can be considered credible sources. People who are experts in their field and those you know and trust personally are also credible sources.
- Use caution when using Web sites, movies, and television as sources. Many Web sites offer the opinion of the people who created them, not necessarily the facts about a topic. Check several Web sites and some printed sources on the same topic to be sure you are getting "just the facts." Also, Web sites often move or become outdated, so check to see that the ones you are using are still in operation. Finally, make sure you have an adult—a teacher or parent—help you as you do research on the Internet.
- Movies and television offer a lot of information, but it is often difficult to tell if the information is fact, fiction, or someone's opinion. Again, double check with other sources and with an adult to be sure you are getting accurate information.

	Printed	Electronic	Personal
Sources	Books, Magazines, Newspapers, Reference Materials, Letters, Journals/Diaries	The Internet, Television, Radio, Videos	Self, Other People
Where to Find Them	Library, Home, School, Bookstores, Discount Department Stores	The Internet, Television, Radio, Stores, Library	**Home:** Parents, Siblings, Grandparents **School:** Teachers, Principals, Librarians, Friends, Other Family Members, People in the Community
How to Use Them	Use headings to find useful information. Read. Take notes while reading.	Read Web sites. Watch the news on television. Listen to radio programs. Rent or check out videos. Take notes as you are reading, watching, and listening.	Listen to people when they tell stories. Interview people who know something about your topic. Ask questions. Take notes.
How to Cite Them (Use punctuation and capitalization as shown.)	**Books:** Author's Last Name, First Name. <u>Book Title</u>. City: Publishing Company, year. **Magazine Articles:** Author's Last Name, First Name. "Title of Article." Title of Magazine, volume number (if there is one), date, month, or season, and year of publication: page number. (If the article is longer than one page, state the first page and the last page of the article with a dash between them.) **Encyclopedias/Dictionaries:** Title of Encyclopedia or Dictionary, edition number (ed. __), s.v. "item." (If you looked up Olympic Games, it would be s.v. "Olympic Games.") **Letters/Diaries/Journals:** Mention them in the text as you are writing, rather than citing them later.	**Internet:** State the Web address of the Web sites you used. Most Web addresses will begin with http:// and end with .com, .net, .org, or .edu. **Films/Videos:** Title of Film or Video. City where the production company is located: Production Company Name, year. **Television/Radio:** Mention them in the text as you are writing, rather than citing them later.	Personal sources should be mentioned in the text as you are writing. When interviewing, you can quote the person by enclosing his or her exact words in quotation marks. You can also use phrases such as "according to" to give credit to your source. To give credit to personal sources other than people you interview, simply state where you found the information.

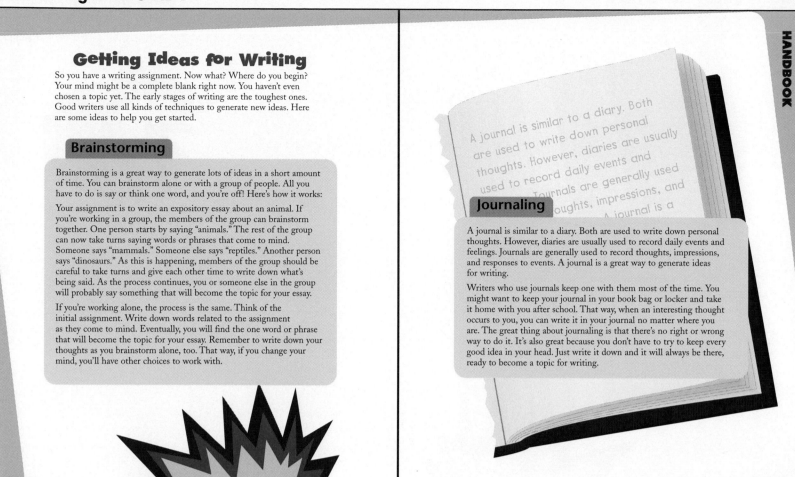

HANDBOOK

Getting Ideas for Writing

So you have a writing assignment. Now what? Where do you begin? Your mind might be a complete blank right now. You haven't even chosen a topic yet. The early stages of writing are the toughest ones. Good writers use all kinds of techniques to generate new ideas. Here are some ideas to help you get started.

Brainstorming

Brainstorming is a great way to generate lots of ideas in a short amount of time. You can brainstorm alone or with a group of people. All you have to do is say or think one word, and you're off! Here's how it works:

Your assignment is to write an expository essay about an animal. If you're working in a group, the members of the group can brainstorm together. One person starts by saying "animals." The rest of the group can now take turns saying words or phrases that come to mind. Someone says "mammals." Someone else says "reptiles." Another person says "dinosaurs." As this is happening, members of the group should be careful to take turns and give each other time to write down what's being said. As the process continues, you or someone else in the group will probably say something that will become the topic for your essay.

If you're working alone, the process is the same. Think of the initial assignment. Write down words related to the assignment as they come to mind. Eventually, you will find the one word or phrase that will become the topic for your essay. Remember to write down your thoughts as you brainstorm alone, too. That way, if you change your mind, you'll have other choices to work with.

Journaling

A journal is similar to a diary. Both are used to write down personal thoughts. However, diaries are usually used to record daily events and feelings. Journals are generally used to record thoughts, impressions, and responses to events. A journal is a great way to generate ideas for writing.

Writers who use journals keep one with them most of the time. You might want to keep your journal in your book bag or locker and take it home with you after school. That way, when an interesting thought occurs to you, you can write it in your journal no matter where you are. The great thing about journaling is that there's no right or wrong way to do it. It's also great because you don't have to try to keep every good idea in your head. Just write it down and it will always be there, ready to become a topic for writing.

HB 6 Writer's Handbook

Writer's Handbook HB 7

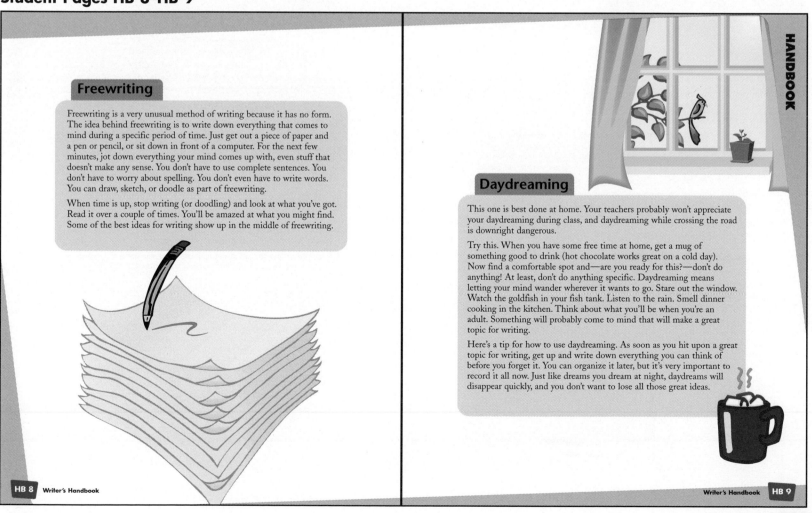

HANDBOOK

Freewriting

Freewriting is a very unusual method of writing because it has no form. The idea behind freewriting is to write down everything that comes to mind during a specific period of time. Just get out a piece of paper and a pen or pencil, or sit down in front of a computer. For the next few minutes, jot down everything your mind comes up with, even stuff that doesn't make any sense. You don't have to use complete sentences. You don't have to worry about spelling. You don't even have to write words. You can draw, sketch, or doodle as part of freewriting.

When time is up, stop writing (or doodling) and look at what you've got. Read it over a couple of times. You'll be amazed at what you might find. Some of the best ideas for writing show up in the middle of freewriting.

Daydreaming

This one is best done at home. Your teachers probably won't appreciate your daydreaming during class, and daydreaming while crossing the road is downright dangerous.

Try this. When you have some free time at home, get a mug of something good to drink (hot chocolate works great on a cold day). Now find a comfortable spot and—are you ready for this?—don't do anything! At least, don't do anything specific. Daydreaming means letting your mind wander wherever it wants to go. Stare out the window. Watch the goldfish in your fish tank. Listen to the rain. Smell dinner cooking in the kitchen. Think about what you'll be when you're an adult. Something will probably come to mind that will make a great topic for writing.

Here's a tip for how to use daydreaming. As soon as you hit upon a great topic for writing, get up and write down everything you can think of before you forget it. You can organize it later, but it's very important to record it all now. Just like dreams you dream at night, daydreams will disappear quickly, and you don't want to lose all those great ideas.

HB 8 Writer's Handbook

Writer's Handbook HB 9

Writer's Handbook

Reading

Sometimes the easiest way to get ideas for writing is to read. For example, let's say you have been asked to write a piece of narrative historical fiction. You don't know much about history. How do you write about something you don't know? Make use of your library.

Talk to your school librarian or go to the public library and ask for help at the information desk. These people are experts. Tell them you are looking for a few books about history. They will probably ask you some questions such as, "What kind of history are you interested in reading about?" or, "Would you like books about U.S. history or world history?" These questions will help you to make some early decisions about your writing. Once you decide what kind of history you want to read about, pick a few books that are short enough to read quickly, but long enough to have lots of interesting information. Again, people who work at libraries can help you through this process.

As you read about history, you will spot things that interest you. Write down those things. Skip over the stuff you don't find interesting, at least for now. When you are finished reading, look at the notes you took. Do they have anything in common? Do most of them have something to do with specific time periods, people, or things in history? For example, in reading about U.S. history, did you always stop at the sections about inventions because you found that information interesting? Maybe you can focus your writing assignment on an invention or an inventor.

Don't forget to read for your own interest and pleasure. The more you read, the more you'll know. The more you know, the more ideas for writing you will have.

TV/Movies

Great ideas for writing may be as close as your television or movie theater. There are cable channels that run programs specifically about science, technology, history, animals, cooking, music, sports, and just about any other topic you can think of. Public television also has great documentaries and programs about interesting and unusual topics.

Movies can also be good for generating ideas for writing—especially movies that deal with specific topics. Are you a fan of sci-fi movies? You can use your favorite sci-fi movie to come up with ideas for an expository essay about artificial intelligence or a compare-and-contrast report about robots and computers.

Just as you should use caution when using television and movies as sources when you write, be cautious in using them to generate ideas. Make sure you talk to an adult about appropriate and safe choices in movies and television programs.

Interviewing

An interview is the process of asking questions of another person and listening to and recording that person's answers. Interviews make good sources for writing projects, especially if the person you interview is an expert about your topic. Interviews can also be good ways to generate ideas for writing.

Some of the most interesting stories come from people in your community and family. Your parents and grandparents have lived through many events. Sit down with a family member or another trusted adult and ask that person to tell you about a memorable event he or she experienced or an interesting person he or she knew. You'll be amazed at the stories you will hear. Many famous authors say that their stories were inspired by what other people have told them.

As you listen to people's stories, jot down notes. It's safe to say that something the person said during the interview will probably give you a good idea for your own writing project.

Prewriting Organize

Note Taking

As you are doing research for your writing project, you will want to take notes. That way you will have the most important information in small pieces that you can use easily. However, taking notes can be tricky, especially for the beginner. Here are some things to keep in mind:

- Keep your notes short. You don't have to use complete sentences, as long as you include the important information.

- Make sure your handwriting is legible. If you scribble, you may not be able to read your own notes later.

- Use note cards. That way you can arrange your notes without having to rewrite them. Try using different colors of note cards to help you organize your notes.

- When listening to a speaker and taking notes, don't try to write down what the speaker is saying "word for word." Just make sure you get the important stuff.

- When you are interviewing, however, you will want to get the exact words down on paper. In this case, ask the speaker to repeat what he or she said, so you can write the quote. If it's possible, use a tape recorder during the interview, so you can listen to the quote as often as you need to. Just make sure you get the speaker's permission to record the interview.

- It's important to write down the source of your information on your note cards as you are taking notes. That way you can cite or credit your sources easily.

Graphic Organizers

A graphic organizer is a tool that helps writers put information in order before they start a draft. Graphic organizers include storyboards, sequence chains, spider maps, network trees, support patterns, attribute charts, cause-and-effect chains, story maps, pros-and-cons charts, 5 W's charts, order-of-importance organizers, main idea tables, Venn diagrams, and outlines. When you do other writing projects, you'll want to continue to use them to help you keep track of information. What kind of graphic organizers you use depends on what kind of writing project you use. Check back with this book to see what kind of graphic organizer works best for different writing projects.

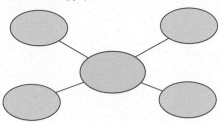

Outlining

There are many ways to organize information. One very useful organizer that you have used is an outline. The outline helps you put your information in the order it will appear in your writing. The outline can be divided into several basic pieces—the introduction, the body, and the conclusion—just like a basic essay. Every letter and number in the outline stands for something in your essay. Words or phrases that are designated with Roman numerals represent entire chunks of an essay. Words or phrases that are designated with capital letters represent paragraphs which support a main statement or idea. Words or phrases that are designated with regular numbers represent specific details. Here's a basic outline.

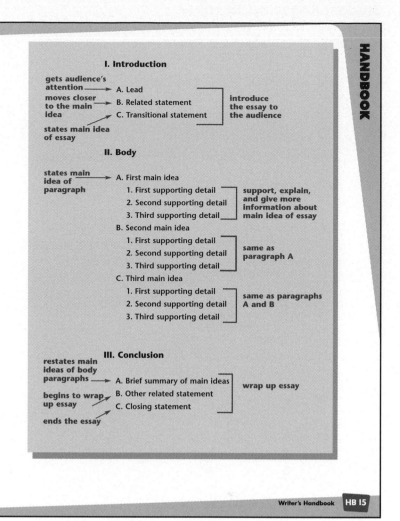

I. Introduction

gets audience's attention → A. Lead
moves closer to the main idea → B. Related statement
states main idea of essay → C. Transitional statement
⎫ introduce the essay to the audience

II. Body

states main idea of paragraph → A. First main idea
1. First supporting detail
2. Second supporting detail
3. Third supporting detail
⎫ support, explain, and give more information about main idea of essay

B. Second main idea
1. First supporting detail
2. Second supporting detail
3. Third supporting detail
⎫ same as paragraph A

C. Third main idea
1. First supporting detail
2. Second supporting detail
3. Third supporting detail
⎫ same as paragraphs A and B

III. Conclusion

restates main ideas of body paragraphs → A. Brief summary of main ideas
begins to wrap up essay → B. Other related statement
ends the essay → C. Closing statement
⎫ wrap up essay

Drafting
Write

Writing Paragraphs

A paragraph is a group of related sentences. The main idea of a paragraph is usually in the first sentence, called the **topic sentence**. The rest of the sentences in a paragraph give more information about the topic sentence. Start with the idea you want your audience to know. This will become the topic sentence for your paragraph. For example, let's say your essay is an expository piece about horses. You have gathered information about horses and made a web to put your information in order.

Your web may look something like this:

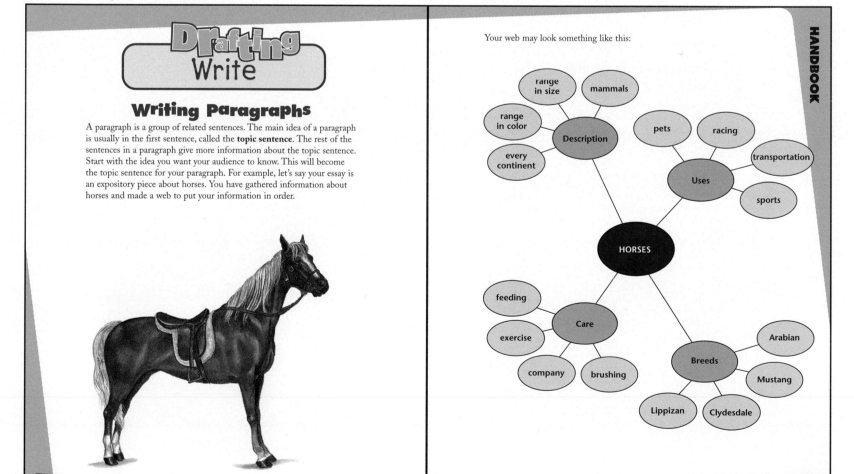

Take one part of your web—Breeds. Write it as a sentence. You might come up with this:

> There are many different kinds, or breeds, of horses.

This is now your topic sentence. Now it's time to tell your audience more information about the main idea. If you have gathered information about horses, you might have these facts.

1. Arabian horses were prized by Bedouin tribes in the desert for their speed, beauty, and intelligence.
2. The Mustang is a well-known breed in North America and descends from Spanish horses.
3. The Clydesdale is native to Scotland and is one of the largest breeds.
4. The Lippizan horses were bred for the royal family of Spain, who valued them for their dazzling white coats, graceful appearance, and gentleness.

When you combine your topic sentence with these supporting sentences, you have a paragraph.

> There are many different kinds, or breeds, of horses. Arabian horses were prized by Bedouin tribes in the desert for their speed, beauty, and intelligence. The Mustang is a well-known breed in North America and descends from Spanish horses. The Clydesdale is native to Scotland and is one of the largest breeds. The Lippizan horses were bred for the royal family of Spain, who valued them for their dazzling white coats, graceful appearance, and gentleness.

Following the same steps for the other three parts of your web will give you three more paragraphs. Put these together, and you will have the body of a well-organized essay. All you need now is an introduction and a conclusion. For tips about writing good introductions and conclusions see "Writing a Five-Paragraph Essay" on page HB20.

Writing a Five-Paragraph Essay

An essay is a piece of nonfiction writing about one topic. In grades 5 and 6, you practice writing a descriptive essay, a compare-and-contrast essay, a cause-and-effect essay, and a persuasive essay. Essays are made up of three basic parts—the introduction, the body, and the conclusion.

Write the body of your essay first. It doesn't matter that you don't have an introduction yet. It's very difficult to write a good introduction until you have written the body. Imagine trying to introduce a person you don't know to an audience. What would you say? That's kind of what it's like to try writing an introduction first. You don't know your essay yet. Write the body first and then you'll know what to say in your introduction.

Body

The body of your essay is where you explain, describe, prove, and give information about your main idea. Look at your graphic organizer. There's a good chance that you already have the makings of several good paragraphs.

Let's pretend you're writing a descriptive essay on your favorite vacation spot—the beach. After gathering and organizing your information, you may have three main points in your graphic organizer—how it looks, how it feels, and how it sounds. Look at the web on page HB21.

To move from one paragraph to the next, use a trick good writers know. It's called a "signal word." There's a list of these words on page HB41.

Once you have written all the paragraphs of the body of your essay, it's time to write the introduction and the conclusion.

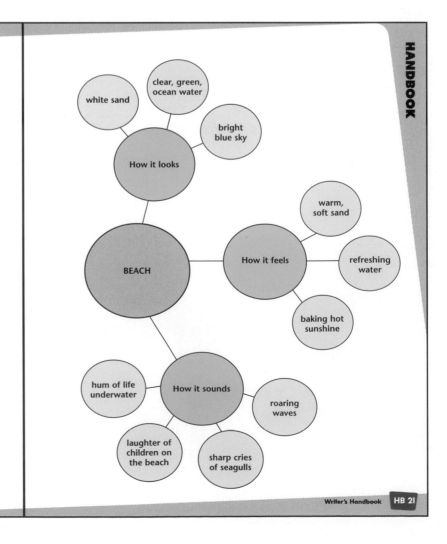

HANDBOOK

Introduction

The introduction is the first part of the essay that your audience will read or hear. You want it to get their attention and make them interested enough to keep reading or listening. You don't want to give away what's in the essay.

The Upside-Down Pyramid

If your introduction were a graphic organizer, it would look like an upside-down pyramid with more general information at the beginning and more specific information at the end. Let's write an introduction for our descriptive essay about the beach.

The first sentence of your introduction should say something true but general about your topic.

There are many great places to go on vacation.

This sentence gives some examples of vacation spots. It's still pretty general, but it gets closer to the main idea.

Amusement parks, campgrounds, and cities are some good choices for vacation spots.

This sentence should be the main idea of your essay.

For the sights, the sounds, and feeling good, nothing beats my favorite vacation spot—the beach.

Here's the complete introduction:

There are many great places to go on vacation. Amusement parks, campgrounds, and cities are some good choices for vacation spots. For the sights, the sounds, and feeling good, nothing beats my favorite vacation spot—the beach.

Remember—start with something general and true. Then say something a little more specific. Finish with the main idea of the essay. Now your introduction is complete.

Conclusion

The conclusion of an essay does two things. It restates the main idea of the essay, and it wraps up the essay. Restating the main idea is important. You want to make sure your audience remembers what the essay was about. Wrapping things up helps the audience feel that they have read a complete work and that nothing is missing.

The Right-Side-Up Pyramid

If the introduction of your essay looks like an upside-down pyramid, the conclusion looks like a pyramid right-side-up with more specific information at the beginning and more general information at the end. Here's how:

The first sentence of the conclusion should restate the main idea.

The beach is an amazing place to go on vacation if you want to see beautiful things, hear interesting and fun sounds, and feel great.

The next sentence should say something a little more general but still stay on the main idea.

It's a good idea to visit different and interesting places on vacation.

The final sentence should wrap things up and finish the essay. It should be very general.

Beaches all over the world offer a wonderful way to relax and enjoy your vacation.

When you put your conclusion together, it will look like this:

The beach is an amazing place to go on vacation if you want to see beautiful things, hear interesting and fun sounds, and feel great. It's a good idea to visit different and interesting places on vacation. Beaches all over the world offer a wonderful way to relax and enjoy your vacation.

HANDBOOK

Writing Poetry

Poetry is different from other forms of writing. Some poems are written in lines and stanzas and follow a rhyme or rhythm. Some poems are simply words or phrases with no rhyme. Most poems are full of imagery or word pictures. Whatever form a poem takes, it's one of the most creative forms of writing.

When you start to write a poem, the first thing to do is to pick a subject. It's a good idea to pick a subject that you know something about or a subject that means a lot to you. Next you should try to write down interesting ideas about your subject. You can write down your ideas however you like.

Then it is time to write your first draft. Once again, you can use any form you like to write your poem. Be sure to use plenty of descriptive words, or words that describe sounds, smells, tastes, and how things look and feel. As you begin to write, your poem might already be taking on its own form.

Revising is an important part of all writing, including writing poetry. You'll probably revise your poem many times. You might want to try changing the form of your poem. Once it's written, you may think it would be better stated in rhyme. You may think your poem is better if it doesn't rhyme. Just make sure your poem's message and ideas are clear to your readers.

Once you have written your final version, read it over to yourself. Then read it out loud. You may find more areas to improve.

Types of Poetry

Ballad: A ballad tells a story. Ballads are usually written as quatrains (four-line stanzas). Often, the first and third lines have four accented syllables; the second and fourth have three.

Blank Verse: Blank verse poems do not rhyme, but they have meter. Beginning with the second syllable of a line, every other syllable is accented.

Epic: An epic is a long poem that tells a story. The story describes adventures of heroes.

Free Verse: Free verse poems do not rhyme and do not have meter.

Haiku: Haiku is a form of poetry developed in Japan. The words of a haiku poem represent nature. A haiku is three lines in length. The first line is five syllables; the second is seven syllables; and the third is five syllables in length.

Limerick: A limerick is a funny poem that has five lines. Lines one, two, and five rhyme and have three stressed syllables. Lines three and four rhyme and have two stressed syllables.

Lyric: A lyric is a short poem that expresses personal feeling.

Ode: An ode is a long lyric. It expresses deeper feelings and uses poetic devices and imagery.

Sonnet: A sonnet is a fourteen-line poem that expresses personal feeling. Each line in a sonnet is ten syllables in length; every other syllable is stressed, beginning with the second syllable.

Poetry Terms

Alliteration: Alliteration is the repeating of the beginning consonant sounds:

cute, cuddly, calico cats

End Rhyme: End rhyme refers to the rhyming words at the ends of two or more lines of poetry:

Her favorite pastime was to take a **hike**.
His first choice was to ride a **bike**.

Foot: A foot is one unit of meter.

Meter: Meter is the pattern of accented and unaccented syllables in the lines of a traditional poem.

Onomatopoeia: Onomatopoeia is the use of a word whose sound makes you think of its meaning. Here are some examples:

bang, beep, buzz, clang, swish, thump, zoom

Quatrain: A quatrain is a four-line stanza:

At night she looks up at the stars
And thinks of what might be.
By day she works and studies so
To someday live her dreams.

Stanza: A stanza is a section in a poem named for the number of lines it contains.

Verse: Verse is a name for a line of traditional poetry.

Revising
Elaborate and Clarify

Thesaurus

When it comes to saying things in different, more interesting ways, the thesaurus is one of the best friends a writer can have.

A thesaurus is a reference book that lists the *synonyms* (words that have the same or similar meaning) of words, and the *antonyms* (words that have the opposite meaning) of words.

Many times writers get stuck using the same words over and over. It's difficult to think of new and more colorful words. The next time you are writing, ask yourself, "Have I used a word too many times? Is there a better way to say this?" Chances are, the answer will be yes. That's where a thesaurus can help.

For example, let's say you are writing a descriptive essay about a place, and you have picked a beach where you vacationed last summer. You have written that the ocean was **beautiful**. You have said that the sky was a **beautiful** shade of blue. You have stated that the tropical plants were **beautiful**. Do you see a pattern yet?

All those things were beautiful, but there are more colorful words you can use. Maybe the ocean is **stunning** or **spectacular**. The sky might be a **lovely** or even an **exquisite** shade of blue. And how about those tropical plants? Are they **extravagant**, **magnificent**, or **dramatic** in their beauty? Use rich words and your writing becomes truly **fabulous**.

Dictionary

One of the most helpful tools for writers is the dictionary. Just think of it! Every word you could possibly need is in there. Until now, you might have used your dictionary only to look up the spellings of difficult words. That's important because good spelling makes writing clearer, but it's not the only information in a dictionary.

Your dictionary contains valuable information, such as the history of words, a guide for pronunciation, foreign words and phrases, the names of historical people, the names of places in the world, and lots of other interesting things. Some dictionaries even contain the Declaration of Independence and the Constitution of the United States! The next time you are looking for more than just the spelling of a word, try your dictionary.

Web Sites

With the help of an adult, try these Web sites for even more help in building your vocabulary and making your writing richer and clearer.

http://www.writetools.com
This is a one-stop Web site for writers. It contains links to reference materials, almanacs, calendars, historical documents, government resources, grammar and style guides, and all kinds of other tools for writing and editing.

http://www.bartleby.com
This Web site has links to several on-line dictionaries, encyclopedias, thesauri, and many other useful and interesting sources. It also contains links to on-line fiction and nonfiction books. It's like having a library of your own.

Editing
Proofread

Capitalization

Capitalize:

- the first word in a sentence.
- all proper nouns, including people's names and the names of particular places.
- titles of respect.
- family titles used just before people's names and titles of respect that are part of names.
- initials of names.
- place names.
- proper adjectives, adjectives that are made from proper nouns.
- the months of the year and the days of the week.
- important words in the names of organizations.
- important words in the names of holidays.
- the first word in the greeting or closing of a letter.
- the word *I*.
- the first, last, and most important words in a title. Be sure to capitalize all verbs including *is* and *was*.
- the first word in a direct quotation.

Sentence Structure

The Sentence

A sentence is a group of words that tells a complete thought. A sentence has two parts: a **subject** and a **predicate**.

- The complete subject tells who or what.
  A famous artist painted the picture.
- The complete predicate tells what happened.
  A famous artist **painted the picture**.

Subject

The **subject** of a sentence tells whom or what the sentence is about.

- The **complete** subject includes all the words that name and tell about the subject.
  A **famous artist** painted the picture.

- The **simple** subject is the most important noun or pronoun in the complete subject.
  A famous **artist** painted the picture.

- A sentence can have one subject.
  Jessica walked home.

- A sentence can have a **compound** subject, two or more subjects that share the same predicate.
  Jessica and Joan walked home.

Predicate

The **predicate** of a sentence tells what happened.
The **complete** predicate includes a verb and all the words that tell what happened.

- A **complete** predicate can tell what the subject of the sentence did. This kind of predicate includes an action verb.
  A famous artist **painted the picture**.

- A complete predicate can also tell more about the subject. This kind of predicate includes a **linking verb**.
  The coat **was** red wool.

- A **predicate noun** follows a linking verb and renames the subject.
  The garment was **a coat**.

- A **predicate adjective** follows a linking verb and describes the subject.
  The coat was **red**.

- A **compound** predicate is two or more predicates that share the same subject. Compound predicates are often joined by the conjunction *and* or *or*.
  James **ran** across the deck and **jumped** into the pool.

- The **simple** predicate is the most important word or words in the complete predicate. The simple predicate is always a verb.
  A famous artist **painted** the picture.

Simple, Compound, and Complex Sentences

- A **simple** sentence tells one complete thought.
  A famous artist painted the picture.

- A **compound** sentence is made up of two simple sentences joined by a comma and a conjunction *(and, or, but)*. The two simple sentences in a compound sentence can also be joined by a semicolon. Two simple sentences can go together to make one compound sentence if the ideas in the simple sentences are related.
  Tony cut out the letters, **and** Shanna glued them to the poster.

- A **complex** sentence is made up of one **independent clause** (or simple sentence), and at least one **dependent clause**. A **dependent clause** is a group of words that has a subject and a predicate but cannot stand on its own.
  Dependent Clause: while Shanna glued them to the poster
  Independent Clause: Tony cut out the letters
  Complex Sentence: Tony cut out the letters, while Shanna glued them to the poster.

Subject-Verb Agreement

- The subject and its verb must agree in number.
  One **part** of speech **is** a noun.
  (*Part* is singular; it requires the verb *is*.)

  The **sweatshirts** on the rack **were** on sale.
  (*Sweatshirts* is plural; it requires the verb *were*.)

- Sometimes a **helping verb** is needed to help the main verb show action. A helping verb comes before a main verb.
  Joe **has watched** the team practice.

- An **action verb** shows action in a sentence.
  A penguin **waddles** and **slides** on the ice.

- A **linking verb** does not show action. It connects the subject of a sentence to a word or words in the predicate that tell about the subject. Linking verbs include *am, is, are, was,* and *were. Seem* and *become* are linking verbs, too.
  The coat **is** red wool.
  This milk **seems** sour.

Abbreviations

Abbreviations are shortened forms of words. Many abbreviations begin with a capital letter and end with a period.

Abbreviate:

- titles of address and titles of respect.
  Mister (Mr. Robert Sing)
  Mistress (Mrs. Amy Walters)
  Doctor (Dr. Donna Rodrigues)

- words used in addresses.
  Street (St.)
  Avenue (Ave.)
  Route (Rt.)
  Boulevard (Blvd.)
  Road (Rd.)

- certain words in the names of businesses.
  Incorporated (Inc.)
  Corporation (Corp.)
  Limited (Ltd.)

- days of the week when you take notes.
  Sunday (Sun.)
  Monday (Mon.)
  Tuesday (Tues.)
  Wednesday (Wed.)
  Thursday (Thurs.)
  Friday (Fri.)
  Saturday (Sat.)

- most months of the year.
  January (Jan.)
  February (Feb.)
  March (Mar.)
  April (Apr.)
  August (Aug.)
  September (Sept.)
  October (Oct.)
  November (Nov.)
  December (Dec.)
  (May, June, and July do not have abbreviated forms.)

- directions.
  North (N)
  East (E)
  South (S)
  West (W)

Quotation Marks

Quotation marks are used to separate a speaker's exact words from the rest of the sentence. Begin a **direct quotation** with a capital letter. Use a comma to separate the direct quotation from the speaker's name. When a direct quotation comes at the end of a sentence, put the end mark inside the last quotation mark. When writing a conversation, begin a new paragraph with each change of speaker. For example:

> Tim said, "My homework is done." He was hoping to go rollerblading before dinner.

> "You can go," his mom answered. "Just be back before dinnertime."

End Marks

Every sentence must end with a **period,** an **exclamation point,** or a **question mark.**

- Use a **period** at the end of a statement (declarative sentence) or a command (imperative sentence).
  Statement: The sky is blue.
  Command: Please come here.

- Use an **exclamation point** at the end of a firm command (imperative sentence)
  Shut the door!

  or at the end of a sentence that shows great feeling or excitement (exclamatory sentence)
  It's hot!

- Use a **question mark** at the end of an asking sentence (interrogative sentence).
  Is it raining?

Commas

Use a **comma:**

- after an introductory word in a sentence.
  Wow, you're here.

- to separate items in a series. Put the last comma before *and* or *or.*
  Jessica bought paper, pens, and a pencil.

- when speaking directly to a person.
  Alan, take your seat.

- to separate a direct quotation from the speaker's name.
  Tim said, "My homework is done."

- with the conjunctions *and, or,* or *but* when combining independent clauses in a compound sentence.
  He could play soccer, or he could run track.

Parts of Speech

Nouns

- A **singular noun** names one person, place, thing, or idea.
  boy   watch   cat

- A **plural noun** names more than one person, place, thing or idea. To make most singular nouns plural, add *-s.*
  boys   cats

- For nouns ending in *sh, ch, x,* or *z,* add *-es* to make the word plural.
  watch/watches   box/boxes

- For nouns ending in a consonant and *y,* change the *y* to *i* and add *-es.*
  pony/ponies   story/stories

- For many nouns that end in *f* or *fe,* replace *f* or *fe* with *ves* to make the noun plural.
  hoof/hooves   shelf/shelves

- Some words change spelling when the plural is formed.
  man/men   child/children

- Some words have the same singular and plural form.
  deer/deer   fish/fish

HANDBOOK

Possessive Nouns

A **possessive noun** shows ownership.

- To make a singular noun possessive, add an apostrophe and *-s.*
  boy/boy's   cat/cat's   watch/watch's

- When a singular noun ends in *s,* add an apostrophe and *-s.*
  dress/dress's   class/class's

- To make a plural noun that ends in *s* possessive, add an apostrophe.
  boys/boys'   cats/cats'   watches/watches'

- When a plural noun does not end in *s,* add an apostrophe and *-s* to show possession.
  women/women's   children/children's

Verbs

Verbs can tell about the present, the past, or the future.

- The **present tense** is used to show that something happens regularly or is true now.
  Add *-s* to most verbs to show present tense when the subject is *he, she, it,* or a singular noun.
  He walks to school.

  Add *-es* to verbs ending in *s, ch, sh, x,* or *z.*
  Joe watches the team practice.

  Do not add *-s* or *-es* if the subject is a plural noun or *I, you, we,* or *they.*
  I want to go to the park.

  Change *y* to *i* and add *-es* to form some present tense verbs.
  Sam hurries to school.

- The **past tense** shows past action. Add *-ed* to most verbs to form the past tense.
  climb/climbed   watch/watched   show/showed

- Past tense verbs that do not add *-ed* are called **irregular verbs.**

Present	Past	Past Participle (with *have, has,* or *had*)
bring	brought	brought
go	went	gone
grow	grew	grown
know	knew	known
take	took	taken

- The **future tense** indicates future action. Use the helping verb *will* to form the future tense.
  Joe will watch the team practice.

- The **present perfect tense** shows action that began in the past and may still be happening. To form the present perfect tense, add the helping verb *has* or *have* to the past participle of a verb.
  Joe has watched the team practice.

Pronouns

A **pronoun** can replace a **noun** naming a person, place, thing, or idea. Personal pronouns include *I, me, you, we, us, he, she, it, they,* and *them.*

- A **subject** pronoun takes the place of the subject of a sentence. Subject pronouns are said to be in the **subjective case.** Do not use both the pronoun and the noun it replaces together.
  Incorrect: Marla she answered the question.
  Correct: Marla answered the question.

HANDBOOK

- An **object** pronoun replaces a noun that is the object of a verb or preposition. Object pronouns are said to be in the **objective case**. Rosco came with **us**.

- Use a **subject** pronoun as part of a **compound subject**. Use an **object** pronoun as part of a **compound object**. To test whether a pronoun is correct, say the sentence *without* the other part of a compound subject or object.
  Incorrect: Rosco and **him** came with Jessica and **we**.
  Correct: Rosco and **he** came with Jessica and **us**.

- An **antecedent** is the word or phrase a pronoun refers to. The antecedent always includes a noun.
  Joan cleaned **her** room.

- A pronoun must match its antecedent. An antecedent and pronoun agree when they have the same **number** (singular or plural) and **gender** (male or female).

- **Possessive** pronouns show ownership. The words *my, your, his, her, its, their,* and *our* are possessive pronouns.

- The **interrogative** pronouns *who, what,* and *which* are used to ask questions.
  Who opened the window?

- *This, that, these,* and *those* can be used as **demonstrative** pronouns. Use *this* and *these* to talk about one or more things that are nearby. Use *that* and *those* to talk about one or more things that are far away.
  This is interesting.
  That is his new car.
  Those are my favorite.

Prepositions

A **preposition** shows a relationship between a word in a sentence and a noun or pronoun that follows the preposition. Prepositions help tell *when, where, what kind, how,* or *how much.*

Common Prepositions

aboard	behind	from	throughout
about	below	in	to
above	beneath	into	toward
across	beside	like	under
after	between	near	underneath
against	beyond	of	until
along	but (except)	off	unto
amid	by	on	up
among	down	over	upon
around	during	past	with
at	except	since	within
before	for	through	without

Conjunctions

The words *and, or,* and *but* are **coordinating conjunctions**.

- Coordinating conjunctions may be used to join words within a sentence.
  Jessica bought paper, pens, **and** a pencil.

- A comma and a coordinating conjunction can be used to join two or more simple sentences.
  Tony cut out the letters**, and** Shanna glued them to the poster.

Negatives

A negative word says "no" or "not."

- Often negatives are in the form of contractions.
  isn't, doesn't, haven't

- It is not correct to use two negatives to refer to the same thing.
  Incorrect: Tina **hasn't never** seen the ocean.
  Correct: Tina **hasn't ever** seen the ocean.

Homophones

Homophones are words that sound alike but have different spellings and meanings.

- Here is a list of some homophones often confused in writing.

are	**Are** is a form of the verb *be*.
our	**Our** is a possessive noun.
hour	An **hour** is sixty minutes.
its	**Its** is a possessive pronoun.
it's	**It's** is a contraction of the words *it is*.
there	**There** means "in that place." It can also be used as an introductory word.
their	**Their** is a possessive pronoun. It shows something belongs to more than one person or thing.
they're	**They're** is a contraction made from the words *they are*.
two	**Two** is a number.
to	**To** means "toward."
too	**Too** means "also." **Too** can mean "more than enough."
your	**Your** is a possessive pronoun.
you're	**You're** is a contraction made from the words *you are*.
whose	**Whose** is a possessive pronoun.
who's	**Who's** is a contraction made from the words *who* and *is* or *who* and *has*.

ate	**Ate** is a form of the verb *eat*.
eight	**Eight** is a number word.
principal	A **principal** is a person with authority.
principle	A **principle** is a general rule or code of behavior.
waist	The **waist** is the middle part of the body.
waste	To **waste** something is to use it in a careless way.
aloud	**Aloud** means out loud, or able to be heard.
allowed	**Allowed** is a form of the verb *allow*.

Signal Words

Signal words help writers move from one idea to another. Here is a list of some common signal words.

Time-Order Signal Words

after	third	later	as soon as
before	till	immediately	when
during	until	finally	then
first	meanwhile	soon	next
second			

Comparison/Contrast Signal Words

in the same way	likewise	as	also
similarly	like	as well	
but	however	otherwise	yet
still	even though	although	on the other hand

Concluding or Summarizing Signal Words

as a result	finally	in conclusion	to sum up
therefore	lastly	in summary	all in all

Writing a Letter

Friendly Letters

A friendly letter is an informal letter written to a friend or family member. In a friendly letter, you might send a message, invite someone to a party, or thank someone for a gift. A friendly letter has five parts:

- The **heading** gives your address and the date.
- The **greeting** includes the name of the person you are writing to. It begins with a capital letter and ends with a comma.
- The **body** of the letter gives your message.
- The **closing** is a friendly or polite way to say good-bye. It begins with a capital letter and ends with a comma.
- The **signature** is your name.

Business Letters

A business letter is a formal letter. You would write a business letter to a company, an employer, a newspaper, or any person you do not know well. A business letter looks a lot like a friendly letter, but a business letter includes the name and address of the business you are writing to. The greeting of a business letter begins with a capital letter and ends with a **colon (:)**.

Addressing Letters

The envelope below shows how to address a letter. A friendly letter and a business letter are addressed the same way.

Arthur Quinn
35 Rand St.
Chicago, IL 60606

Kim Lee
1555 Montague Blvd.
Memphis, TN 38106

Publishing
Share

This is the last step of the writing process. You have gathered and organized information. You have drafted, revised, and edited your writing. Your project is completed. Here are some tips for publishing your work.

Ways to Publish

There are lots of ways to publish your work. Keep your audience in mind as you choose different publishing methods. Your teacher might ask you to publish your work by writing your final draft on a clean piece of paper, with a title and your name at the top. You might try one of the publishing methods from this book, like an author's circle or a letter with an addressed envelope. It all depends on who is going to read or listen to your work.

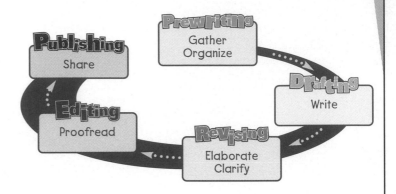

Listening, Speaking, and Thinking Skills

Listening

These tips will help you be a good listener:

- Listen carefully when others are speaking.

- Keep in mind your reason for listening. Are you listening to learn about a topic? To be entertained? To get directions? Decide what you should get out of the listening experience.

- Look directly at the speaker. Doing this will help you concentrate on what he or she has to say.

- Do not interrupt the speaker or talk to others while the speaker is talking.

- Ask questions when the speaker is finished talking if there is anything you did not understand.

Speaking

Being a good speaker takes practice. These guidelines can help you become an effective speaker.

Giving Oral Reports

- Be prepared. Know exactly what you are going to talk about and how long you will speak. Have your notes in front of you.

- Speak slowly and clearly. Speak loudly enough so everyone can hear you.

- Look at your audience.

Taking Part in Discussions

- Listen to what others have to say.

- Disagree politely. Let others in the group know you respect their points of view.

- Try not to interrupt others. Everyone should have a chance to speak.

Thinking

Writers use a variety of thinking skills as they work through the writing process. These skills include **logic, analyzing, setting goals, creativity,** and **problem solving**. As you write, keep these skills in mind and try to put them to use as much as possible.

- **Logic** Writers use logic to support a point of view by using reasoning, facts, and examples.

- **Analyzing** Analyzing is a thinking skill that requires the writer to think about and examine the information learned about a topic. Once the information is examined, a general conclusion or more meaningful understanding can be made about the topic.

- **Setting Goals** When setting goals, writers must think about deadlines (when the assignment is due; how much time there is for prewriting, drafting, revising, editing, and publishing), the objective of the writing assignment, and the amount of research required.

- **Creativity** Using creativity means using the imagination. Writers let their minds wonder about many different ways to tackle an assignment before finally settling on one. It is often necessary to start an assignment, stop, try it a different way, stop again, and maybe even go back to the original idea. Thinking creatively and openly allows the writer to examine many options.

- **Problem Solving** Learning to problem solve helps writers make decisions about the writing assignment and helps them use facts and opinions correctly. Strategies for problem solving include: naming the problem; thinking of everything about the problem; thinking of ways to solve the problem; choosing the best plan to solve the problem and trying it out; and analyzing the result.

Appendix
Table of Contents

Using the Mode-Specific Rubrics

Rubrics are central to instruction in *Strategies for Writers*. Each chapter includes a strategy-specific rubric that measures students' performance on the targeted strategies within that chapter.

More general, mode-specific rubrics are included on the following pages. One rubric is included for each of the four writing modes: narrative, descriptive, expository, and persuasive. You may wish to duplicate these rubrics and use them as instruments to assess students' writing within that mode both before (as a pretest rubric) and after (as a posttest rubric) instruction within that mode.

The strands on each of the rubrics are:

Audience...meaning the ways in which the writer identifies her audience and keeps that audience in mind as she writes.

Organization...meaning the way in which the writer moves from one main idea to the next, carefully presenting supporting information in clear relationship to each main idea.

Elaboration...meaning the way the writer adds supporting information to flesh out his writing.

Clarification...meaning the way in which the writer makes the meaning clearer by changing words, deleting unnecessary information, and effectively using transitions.

Conventions & Skills...meaning the ways in which the writer observes grammar, usage, mechanics, and spelling guidelines.

Narrative Writing Rubric

	(Novice) Score 1 Point	(Apprentice) Score 2 Points	(Proficient) Score 3 Points	(Distinguished) Score 4 Points
Audience Does the writer get the audience's attention at the beginning and keep it throughout the story?	The writer doesn't get the audience's attention.	The writer gets the audience's attention at the beginning but doesn't hold it throughout the story.	The writer gets the audience's attention at the beginning and keeps it for most of the story.	The writer gets the audience's attention right away and keeps it throughout the story.
Organization Does the writer organize the story so that events follow one another?	Events in the story are out of order. The story is confusing.	Some events in the story are told in order.	Most of the events in the story follow one another.	All events in the story follow one another.
Elaboration Does the writer include information about who or what the story is about and when and where the story takes place?	There is very little information about who or what the story is about and when and where it takes place.	There is some information about who or what the story is about and when and where it takes place.	The writer includes information about who or what the story is about and when and where it takes place.	The writer includes a lot of interesting information about who or what the story is about and when and where it takes place.
Clarification Does the writer include details that make the story clear and the characters more real?	There are almost no details to make the story clear and the characters seem more real.	There are a few details that make the story clear and the characters seem more real.	The writer includes enough details to make the story clear and the characters seem real most of the time.	The writer includes many interesting details that make the story clear and the characters seem real.
Conventions & Skills Does the writer use conventions and skills correctly?	There are many errors in grammar, usage, mechanics, and spelling.	There are some errors in grammar, usage, mechanics, and spelling.	There are only a few errors in grammar, usage, mechanics, and spelling.	There are no errors in grammar, usage, mechanics, and spelling.

Descriptive Writing Rubric

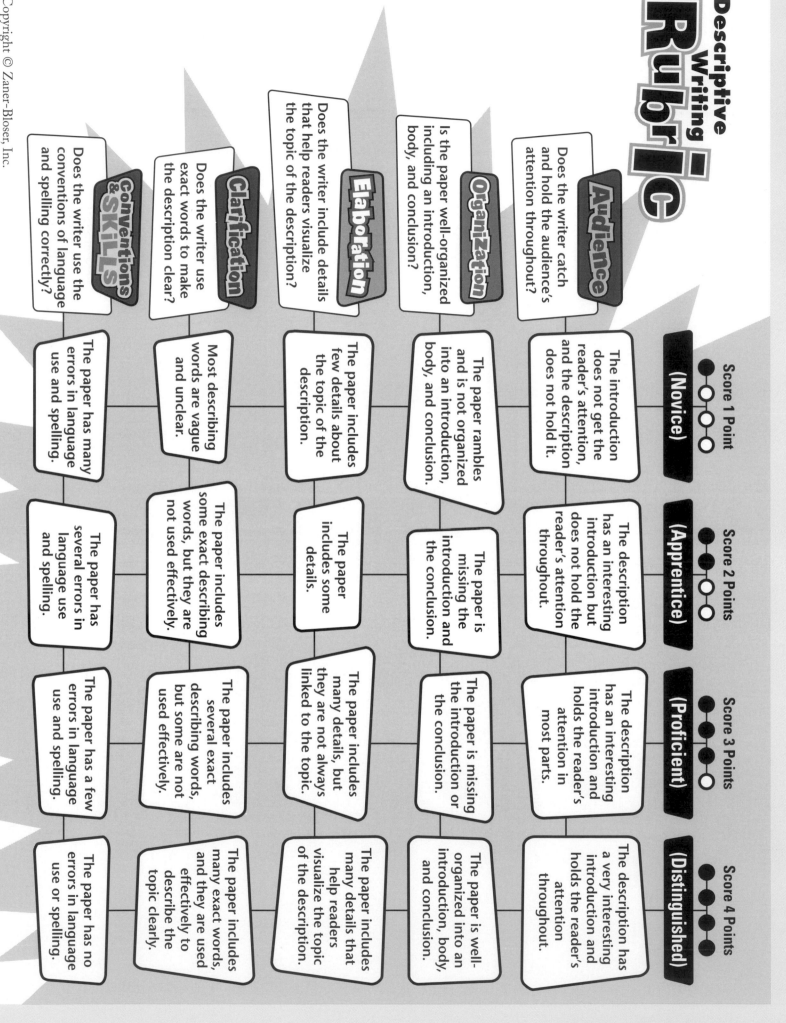

	Score 1 Point (Novice)	Score 2 Points (Apprentice)	Score 3 Points (Proficient)	Score 4 Points (Distinguished)
Audience — Does the writer catch and hold the audience's attention throughout?	The introduction does not get the reader's attention, and the description does not hold it.	The description has an interesting introduction but does not hold the reader's attention throughout.	The description has an interesting introduction and holds the reader's attention in most parts.	The description has a very interesting introduction and holds the reader's attention throughout.
Organization — Is the paper well-organized, including an introduction, body, and conclusion?	The paper rambles and is not organized into an introduction, body, and conclusion.	The paper is missing the introduction and the conclusion.	The paper is missing the introduction or the conclusion.	The paper is well-organized into an introduction, body, and conclusion.
Elaboration — Does the writer include details that help readers visualize the topic of the description?	The paper includes few details about the topic of the description.	The paper includes some details.	The paper includes many details, but they are not always linked to the topic.	The paper includes many details that help readers visualize the topic of the description.
Clarification — Does the writer use exact words to make the description clear?	Most describing words are vague and unclear.	The paper includes some exact describing words, but they are not used effectively.	The paper includes several exact describing words, but some are not used effectively.	The paper includes many exact words, and they are used effectively to describe the topic clearly.
Conventions & Skills — Does the writer use the conventions of language and spelling correctly?	The paper has many errors in language use and spelling.	The paper has several errors in language use and spelling.	The paper has a few errors in language use and spelling.	The paper has no errors in language use or spelling.

Expository Writing Rubric

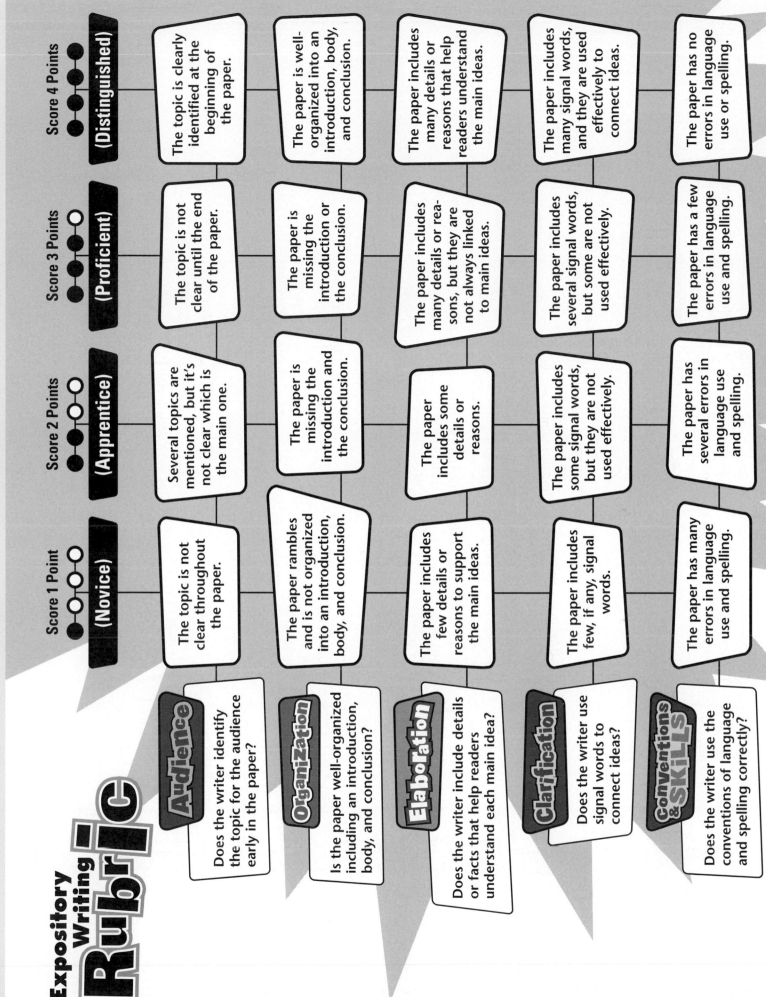

	Score 1 Point (Novice)	Score 2 Points (Apprentice)	Score 3 Points (Proficient)	Score 4 Points (Distinguished)
Audience — Does the writer identify the topic for the audience early in the paper?	The topic is not clear throughout the paper.	Several topics are mentioned, but it's not clear which is the main one.	The topic is not clear until the end of the paper.	The topic is clearly identified at the beginning of the paper.
Organization — Is the paper well-organized including an introduction, body, and conclusion?	The paper rambles and is not organized into an introduction, body, and conclusion.	The paper is missing the introduction and the conclusion.	The paper is missing the introduction or the conclusion.	The paper is well-organized into an introduction, body, and conclusion.
Elaboration — Does the writer include details or facts that help readers understand each main idea?	The paper includes few details or reasons to support the main ideas.	The paper includes some details or reasons.	The paper includes many details or reasons, but they are not always linked to main ideas.	The paper includes many details or reasons that help readers understand the main ideas.
Clarification — Does the writer use signal words to connect ideas?	The paper includes few, if any, signal words.	The paper includes some signal words, but they are not used effectively.	The paper includes several signal words, but some are not used effectively.	The paper includes many signal words, and they are used effectively to connect ideas.
Conventions & Skills — Does the writer use the conventions of language and spelling correctly?	The paper has many errors in language use and spelling.	The paper has several errors in language use and spelling.	The paper has a few errors in language use and spelling.	The paper has no errors in language use or spelling.

Persuasive Writing Rubric

Audience
How quickly and clearly is the writer's opinion presented to the audience?

Organization
How clearly and effectively has the writer organized the writing?

Elaboration
How effectively does the writer use facts and examples to support reasons for the opinion?

Clarification
How well does the writer avoid confusing or unnecessary ideas to make sure reasons are sound and to the point?

Conventions & SKILLS
How carefully does the writer follow conventions of language and spelling?

Score 1 Point (Novice)

- The writer's opinion is never made clear.
- Ideas run together with no clear organization.
- There are no facts or examples to support the writer's opinion.
- The writer includes several confusing or unnecessary ideas. The essay rambles.
- Too many errors in grammar, spelling, and punctuation make the essay difficult to understand.

Score 2 Points (Apprentice)

- The writer's opinion is stated, but it is mixed in with reasons for the opinion.
- Some paragraphs are unclear and there is little evidence of a logical organization.
- Many of the facts and examples are unrelated to the writer's opinion.
- The writer includes some confusing or unnecessary ideas.
- There are several errors with grammar, spelling, and punctuation.

Score 3 Points (Proficient)

- The writer's opinion is given in a somewhat long introductory paragraph.
- Most paragraphs give clear reasons for the writer's opinion, but one or two are unclear.
- Most facts and examples support the writer's opinion.
- The writer occasionally includes a confusing or unnecessary idea.
- There are a few errors with grammar, spelling, and punctuation.

Score 4 Points (Distinguished)

- The writer's opinion is given in a brief, clear introductory paragraph.
- Well-constructed paragraphs present the writer's opinion and reasons clearly and logically.
- All facts and examples provide strong support for the writer's opinion.
- Reasons are sound and to the point. There are no confusing or unnecessary ideas.
- There are no errors with grammar, spelling, or punctuation.

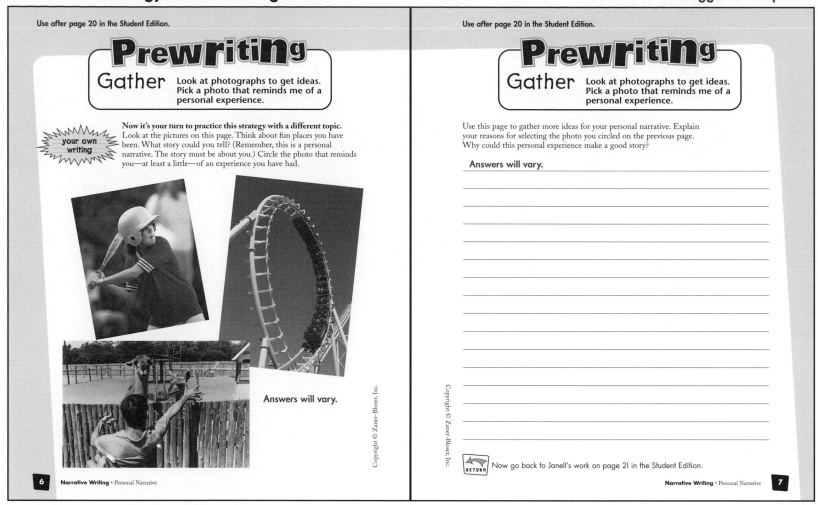

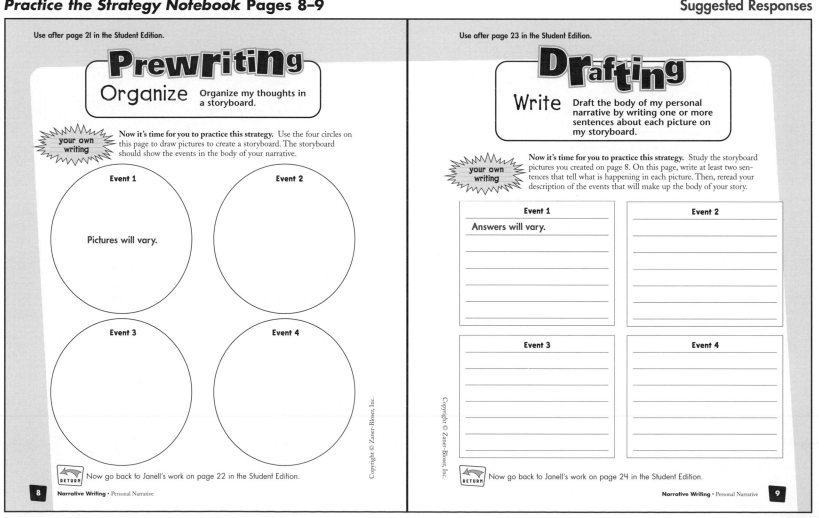

Use after page 25 in the Student Edition.

REVISING

Elaborate
Write an introduction and a conclusion that will interest my reader.

Remember the picture of the roller coaster on page 6? One student writer chose to write about a roller coaster ride. Here is this writer's introduction. Read the introduction and then rewrite it to make it better. Remember, a good introduction grabs the reader's attention.

> I was happy because we were going to the amusement park. I wanted to ride the **Apollo** for the first time. I couldn't wait. I told my friends about it.

Answers will vary.

Now read and rewrite this writer's conclusion. Make it better, too. A good conclusion ties up loose ends, provides a good summary, and leaves the reader satisfied.

> I was disappointed. I couldn't ride the **Apollo** roller coaster because I was too short. My brother and I rode the **Junior Apollo**. It made me feel a little better.

Answers will vary.

Copyright © Zaner-Bloser, Inc.

Use after page 25 in the Student Edition.

REVISING

Elaborate
Write an introduction and a conclusion that will interest my reader.

your own writing

Now it's time for you to practice this strategy. On the following lines, write a good introduction and a good conclusion for your own personal narrative about your experience.

My Introduction

Answers will vary.

My Conclusion

Answers will vary.

 Now go back to Janell's work on page 26 in the Student Edition.

Copyright © Zaner-Bloser, Inc.

Use after page 27 in the Student Edition.

REVISING

Clarify
Replace overused words and clichés with more exact words and fresh language.

Now it's time for you to practice this strategy. Revise this draft of a personal narrative about a roller coaster ride. Delete or replace the underlined words with words that are more exact and fresh. Correct any other errors you find, too.

I thought we would never get to the front of the line ~~in a million years~~!

Every time a coaster roared by us, I got ~~really~~ excited. Finally, it was our

turn. As I started through the gate, a gigantic hand ~~came out of nowhere~~

~~and held~~ [reached out to hold] me back. "Say there, young lady," a loud voice ~~said~~ [bellowed]. "I believe

that ~~your~~ [you're] a bit ~~too~~ short to ride the **Apollo**."

~~I couldn't believe my ears!~~ [It couldn't be true!] I stood beside the ~~really~~ colorful sign that

showed how tall riders had to be. My family sighed and shook their heads.

"You're an inch too short," they ~~said really~~ [pointed out] sadly. My older brother put his

arm around my shoulders and ~~said~~ [whispered], "Follow me. I have a ~~really~~ good

idea!" The rest of our family got on the **Apollo**. My brother led me through

the park. I followed behind him ~~as slow as a turtle~~ [slowly] until I saw another

roller coaster, the **Junior Apollo**.

Remember: Use this strategy in your own writing

 Now go back to Janell's work on page 28 in the Student Edition.

Copyright © Zaner-Bloser, Inc.

Use after page 29 in the Student Edition.

Proofreading marks:
⌐ Indent.
≡ Make a capital.
/ Make a small letter.
∧ Add something.
𝒆 Take out something.
⊙ Add a period.
New paragraph.
(SP) Spelling error

Editing

Proofread
Make sure I have avoided run-on sentences by joining compound sentences correctly.

Now it's time for you to practice this strategy. Here is part of the revised draft of the story about the roller coaster. Use the proofreading marks to correct any errors. Use a dictionary to help with spelling.

I couldn't believe we were finally on our way to the amusement park! I was six years old, and I had been waiting for this trip for a long time. This park had fourteen sensational roller coasters, that was more than any other amusement park in the entire world! I had counted down the weeks, the days, the hours, and the minutes! I rode up and down roller coasters in my dreams at night. My friends at school got tired of hearing about the park but I didn't get tired of talking about it.

My goal was to ride the **Apollo**. It had two tracks with two trains, and they raced each other! this roller coaster was almost 4,000 feet tall, and it went 60 miles per hour, which is unbelievably fast. When we got to the park, my family had a hard time holding me back. We soon located the **Apollo** on the map and set off to find it. Suddenly I shrieked, "Look! There's the **Apollo**!" I ran as fast as I could, and I got in line. It took a while for my parents to catch up with me.

I thought we would never get to the front of the line! Every time a coaster roared by us, I got excited. Finally, it was our turn. I started through the gate, and a gigantic hand reached out to hold me back. "Say there, young lady," a loud voice bellowed. "I believe that you're a bit too short to ride the **Apollo**."

Remember: Use this strategy in your own writing

 Now go back to Janell's work on page 30 in the Student Edition.

Copyright © Zaner-Bloser, Inc.

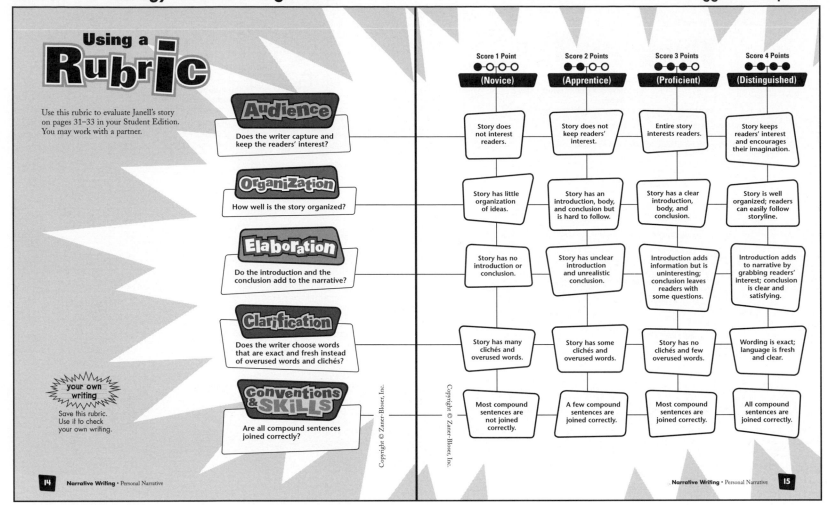

Using a Rubric

Use this rubric to evaluate Janell's story on pages 31–33 in your Student Edition. You may work with a partner.

your own writing
Save this rubric. Use it to check your own writing.

	Score 1 Point (Novice)	Score 2 Points (Apprentice)	Score 3 Points (Proficient)	Score 4 Points (Distinguished)
Audience — Does the writer capture and keep the readers' interest?	Story does not interest readers.	Story does not keep readers' interest.	Entire story interests readers.	Story keeps readers' interest and encourages their imagination.
Organization — How well is the story organized?	Story has little organization of ideas.	Story has an introduction, body, and conclusion but is hard to follow.	Story has a clear introduction, body, and conclusion.	Story is well organized; readers can easily follow storyline.
Elaboration — Do the introduction and the conclusion add to the narrative?	Story has no introduction or conclusion.	Story has unclear introduction and unrealistic conclusion.	Introduction adds information but is uninteresting; conclusion leaves readers with some questions.	Introduction adds to narrative by grabbing readers' interest; conclusion is clear and satisfying.
Clarification — Does the writer choose words that are exact and fresh instead of overused words and clichés?	Story has many clichés and overused words.	Story has some clichés and overused words.	Story has no clichés and few overused words.	Wording is exact; language is fresh and clear.
Conventions & Skills — Are all compound sentences joined correctly?	Most compound sentences are not joined correctly.	A few compound sentences are joined correctly.	Most compound sentences are joined correctly.	All compound sentences are joined correctly.

Copyright © Zaner-Bloser, Inc.

Copyright © Zaner-Bloser, Inc.

14 **Narrative Writing** • Personal Narrative

Narrative Writing • Personal Narrative 15

Use after page 44 in the Student Edition.

PrewRiting

Gather
Draw on my memory of an incident. Jot down what I saw and heard.

Now it's your turn to practice this strategy with a different topic. Read the following memories about watching a shuttle launch at the Kennedy Space Center. A writer might include these memories in an eyewitness account.

- feeling excitement in the crowd before blast-off
- watching huge clouds of smoke and steam
- seeing flames coming out of the rockets
- feeling the earth shake
- hearing a huge roar
- watching all the birds fly away
- cheering as Discovery rose into the sky
- counting down to blast-off
- wondering if the launch would be postponed
- finding marshes close to the space center

Use after page 44 in the Student Edition.

PrewRiting

Gather
Draw on my memory of an incident. Jot down what I saw and heard.

your own writing   Now think of an incident that you remember. Jot down what you saw and heard during the incident.

Answers will vary.

Now go back to William's work on page 45 in the Student Edition.

Use after page 45 in the Student Edition.

PrewRiting

Organize
Make a sequence chain of the most important events.

Here's how one writer filled in the sequence chain of an eyewitness account of the shuttle launch.

Topic:	Shuttle launch
First Event:	driving to the space center
Next Event:	feeling excitement in the crowd at the site
Next Event:	counting down to the blast-off
Next Event:	seeing the flames and feeling the rumble
Final Event:	cheering as Discovery rose into the sky

Use after page 45 in the Student Edition.

PrewRiting

Organize
Make a sequence chain of the most important events.

your own writing   **Now it's time for you to practice this strategy.** Think about the important events in the incident you selected. Make a sequence chain that shows the events in the order they happened. You can add more event boxes to your sequence chain if you need them.

Topic:	Answers will vary.
First Event:	
Next Event:	
Next Event:	
Next Event:	
Final Event:	

Now go back to William's work on page 46 in the Student Edition.

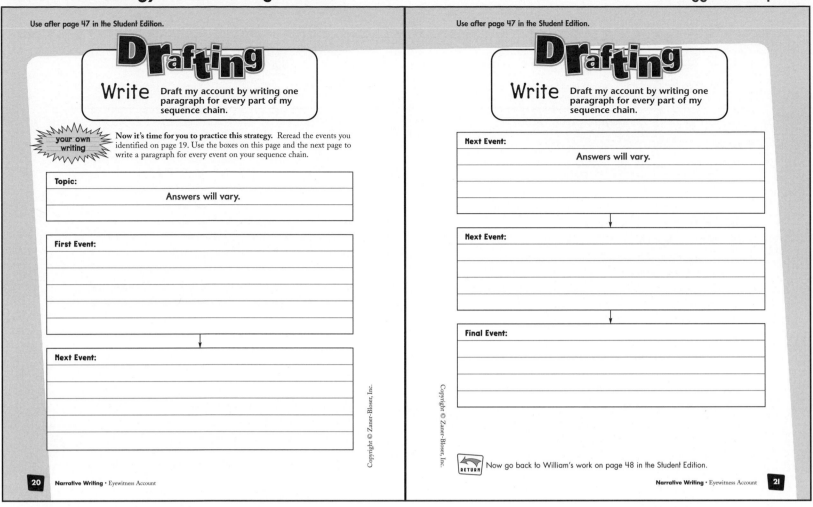

Use after page 47 in the Student Edition.

Drafting

Write Draft my account by writing one paragraph for every part of my sequence chain.

your own writing **Now it's time for you to practice this strategy.** Reread the events you identified on page 19. Use the boxes on this page and the next page to write a paragraph for every event on your sequence chain.

Topic:
Answers will vary.

First Event:

Next Event:

Copyright © Zaner-Bloser, Inc.

20 **Narrative Writing** • Eyewitness Account

Use after page 47 in the Student Edition.

Drafting

Write Draft my account by writing one paragraph for every part of my sequence chain.

Next Event:
Answers will vary.

Next Event:

Final Event:

Copyright © Zaner-Bloser, Inc.

RETURN Now go back to William's work on page 48 in the Student Edition.

21 **Narrative Writing** • Eyewitness Account

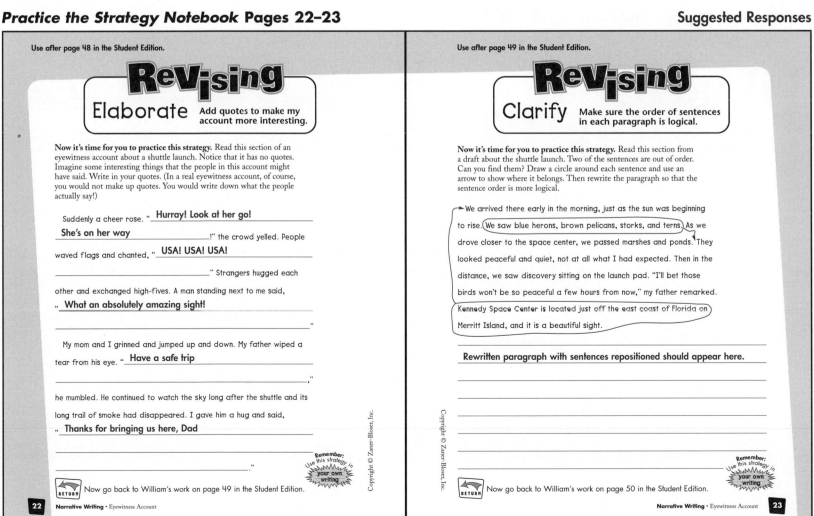

Use after page 48 in the Student Edition.

Revising

Elaborate Add quotes to make my account more interesting.

Now it's time for you to practice this strategy. Read this section of an eyewitness account about a shuttle launch. Notice that it has no quotes. Imagine some interesting things that the people in this account might have said. Write in your quotes. (In a real eyewitness account, of course, you would not make up quotes. You would write down what the people actually say!)

Suddenly a cheer rose. "__Hurray! Look at her go!__ __She's on her way__!" the crowd yelled. People waved flags and chanted, "__USA! USA! USA!__ _____" Strangers hugged each other and exchanged high-fives. A man standing next to me said, "__What an absolutely amazing sight!__ _____"

My mom and I grinned and jumped up and down. My father wiped a tear from his eye. "__Have a safe trip__ _____," he mumbled. He continued to watch the sky long after the shuttle and its long trail of smoke had disappeared. I gave him a hug and said, "__Thanks for bringing us here, Dad__ _____"

Remember: Use this strategy in your own writing

RETURN Now go back to William's work on page 49 in the Student Edition.

22 **Narrative Writing** • Eyewitness Account

Copyright © Zaner-Bloser, Inc.

Use after page 49 in the Student Edition.

Revising

Clarify Make sure the order of sentences in each paragraph is logical.

Now it's time for you to practice this strategy. Read this section from a draft about the shuttle launch. Two of the sentences are out of order. Can you find them? Draw a circle around each sentence and use an arrow to show where it belongs. Then rewrite the paragraph so that the sentence order is more logical.

We arrived there early in the morning, just as the sun was beginning to rise. We saw blue herons, brown pelicans, storks, and terns. As we drove closer to the space center, we passed marshes and ponds. They looked peaceful and quiet, not at all what I had expected. Then in the distance, we saw discovery sitting on the launch pad. "I'll bet those birds won't be so peaceful a few hours from now," my father remarked. Kennedy Space Center is located just off the east coast of Florida on Merritt Island, and it is a beautiful sight.

__Rewritten paragraph with sentences repositioned should appear here.__

Remember: Use this strategy in your own writing

RETURN Now go back to William's work on page 50 in the Student Edition.

23 **Narrative Writing** • Eyewitness Account

Copyright © Zaner-Bloser, Inc.

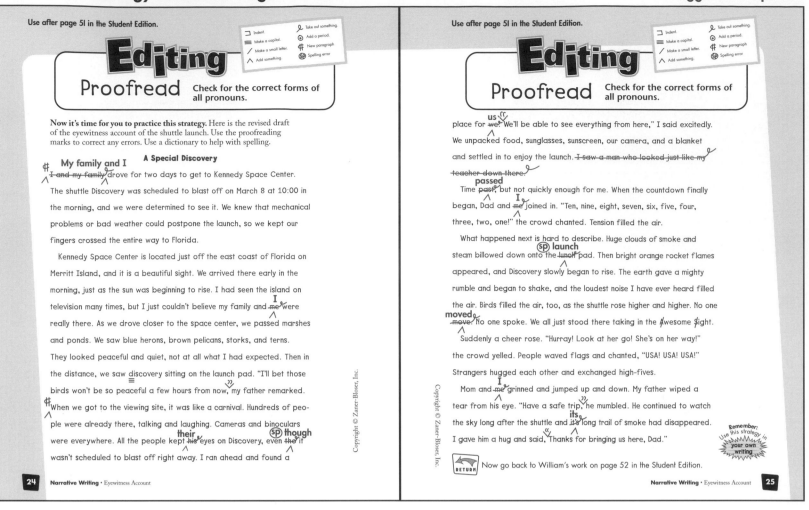

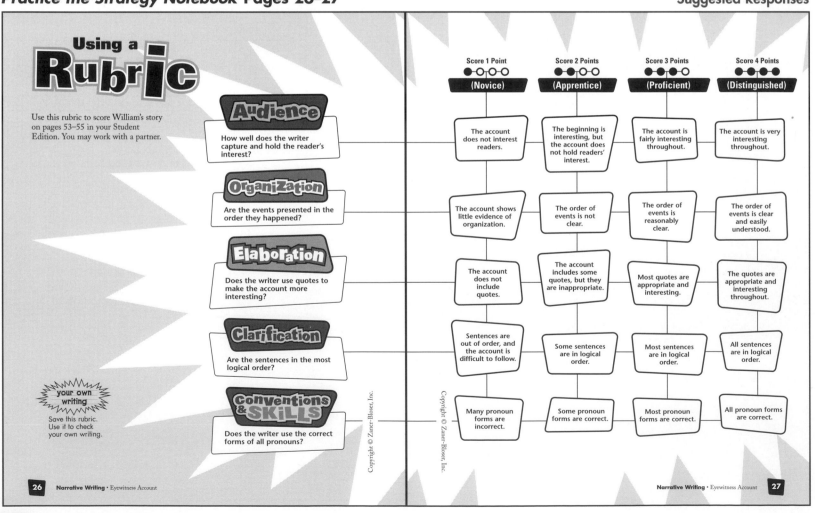

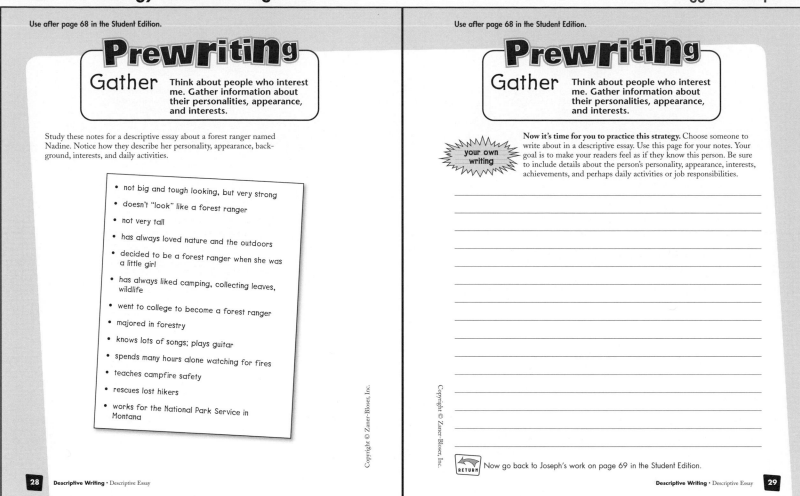

Use after page 68 in the Student Edition.

PrewRitiNg

Gather
Think about people who interest me. Gather information about their personalities, appearance, and interests.

Study these notes for a descriptive essay about a forest ranger named Nadine. Notice how they describe her personality, appearance, background, interests, and daily activities.

- not big and tough looking, but very strong
- doesn't "look" like a forest ranger
- not very tall
- has always loved nature and the outdoors
- decided to be a forest ranger when she was a little girl
- has always liked camping, collecting leaves, wildlife
- went to college to become a forest ranger
- majored in forestry
- knows lots of songs; plays guitar
- spends many hours alone watching for fires
- teaches campfire safety
- rescues lost hikers
- works for the National Park Service in Montana

Copyright © Zaner-Bloser, Inc.

28 **Descriptive Writing** • Descriptive Essay

Use after page 68 in the Student Edition.

PrewRitiNg

Gather
Think about people who interest me. Gather information about their personalities, appearance, and interests.

your own writing

Now it's time for you to practice this strategy. Choose someone to write about in a descriptive essay. Use this page for your notes. Your goal is to make your readers feel as if they know this person. Be sure to include details about the person's personality, appearance, interests, achievements, and perhaps daily activities or job responsibilities.

RETURN Now go back to Joseph's work on page 69 in the Student Edition.

Copyright © Zaner-Bloser, Inc.

29 **Descriptive Writing** • Descriptive Essay

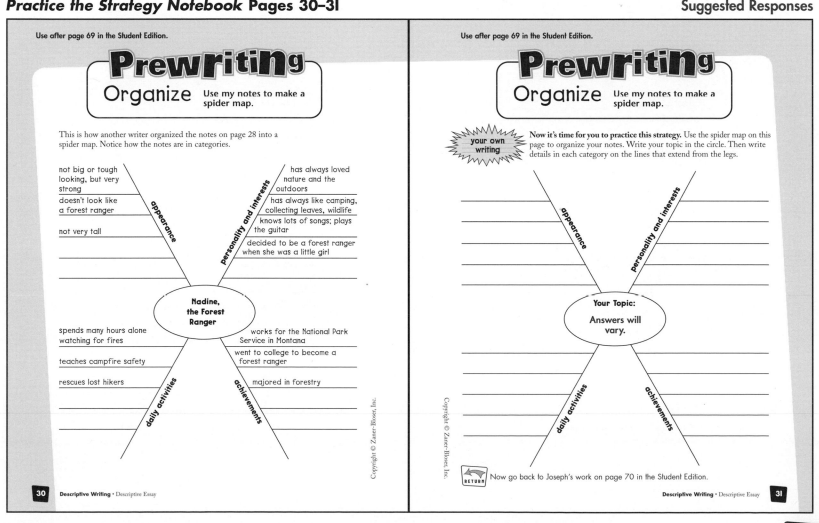

Use after page 69 in the Student Edition.

PrewRitiNg

Organize
Use my notes to make a spider map.

This is how another writer organized the notes on page 28 into a spider map. Notice how the notes are in categories.

appearance
- not big or tough looking, but very strong
- doesn't look like a forest ranger
- not very tall

personality and interests
- has always loved nature and the outdoors
- has always like camping, collecting leaves, wildlife
- knows lots of songs; plays the guitar
- decided to be a forest ranger when she was a little girl

Nadine, the Forest Ranger

daily activities
- spends many hours alone watching for fires
- teaches campfire safety
- rescues lost hikers

achievements
- works for the National Park Service in Montana
- went to college to become a forest ranger
- majored in forestry

Copyright © Zaner-Bloser, Inc.

30 **Descriptive Writing** • Descriptive Essay

Use after page 69 in the Student Edition.

PrewRitiNg

Organize
Use my notes to make a spider map.

your own writing

Now it's time for you to practice this strategy. Use the spider map on this page to organize your notes. Write your topic in the circle. Then write details in each category on the lines that extend from the legs.

appearance

personality and interests

Your Topic:
Answers will vary.

daily activities

achievements

RETURN Now go back to Joseph's work on page 70 in the Student Edition.

Copyright © Zaner-Bloser, Inc.

31 **Descriptive Writing** • Descriptive Essay

Use after page 71 in the Student Edition.

Drafting

Write
Draft my description. Begin by describing the most interesting thing about my topic.

Now it's time for you to practice this strategy. On this page, you are going to write a draft of the first paragraph of your descriptive essay. Study the spider map you made on the last page.

your own writing

What is the most interesting thing about the person you chose?
Answers will vary.

Why is this piece of information interesting?

Now draft the first paragraph of your descriptive essay. Be sure to include the interesting thing you chose. Continue writing your essay on the next page.
Answers will vary.

32   **Descriptive Writing** • Descriptive Essay

Copyright © Zaner-Bloser, Inc.

Use after page 71 in the Student Edition.

Drafting

Write
Draft my description. Begin by describing the most interesting thing about my topic.

On this page, you can continue writing your draft of your descriptive essay. Do not forget to refer to the spider map you made.

Answers will vary.

Now go back to Joseph's work on page 72 in the Student Edition.

Copyright © Zaner-Bloser, Inc.

Descriptive Writing • Descriptive Essay   33

Use after page 72 in the Student Edition.

Revising

Elaborate
Add similes to make my description clearer.

Remember that a simile must compare two different things.

Not a simile: You look as tired as I am. (compares two similar things: two people)

Simile: You look as tired as my dog after he runs for a mile. (compares two different things: a person and a dog)

Now it's time for you to practice this strategy. First, underline the three similes below. Identify the two things that are being compared in each simile.

Nadine is a good musician. She named her guitar "Woody," and she **(compares a guitar and a friend)** treats it like a favorite old friend. Nadine's weathered fingers dance **(compares the movements of fingers and a butterfly)** across the strings as delicately as a butterfly, and wonderful music fills **(compares a human voice and a bird's song)** the air. Nadine loves to sing, and her voice is as high and clear as a bird's song.

Now decide which of the sentences below contains a simile. Rewrite the two sentences that are not similes, making them into "real" similes. **Answers will vary.**

1. We ran as fast as we could.
   We ran as fast as a squirrel being chased by a dog.

2. His head was nodding like a sunflower in a slight breeze.
   simile

3. The smell was like nothing I ever smelled before.
   The smell was like a dark corner in an old basement.

Now go back to Joseph's work on page 73 in the Student Edition.

Remember: Use this strategy in your own writing

Copyright © Zaner-Bloser, Inc.

34   **Descriptive Writing** • Descriptive Essay

Use after page 73 in the Student Edition.

Revising

Clarify
Combine short, choppy sentences.

Now it's time for you to practice this strategy. Read this paragraph from the descriptive essay about Nadine. Did you notice how awkward the short, choppy sentences sounded? Revise the paragraph, combining some of the short sentences so they will be easier to read.

> My aunt Nadine decided to become a forest ranger. She was eight years old. She loved nature. She was happiest when she was outdoors. Nadine went camping. She collected leaves. She read about wildlife. Actually, it was her reading that helped her choose her profession. She read a comic book about Smokey the Bear. She knew right away what she wanted to do. Not only would she help prevent forest fires, she would help protect the entire forest! That year she decided to become a forest ranger. She dressed like Smokey the Bear on Halloween. She would have worn the costume every day for the rest of the year. Her mother wouldn't let her.

My aunt Nadine decided to become a forest ranger when she was eight years old. She loved nature, and she was happiest when she was outdoors. Nadine went camping, collected leaves, and read everything she could find about wildlife. Actually, it was her reading that helped her choose her profession. When she read a comic book about Smokey the Bear, she knew right away what she wanted to do. Not only would she help prevent forest fires, she would help protect the entire forest! That year she decided to become a forest ranger and dressed like Smokey the Bear on Halloween. She would have worn the costume every day for the rest of the year, but her mother wouldn't let her.

Now go back to Joseph's work on page 74 in the Student Edition.

Remember: Use this strategy in your own writing

Copyright © Zaner-Bloser, Inc.

Descriptive Writing • Descriptive Essay   35

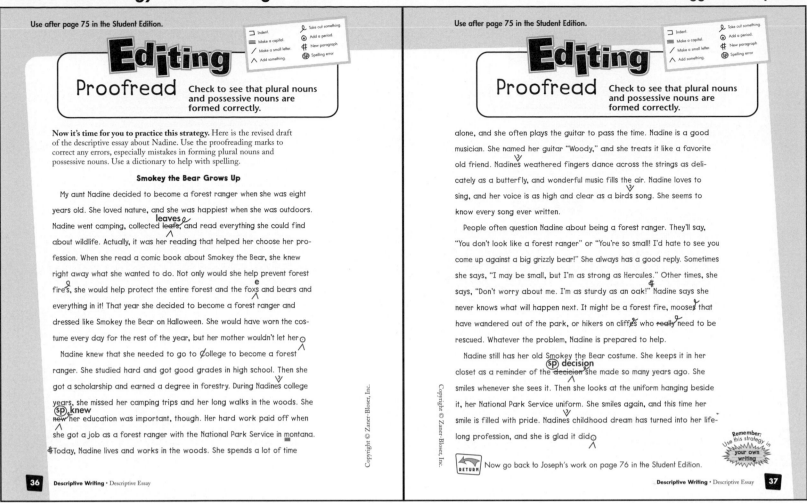

Use after page 75 in the Student Edition.

⌐ Indent.	ℓ Take out something.
≡ Make a capital.	⊙ Add a period.
/ Make a small letter.	¶ New paragraph.
∧ Add something.	sp Spelling error

Editing
Proofread
Check to see that plural nouns and possessive nouns are formed correctly.

Now it's time for you to practice this strategy. Here is the revised draft of the descriptive essay about Nadine. Use the proofreading marks to correct any errors, especially mistakes in forming plural nouns and possessive nouns. Use a dictionary to help with spelling.

Smokey the Bear Grows Up

My aunt Nadine decided to become a forest ranger when she was eight years old. She loved nature, and she was happiest when she was outdoors. Nadine went camping, collected leaves, and read everything she could find about wildlife. Actually, it was her reading that helped her choose her profession. When she read a comic book about Smokey the Bear, she knew right away what she wanted to do. Not only would she help prevent forest fires, she would help protect the entire forest and the foxes and bears and everything in it! That year she decided to become a forest ranger and dressed like Smokey the Bear on Halloween. She would have worn the costume every day for the rest of the year, but her mother wouldn't let her.

Nadine knew that she needed to go to college to become a forest ranger. She studied hard and got good grades in high school. Then she got a scholarship and earned a degree in forestry. During Nadines college years, she missed her camping trips and her long walks in the woods. She knew her education was important, though. Her hard work paid off when she got a job as a forest ranger with the National Park Service in montana. Today, Nadine lives and works in the woods. She spends a lot of time

Copyright © Zaner-Bloser, Inc.

Use after page 75 in the Student Edition.

⌐ Indent.	ℓ Take out something.
≡ Make a capital.	⊙ Add a period.
/ Make a small letter.	¶ New paragraph.
∧ Add something.	sp Spelling error

Editing
Proofread
Check to see that plural nouns and possessive nouns are formed correctly.

alone, and she often plays the guitar to pass the time. Nadine is a good musician. She named her guitar "Woody," and she treats it like a favorite old friend. Nadines weathered fingers dance across the strings as delicately as a butterfly, and wonderful music fills the air. Nadine loves to sing, and her voice is as high and clear as a birds song. She seems to know every song ever written.

People often question Nadine about being a forest ranger. They'll say, "You don't look like a forest ranger" or "You're so small! I'd hate to see you come up against a big grizzly bear!" She always has a good reply. Sometimes she says, "I may be small, but I'm as strong as Hercules." Other times, she says, "Don't worry about me. I'm as sturdy as an oak!" Nadine says she never knows what will happen next. It might be a forest fire, mooses that have wandered out of the park, or hikers on cliffs who really need to be rescued. Whatever the problem, Nadine is prepared to help.

Nadine still has her old Smokey the Bear costume. She keeps it in her closet as a reminder of the decision she made so many years ago. She smiles whenever she sees it. Then she looks at the uniform hanging beside it, her National Park Service uniform. She smiles again, and this time her smile is filled with pride. Nadines childhood dream has turned into her lifelong profession, and she is glad it did.

Remember: Use this strategy in your own writing

↩ RETURN Now go back to Joseph's work on page 76 in the Student Edition.

Copyright © Zaner-Bloser, Inc.

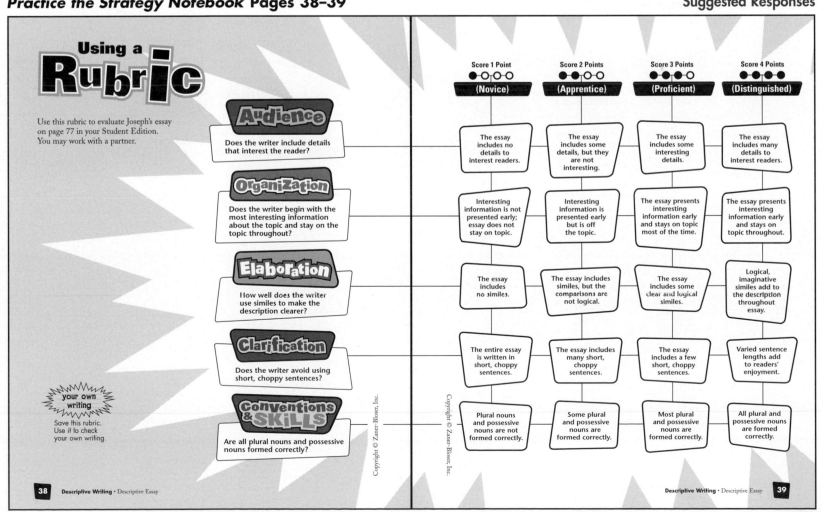

Using a Rubric

Use this rubric to evaluate Joseph's essay on page 77 in your Student Edition. You may work with a partner.

your own writing — Save this rubric. Use it to check your own writing.

	Score 1 Point ●○○○ (Novice)	Score 2 Points ●●○○ (Apprentice)	Score 3 Points ●●●○ (Proficient)	Score 4 Points ●●●● (Distinguished)
Audience — Does the writer include details that interest the reader?	The essay includes no details to interest readers.	The essay includes some details, but they are not interesting.	The essay includes some interesting details.	The essay includes many details to interest readers.
Organization — Does the writer begin with the most interesting information about the topic and stay on the topic throughout?	Interesting information is not presented early; essay does not stay on topic.	Interesting information is presented early but is off the topic.	The essay presents interesting information early and stays on topic most of the time.	The essay presents interesting information early and stays on topic throughout.
Elaboration — How well does the writer use similes to make the description clearer?	The essay includes no similes.	The essay includes similes, but the comparisons are not logical.	The essay includes some clear and logical similes.	Logical, imaginative similes add to the description throughout essay.
Clarification — Does the writer avoid using short, choppy sentences?	The entire essay is written in short, choppy sentences.	The essay includes many short, choppy sentences.	The essay includes a few short, choppy sentences.	Varied sentence lengths add to readers' enjoyment.
Conventions & Skills — Are all plural nouns and possessive nouns formed correctly?	Plural nouns and possessive nouns are not formed correctly.	Some plural and possessive nouns are formed correctly.	Most plural and possessive nouns are formed correctly.	All plural and possessive nouns are formed correctly.

Copyright © Zaner-Bloser, Inc.

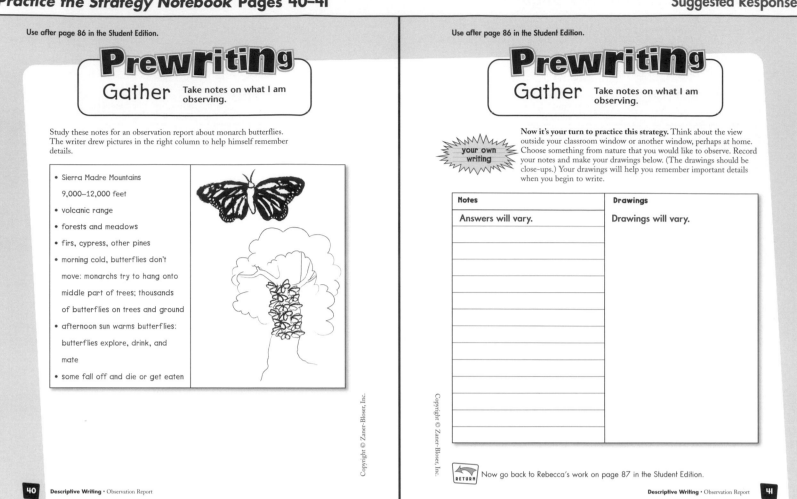

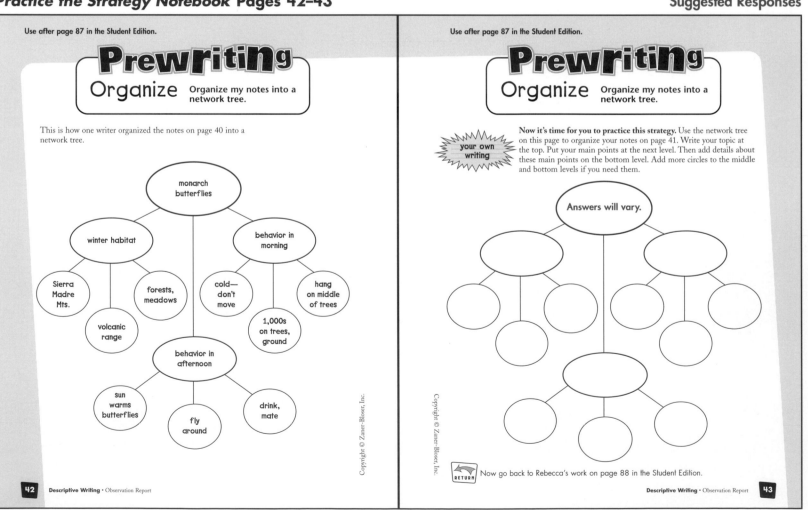

Use after page 89 in the Student Edition.

Drafting

Write Draft my report. For each main point in my network tree, write a topic sentence and add details.

Now it's time for you to practice this strategy. On this page and the next page, you are going to begin writing your observation report. First, review your network tree on page 43. Then start your report below. Remember that each paragraph should begin with a topic sentence and include three or four more sentences with details.

Answers will vary.

Copyright © Zaner-Bloser, Inc.

44 | **Descriptive Writing** • Observation Report

Use after page 89 in the Student Edition.

Drafting

Write Draft my report. For each main point in my network tree, write a topic sentence and add details.

Answers will vary.

Copyright © Zaner-Bloser, Inc.

Now go back to Rebecca's work on page 90 in the Student Edition.

45 | **Descriptive Writing** • Observation Report

Use after page 90 in the Student Edition.

Revising

Elaborate Fill in any gaps in my description.

Now it's time for you to practice this strategy. Read this paragraph from an observation report about monarch butterflies. Do any questions come to mind as you read? Do any important details or explanations seem to be missing? You will find more details in the box. Add them to the paragraph wherever you see a gap in the description. Make any other changes necessary to work in the details.

Details

to protect them from the cool temperatures

The forest was mostly firs, cypress trees, and other pines.

They were hanging on trunks and branches and covered the ground like a carpet.

in the Sierra Madre Mountains

in the Sierra Madre Mountains
We first found the butterflies in the early morning. This forest was cool **The forest was mostly firs, cypress trees, and other pines.** and still somewhat dark. The forest floor and all the trees seemed to be covered with brown leaves. When we looked closely at these leaves, we realized they were all monarch butterflies. There must have **They were hanging on trunks and branches and covered the ground like a carpet.** been millions of them! They were absolutely everywhere! The butterflies' **to protect them from the cool temperatures** wings were tightly closed. Because the butterflies were cold, they did not move.

Remember: Use this strategy in your own writing

Now go back to Rebecca's work on page 91 in the Student Edition.

46 | **Descriptive Writing** • Observation Report

Use after page 91 in the Student Edition.

Revising

Clarify Make sure my sentences begin in a variety of ways.

Now it's time for you to practice this strategy. Rewrite the sentences below. Make them more interesting by beginning them with prepositional phrases, other kinds of phrases, and adverbs. Of course, in most of your writing, some of your sentences will begin with the subject. **Answers will vary. Possible answers appear below.**

1. My mother and I drove to the forest early this morning.
   Early this morning, my mother and I drove to the forest.

2. We had wanted to make this trip for a long time.
   For a long time, we had wanted to make this trip.

3. We finally stopped the car by some thick evergreens.
   Finally, we stopped the car by some thick evergreens.

4. We peered closely at the trees and realized they were covered with butterflies.
   Peering closely at the trees, we realized they were covered with butterflies.

5. The air temperature slowly rose.
   Slowly, the air temperature rose.

6. The butterflies became more active in the warmer air.
   In the warmer air, the butterflies became more active.

7. I was fascinated as I watched them begin to open their wings.
   Fascinated, I watched them begin to open their wings.

8. They soon were ready to fly.
   Soon, they were ready to fly.

9. They fluttered from tree to tree up and down the mountain slopes.
   Up and down the mountain slopes, they fluttered from tree to tree.

10. They paused in the sunshine and drank from pools of water.
    Pausing in the sunshine, they drank from pools of water.

Remember: Use this strategy in your own writing

Now go back to Rebecca's work on page 92 in the Student Edition.

47 | **Descriptive Writing** • Observation Report

Copyright © Zaner-Bloser, Inc.

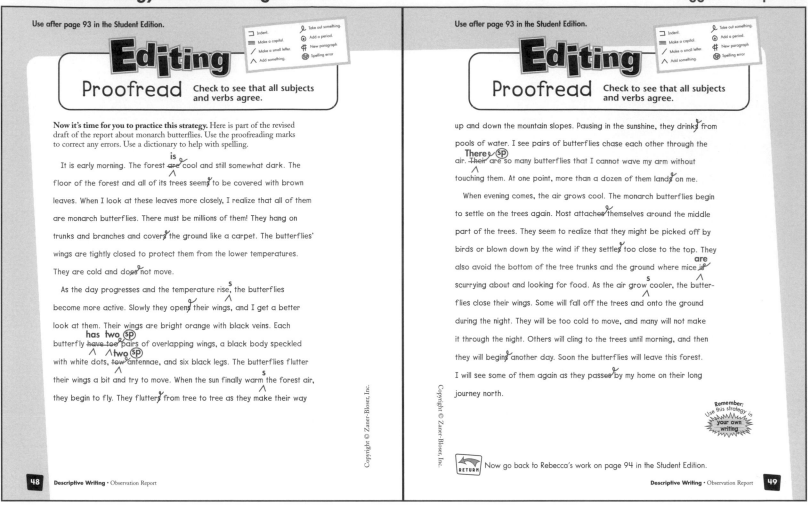

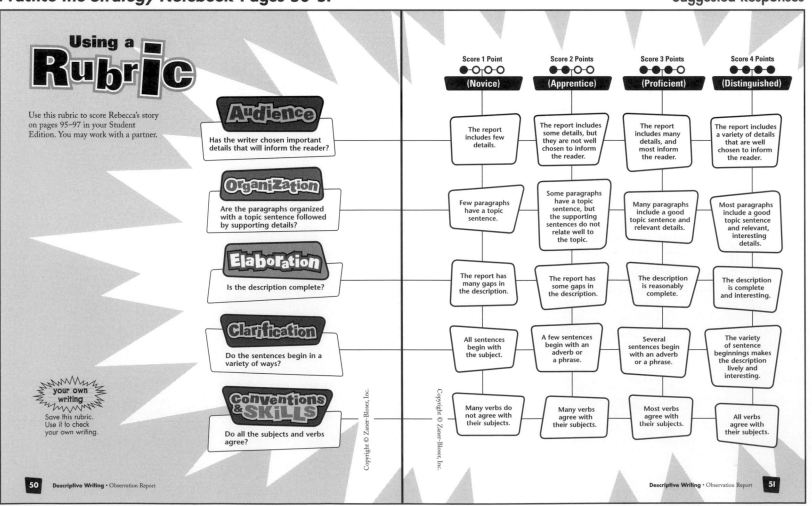

Practice the Strategy Notebook Pages 52–53

Suggested Responses

Use after page 109 in the Student Edition.

PrewRitiNg

Gather Take notes from the Internet and at least one other source. Cite my sources.

Study these notes for a research report about Teddy Roosevelt. You will notice that each note card includes the source of the information.

Conservation Goals
Environmental issues that TR worked on while president
1. Water/irrigation
2. Responsible use and preservation of forest
3. Wildlife refuges
Theodore Roosevelt: Conservation President, pp. 61–63

Conservation Accomplishments
• established 18 national monuments (like Grand Canyon)
• created five national parks
• designated 51 wildlife refuges
• added 150 million acres of woods to forest reserves
Theodore Roosevelt: Conservation President, p. 74

Personal Interests
TR led an active life—
• liked hiking and camping
• lived in the West, drove cattle
• went on African safari
"Theodore Roosevelt. The White House Presidential Biographies" (Web site)

Copyright © Zaner-Bloser, Inc.

52 **Expository Writing** • Research Report

Use after page 109 in the Student Edition.

PrewRitiNg

Gather Take notes from the Internet and at least one other source. Cite my sources.

your own writing

Now it's your turn to practice this strategy with a different topic. Select a topic that interests you. Choose another president or world leader. Then choose an Internet site that you believe provides accurate, reliable, up-to-date information. Ask an adult for help, if you wish. Record notes about the person you chose from this Web site and from one other source. You can use the space below or real note cards. Be sure to cite the source of your information.

Answers will vary.

Answers will vary.

Copyright © Zaner-Bloser, Inc.

 Now go back to Selena's work on page 110 in the Student Edition.

53 **Expository Writing** • Research Report

Practice the Strategy Notebook Pages 54–55

Suggested Responses

Use after page 111 in the Student Edition.

PrewRitiNg

Organize Use my notes to make a support pattern.

The support pattern on the next page was created for a research report on Teddy Roosevelt. It has three main points written on it. Read the facts and notes below and write each one under the appropriate main point on the support pattern on page 55.

Notes

- Environmental issues that TR worked on while President
  1. Water/irrigation
  2. Responsible use and preservation of forest
  3. Wildlife refuges
- TR's accomplishments in conservation
  − established 18 national monuments (like Grand Canyon)
  − created five national parks
  − designated 51 wildlife refuges
  − added 150 million acres of woods to forest reserves
- TR led an active life—
  − liked hiking and camping
  − lived in the West, drove cattle
  − went on African safari
- Before becoming president, served in Spanish-American War: Rough Riders
- Earned 1906 Nobel Peace Prize for ending Russo-Japanese War
- Set up the U.S. Forest Service in 1905
- Governor of NY 1899–1901
- Acquired the Panama Canal Zone in 1903
- President 1901–1909
- 26th president; born 1858; died 1919
- First conservation president
- Youngest president in history: age 42
- Foreign policy: "Speak softly and carry a big stick."

Copyright © Zaner-Bloser, Inc.

54 **Expository Writing** • Research Report

Use after page 111 in the Student Edition.

PrewRitiNg

Organize Use my notes to make a support pattern.

Now it's time for you to practice this strategy. Write the facts from page 54 under the appropriate main points. Use another sheet of paper, if you need more room.

Topic: Teddy Roosevelt

Main Point: Basic facts about his presidency and personal life

Supporting facts President 1901–1909; Youngest president in history: age 42; 26th president; born 1858; died 1919; TR led an active life: liked hiking and camping; lived in the West, drove cattle; went on African safari; Governor of NY 1899–1901; Served in Spanish-American War: Rough Riders

Main Point: Role in conservation First conservation president; Environmental issues that TR worked on:

Supporting facts
1. Water/irrigation, 2. Responsible use and preservation of forest, 3. Wildlife refuges; Accomplishments in conservation: established 18 national monuments (like Grand Canyon), created five national parks, designated 51 wildlife refuges, added 150 million acres to forest reserves; Set up U.S. Forest Service 1905

Main Point: Other high points of presidency

Supporting facts Earned 1906 Nobel Peace Prize for ending Russo-Japanese War; Foreign policy: "Speak softly and carry a big stick."; Acquired the Panama Canal Zone in 1903

your own writing You may wish to organize your notes on another topic on a separate sheet of paper.

Now go back to Selena's work on page 112 in the Student Edition.

Copyright © Zaner-Bloser, Inc.

55 **Expository Writing** • Research Report

Practice the Strategy Notebook Suggested Responses **T225**

Use after page 113 in the Student Edition.

Drafting

Write — Draft the body of my report. Write a paragraph for each main point on my organizer.

your own writing

Now it's time for you to practice this strategy. On this page, you are going to write one or two paragraphs for the research report on Teddy Roosevelt or on your own topic. Choose one main point from the previous page or your own notes. Then use most or all of the facts you listed under that point in a paragraph or two.

Students' paragraphs should begin with a clear topic sentence and include

only facts and ideas related to that topic.

Now go back to Selena's work on page 114 in the Student Edition.

Copyright © Zaner-Bloser, Inc.

56   Expository Writing • Research Report

Use after page 114 in the Student Edition.

Revising

Elaborate — Complete my report by adding an introduction and a conclusion.

Now it's time for you to practice this strategy. Read the two introductions below. Decide which one is better and explain why you think so on the lines. (You may see some errors.)

1. Theodore Roosevelt became president in 1901. He was the first conservation president. Before him, people did not care much about the environment. He made them more aware of the need to conserve our natural resources.

2. When Theodore Roosevelt became president of the United States in 1901, he brought his love of nature and the outdoors. He enjoyed hiking and camping and had lived in the West. Roosevelt realized that America was in danger of using up its resources, and he vowed to do something about it.

Students should select introduction #2, as it does a much better job of

grabbing readers' attention than the first one. #2 has more interesting

details and livelier writing. Both introductions do clearly introduce the topic.

Now read these two conclusions. Choose the better one and explain why you made that choice below. (You may see some errors.)

1. After Theodore Roosevelt left office, the movement to preserve natural resources continued. Today, Americans can hike, camp, boat, see wild animals, and breathe clean air in our National Parks and Refuges. Thanks to roosevelt and the people who continue his work, Earth's natural resources are being preserved and enjoyed.

2. Theodore Roosevelt's term ended in 1909. Fortunately, his work on the environment continued after that. He ran for president in 1912 but was defeated. He died in 1919.

Students should select conclusion #1, as it summarizes the main points of

the research report and leaves readers feeling satisfied. #2 is dry and

uninteresting.

Remember: Use this strategy in your own writing

Now go back to Selena's work on page 115 in the Student Edition.

Copyright © Zaner-Bloser, Inc.

57   Expository Writing • Research Report

Use after page 115 in the Student Edition.

Revising

Clarify — Delete any unnecessary information.

Now it's time for you to practice this strategy. Here is a paragraph from one writer's research report about Theodore Roosevelt. Read the paragraph and cross out any unnecessary information.

Theodore Roosevelt promised the American people that he would work on three important issues related to natural resources. ~~He also told them about the time he spent in the Badlands of the Dakotas.~~ The first issue was water. Roosevelt had traveled throughout the western United States, and he understood how streams and rivers could be used to irrigate dry areas. ~~He explained how much he had enjoyed bird watching in the West.~~ He knew that storing water could make it possible for more people to live in the West. ~~He thought the East was getting too crowded.~~ Roosevelt's second issue was forests. He wanted to make sure that the U.S. government managed woodlands responsibly so the forests would be preserved. His third issue was wildlife. Roosevelt knew that many plants and animals were dying out in the United States. He wanted to create wildlife preserves where plants and animals could live and grow.

Explain why the information you crossed out is unnecessary.

Answers will vary, but students should explain that the information they

deleted is off the topic or irrelevant.

Remember: Use this strategy in your own writing

Now go back to Selena's work on page 116 in the Student Edition.

Copyright © Zaner-Bloser, Inc.

58   Expository Writing • Research Report

Use after page 117 in the Student Edition.

Editing

Proofread — Check to see that I have capitalized words correctly.

Now it's time for you to practice this strategy. Here is part of the revised draft of the report about Theodore Roosevelt. Use the proofreading marks to correct any errors. Use a dictionary to help with spelling.

¶ Some of the greatest acomplishments of Theodore Roosevelt's presidency were related to Conservation. He protected 150 million acres of woods by adding them to the u.s. forest preserves. He turned 18 places, including the grand canyon, into national monuments. He established five national parks and more than fifty wildlife refuges. Roosevelt did not do these things for political reasons. He really believed that Conservation was important. He wanted future generations of americans to be able to use and enjoy these natural resources.

After Theodore Roosevelt left office, the movement to preserve natural resources continued. Today, Americans can hike, camp, boat, see wild animals, and breathe clean air in our National Parks and Refuges. in fact, countries all over the world are now working to protect the water, air, oceans, and land. Thanks to roosevelt and the people who continue his work, Earth's natural resources are being preserved and enjoyed.

Remember: Use this strategy in your own writing

Now go back to Selena's work on page 118 in the Student Edition.

Copyright © Zaner-Bloser, Inc.

59   Expository Writing • Research Report

Using a Rubric

Use this rubric to evaluate Selena's report on pages 119–121 in your Student Edition. You may work with a partner.

your own writing

Save this rubric. Use it to check your own writing.

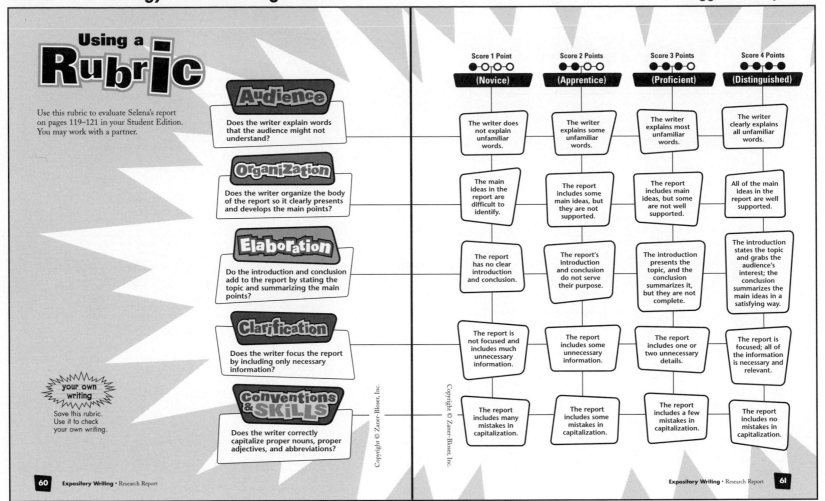

	Score 1 Point ●○○○ (Novice)	Score 2 Points ●●○○ (Apprentice)	Score 3 Points ●●●○ (Proficient)	Score 4 Points ●●●● (Distinguished)
Audience Does the writer explain words that the audience might not understand?	The writer does not explain unfamiliar words.	The writer explains some unfamiliar words.	The writer explains most unfamiliar words.	The writer clearly explains all unfamiliar words.
Organization Does the writer organize the body of the report so it clearly presents and develops the main points?	The main ideas in the report are difficult to identify.	The report includes some main ideas, but they are not supported.	The report includes main ideas, but some are not well supported.	All of the main ideas in the report are well supported.
Elaboration Do the introduction and conclusion add to the report by stating the topic and summarizing the main points?	The report has no clear introduction and conclusion.	The report's introduction and conclusion do not serve their purpose.	The introduction presents the topic, and the conclusion summarizes it, but they are not complete.	The introduction states the topic and grabs the audience's interest; the conclusion summarizes the main ideas in a satisfying way.
Clarification Does the writer focus the report by including only necessary information?	The report is not focused and includes much unnecessary information.	The report includes some unnecessary information.	The report includes one or two unnecessary details.	The report is focused; all of the information is necessary and relevant.
Conventions & Skills Does the writer correctly capitalize proper nouns, proper adjectives, and abbreviations?	The report includes many mistakes in capitalization.	The report includes some mistakes in capitalization.	The report includes a few mistakes in capitalization.	The report includes no mistakes in capitalization.

Use after page 130 in the Student Edition.

PreWRITiNg
Gather   Interview others and take notes.

Now it's your turn to practice this strategy with a different topic.
Suppose you are writing a compare-and-contrast essay about mysteries
on TV and mysteries on the radio. You plan to interview Angela
Murphy, a writer for Radio Mystery Theater. Put a star in front of each
question that should help you gather good information for your essay.

★ How long is a radio mystery?

___ What kind of radio do you have?

★ How important is imagination when
you're creating a radio mystery?

★ How do you make the sound effects for
a radio mystery?

___ What is your favorite sport?

★ Where do you get the stories you make
into radio mysteries?

★ How is listening to a mystery different
from watching one?

 Now write two questions you would like to ask Angela Murphy.
Choose questions that will help you gather interesting information
for your essay.

Questions will vary but should be designed to obtain relevant information

for a compare-and-contrast essay.

_____

_____

Copyright © Zaner-Bloser, Inc.

Use after page 130 in the Student Edition.

PreWRITiNg
Gather   Interview others and take notes.

Here are the answers one writer received when he asked Angela Murphy
two of the questions on page 62. The writer tape-recorded her answers
so he would remember them. Read the answers and think about what
information you will use in your essay. You will make notes on the
next page.

Q: How important is imagination when you're creating a radio mystery?

A: Imagination is very important. Suppose you have a story and you
want to make it into a radio show. When you read the story, you
have to imagine that you're hearing it. Imagine what a scream sounds
like. Imagine what a slamming door sounds like.

It's fun to put the sounds in. Sometimes I read a story out loud to
myself and do the sound effects as I go along. It helps me plan what
the audience will hear—and what the audience needs to hear. I have
to remember that I can't show them anything. I have to present every
clue with sound.

Q: How do you make the sound effects for a radio mystery?

A: Making sound effects can be so much fun. In the old days, there was at
least one sound person on a radio show. He or she would use things
like squeaky hinges, buckets of water, coconut shells, and people's voices
to create the sound effects.

Today most of our sounds are already recorded. We just play them
when and where we need them. Television and movies use recorded
sound, too. Sometimes we get to be more creative. I always enjoy
looking for new sounds to make and use.

Copyright © Zaner-Bloser, Inc.

 Now go back to Henry's work on page 131 in the Student Edition.

Use after page 131 in the Student Edition.

PreWRITiNg
Organize   Organize my interview notes into an attribute chart. Include my own ideas, too.

Now it's time for you to practice this strategy. Review the questions
and answers on page 63. Organize that information into this attribute
chart. Add your own ideas, too.

TV Mystery	Attribute	Radio Mystery
You can see people's expressions. You can watch a scene.	What You See	There is no visual. You can't see anything. You need your imagination.
Sounds are recorded. Sound is important, but what you see tells a lot of the story.	What You Hear	Sounds are recorded. There's no picture, so you have to pay attention to every sound.
You can hear and see clues.	Source of Clues	You can only hear the clues.

 Now go back to Henry's work on page 132 in the Student Edition.

Copyright © Zaner-Bloser, Inc.

Use after page 133 in the Student Edition.

DRafTiNg
Write   Draft my essay. Discuss the likenesses and differences in separate paragraphs.

Now it's time for you to practice this strategy. Review your notes and
the chart on page 64. Then write a paragraph telling how TV mysteries
and radio mysteries are alike. You can add your own ideas, too. Then
read the directions on the next page.

Students should point out that they both tell a story and they both use

sound effects.

Copyright © Zaner-Bloser, Inc.

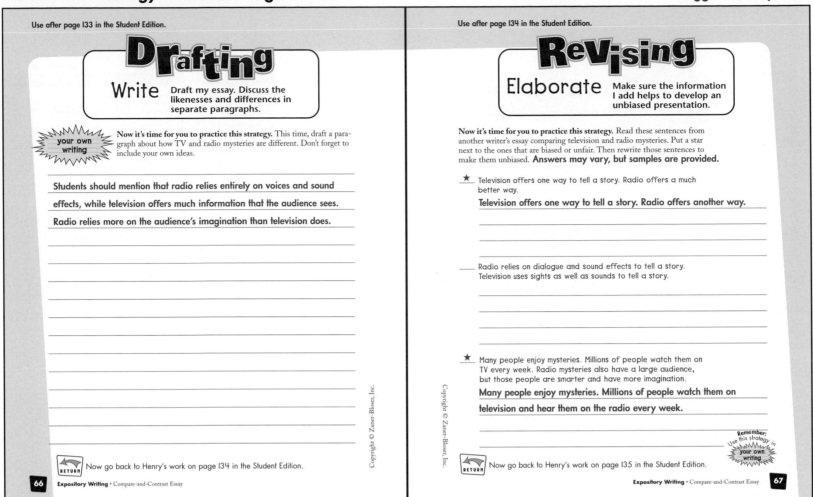

Use after page 133 in the Student Edition.

Drafting

Write
Draft my essay. Discuss the likenesses and differences in separate paragraphs.

your own writing

Now it's time for you to practice this strategy. This time, draft a paragraph about how TV and radio mysteries are different. Don't forget to include your own ideas.

Students should mention that radio relies entirely on voices and sound effects, while television offers much information that the audience sees. Radio relies more on the audience's imagination than television does.

Now go back to Henry's work on page 134 in the Student Edition.

66 **Expository Writing** · Compare-and-Contrast Essay

Copyright © Zaner-Bloser, Inc.

Use after page 134 in the Student Edition.

Revising

Elaborate
Make sure the information I add helps to develop an unbiased presentation.

Now it's time for you to practice this strategy. Read these sentences from another writer's essay comparing television and radio mysteries. Put a star next to the ones that are biased or unfair. Then rewrite those sentences to make them unbiased. **Answers may vary, but samples are provided.**

★ Television offers one way to tell a story. Radio offers a much better way.

Television offers one way to tell a story. Radio offers another way.

___ Radio relies on dialogue and sound effects to tell a story. Television uses sights as well as sounds to tell a story.

★ Many people enjoy mysteries. Millions of people watch them on TV every week. Radio mysteries also have a large audience, but those people are smarter and have more imagination.

Many people enjoy mysteries. Millions of people watch them on television and hear them on the radio every week.

Remember: Use this strategy in your own writing

Now go back to Henry's work on page 135 in the Student Edition.

Expository Writing · Compare-and-Contrast Essay 67

Copyright © Zaner-Bloser, Inc.

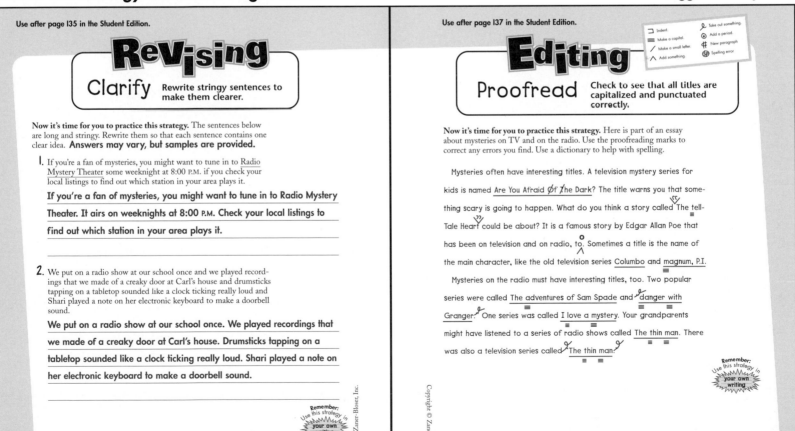

Use after page 135 in the Student Edition.

Revising

Clarify
Rewrite stringy sentences to make them clearer.

Now it's time for you to practice this strategy. The sentences below are long and stringy. Rewrite them so that each sentence contains one clear idea. **Answers may vary, but samples are provided.**

1. If you're a fan of mysteries, you might want to tune in to Radio Mystery Theater some weeknight at 8:00 P.M. if you check your local listings to find out which station in your area plays it.

If you're a fan of mysteries, you might want to tune in to Radio Mystery Theater. It airs on weeknights at 8:00 P.M. Check your local listings to find out which station in your area plays it.

2. We put on a radio show at our school once and we played recordings that we made of a creaky door at Carl's house and drumsticks tapping on a tabletop sounded like a clock ticking really loud and Shari played a note on her electronic keyboard to make a doorbell sound.

We put on a radio show at our school once. We played recordings that we made of a creaky door at Carl's house. Drumsticks tapping on a tabletop sounded like a clock ticking really loud. Shari played a note on her electronic keyboard to make a doorbell sound.

Remember: Use this strategy in your own writing

Now go back to Henry's work on page 136 in the Student Edition.

68 **Expository Writing** · Compare-and-Contrast Essay

Copyright © Zaner-Bloser, Inc.

Use after page 137 in the Student Edition.

⊐ Indent.	ℓ Take out something.
≡ Make a capital.	⊙ Add a period.
/ Make a small letter.	# New paragraph
∧ Add something.	⦿ Spelling error

Editing

Proofread
Check to see that all titles are capitalized and punctuated correctly.

Now it's time for you to practice this strategy. Here is part of an essay about mysteries on TV and on the radio. Use the proofreading marks to correct any errors you find. Use a dictionary to help with spelling.

Mysteries often have interesting titles. A television mystery series for kids is named Are You Afraid Øf The Dark? The title warns you that something scary is going to happen. What do you think a story called The tell-Tale Heart could be about? It is a famous story by Edgar Allan Poe that has been on television and on radio, to. Sometimes a title is the name of the main character, like the old television series Columbo and magnum, P.I.

Mysteries on the radio must have interesting titles, too. Two popular series were called The adventures of Sam Spade and danger with Granger. One series was called I love a mystery. Your grandparents might have listened to a series of radio shows called The thin man. There was also a television series called The thin man.

Remember: Use this strategy in your own writing

Now go back to Henry's work on page 138 in the Student Edition.

Expository Writing · Compare-and-Contrast Essay 69

Copyright © Zaner-Bloser, Inc.

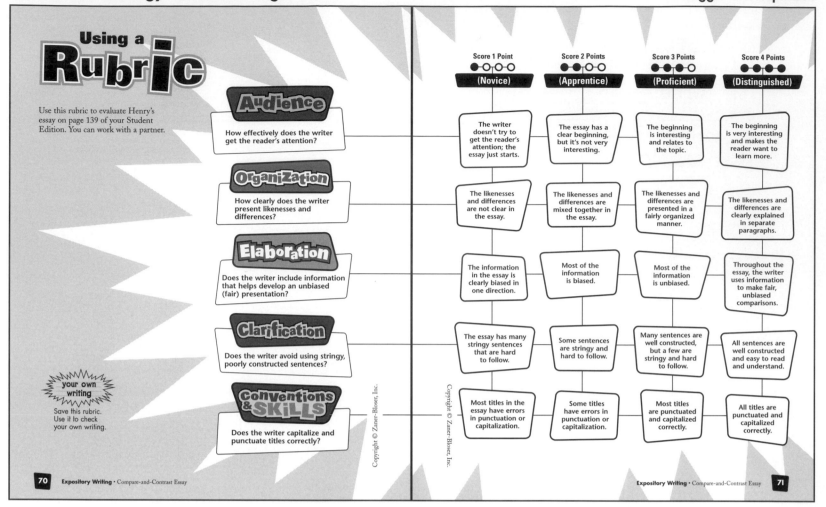

Using a Rubric

Use this rubric to evaluate Henry's essay on page 139 of your Student Edition. You can work with a partner.

Audience
How effectively does the writer get the reader's attention?

Organization
How clearly does the writer present likenesses and differences?

Elaboration
Does the writer include information that helps develop an unbiased (fair) presentation?

Clarification
Does the writer avoid using stringy, poorly constructed sentences?

your own writing
Save this rubric. Use it to check your own writing.

Conventions & Skills
Does the writer capitalize and punctuate titles correctly?

Score 1 Point (Novice)	Score 2 Points (Apprentice)	Score 3 Points (Proficient)	Score 4 Points (Distinguished)
The writer doesn't try to get the reader's attention; the essay just starts.	The essay has a clear beginning, but it's not very interesting.	The beginning is interesting and relates to the topic.	The beginning is very interesting and makes the reader want to learn more.
The likenesses and differences are not clear in the essay.	The likenesses and differences are mixed together in the essay.	The likenesses and differences are presented in a fairly organized manner.	The likenesses and differences are clearly explained in separate paragraphs.
The information in the essay is clearly biased in one direction.	Most of the information is biased.	Most of the information is unbiased.	Throughout the essay, the writer uses information to make fair, unbiased comparisons.
The essay has many stringy sentences that are hard to follow.	Some sentences are stringy and hard to follow.	Many sentences are well constructed, but a few are stringy and hard to follow.	All sentences are well constructed and easy to read and understand.
Most titles in the essay have errors in punctuation or capitalization.	Some titles have errors in punctuation or capitalization.	Most titles are punctuated and capitalized correctly.	All titles are punctuated and capitalized correctly.

Copyright © Zaner-Bloser, Inc.

Copyright © Zaner-Bloser, Inc.

70   Expository Writing • Compare-and-Contrast Essay

Expository Writing • Compare-and-Contrast Essay   71

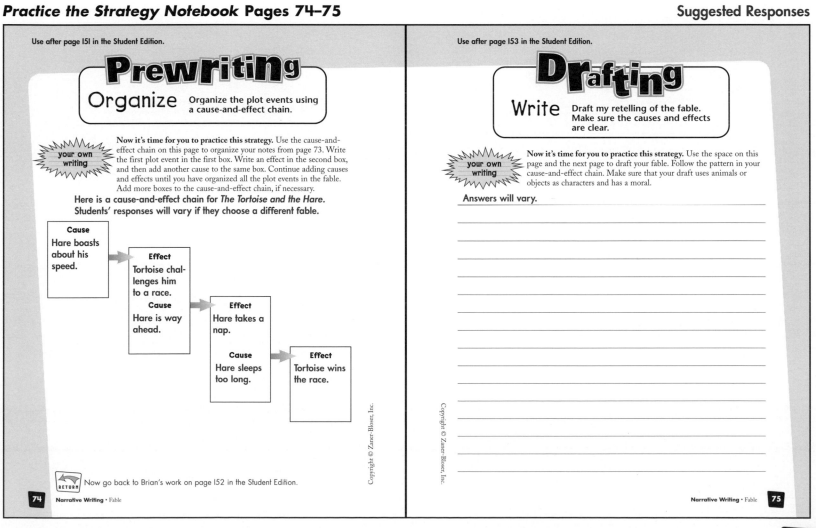

Use after page 150 in the Student Edition.

PreWritiNg

Gather
Pick a fable that interests me. Take notes on it so I can rewrite it in my own words.

You are going to rewrite one of your favorite fables. You can choose the fable below or another one, such as *The Fox and the Grapes, The Town Mouse and the Country Mouse, The Lion and the Mouse, The Ants and the Grasshopper, The Goose That Laid the Golden Eggs,* or others.

Read the fable below or another one of your choice.

The Tortoise and the Hare

One day, a hare was boasting about how fast he could run. To the hare's surprise, a tortoise challenged him to a race. The hare laughed at the tortoise, but he agreed to race. The race began, and the hare quickly left the tortoise far behind.

Halfway to the finish line, the hare was so far ahead of the tortoise that he decided to rest a while. He found a shady spot and took a nap. He thought that if the tortoise passed him while he was sleeping, he could easily catch up. However, the hare slept longer than he had planned. Meanwhile, the tortoise just kept plodding along.

When the hare woke up, the tortoise was nowhere to be seen. The hare sprinted toward the finish line as fast as he could. When he arrived, however, he saw that the tortoise had beaten him and won the race.

Moral: Slow and steady wins the race.

Copyright © Zaner-Bloser, Inc.

Use after page 150 in the Student Edition.

PreWritiNg

Gather
Pick a fable that interests me. Take notes on it so I can rewrite it in my own words.

your own writing

Now it's your turn to practice this strategy. After you have chosen and read a fable, use this page to make notes on the plot events, the characters, and the moral. You can also use this space to brainstorm ways to make small changes in the fable and rewrite it in your own words. You do need to change the fable in some way, not just retell the same story.

Here are some notes on *The Tortoise and the Hare.*

• Hare boasts that he can run the fastest.

• Tortoise challenges him to a race.

• Hare is overconfident and foolish because he takes a long nap.

• Tortoise wins the race.

• Tortoise's victory shows that the fastest runner doesn't always win.

Students' responses will vary if they choose different fables.

Now go back to Brian's work on page 151 in the Student Edition.

Copyright © Zaner-Bloser, Inc.

Use after page 151 in the Student Edition.

PreWritiNg

Organize
Organize the plot events using a cause-and-effect chain.

your own writing

Now it's time for you to practice this strategy. Use the cause-and-effect chain on this page to organize your notes from page 73. Write the first plot event in the first box. Write an effect in the second box, and then add another cause to the same box. Continue adding causes and effects until you have organized all the plot events in the fable. Add more boxes to the cause-and-effect chain, if necessary.

Here is a cause-and-effect chain for *The Tortoise and the Hare.* Students' responses will vary if they choose a different fable.

Cause
Hare boasts about his speed.

Effect
Tortoise challenges him to a race.

Cause
Hare is way ahead.

Effect
Hare takes a nap.

Cause
Hare sleeps too long.

Effect
Tortoise wins the race.

Now go back to Brian's work on page 152 in the Student Edition.

Copyright © Zaner-Bloser, Inc.

Use after page 153 in the Student Edition.

DraftiNg

Write
Draft my retelling of the fable. Make sure the causes and effects are clear.

your own writing

Now it's time for you to practice this strategy. Use the space on this page and the next page to draft your fable. Follow the pattern in your cause-and-effect chain. Make sure that your draft uses animals or objects as characters and has a moral.

Answers will vary.

Copyright © Zaner-Bloser, Inc.

Use after page 153 in the Student Edition.

Drafting

Write
Draft my retelling of the fable. Make sure the causes and effects are clear.

your own writing Use this space to write the rest of your fable.

Answers will vary.

Now go back to Brian's work on page 154 in the Student Edition.

76 **Narrative Writing** • Fable

Use after page 154 in the Student Edition.

Revising

Elaborate
Add dialogue to make the story and characters come alive.

Now it's time for you to practice this strategy. Read these sentences from a retelling of *The Tortoise and the Hare.* Each sentence describes what a character says but does not contain dialogue. Rewrite the sentence so it contains dialogue. **Possible answers appear below.**

1. One day, a swift hare was bragging about how fast he could run and how slow the tortoise was.
   One day, a swift hare bragged, "I'm the fastest runner in the forest, and you, Tortoise, are without a doubt the slowest."

2. After listening to the hare's boasting, the tortoise challenged him to a race.
   After listening to the hare's boasting, the tortoise answered, "Why don't we race, just to make sure you know what you're talking about?"

3. The hare said with a laugh that he was quite surprised at the tortoise's challenge.
   The hare said with a laugh, "I'm really surprised that you are challenging me to a race!"

4. The hare thought the whole thing was a big joke, but he agreed to race the tortoise.
   "The whole idea is one huge joke," said the hare, "but if you want to make a fool of yourself, I'll race you."

Remember: Use this strategy in **your own writing**

Now go back to Brian's work on page 155 in the Student Edition.

77 **Narrative Writing** • Fable

Use after page 155 in the Student Edition.

Revising

Clarify
Make sure that all the plot events lead to the moral of the fable.

Now it's time for you to practice this strategy. Read this paragraph from another writer's retelling of *The Tortoise and the Hare.* The moral of the fable is "Slow and steady wins the race." Cross out any plot events that do not lead to this moral.

With all the other animals watching and cheering, the race began. To nobody's surprise, the hare took off like a shot. ~~He had learned to run fast from his mother.~~ The tortoise crawled along after him. Within a few minutes, the hare was so far ahead that he started to slow down. Then he happened to glance into a store window as he was passing. There, he saw the most incredible large-screen TV he had ever seen. ~~It was on sale!~~ Because he was so far ahead, he decided to go into the store and have a look at the TV. ~~The hare had always wanted a large-screen TV because he was fond of watching nature specials and golf on television.~~

Remember: Use this strategy in **your own writing**

Now go back to Brian's work on page 156 in the Student Edition.

78 **Narrative Writing** • Fable

Use after page 157 in the Student Edition.

Editing

Proofread
Check to see that I have not used double negatives.

Proofreading marks legend:
⊐ Indent.
≡ Make a capital.
/ Make a small letter.
∧ Add something.
⌝ Take out something.
⊙ Add a period.
New paragraph
(SP) Spelling error

Now it's time for you to practice this strategy. This is the first part of one writer's retelling of *The Tortoise and the Hare.* Use the proofreading marks to correct any errors, especially double negatives. Use a dictionary to help with spelling.

The Tortoise and the Hare

One day, all the animals were gathered together in the forest. A swift hare ⓢⓟ braged, "I'm the fastest runner in the forest, and you, Tortoise, are without a doubt the slowest. You could not ~~ever~~ beat me in a race!"

The tortoise listened to the hare's boasting, but he was very tired of it. He did not say ~~nothing~~ anything. He pulled his head back into his shell, but he could still hear the hare bragging. When he could not stand it ~~no~~ any longer, the tortoise answered, "Why don't we race, just to make sure you know what you're talking about?"

The hare's eyes bugged out, and he said with a laugh, "I'm really surprised that you are challenging me to a race! ≡of course, the whole idea is one huge joke, but if you want to make a fool of yourself, I'll race you."

Remember: Use this strategy in **your own writing**

Now go back to Brian's work on page 158 in the Student Edition

79 **Narrative Writing** • Fable

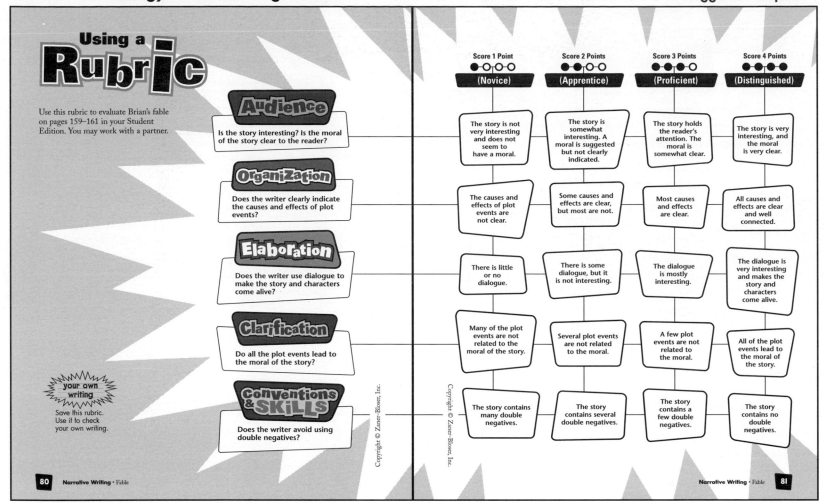

Using a Rubric

Use this rubric to evaluate Brian's fable on pages 159–161 in your Student Edition. You may work with a partner.

your own writing

Save this rubric. Use it to check your own writing.

Audience
Is the story interesting? Is the moral of the story clear to the reader?

Organization
Does the writer clearly indicate the causes and effects of plot events?

Elaboration
Does the writer use dialogue to make the story and characters come alive?

Clarification
Do all the plot events lead to the moral of the story?

Conventions & Skills
Does the writer avoid using double negatives?

Copyright © Zaner-Bloser, Inc.

Score 1 Point (Novice)	Score 2 Points (Apprentice)	Score 3 Points (Proficient)	Score 4 Points (Distinguished)
The story is not very interesting and does not seem to have a moral.	The story is somewhat interesting. A moral is suggested but not clearly indicated.	The story holds the reader's attention. The moral is somewhat clear.	The story is very interesting, and the moral is very clear.
The causes and effects of plot events are not clear.	Some causes and effects are clear, but most are not.	Most causes and effects are clear.	All causes and effects are clear and well connected.
There is little or no dialogue.	There is some dialogue, but it is not interesting.	The dialogue is mostly interesting.	The dialogue is very interesting and makes the story and characters come alive.
Many of the plot events are not related to the moral of the story.	Several plot events are not related to the moral.	A few plot events are not related to the moral.	All of the plot events lead to the moral of the story.
The story contains many double negatives.	The story contains several double negatives.	The story contains a few double negatives.	The story contains no double negatives.

Copyright © Zaner-Bloser, Inc.

Use after page 172 in the Student Edition.

PrewRiTiNg

Gather — Brainstorm some people and events for my mystery.

Here's how one writer got ready to write a mystery. She started by listing people and events her mystery could be about. Then she circled the one that interested her most: a lost homework assignment. Read what she wrote below.

People and Events My Mystery Could Be About

- The county fair: A stranger enters an animal in a contest at the fair, but he keeps the animal out of sight.

- A lost homework assignment: The assignment is done, but it disappears overnight.

- My great aunt Tilda: She has disappeared!

- A strange smell in the air: The air at school suddenly smells like peaches.

- An old box in the basement: A clear, sticky liquid is leaking out of one corner.

- Our new neighbor: Why does she seem to be hiding from us?

- A new teacher: What does she carry back and forth to school in that long, narrow box?

- A neighbor who disappears: He used to wave at me every morning, but now his house is dark and looks deserted.

- A new pet that does something strange: It might be a parrot that seems to be telling me something in a language I don't understand.

Copyright © Zaner-Bloser, Inc.

Use after page 172 in the Student Edition.

PrewRiTiNg

Gather — Brainstorm some people and events for my mystery.

 your own writing

Now it's your turn to practice this strategy with a different topic. Start by listing several people and events that your mystery could be about. Then choose the one that interests you most and circle it.

People and Events My Mystery Could Be About

Answers will vary.

Copyright © Zaner-Bloser, Inc.

RETURN Now go back to Tia's work on page 173 in the Student Edition.

Use after page 173 in the Student Edition.

PrewRiTiNg

Organize — Make a story map to plan my mystery.

On this page, you can see the story map for one writer's mystery about the missing homework. Read it and then use the boxes on the next page to make a story map for your mystery.

Setting:
   Place: home of fifth grader, a fifth-grade classroom
   Time: now

Main Characters: Josh, a fifth grader; his mom; Mr. Randolph, his teacher

Problem/Mystery: Josh's homework assignment is missing. He did it one evening, but it is gone the next morning.

Plot:
   Event 1: One morning, Josh goes to put his homework in his backpack, but he can't find it.
   Event 2: He tells his teacher that the assignment is missing. The teacher gives him another day to find it.
   Event 3: Josh looks for clues to the mystery.

Outcome: Josh finally solves the puzzle and turns in his assignment.

Copyright © Zaner-Bloser, Inc.

Use after page 173 in the Student Edition.

PrewRiTiNg

Organize — Make a story map to plan my mystery.

 your own writing

Now it's time to practice this strategy. Use the boxes on this page to make a story map for your mystery. Add more events to the story map, if needed.

Setting:
   Place: Answers will vary.
   Time:

Main Characters:

Problem/Mystery:

Plot:
   Event 1:
   Event 2:
   Event 3:

Outcome:

Copyright © Zaner-Bloser, Inc.

RETURN Now go back to Tia's work on page 174 in the Student Edition.

Use after page 175 in the Student Edition.

Drafting

Write — Draft my mystery, using the story map and paying special attention to the clues.

your own writing

Now it's time for you to practice this strategy. Below, list the clues you want to use in your mystery. You might change the clues as you write, but your list will give you a good starting point. Be careful not to give too much away!

Clues I Want to Include in My Mystery

Answers will vary.

Now use the rest of this page and the next page to write the first draft of your mystery. Follow your story map and work in the clues you listed above.

Students' mysteries will vary, but they should follow their story maps on page 85.

86 Narrative Writing • Mystery

Use after page 175 in the Student Edition.

Drafting

Write — Draft my mystery, using the story map and paying special attention to the clues.

RETURN — Now go back to Tia's work on page 176 in the Student Edition.

Narrative Writing • Mystery 87

Use after page 176 in the Student Edition.

Revising

Elaborate — Add suspenseful words. Use a thesaurus to find new words.

Now it's time for you to practice this strategy. Here are some sentences from one writer's mystery. Notice that some words are underlined. Use a thesaurus to find a more suspenseful and interesting word to replace each underlined word.

Answers will vary, but sample answers are provided.

1. Josh was completely confused **bewildered, befuddled, flustered**

   The folder with his homework had been sitting on the counter when he went to bed last night. Now it had disappeared **vanished, evaporated**!

2. As he walked into class, Josh was worried **anxious, upset, troubled** What would Mr. Randolph say about the missing assignment?

3. As Josh slowly pushed open the door of the barn, he heard a sound **moan, squeak, rattle, creak**. It took a while for his eyes to adjust to the black **inky, murky, shadowy** darkness.

4. His hand was shaking **trembling, quivering, shivering** as he reached toward the sleeping pig.

5. Quickly, he reached behind the pig and took **snatched, grabbed, seized** the papers it had been lying on.

Remember: Use this strategy in your own writing

RETURN — Now go back to Tia's work on page 177 in the Student Edition.

88 Narrative Writing • Mystery

Use after page 177 in the Student Edition.

Revising

Clarify — Check for conflicting information.

Now it's time for you to practice this strategy. Read the paragraph on this page. What conflicting information did you find? Explain the problem on the lines. Then revise the paragraph so the information in it does not conflict.

Josh ate his breakfast under a deep, dark cloud. The folder with his assignment was gone. It was as if one of the farm animals had come into the house last night and eaten his homework! Of course, he could make another copy of his report from his notes, but what about the illustrations he had drawn? It would take a week to redo them. He decided to skip breakfast and take one more look around the house.

The Problem:

Students should point out that the first sentence says Josh ate his breakfast, but the last sentence says he skipped it. To correct this error, students might change the last sentence to something like this: "After eating breakfast, he decided to take one more look around the house."

Remember: Use this strategy in your own writing

RETURN — Now go back to Tia's work on page 178 in the Student Edition.

Narrative Writing • Mystery 89

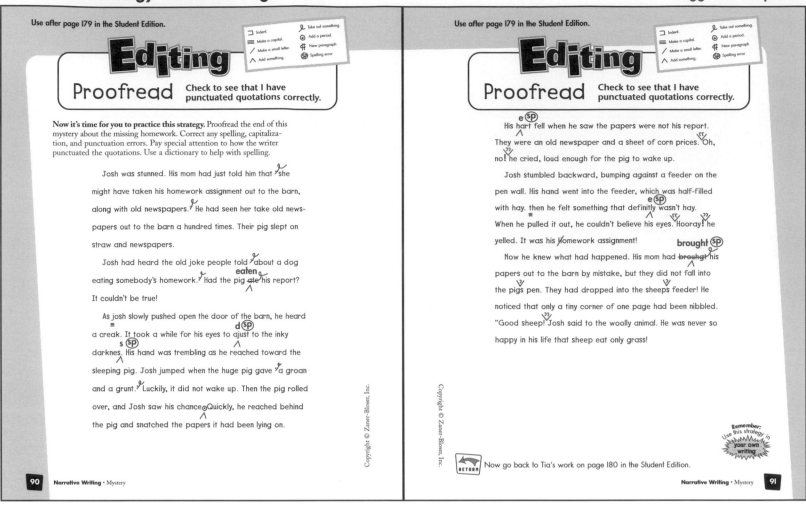

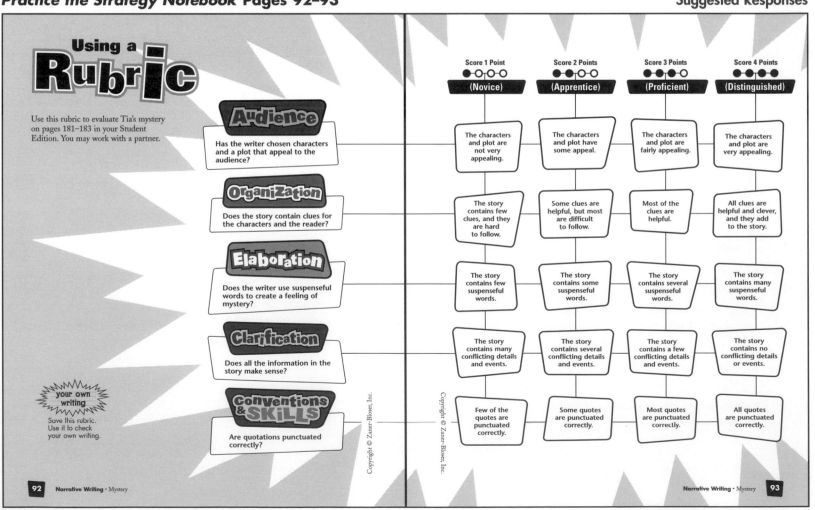

Use after page 194 in the Student Edition.

PreWriting
Gather
As I read my book, take notes on ideas I might include in my review.

Read these notes that a writer took as she read *Terrible Things* by Eve Bunting.

Notes About Terrible Things
by Eve Bunting

- According to the cover, the story is an **allegory**, or retelling, of the Holocaust.
- Different animals live peacefully in a forest.
- One day, the Terrible Things come and take away "every creature with feathers."
- The Terrible Things represent the Nazis.
- After the birds are taken, the other animals feel relieved they were not captured.
- The main character is Little Rabbit, who asks the other animals why the birds were taken. However, the other animals don't want to think about what happened.
- Soon the Terrible Things come back for more animals (creatures with bushy tails, creatures that swim, creatures that sprout quills).
- Finally, the Terrible Things come for white creatures.
- All the rabbits are taken except Little Rabbit, who hides. As the story ends, he goes off to warn creatures in other parts of the forest.
- The story ends with this question: "If we had stuck together, would things have turned out differently?"

Copyright © Zaner-Bloser, Inc.

Use after page 194 in the Student Edition.

PreWriting
Gather
As I read my book, take notes on ideas I might include in my review.

your own writing

Now it's your turn to practice this strategy with a different topic. Choose a book to review and use this page to take notes on it. You will use these notes to organize and draft your own book review.

Notes on _____ Answers will vary. _____ by _____

Students' notes will vary, but they should follow the model on page 94 of this book and on page 194 of the Student Edition.

_____

_____

_____

_____

_____

_____

_____

_____

_____

_____

RETURN Now go back to Jared's work on page 195 in the Student Edition.

Copyright © Zaner-Bloser, Inc.

Use after page 195 in the Student Edition.

PreWriting
Organize
Use my notes to make a pros-and-cons chart.

Below is a pros-and-cons chart that one writer made using the notes on *Terrible Things* on page 94. Notice how the writer has organized the notes into categories, such as plot, theme, and setting.

	Pros (what I liked)	Cons (what I disliked)
Plot	The story echoed the events of the Holocaust.	
Theme	The message is that we must all stick together if we want to defeat evil.	
Setting		The setting wasn't very well described; it's just a forest.
Characters	The Terrible Things were spooky. It was good that the author didn't describe them very much. They remain mysterious and frightening.	Little Rabbit was kind of blah.
Language	The animals make excuses and try not to think about what is happening—just like some people do when bad things happen.	
Other	It seemed almost like a fable with talking animal characters, but it explains how some people living in Nazi Germany must have felt.	

Copyright © Zaner-Bloser, Inc.

Use after page 195 in the Student Edition.

PreWriting
Organize
Use my notes to make a pros-and-cons chart.

your own writing

Now it's time for you to practice this strategy. Use the blank chart on this page to make a pros-and-cons chart for your own book review. This chart will help you decide what you like and dislike about the book and organize your review of it.

Title of book: _____ Answers will vary. _____

Author: _____

	Pros (what I liked)	Cons (what I disliked)
Plot		
Theme	Answers will vary. Students' likes and dislikes should indicate their understanding of the book they chose to review.	
Setting		
Characters		
Language		
Other		

RETURN Now go back to Jared's work on page 196 in the Student Edition.

Copyright © Zaner-Bloser, Inc.

Practice the Strategy Notebook Suggested Responses

Use after page 197 in the Student Edition.

Drafting

Write — Draft my book review, starting with my thesis statement.

Now it's time for you to practice this strategy. Here is the opening paragraph from a review of *Terrible Things*. Find and underline the writer's thesis statement. **Thesis statement should be underlined, as shown.**

In <u>Terrible Things</u>, Eve Bunting creates an allegory, or retelling, of the events of the Holocaust. <u>Everyone should read this thought-provoking book.</u> Using animals, the author helps readers better understand the thoughts and feelings of those caught in a terrible situation. The characters represent the people living in Germany in the 1930s. They are forest animals, including rabbits, birds, and fish. The evil Terrible Things in the story represent the Nazis.

your own writing — Now write the opening paragraph of your own book review. Include a thesis statement that expresses your opinion of the book.

Answers will vary. Students' paragraphs should show careful thinking about their chosen books and include a thesis statement expressing their opinion about the book.

RETURN Now go back to Jared's work on page 198 in the Student Edition.

98 **Persuasive Writing** · Book Review

Copyright © Zaner-Bloser, Inc.

Use after page 198 in the Student Edition.

Revising

Elaborate — Include quotations and examples to support my opinion.

Now it's time for you to practice this strategy. Here is part of the book review of *Terrible Things*. Place a check mark where the author could have included a quotation or example to support her opinion. Then explain why you think a quotation or example is needed at that particular place.

Bunting's use of language is especially effective when different animals make excuses. In other parts of the book, she often repeats words to strengthen the feeling of approaching evil. ✔

Answers will vary. Likely placements of check marks and reasons are shown.

✔ The writer should give an example or quotation here to show how different animals talk.

✔ The writer should provide a quotation here to show the author's use of repetition.

Remember: Use this strategy in your own writing

RETURN Now go back to Jared's work on page 199 in the Student Edition.

Persuasive Writing · Book Review 99

Use after page 199 in the Student Edition.

Revising

Clarify — Restate my opinion at the end of the book review.

Now it's time for you to practice this strategy. Here are three possible paragraphs to end the review of *Terrible Things*. Read them and decide which one you would use. Then explain why each paragraph should—or should not—end the review. You might begin by rereading the author's opening paragraph on page 98.

Paragraph 1
   The setting of the book is a forest clearing. Here, the animals have lived in peace for a long time. As Bunting writes, "They were content. Until the day the Terrible Things came." The setting is not well described in the book, although the drawings show it.

Paragraph 2
   Bunting's language, plot, and characters create a powerful story that most readers will enjoy. The theme is clear: only by uniting and working together can the forest creatures—as well as we human beings—defeat the evil around us. As Little Rabbit explains, "I should have tried to help the other rabbits. If only we creatures had stuck together, it could have been different."

Paragraph 3
   Bunting's book is interesting and well written but somewhat depressing. Most readers would probably enjoy one of her other books more, such as *Riding the Tiger*. That book is about a boy who finds out that it's easier to get on a tiger than to get off. **Students should select Paragraph 2.**

Their explanations may vary, but sample answers are provided.

Paragraph I: This paragraph does not sum up the book or repeat the writer's thesis statement. Paragraph 2: This paragraph would make an excellent conclusion because it restates the thesis statement in the first sentence.

Paragraph 3: This paragraph should not be used because it contradicts the writer's thesis statement in the opening paragraph. It suggests that she did not like Terrible Things.

Remember: Use this strategy in your own writing

RETURN Now go back to Jared's work on page 200 in the Student Edition.

100 **Persuasive Writing** · Book Review

Copyright © Zaner-Bloser, Inc.

Use after page 201 in the Student Edition.

Proofreading marks	
⊐ Indent	ℒ Take out something
≡ Make a capital	⊙ Add a period
/ Make a small letter	# New paragraph
∧ Add something	SP Spelling error

Editing

Proofread — Make sure pronoun antecedents are clear. Check to see that pronouns agree with their antecedents in number.

Now it's time for you to practice this strategy. Here is part of the book review of *Terrible Things*. Use the proofreading marks to correct any errors. Use a dictionary to help with spelling.

The plot of the book echoes the events of the
Holocaust in Nazi Germany, when Jews and other people
were arrested. He were taken to concentration camps
and later killed. Like most people in Germany, the
forest creatures at first cannot believe what is happening to him. They try to convince themselves that the
evil will be limited to others and that she will be safe.
However, he soon learns that no one is safe from the
Terrible Things.
   The book's theme is stated at the end. Little Rabbit
says that if the animals had all stuck together and
supported each other in the face of danger, he might
have been able to save himself. Little Rabbit manages
to save himself by hiding behind a rock.

Remember: Use this strategy in your own writing

RETURN Now go back to Jared's work on page 202 in the Student Edition.

Persuasive Writing · Book Review 101

Copyright © Zaner-Bloser, Inc.

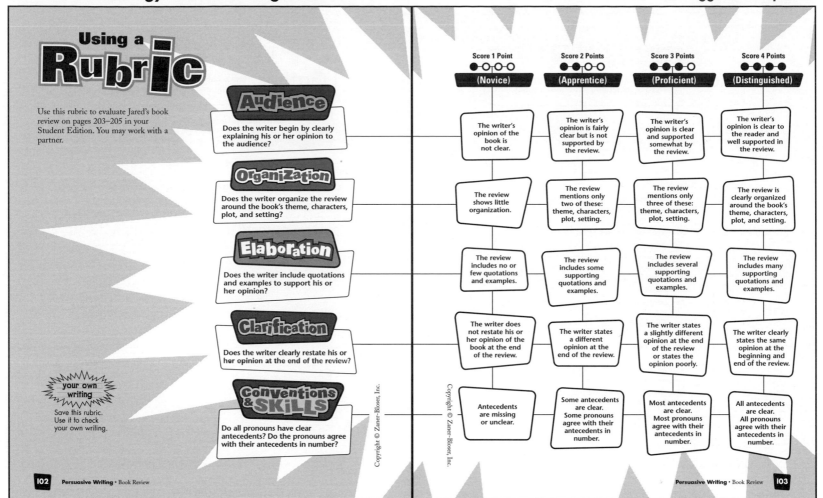

Using a Rubric

Use this rubric to evaluate Jared's book review on pages 203–205 in your Student Edition. You may work with a partner.

your own writing
Save this rubric. Use it to check your own writing.

102 **Persuasive Writing** • Book Review

Copyright © Zaner-Bloser, Inc.

Copyright © Zaner-Bloser, Inc.

Persuasive Writing • Book Review 103

	Score 1 Point (Novice)	Score 2 Points (Apprentice)	Score 3 Points (Proficient)	Score 4 Points (Distinguished)
Audience Does the writer begin by clearly explaining his or her opinion to the audience?	The writer's opinion of the book is not clear.	The writer's opinion is fairly clear but is not supported by the review.	The writer's opinion is clear and supported somewhat by the review.	The writer's opinion is clear to the reader and well supported in the review.
Organization Does the writer organize the review around the book's theme, characters, plot, and setting?	The review shows little organization.	The review mentions only two of these: theme, characters, plot, setting.	The review mentions only three of these: theme, characters, plot, setting.	The review is clearly organized around the book's theme, characters, plot, and setting.
Elaboration Does the writer include quotations and examples to support his or her opinion?	The review includes no or few quotations and examples.	The review includes some supporting quotations and examples.	The review includes several supporting quotations and examples.	The review includes many supporting quotations and examples.
Clarification Does the writer clearly restate his or her opinion at the end of the review?	The writer does not restate his or her opinion of the book at the end of the review.	The writer states a different opinion at the end of the review.	The writer states a slightly different opinion at the end of the review or states the opinion poorly.	The writer clearly states the same opinion at the beginning and end of the review.
Conventions & Skills Do all pronouns have clear antecedents? Do the pronouns agree with their antecedents in number?	Antecedents are missing or unclear.	Some antecedents are clear. Some pronouns agree with their antecedents in number.	Most antecedents are clear. Most pronouns agree with their antecedents in number.	All antecedents are clear. All pronouns agree with their antecedents in number.

Use after page 214 in the Student Edition.

Gather Use what I read and learn from others to form an opinion about a topic.

Read these notes that one student made for a letter to the editor. The notes are based on his observations, plus interviews with other students and school staff. As you can tell, the writer has already gathered enough information to decide that the school grounds need help.

> **My Notes on the School Grounds**
> • Our school grounds are messy.
>   – They have lots of litter, paper, pop bottles, and other trash.
>   – Bike racks are tipped over.
>   – Bushes need trimming.
>   – The grounds need new flowers, plants, and trees.
>   – The sports fields need to be cleaned and fixed up.
>   – New paint is needed at several locations.
>
> • Here is why we should clean up the school grounds:
>   – We will enjoy coming to school more.
>   – We will have more pride in our school.
>   – Parents and other adults will have more respect for us.
>   – We can build school spirit by working together.

Use after page 214 in the Student Edition.

Gather Use what I read and learn from others to form an opinion about a topic.

your own writing

Now it's your turn to practice this strategy with a different topic. Use this page to take notes on a topic or issue you feel strongly about. It could be an issue of concern in your school, community, or state. You will use these notes to organize and draft your own letter to the editor.

Notes on _____

• **Answers will vary. Students' answers should follow the model on page 104 of this book and on page 214 of the Student Edition.**

• _____

• _____

• _____

• _____

• _____

RETURN Now go back to Halle's work on page 215 in the Student Edition.

Use after page 215 in the Student Edition.

Organize Make an outline to focus and support my opinion.

Below is part of a topic outline that a writer made using the notes on page 104. Read his notes.

> I. Problems with the school grounds
>   A. Litter and trash
>   B. Bike racks tipped over
>   C. Bushes overgrown and unhealthy
>   D. New plantings needed
>   E. Sports fields need cleaning
>   F. New paint needed in many places
>
> II. Benefits of making school grounds more attractive
>   A. More pleasant to come to school
>   B. Increased pride among students
>   C. Increased respect from parents, other adults, and community members
>   D. Increased school spirit from working together on a project

Now it's time for you to practice this strategy. You will help this writer organize each section of his letter. Decide which of the problems listed in the first section (I.) of his outline is most important. Write the letter of that problem (A.–F.) below and explain why you think it is the most important. Then decide which of the benefits (II.) is most important. Write its letter (A.–D.) and explain your choice.

Most Important Problem: _____
Answers will vary, but students should support their choices with clear, logical reasons.
_____
_____

Most Important Benefit: _____

Use after page 215 in the Student Edition.

Organize Make an outline to focus and support my opinion.

your own writing

Now it's time for you to practice this strategy. Make an outline below for your own letter to the editor. You can use a sentence outline or a topic outline. Use your notes on page 105. Outline only the reasons you will use to support your opinion. Put them in order from most important to least important. Use another sheet of paper if you need more room.

I. _____ **Answers will vary.**
  A. _____
  B. _____
  C. _____

II. _____
  A. _____
  B. _____
  C. _____

III. _____
  A. _____
  B. _____
  C. _____

RETURN Now go back to Halle's work on page 216 in the Student Edition.

Use after page 217 in the Student Edition.

Drafting

Write Draft my letter to the editor. State my opinion, support it, and sum up my argument.

your own writing

Now it's time for you to practice this strategy. On these two pages, draft your own letter to the editor, using your notes on page 105 and your outline on page 107. Start with your opinion, support it, and sum up your argument at the end of your letter. You do not need to include all the parts of a business letter, such as the heading and salutation, in this draft.

Answers will vary. Students' letters should state their opinion about the

topic they chose, include at least a few reasons to support their opinion,

and summarize their argument in the concluding paragraph.

Use after page 217 in the Student Edition.

Drafting

Write Draft my letter to the editor. State my opinion, support it, and sum up my argument.

Answers will vary.

 Now go back to Halle's work on page 218 in the Student Edition.

Use after page 218 in the Student Edition.

Revising

Elaborate Add reasons and facts to support my opinion.

Now it's time for you to practice this strategy. Read this paragraph from a draft of a letter to the editor about the school grounds. Use the space below to write a note to this writer. Explain where he might add more reasons and facts. Describe the kinds of reasons and facts he might include. Refer to this writer's notes and outline on pages 104 and 106. (You will see some errors in this paragraph, as this is his first draft.)

> Making the school grounds more attactive will have many benefits for our school and for the community. Because of these many benefits, I suggest we start a project to improve the apearance of our school grounds. The work force could include current and former students, parents, and teachers. And any community member. I believe that the largest group should be students We are the ones who will benefit most from an attractive, clean, and safe school.

Answers will vary, but students should suggest that the writer include

some or all of the benefits he listed in section II on page 106, such as

increased pride among students and increased respect from parents.

Remember: Use this strategy in **your own writing**

 Now go back to Halle's work on page 219 in the Student Edition.

Use after page 219 in the Student Edition.

Revising

Clarify Add signal words to clarify my ideas.

Now it's time for you to practice this strategy. Signal words act like road signs. They show that the writer is making an important point, changing direction, or coming to the conclusion. Read the following paragraph from the draft of one writer's letter to the editor. Then insert signal words where they will help make the ideas clearer. Choose from the signal words in the box.

Signal Words

therefore	on the other hand
for this reason	but
in addition	in the same way
as a result	in fact
meanwhile	for example

Dear Editor:

I am a student at Somerset elementary School. I am writing to address a serious problem at our school. Our school grounds are unattractive. **For example,** They are littered with trash. The plantings are weedy and overgrown. **In addition,** New paint and repairs are needed in many locations. **As a result,** People must think that we do not care about our school. **In fact,** I know this is not true. It's time for us to get buzy and make the school grounds a more beautiful place.

Answers will vary. Sample revisions are shown.

Remember: Use this strategy in **your own writing**

 Now go back to Halle's work on page 220 in the Student Edition.

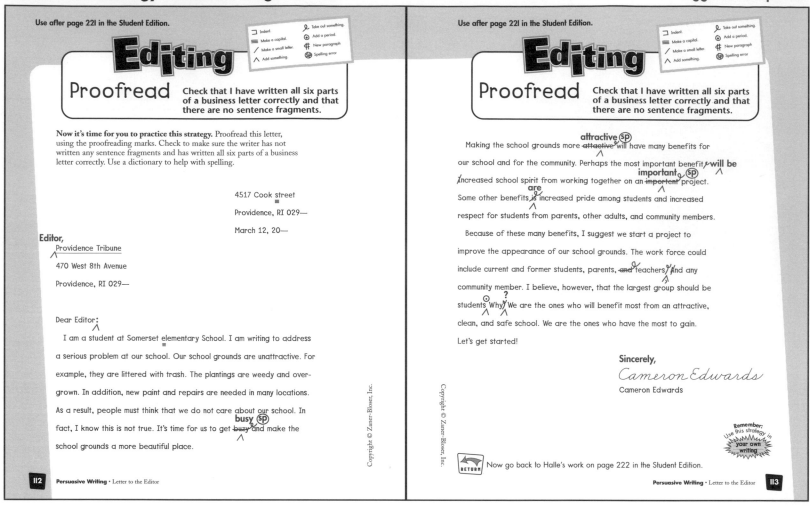

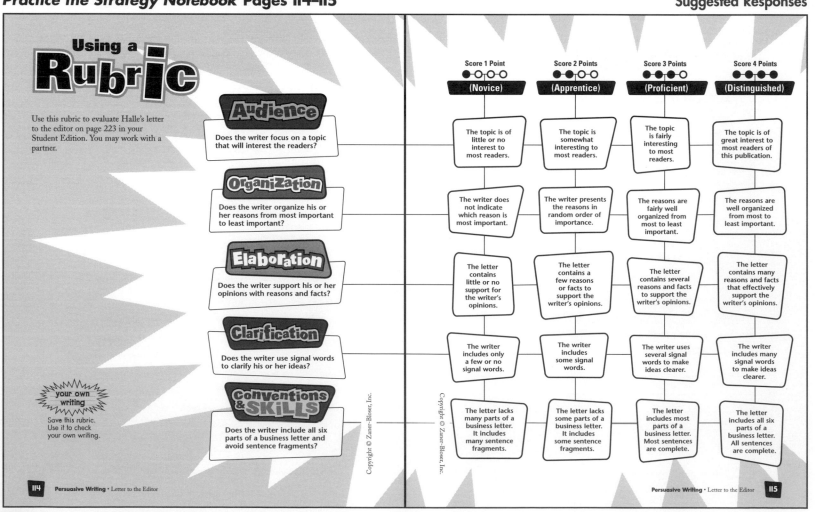

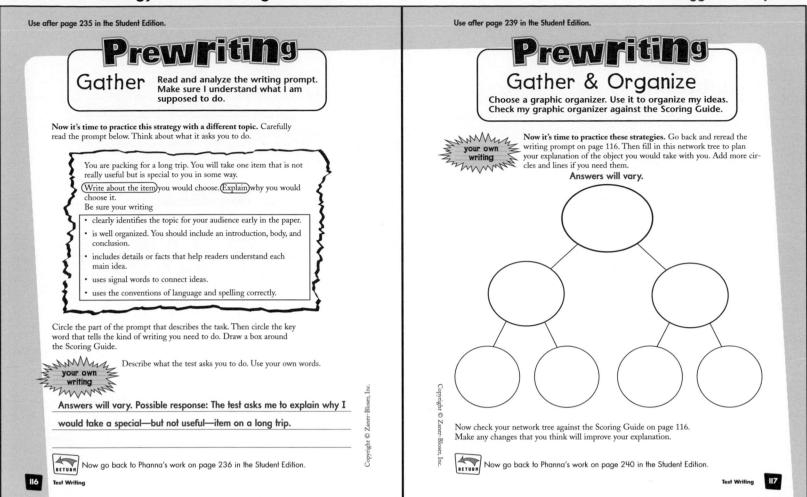

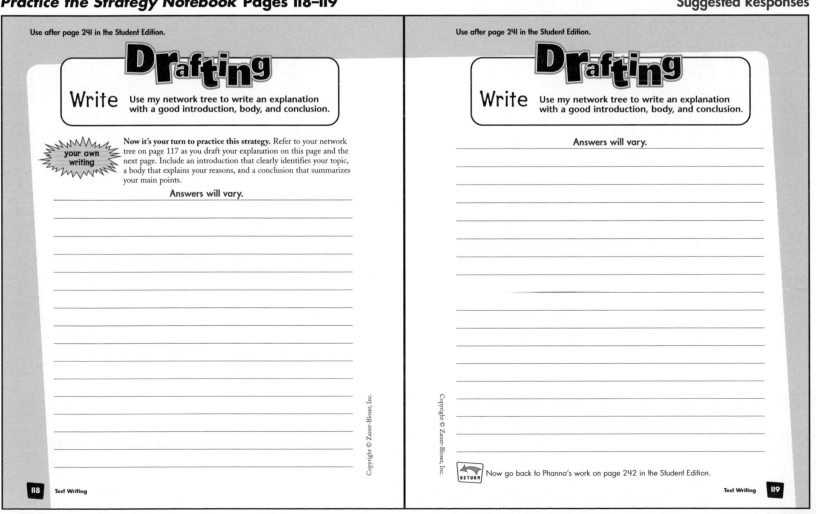

Use after page 242 in the Student Edition.

ReVising

Elaborate
Check what I have written against the Scoring Guide. Add any missing facts or details.

Now it's time for you to practice this strategy. The paragraphs below are part of one student's draft response to the writing prompt on page 116. The student is explaining why he would pack a rabbit puppet. Rewrite the paragraphs. Add two or more sentences with details that tell who, what, when, where, or how. You can make up details if you wish.

> Their is something that's not really useful that I would pack, too. It's a silly old sock puppet named Jack.
>
> I enjoy playing with Jack sometimes, making him move like a real rabbit.

Answers will vary. Possible response: . . . puppet named Jack. I keep him under my pillow at home. . . . like a real rabbit. I make him hop so his ears flop up and down. Sometimes my cat tries to pounce on him when I do this.

Remember: Use this strategy in *your own writing*

Now go back to Phanna's work on page 243 in the Student Edition.

Use after page 243 in the Student Edition.

ReVising

Clarify
Check what I have written against the Scoring Guide. Make sure I have used signal words so that everything is clear.

Now it's time for you to practice this strategy. Decide where the signal words below belong in this draft. At each place where you see a ^, add signal words from the Word Bank that will help clarify and connect the ideas. This is a draft, so you will see some errors that you can correct now or later.

Word Bank

, but	Next,
because	First,
As a finishing touch,	

Jack don't actually belong to me. I've been taking
, but
care of him ^ Jack belongs to my big sister Pam. He is
First,
special partly because Pam made him. ^ She got an old
Next,
sock and sewed on a couple of buttons for eyes. ^ She
As a finishing touch,
cut up an old bath towel to make his ears. ^ She sewed
some pieces of fishing line to his nose to make whiskers.
because
You can bend his ears ^ Pam put pipe cleaners inside them.

Remember: Use this strategy in *your own writing*

Now go back to Phanna's work on page 244 in the Student Edition.

Use after page 246 in the Student Edition.

Proofreading marks:
- Indent.
- Make a capital.
- Make a small letter.
- Add something.
- Take out something.
- Add a period.
- New paragraph.
- Spelling error

Editing

Proofread
Check that I have used correct grammar, capitalization, punctuation, and spelling.

Now it's time for you to practice this strategy. Below is a revised explanation about the object one student would take on a trip. Use the proofreading marks to correct any errors in grammar, capitalization, punctuation, and spelling.

I'd Pack Jack
by Tracy Dobbins

If I went away from home, of course I'd pack clean socks
(sp) There
and my toothbrush. ~~Their~~ is another item that's not really

useful that I would pack, too. It's a silly old sock puppet

named Jack. His full name is Jack rabbit.
doesn't
Jack ~~don't~~ actually belong to me. I've been taking care of
, but ^
him ^ Jack really belongs to my big sister Pam. He is special
First,
partly because Pam made him. She got an old sock and
Next,
sewed on a couple of buttons for eyes. She cut up an old
As a finishing touch, ^
bath towel to make his ears. She sewed some pieces of
because
fishing line to his nose to make whiskers. You can bend his
because
ears Pam put pipe cleaners inside them.
^ Pam and I
~~Me and Pam~~ are really close, even though we are not
^
~~nothing~~ close in age. Pam is a soldier in the National guard.
so
She's really far away from home right now, ~~And~~ I try to

Use after page 246 in the Student Edition.

Proofreading marks:
- Indent.
- Make a capital.
- Make a small letter.
- Add something.
- Take out something.
- Add a period.
- New paragraph.
- Spelling error

Editing

Proofread
Check that I have used correct grammar, capitalization, punctuation, and spelling.

(sp) write
~~right~~ to her a few times a week. Pam gave me Jack long

before she joined the National Guard. After Pam made Jack

for a school play, she said I could borrow him if I took really

good care of him. She really meant I could have him.

Every time I get one of Pam's letters, she asks how Jack is

and reminds me to take good care of him. Somehow it seems

that if I take good care of Jack, then Pam will be okay, too.
, but
I miss her. I don't ~~never~~ worry about her so much if I hold Jack

while I read her letters.
(sp) h
If I were taking a trip anywere in the world, I would pack

Jack. Even though he might take up room for something more

useful, I'd rather have Jack. He reminds me of my sister.
(sp) promised **him**
Besides, I ~~promized~~ I would always be responsible for ~~them~~.

Remember: Use this strategy in *your own writing*

Now go back to page 247 in the Student Edition.

Using a Rubric

This rubric for expository writing was developed from the Scoring Guide on page 227 in the Student Edition.

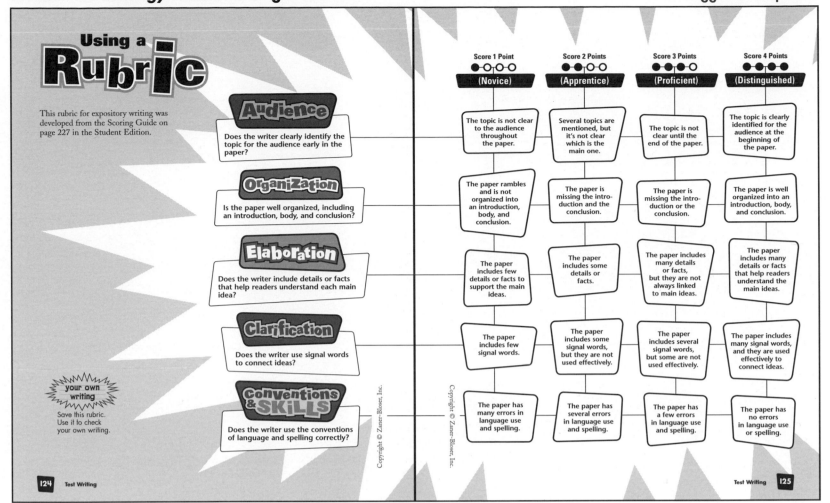

Audience
Does the writer clearly identify the topic for the audience early in the paper?

Organization
Is the paper well organized, including an introduction, body, and conclusion?

Elaboration
Does the writer include details or facts that help readers understand each main idea?

Clarification
Does the writer use signal words to connect ideas?

your own writing
Save this rubric. Use it to check your own writing.

Conventions & Skills
Does the writer use the conventions of language and spelling correctly?

Copyright © Zaner-Bloser, Inc.

	Score 1 Point (Novice)	**Score 2 Points** (Apprentice)	**Score 3 Points** (Proficient)	**Score 4 Points** (Distinguished)
Audience	The topic is not clear to the audience throughout the paper.	Several topics are mentioned, but it's not clear which is the main one.	The topic is not clear until the end of the paper.	The topic is clearly identified for the audience at the beginning of the paper.
Organization	The paper rambles and is not organized into an introduction, body, and conclusion.	The paper is missing the introduction and the conclusion.	The paper is missing the introduction or the conclusion.	The paper is well organized into an introduction, body, and conclusion.
Elaboration	The paper includes few details or facts to support the main ideas.	The paper includes some details or facts.	The paper includes many details or facts, but they are not always linked to main ideas.	The paper includes many details or facts that help readers understand the main ideas.
Clarification	The paper includes few signal words.	The paper includes some signal words, but they are not used effectively.	The paper includes several signal words, but some are not used effectively.	The paper includes many signal words, and they are used effectively to connect ideas.
Conventions & Skills	The paper has many errors in language use and spelling.	The paper has several errors in language use and spelling.	The paper has a few errors in language use and spelling.	The paper has no errors in language use or spelling.

Writing Modes and Genres	LEVEL C	LEVEL D	LEVEL E	LEVEL F	LEVEL G	LEVEL H
Adventure Story		●				
Biographic Sketch		●				●
Book Report			●	●		●
Cause and Effect Report				●	●	
Character Sketch		●				
Compare and Contrast Essay		●	●			
Contemporary Story		●				
Descriptive Essay	●		●	●	●	●
Descriptive Paragraph	●	●				
E-mail					●	
Editorial					●	●
Explanation of a Complex Process						●
Eyewitness Account			●	●		
Fable			●			
Factual Report	●	●				
Folktale	●					
Historical Fiction/Episode				●	●	●
How-To Essay	●					
Letters (Friendly, Business)	●	●	●	●	●	●
Mystery			●			
Observation Report			●	●	●	●
Personal Narrative	●	●	●		●	
Persuasive Essay	●	●		●	●	●
Persuasive Paragraph	●					

	LEVEL C	LEVEL D	LEVEL E	LEVEL F	LEVEL G	LEVEL H
Writing Modes and Genres continued						
Realistic Story	●					
Research Report			●	●	●	●
Summary				●	●	
TV Commercial Script						●
Graphic Organizers						
Attribute Chart		●	●			
Cause-and-Effect Chain			●	●	●	●
Character Chart		●				
5 W's Chart; 3 W's Chart	●			●	●	●
K-W-S Chart					●	
Main-Idea Table	●				●	●
Network Tree	●	●	●	●		
Observation Chart	●				●	
Order-of-Importance Organizer		●		●	●	
Outline			●	●	●	●
Persuasion Map					●	
Problem-Solution Frame					●	●
Pros-and-Cons Chart			●			●
Sequence Chain	●	●	●	●		●
Spider Map	●	●	●	●		
Storyboard	●		●			●
Story Map	●	●	●	●	●	●
Support Pattern			●			
Time Line		●				●
Venn Diagram				●		
Web		●			●	●

Writing Strategies

	LEVEL C	LEVEL D	LEVEL E	LEVEL F	LEVEL G	LEVEL H
Adding dialogue/quotations	●	●	●	●	●	●
Adding figurative language			●	●	●	●
Adding or rewriting details/facts/examples	●	●	●	●	●	●
Adding transitions/signal words	●	●	●	●	●	●
Assessing personal experience/knowledge	●	●	●	●	●	●
Assessing personal interests	●	●	●	●	●	●
Clear beginning, middle, end; introduction, conclusion	●	●	●	●	●	●
Correcting sentence fragments/run-ons/confusing sentences	●	●	●	●	●	●
Deleting unnecessary or confusing information/wordy phrases	●		●	●	●	●
Determining Audience	●	●	●	●	●	●
End Notes, Bibliography					●	●
Generating ideas/statements/questions	●	●	●	●	●	●
Interviewing	●	●	●	●	●	●
Listing	●	●	●	●	●	●
Making Notecards				●	●	●
Paraphrasing					●	●
Recognizing and developing parts of genre	●	●	●	●	●	●
Recognizing and using genre conventions	●	●	●	●	●	●
Reordering sentences/paragraphs	●	●	●	●	●	●
Replacing vague/loaded/cliché language		●	●	●		●
Restating opinion, purpose	●	●	●	●		
Rewriting unclear/confusing/incorrect information	●		●	●		●
Taking Notes	●	●	●	●	●	●
Thesis Statement			●	●	●	
Topic and Detail Sentences	●	●	●	●	●	●
Using appropriate text structure	●	●	●	●	●	●

Writing Strategies continued	LEVEL C	LEVEL D	LEVEL E	LEVEL F	LEVEL G	LEVEL H
Using appropriate voice/tone/point of view	●	○	●	○	●	○
Using a thesaurus		○	●			
Using exact/precise/interesting words	●	○	●	○	●	○
Using graphic organizers to generate draft	●	○	●	○	●	○
Using references/resources	●	○	●	○	●	○
Visual aids/Illustrations			●	○	●	○
Writing effective sentences	●	○	●	○	●	○
Writing paragraphs	●	○	●	○	●	○

Sharing Writing	LEVEL C	LEVEL D	LEVEL E	LEVEL F	LEVEL G	LEVEL H
Author's circle		○				
Big books		○				
Mail to appropriate person or publication	●	○	●	○	●	○
Multimedia presentation			●	○	●	○
Observation journal			●		●	○
Part of a display		○	●	○	●	○
Perform as play/newscast/commercial			●			○
Post on Web site	●	○			●	○
Post on bulletin board	●	○		○	●	○
Present as speech or read aloud	●	○	●	○		○
Publish for class library	●	○	●	○		
Publish in class or school newspaper/collection/magazine/newsletter/journal/diary	●	○	●	○	●	○
Record on audiotape	●					
Send as e-mail					●	
Time capsule			●			
Travel brochure		○				

Grammar, Usage, and Mechanics

	LEVEL C	LEVEL D	LEVEL E	LEVEL F	LEVEL G	LEVEL H
Active and passive voice				○	●	○
Adjectives	●	○			●	○
Adverbs		○			●	○
Apostrophes				○	●	
Appositives				○	●	○
Capitalization	●	○	●	○	●	
Double negatives			●		●	
Easily confused words/homophones	●	○		○	●	
Introductory verbal phrases						○
Letters: Friendly, Business	●	○	●	○	●	
Nouns (plural, possessive)		○	●		●	
Pronoun forms/antecedents	●	○	●	○	●	○
Punctuation	●	●	●	○	●	○
Quotations/dialogue	●	○	●	○	●	○
Sentence Patterns	●	○	●	○	●	○
Sentences: complex				○		○
Sentences: compound	●		●	○		○
Sentences: fragments	●	○	●	○	●	○
Sentences: run-ons		○	●	○	○	○
Subject-verb agreement	●	○	●	○	●	○
Verb forms/tenses	●				●	
More instruction on grammar, usage, and mechanics can be found in the *Conventions and Skills Practice Book* for each level.	●	○	●	○	●	○

Teacher Notes